FREE Study Skills DV

Dear Customer,

Thank you for your purchase from Mometrix! We consider it an honor and privilege that you have purchased our product and want to ensure your satisfaction.

As a way of showing our appreciation and to help us better serve you, we have developed a Study Skills DVD that we would like to give you for <u>FREE</u>. **This DVD covers our "best practices" for studying for your exam, from using our study materials to preparing for the day of the test.**

All that we ask is that you email us your feedback that would describe your experience so far with our product. Good, bad or indifferent, we want to know what you think!

To get your **FREE Study Skills DVD**, email <u>freedvd@mometrix.com</u> with "FREE STUDY SKILLS DVD" in the subject line and the following information in the body of the email:

    a. The name of the product you purchased.

    b. Your product rating on a scale of 1-5, with 5 being the highest rating.

    c. Your feedback. It can be long, short, or anything in-between, just your impressions and experience so far with our product. Good feedback might include how our study material met your needs and will highlight features of the product that you found helpful.

    d. Your full name and shipping address where you would like us to send your free DVD.

If you have any questions or concerns, please don't hesitate to contact me directly.

Thanks again!

Sincerely,

Jay Willis
Vice President
<u>jay.willis@mometrix.com</u>
1-800-673-8175

TExES

Core Subjects 4-8 (211)

SECRETS

Study Guide
Your Key to Exam Success

TExES Test Review for the
Texas Examinations of Educator Standards

Published by

Mometrix Test Preparation

TExES Exam Secrets Test Prep Team

Written and edited by the TExES Exam Secrets Test Prep Staff

Printed in the United States of America

This paper meets the requirements of ANSI/NISO Z39.48-1992 (Permanence of Paper).

Mometrix offers volume discount pricing to institutions. For more information or a price quote, please contact our sales department at sales@mometrix.com or 888-248-1219.

*TExES Texas Examinations of Educator Standards™ is a registered trademark of the Texas Education Agency, which was not involved in the production of, and does not endorse, this product.

ISBN 13: 978-1-5167-0044-8
ISBN 10: 1-51670-044-9

Dear Future Exam Success Story:

Congratulations on your purchase of our study guide. Our goal in writing our study guide was to cover the content on the test, as well as provide insight into typical test taking mistakes and how to overcome them.

Standardized tests are a key component of being successful, which only increases the importance of doing well in the high-pressure high-stakes environment of test day. How well you do on this test will have a significant impact on your future, and we have the research and practical advice to help you execute on test day.

The product you're reading now is designed to exploit weaknesses in the test itself, and help you avoid the most common errors test takers frequently make.

How to use this study guide

We don't want to waste your time. Our study guide is fast-paced and fluff-free. We suggest going through it a number of times, as repetition is an important part of learning new information and concepts.

First, read through the study guide completely to get a feel for the content and organization. Read the general success strategies first, and then proceed to the content sections. Each tip has been carefully selected for its effectiveness.

Second, read through the study guide again, and take notes in the margins and highlight those sections where you may have a particular weakness.

Finally, bring the manual with you on test day and study it before the exam begins.

Your success is our success

We would be delighted to hear about your success. Send us an email and tell us your story. Thanks for your business and we wish you continued success.

Sincerely,

Mometrix Test Preparation Team

Need more help? Check out our flashcards at: http://MometrixFlashcards.com/TExES

TABLE OF CONTENTS

Top 20 Test Taking Tips

1. Carefully follow all the test registration procedures
2. Know the test directions, duration, topics, question types, how many questions
3. Setup a flexible study schedule at least 3-4 weeks before test day
4. Study during the time of day you are most alert, relaxed, and stress free
5. Maximize your learning style; visual learner use visual study aids, auditory learner use auditory study aids
6. Focus on your weakest knowledge base
7. Find a study partner to review with and help clarify questions
8. Practice, practice, practice
9. Get a good night's sleep; don't try to cram the night before the test
10. Eat a well balanced meal
11. Know the exact physical location of the testing site; drive the route to the site prior to test day
12. Bring a set of ear plugs; the testing center could be noisy
13. Wear comfortable, loose fitting, layered clothing to the testing center; prepare for it to be either cold or hot during the test
14. Bring at least 2 current forms of ID to the testing center
15. Arrive to the test early; be prepared to wait and be patient
16. Eliminate the obviously wrong answer choices, then guess the first remaining choice
17. Pace yourself; don't rush, but keep working and move on if you get stuck
18. Maintain a positive attitude even if the test is going poorly
19. Keep your first answer unless you are positive it is wrong
20. Check your work, don't make a careless mistake

English Language Arts and Reading

Oral Language

Development of language skills

Children learn language through interacting with others, by experiencing language in daily and relevant context, and through understanding that speaking and listening are necessary for effective communication. Teachers can promote language development by intensifying the opportunities a child has to experience and understand language. Teachers can assist language development by:

- Modeling enriched vocabulary and teaching new words
- Using questions and examples to extend a child's descriptive language skills
- Providing ample response time to encourage children to practice speech
- Asking for clarification to provide students with the opportunity to develop communication skills
- Promoting conversations among children
- Providing feedback to let children know they have been heard and understood, and providing further explanation when needed

Oral and written language development

Oral and written language develops simultaneously. The acquisition of skills in one area supports the acquisition of skills in the other. However, oral language is not a prerequisite to written language. An immature form of oral language development is babbling, and an immature form of written language development is scribbling. Oral language development does not occur naturally, but does occur in a social context. This means it is best to include children in conversations rather than simply talk at them. Written language development can occur without direct instruction. In fact, reading and writing do not necessarily need to be taught through formal lessons if the child is exposed to a print-rich environment. A teacher can assist a child's language development by building on what the child already knows, discussing relevant and meaningful events and experiences, teaching vocabulary and literacy skills, and providing opportunities to acquire more complex language.

Theories of language development

Four theories of language development are:

- Learning approach – This theory assumes that language is first learned by imitating the speech of adults. It is then solidified in school through drills about the rules of language structures.
- Linguistic approach – Championed by Noam Chomsky in the 1950s, this theory proposes that the ability to use a language is innate. This is a biological approach rather than one based on cognition or social patterning.
- Cognitive approach – Developed in the 1970s and based on the work of Piaget, this theory states that children must develop appropriate cognitive skills before they can acquire language.

- Sociocognitive approach – In the 1970s, some researchers proposed that language development is a complex interaction of linguistic, social, and cognitive influences. This theory best explains the lack of language skills among children who are neglected, have uneducated parents, or lives in poverty.

Literacy

Literacy is commonly understood to refer to the ability to read and write. UNESCO has further defined literacy as the "ability to identify, understand, interpret, create, communicate, compute, and use printed and written materials associated with varying contexts." Under the UNESCO definition, understanding cultural, political, and historical contexts of communities falls under the definition of literacy. While reading literacy may be gauged simply by the ability to read a newspaper, writing literacy includes spelling, grammar, and sentence structure. To be literate in a foreign language, one would also need to have the ability to understand a language by listening and to speak the language. Some argue that visual representation and numeracy should be included in the requirements one must meet to be considered literate. Computer literacy refers to one's ability to utilize the basic functions of computers and other technologies. Subsets of reading literacy include phonological awareness, decoding, comprehension, and vocabulary.

Literacy development

Necessary skills
According to studies by the National Reading Panel, for children to develop literacy, they must have developed skills in phonemic awareness, phonics, vocabulary, comprehension, and fluency. A prerequisite to developing these five skill areas is having an understanding of how literacy works, what it does, and how it is used. While young children exposed to spoken and printed language interactions from birth often develop this understanding of the functions and applications of literacy in a natural way, children with language and learning disabilities may not. A literacy-rich environment is defined as one that provides students having disabilities with stimulation to take part in activities involving language and literacy during their everyday life routines. Stimulating such participation in and integration of language and literacy into daily living is an effective way to help disabled students begin to develop understanding of how spoken and printed language function and are used. Teaching strategies to establish literacy-rich environments can not only remediate language and literacy deficits, but also benefit all elementary-level students.

Vocabulary
When students do not know the meaning of words in a text, their comprehension is limited. As a result, the text becomes boring or confusing. The larger a student's vocabulary is, the better their reading comprehension will be. A larger vocabulary is also associated with an enhanced ability to communicate in speech and writing. It is the teacher's role to help students develop a good working vocabulary. Students learn most of the words they use and understand from listening to the world around them (adults, other students, media, etc.) They also learn from their reading experiences, which include being read to and reading independently. Carefully designed activities can also stimulate vocabulary growth, and should emphasize useful words that students see frequently, important words necessary for understanding text, and difficult words such as idioms or words with more than one meaning.

Vocabulary development

A student's vocabulary can be developed by:
- Calling upon a student's prior knowledge and making comparisons to that knowledge
- Defining a word and providing multiple examples of the use of the word in context
- Showing a student how to use context clues to discover the meaning of a word
- Providing instruction on prefixes, roots, and suffixes to help students break a word into its parts and decipher its meaning
- Showing students how to use a dictionary and a thesaurus
- Asking students to practice new vocabulary by using the words in their own writing
- Providing a print-rich environment with a word wall
- Studying a group of words related to a single subject, such as farm words, transportation words, etc. so that concept development is enhanced.

Elementary/intermediate speaking skills

Children of elementary/intermediate school age should be able to:
- Speak at an appropriate volume, tone, and pace that is understandable and appropriate to the audience
- Pronounce most words accurately
- Use complete sentences
- Make eye contact
- Use appropriate gestures with speech
- Exhibit an awareness of audience and adjust content to fit the audience (adjust word choices and style to be appropriate for peers or adults)
- Ask relevant questions
- Respond appropriately when asked questions about information or an opinion, possibly also being able to provide reasons for opinions
- Speak in turn, not interrupt, and include others in conversations
- Provide a summary or report orally
- Participate in small and large group discussions and debates
- Read orally before an audience
- Conduct short interviews
- Provide directions and explanations orally, including explanations of class lessons

Difficulties related to learning by listening

It is difficult to learn just by listening because the instruction is presented only in spoken form. Therefore, unless students take notes, there is nothing for them to review. However, an active listener will anticipate finding a message in an oral presentation and will listen for it, interpreting tone and gestures as the presentation progresses. In group discussions, students are often too busy figuring out what they will say when it is their turn to talk to concentrate on what others are saying. Therefore, they don't learn from others, but instead come away knowing only what they already knew. Students should be required to respond directly to the previous speaker before launching into their own comments. This practice will force students to listen to each other and learn that their own responses will be better because of what can be added by listening to others.

Volume, pace, pronunciation, body language, word choice, and visual aids in speaking

Key points to remember are as follows:
- Volume – Voice volume should be appropriate to the room and adjusted according to whether or not a microphone is used. The speaker should not shout at the audience, mumble, or speak so softly that his or her voice is inaudible.
- Pace and pronunciation – The speaker shouldn't talk so fast that his or her speech is unintelligible, nor should the speaker speak so slowly as to be boring. The speaker should enunciate words clearly.
- Body language and gestures – Body language can add to or distract from the message, so annoying, repetitive gestures such as waving hands about, flipping hair, or staring at one spot should be avoided. Good posture is critical.
- Word choice – The speaker should use a vocabulary level that fits the age and interest level of the audience. Vocabulary may be casual or formal depending on the audience.
- Visual aids – The speaker should use whatever aids will enhance the presentation, such as props, models, media, etc., but should not use anything that will be distracting or unmanageable.

Listening skills of ESL students

Listening is a critical skill when learning a new language. Students spend a great deal more time listening than they do speaking, and far less time reading and writing than speaking. Two ways to encourage ESL students to listen are to:
- Talk about topics that are of interest to the ESL learner. Otherwise, students may tune out the speaker because they don't want to put in that much effort to learn about a topic they find boring.
- Talk about content or give examples that are easy to understand or are related to a topic that is familiar to ESL students. Culturally relevant materials will be more interesting to ESL students, will make them feel more comfortable, and will contain vocabulary that they may already be familiar with.

Listening is not a passive skill, but an active one. Therefore, a teacher needs to make the listening experience as rewarding as possible and provide as many auditory and visual clues as possible. Three ways that the teacher can make the listening experience rewarding for ESL students are:
- Avoid colloquialisms and abbreviated or slang terms that may be confusing to the ESL listener, unless there is enough time to define them and explain their use.
- Make the spoken English understandable by stopping to clarify points, repeating new or difficult words, and defining words that may not be known.
- Support the spoken word with as many visuals as possible. Pictures, diagrams, gestures, facial expressions, and body language can help the ESL learner correctly interpret the spoken language more easily and also leaves an image impression that helps them remember the words.

Listening lessons
All students, but especially ESL students, can be taught listening through specific training. During listening lessons, the teacher should guide students through three steps:
- Pre-listening activity – This establishes the purpose of the lesson and engages students' background knowledge. This activity should ask students to think about and discuss

something they already know about the topic. Alternatively, the teacher can provide background information.
- The listening activity – This requires the listener to obtain information and then immediately do something with that information. For example, the teacher can review the schedule for the day or the week. The students are being given information about a routine they already know, but need to be able to identify names, tasks, and times.
- Post-listening activity – This is an evaluation process that allows students to judge how well they did with the listening task. Other language skills can be included in the activity. For example, this activity could involve asking questions about who will do what according to the classroom schedule (Who is the lunch monitor today?) and could also involve asking students to produce whole sentence replies.

Top-down and bottom-up processing

ESL students need to be given opportunities to practice both top-down and bottom-up processing. If they are old enough to understand these concepts, they should be made aware that these are two processes that affect their listening comprehension. In top-down processing, the listener refers to background and global knowledge to figure out the meaning of a message. For example, when asking an ESL student to perform a task, the steps of the task should be explained and accompanied by a review of the vocabulary terms the student already understands so that the student feels comfortable tackling new steps and new words. The teacher should also allow students to ask questions to verify comprehension. In bottom-up processing, the listener figures out the meaning of a message by using "data" obtained from what is said. This data includes sounds (stress, rhythm, and intonation), words, and grammatical relationships. All data can be used to make conclusions or interpretations. For example, the listener can develop bottom-up skills by learning how to detect differences in intonation between statements and questions.

Strategies to help ESL students understand subject matter

Spoken English
To help ESL students better understand subject matter, the following teaching strategies using spoken English can be used:
- Read aloud from a textbook, and then ask ESL students to verbally summarize what was read. The teacher should assist by providing new words as needed to give students the opportunity to practice vocabulary and speaking skills. The teacher should then read the passage again to students to verify accuracy and details.
- The teacher could ask ESL students to explain why the subject matter is important to them and where they see it fitting into their lives. This verbalization gives them speaking practice and helps them relate to the subject.
- Whenever small group activities are being conducted, ESL students can be placed with English-speaking students. It is best to keep the groups to two or three students so that the ESL student will be motivated by the need to be involved. English-speaking students should be encouraged to include ESL students in the group work.

Reading
There are supplemental printed materials that can be used to help ESL students understand subject matter. The following strategies can be used to help ESL students develop English reading skills.
- Make sure all ESL students have a bilingual dictionary to use. A thesaurus would also be helpful.

- Try to keep content area books written in the ESL students' native languages in the classroom. Students can use them side-by-side with English texts. Textbooks in other languages can be ordered from the school library or obtained from the classroom textbook publisher.
- If a student lacks confidence in his/her ability to read the textbook, the teacher can read a passage to the student and have him or her verbally summarize the passage. The teacher should take notes on what the student says and then read them back. These notes can be a substitute, short-form, in-their-own-words textbook that the student can understand.

General teaching strategies for ESL students

Some strategies can help students develop more than one important skill. They may involve a combination of speaking, listening, and/or viewing. Others are mainly classroom management aids. General teaching strategies for ESL students include:
- Partner English-speaking students with ESL students as study buddies and ask the English-speaking students to share notes.
- Encourage ESL students to ask questions whenever they don't understand something. They should be aware that they don't have to be able to interpret every word of text to understand the concept.
- Dictate key sentences related to the content area being taught and ask ESL students to write them down. This gives them practice in listening and writing, and also helps them identify what is important.
- Alternate difficult and easy tasks so that ESL students can experience academic success.
- Ask ESL students to label objects associated with content areas, such as maps, diagrams, parts of a leaf, or parts of a sentence. This gives students writing and reading experience and helps them remember key vocabulary.

Developmentally appropriate materials, curriculum, and classrooms for emergent readers

Materials used to teach reading must be developmentally appropriate to the students being taught. Developmental appropriateness typically involves two major elements:
- Age appropriateness - Curriculum and materials should not be too advanced or too simplistic for the age of the student or students being taught. Materials are more likely to facilitate learning if they are relevant and engaging.
- Individual appropriateness - Materials should appeal to individual students, matching both individual ability and individual interest.

In general, materials that focus exclusively on skills often fail to engage students because they do not appeal to age-specific interests nor do they present reading as an entertaining activity. Curriculum that focuses solely on reading skills also tend to exclude writing, which is as important as reading in developing early literacy.

LEA for language acquisition and development

In the language experience approach, or LEA, to language development, children learn from experience rather than from traditional printed classroom materials such as leveled readers. An example of an LEA approach would be having the class write a report based on a group experience such as a field trip. The class writes this report together, reinforcing the ideas that:
- What the students say aloud can be rendered into print

- What is written down can be rendered back into speech
- Not only the student's own report, but also the reports of others can be written down and read back

LEA can be used to facilitate language acquisition and development, but is also used throughout school when groups of students work together to record a specific experience or activity.

Methods for self-monitoring comprehension

Teachers can help students use comprehension strategies and ensure they can monitor student progress in comprehension using a variety of techniques. These can include:
- Encouraging students to reread and/or read ahead to increase comprehension
- Have students discuss parts of the text that are unclear
- Teach students to use discussion, journaling techniques, or notation to keep track of their thought processes while they are reading
- Teach students to be aware when they lose focus and be prepared to backtrack if necessary
- Addressing all student questions
- Teach students to use different strategies depending upon what problems are encountered in the text

Vocabulary instruction

Effective vocabulary instruction is important to nearly every subject, not just language arts. In order to effectively learn vocabulary in any subject, a student needs more than simply a list of words and their definitions. Major elements of vocabulary instruction include:
- Using new vocabulary in a meaningful context
- Repetition
- Relating vocabulary words to students' experience
- Encouraging students to read
- Providing students with opportunities to use new vocabulary

Some specific strategies for enforcing vocabulary instruction include:
- Word wall with new vocabulary posted regularly
- Lessons on decoding unfamiliar words
- Lessons about word classifications such as synonyms and antonyms
- Ways to study words

<u>Instructional strategies for new vocabulary words</u>
Common instructional strategies teachers use to help young students learn new vocabulary words include: (1) Questioning – when reading aloud, teachers stop at unfamiliar words, asking students their meanings. They may also (2) supply definitions and typical applications, asking students for corresponding words, most often in embedded instruction. To elicit targeted words and reinforce word learning, teachers often (3) provide synonyms. Another strategy to clarify and expand word knowledge is (4) giving students and/or eliciting from them examples of target words. This offers opportunities to use target words; and helps students learn relationships to other words and concepts, and connect words to instances of their use. Teachers also (5) correct and/or clarify student responses, completing partial understandings and/or addressing misunderstandings to guide vocabulary knowledge; (6) extend students' word definitions, supplementing their information; (7) labeling picture-book illustrations with corresponding new words; (8) using facial,

gestural, and/or auditory imagery to illustrate word meanings during read-alouds; and (9) teaching morphemic analyses of complex new words for roots and other components to figure out meanings.

Running record

A teacher keeps a running record when he or she observes a child reading aloud and makes notations about problems encountered during the exercise. The teacher can keep a running record of:
- Words the child mispronounces
- Words the child skips while reading
- Words the child repeats while reading
- Words the child does not understand

The teacher can take notes on another copy of the text including the way the child says each mispronounced word and which words are skipped, repeated, or not understood. This gives the teacher a better understanding of where the child's skills need improvement and can show this improvement when records are compared over time.

Informal assessment

Informal assessment often consists simply of observing students as they read, write and communicate. A teacher can gain a great deal of information this way and this is actually one of the best ways to assess a child's development in the elementary years. This type of assessment typically consists of portfolios or narratives about the child's performance rather than standardized testing or letter grades. Watching how a child responds to various tasks and expected work can also play a part in this type of assessment. If children are frustrated with certain tasks, they most likely need assistance in those areas. Informal assessment should be natural rather than performed in an artificial environment and should be continual rather than limited to a certain time period.

Clay's procedure to assess readiness to learn to read

In 1985, Clay proposed an approach to determine a child's understanding of books in general: how they work and what their different parts are. A typical and informal assessment, according to Clay's approach, is to ask the child where the title of the book is, where the child would begin reading, and where the text ends. The assessment could also establish whether the child understands the directionality of print (i.e., that English is read from left to right). A child who demonstrates an understanding of these basic concepts is displaying a readiness to learn to read.

Abilities, skills, and activities important for acquisition of reading and writing

Many children know something about the ABCs when they start kindergarten. It is important for kindergarten teachers to build on this knowledge by helping them to gain fluency in easily identifying and differentiating among letter shapes. Research has established well that kindergarteners' letter-naming proficiency is highly predictive of their achievement at the end of the year, likely due to its mediation of memory for sounds. Learning theorists recommend beginning with the upper-case letters that are visually the easiest, and progressing to lower-case letters. They also find that mastery is facilitated, not by introducing many letters at once, but by introducing only a few at a time. Developmentally, children's ability to name letters easily coincides with their ability to associate letters with speech sounds. However, phonemic awareness also requires practice and time to develop fully. Kindergarteners with good phonemic awareness can identify rhyming and non-rhyming words, and words with the same initial or final sounds; they can segment short words into individual phonemes, and blend phonemes into words

Phonemes and graphemes

Understanding the connection between print and speech involves understanding the connection between phonemes and graphemes. Students do not need to be aware of these terms in order to understand the concept. The term phoneme refers to the actual sounds produced in a spoken word. Graphemes are the symbols, such as our alphabet, diacritical marks, or other parts of written language, that represent individual sounds of speech. When an adult reads aloud to a child while the child observes, the child often begins to recognize that certain combinations of symbols represent specific words. The ability to make these connections indicates reading readiness.

Phonemic awareness

Phonemic awareness consists of being able to hear, identify, and manipulate individual speech sounds or phonemes. The manipulation of speech sounds includes such processes as breaking words down to individual components; blending phonemes and words; and stretching them. For children to read printed language, they must first develop phonemic awareness. This enables their understanding that words are composed of phonemes, which are the smallest units of sound in a spoken word that affect its meaning. For example, changing the phoneme /s/ to /m/ changes the word sat to mat, a different word and meaning. Children can demonstrate phonemic awareness by identifying words in a group that start with the same phoneme, such as book, boy, and bicycle. They can isolate and pronounce the initial or final phoneme in a word, such as /d/ or /g/ in dog. They can blend phonemes to say a word, e.g. "/d/, /o/, /g/--dog." They can conversely segment words into phonemes, e.g. "dog--/d/, /o/, /g/."

Instruction in phonemic awareness

Teachers can use a rhyme-generating strategy with monosyllabic words for kindergarten students and with multisyllabic words for older students. Teachers first introduce the concept of rhyming, asking students for definitions and examples of rhymes. Then the teachers read a rhyming poem or song lyrics aloud to the students, asking them to identify which of the words rhyme. Teachers chart these words for students, color-coding the onset (word-initial phoneme) and rime (word-stem) of each rhyming word. Teachers use a word ladder graphic to show students how they can use existing words to generate new word stems (rimes). Teachers chart word-initial consonants and show students how to change (manipulate) these to make new rhymes. For example, *fat-cat-sat-mat*. The teacher selects sentences from the poems or song that are read aloud and writes them on strips of paper ("sentence strips"). The teacher then has students generate new rhymes by producing sentences of their own to fit the poem or song context. Teachers also develop student manipulation skills by having them generate rhymes with their own and classmates' names.

Teachers can help first-grade students develop phonological processing skills by providing explicit instruction using multiple sensory modalities, aiding comprehension and retention. Technology provides differentiation for ELL students using technology. For example, ELL students view printed words in onscreen text, type in rhyming words, and listen to stories or songs accompanying the text. There are websites offering activities for word-building. For example, www.readwritethink.org features interactive activities like "Construct a Word," wherein ELL students can find rhyming words, generate matching rhymes, and receive feedback and scores on their responses. Teachers can follow this activity by providing ELL students with repeated reading practice via a podcast and accompanying word sheet of paired rhyming words that the site also supplies. Multisensory modalities and repeated exposures also benefit special-needs students. Teachers can differentiate instruction for them by playing a podcast song like "Old MacDonald" for wordplay and rhyme generation and having students make flip-books with pictures of animals illustrating rhyming words and color-coded text. For ongoing practice, students can even trade their flip books with classmates.

Teachers can help develop phonological and phonemic awareness skills in ELL and special-needs students by providing them with games involving systematic, explicit instruction in separating and combining phonemes in words. This teaches the decoding skills necessary for reading. Teachers can differentiate these activities, like a "Treasure Chest" activity using picture cards, pennies, and a Treasure Chest board or sheet, for ELL students by additionally making them a computer podcast giving the names for each picture card. In the podcast, the teacher (or whoever is speaking in the recording) also separates these words into their component phonemes and blends the individual phonemes into words. Students learning English as a new language need repeated phonemic practice. They receive supplementary support by using the picture cards while listening to the podcast as an in-class activity and/or homework. Special-needs students also get more practice by playing a guessing game with this activity: in pairs, they take turns, one giving the other clues to the names for each picture card and the other guessing using segmented words (e.g., "/d/o/g/").

Informal assessment of ability to blend words and segment phonemes

For assessing blending, the teacher tells the student, "Let's play 'Guess My Word.' I'm going to say a word, but I'm going to say it in parts. I want you to guess what the word is. Here's an example: /c/--/at/." Can you guess the word?" The teacher uses a simple, numbered checklist. For each numbered item, the teacher has pre-written/printed the two sounds to present, such as /s/ and /un/, /b/ and /all/, etc. The teacher marks the student's response to each item as Correct or Incorrect. For phoneme segmentation, the teacher says, "I'm going to say a word. I want you to separate the word into the different sounds you hear. Let's practice: If I say 'cat,' you would say, /c/-/a/-/t/." The teacher presents a series of one-syllable words, which s/he has pre-written/printed on a checklist similar to the blending checklist, and marks the student's responses as correct/incorrect. Both assessments can be repeated periodically. Teachers can also analyze student responses for specific problem areas to remediate.

Impact of reading skills on success with school curriculum content

The ability to read is not simply one academic area; it is a basic skill set underlying all academic activity, and determines whether students fail or succeed in school. Research shows that of first-graders with poor reading skills, 88% still read poorly in fourth grade. By this time, most information that students require is provided in text form. For this reason, the focus shifts from learning to read in the earlier grades, to reading to learn by fourth grade. Consequently, students with poor reading skills can find it harder to access and interact with the content in their schools' curricula. Moreover, reading abilities that are delayed or disordered usually are identified in higher elementary grades. Yet research finds remediation attempts then could be too late, because children acquire language and have literacy experiences from birth. Phonemic awareness, the alphabetic principle, and print awareness normally develop in early childhood. Children missing such early experiences will fall behind peers without extra instruction. This means elementary school teachers must give these children literacy-rich environments

Reading problems

While any student can have reading problems for a variety of causes, some students have higher probabilities of encountering difficulty with reading. Adults need to know about these relationships, as their knowledge can inform their monitoring of students at higher risk for deficits in reading skills. Closer monitoring enables earlier detection of problems and intervention to address them. For example, children of parents who have histories of reading problems can be more likely also to present with reading problems. Children with hearing impairments have a higher likelihood of reading problems, since the normal basis for language and reading development is auditory. Children with visual impairments are also more likely to have delays and/or deficits in visually reading print. Children who have received diagnoses of specific language impairments have a greater probability of reading problems, as do students with cognitive disabilities. In addition, children without physical or cognitive deficits who were exposed less to literacy-related knowledge and/or skills during their preschool development are found more likely to develop reading difficulties.

Information sources

There are many different sources of information. On the Internet, there are multiple sites (some more reliable than others) where print information as well as charts and other graphic organizers are available to all. In addition, there are hard copy and online journals, textbooks, magazines, and newspapers; researchers are often overwhelmed with information. It is best to choose only the sources that can be verified or are from a credible author or organization. This information must then be analyzed to see how consistent it is and whether valid discrepancies exist, and why. After, it can be used in a presentation or a discussion.

Early Literacy Development

Emergent literacy

Emergent literacy is a concept developed by Mary M. Clay in 1966. It refers to a stage in educational development when children begin to formally learn how to read and write. During this process, students begin to understand the printed word and how it relates to spoken language. The use of the term has changed over the years. In current usage, it refers to the development of behavior related to literacy, or simply to the developmental phase when children begin to understand printed language. This phase covers childhood development from birth to approximately five years old. Different definitions and concepts exist in regard to emergent literacy. Some educators feel that emergent literacy should be seen as a transitional period rather than as a specific stage as suggested by Clay (1966). During this transitional stage, a student gradually shifts from a nonreader to an emergent, or beginning, reader. The exact age at which this occurs varies from one child to another. With a teacher taking on the role of getting a child ready to read, transmission educators feel that that readiness can be taught. Other theories posit that children must exhibit certain signs of readiness before any reading instruction will be effective.

Successful teaching strategy for language acquisition

In order to be successful, a teaching strategy for language acquisition must appeal to the students. Major characteristics that will increase the likelihood of meaningful engagement include:

- Authenticity - Materials should relate to students' real life experiences, making them more relevant.
- Books with meaningful stories - In addition to working with skills, materials should include actual books that tell a meaningful story.
- Not overly repetitive - Materials should not repeat themselves, but match the students' existing knowledge levels and provide some challenge.
- Appropriate - Teaching materials should be developmentally, individually and age appropriate for the student or students using them.
- Teachers should be prepared to use different strategies for different students, as well as to provide additional, appropriate materials for those students who might be learning more slowly or more quickly than others in the class.

Alphabetic principle and alphabet writing systems

The alphabetic principle refers to the use of letters and combinations of letters to represent speech sounds. The way letters are combined and pronounced is guided by a system of rules that establishes relationships between written and spoken words and their letter symbols. Alphabet writing systems are common around the world. Some are phonological in that each letter stands for an individual sound and words are spelled just as they sound. However, there are other writing systems as well, such as the Chinese logographic system and the Japanese syllabic system.

Alphabetic principle and letter-sound correspondences

Elementary school students must receive systematic, explicit instruction in letter-sound correspondences beginning immediately in kindergarten if not sooner in order to develop the reading skills they will need in future grades. This includes being able to recite the alphabet; being able to identify all alphabet letters, including upper-case, lower-case, and cursive forms by their appearance; being able to connect the speech sounds they hear to the correct alphabet letters that represent them; and reciprocally, being able to see alphabet letters and produce the correct speech sounds that the letters represent. Students in the early elementary grades must gain these and other skills that are prerequisite to developing reading skills, including accuracy and fluency, that will enable them to read printed text on their respective grade levels with good comprehension. For elementary school students to meet the expectations of their teachers and schools, including expectations mandated by federal laws and aligned state and local laws, schools should assess student learning not only by the particular curriculum, but by grade-level benchmarks.

Phonological awareness

A subskill of literacy, phonological awareness is the ability to perceive sound structures in a spoken word, such as syllables and the individual phonemes within syllables. Phonemes are the sounds represented by the letters in the alphabet. The ability to separate, blend, and manipulate sounds is critical to developing reading and spelling skills. Phonological awareness is concerned with not only syllables, but also onset sounds (the sounds at the beginning of words) and rime (the same thing as rhyme, but spelled differently to distinguish syllable rime from poetic rhyme). Phonological awareness is an auditory skill that does not necessarily involve print. It should be developed before the student has learned letter to sound correspondences. A student's phonological awareness is an indicator of future reading success.

Activities that teach phonological awareness
Classroom activities that teach phonological awareness include language play and exposure to a variety of sounds and contexts of sounds. Activities that teach phonological awareness include:
- Clapping to the sounds of individual words, names, or all words in a sentence
- Practicing saying blended phonemes
- Singing songs that involve phoneme replacement (e.g., The Name Game)
- Reading poems, songs, and nursery rhymes out loud
- Reading patterned and predictable texts out loud
- Listening to environmental sounds or following verbal directions
- Playing games with rhyming chants or fingerplays
- Reading alliterative texts out loud
- Grouping objects by beginning sounds
- Reordering words in a well-known sentence or making silly phrases by deleting words from a well-known sentence (perhaps from a favorite storybook)

Teaching reading through phonics

Phonics is the process of learning to read by learning how spoken language is represented by letters. Students learn to read phonetically by sounding out the phonemes in words and then blending them together to produce the correct sounds in words. In other words, the student connects speech sounds with letters or groups of letters and blends the sounds together to determine the pronunciation of an unknown word. Phonics is a commonly used method to teach decoding and reading, but has been challenged by other methods, such as the whole language approach. Despite the complexity of pronunciation and combined sounds in the English language, research shows that phonics is a highly effective way to teach reading. Being able to read or pronounce a word does not mean the student comprehends the meaning of the word, but context aids comprehension. When phonics is used as a foundation for decoding, children eventually learn to recognize words automatically and advance to decoding multisyllable words with practice.

Instruction in phonics and spelling

Many research studies clearly demonstrate that phonics, spelling, and reading have a reciprocal and interactive relationship. According to the National Reading Panel, students improve their application of alphabetic knowledge to spelling via phonics instruction. When they spell words, students must encode them. In encoding, they apply sound-to-symbol relationships at higher levels. This in turn makes their phonics knowledge deeper. Instructional models like LEAD21 (Wright Group, 2010-2013) align phonics with spelling. Thus the model's lessons in spelling adhere to the same skills sequence and range as are covered in its phonics instruction. Both progress in complexity from simplest to most difficult. Students participate in various phonics activities. For example, teachers lead students in a phonemic awareness warm-up activity containing the phonemes in that week's spelling list. Students read sentences containing words using the week's spelling pattern. They may also read decodable books, individually or in small groups, with the related phonics and spelling components. Then teachers give them a spelling pre-test to introduce the week's spelling list.

Literacy development

Fluency
Fluency is the goal of literacy development. It is the ability to read accurately and quickly. Evidence of fluency includes the ability to recognize words automatically and group words for comprehension. At this point, the student no longer needs to decode words except for complex, unfamiliar ones. He or she is able to move to the next level and understand the meaning of a text. The student should be able to self-check for comprehension and should feel comfortable expressing ideas in writing. Teachers can help students build fluency by continuing to provide: reading experiences and discussions about text, gradually increasing the level of difficulty; reading practice, both silently and out loud; word analysis practice; instruction on reading comprehension strategies; and opportunities to express responses to readings through writing.

Comprehension
The whole point of reading is to comprehend what someone else is trying to say through writing. Without comprehension, a student is just reading the words without understanding them or increasing knowledge of a topic. Comprehension results when the student has the vocabulary and reading skills necessary to make sense of the whole picture, not just individual words. Students can self-monitor because they know when they are comprehending the material and when they are not. Teachers can help students solve problems with comprehension by teaching them strategies such as pre-reading titles, sidebars, and follow-up questions; looking at illustrations; predicting what's going to happen in the story; asking questions to check understanding while reading; connecting to background knowledge; and relating to the experiences or feelings of the characters.

Comprehension

Successful reading involves more than simply decoding words. Reading comprehension involves understanding what is being read. Elements of comprehension include:
- Point of view of the text
- Message of the text
- Purpose of the author
- Opinion vs. fact
- Identifying facts and details
- Making inferences
- Identifying and understanding the conclusion

In addition, there are four basic levels of comprehension:
1. Literal
2. Interpretive
3. Critical
4. Creative

The teacher's work in the classroom should focus on helping students develop these specific comprehension skills and progress through the levels of comprehension to develop higher level thinking skills.

In the literal level of reading comprehension, the reader understands the literal, straightforward meaning of the text. To determine if a student has understood the text on a literal level, the teacher can ask questions referring to:
- Facts in the text
- Details found in the text
- Sequence of events
- Comparing one detail of the text to another

In the interpretive level of reading comprehension, the reader begins to interpret various types of language and make inferences based on the text. Questions to determine interpretive comprehension could cover:
- Point of view of the text
- Definitions of terms
- Explanations of figurative language
- The author's basic message or purpose
- Requiring the reader to infer answers from the text

In the critical level of comprehension, the student must make judgments based on the text. Elements the student might address include:
- Is the text reliable?
- What is the reader's emotional response to the text?
- How does the text compare to other texts?
- Is the text based on facts or on the author's opinions?
- Is the author an informed source?

The creative level is the highest level of comprehension. In this level of comprehension, the student has reached a level where he or she can use information from the text and apply it to other similar situations. The teacher could ask the students to:
- Come up with different solutions to a problem presented in the text
- Compose a different ending to a story
- Consider how the story might have progressed if a specific plot element were changed

SQ3R method
SQ3R is an acronym for a reading comprehension method whose steps are:
- Survey - Skim the text and look at major characteristics such as headings of chapters, diagrams, charts or pictures, and words that are emphasized by a different font.
- Question - Produce a list of questions the text might answer. A list of questions at the end of the text might be helpful in this step.
- Read - Read through the text to find answers to the chosen questions.
- Recite - Read through the questions and attempt to answer them without referring to the text.
- Review - Look over the text to see if the answers supplied are correct.

Strategies to improve reading comprehension
Teachers can model in a read-aloud the strategies students can use on their own to better comprehend a text. First, the teacher should do a walk-through of the story illustrations and ask, "What's happening here?" Based on what they have seen, the teacher should then ask students to predict what the story will be about. As the book is read, the teacher should ask open-ended questions such as, "Why do you think the character did this?" and "How do you think the character

feels?" The teacher should also ask students if they can relate to the story or have background knowledge of something similar. After the reading, the teacher should ask the students to retell the story in their own words to check for comprehension. This retelling can take the form of a puppet show or summarizing the story to a partner.

Role of prior knowledge in determining appropriate literacy education

Even preschool children have some literacy skills, and the extent and type of these skills have implications for instructional approaches. Comprehension results from relating two or more pieces of information. One piece comes from the text, and another piece might come from prior knowledge (something from a student's long-term memory). For a child, that prior knowledge comes from being read to at home; taking part in other literacy experiences, such as playing computer or word games; being exposed to a print-rich environment at home; and observing examples of parents' reading habits. Children who have had extensive literacy experience are better prepared to further develop their literacy skills in school than children who have not been read to, have few books or magazines in their homes, are seldom exposed to high-level oral or written language activities, and seldom witness adults engaged in reading and writing. Children with a scant literacy background are at a disadvantage. The teacher must not make any assumptions about their prior knowledge, and should use intense, targeted instruction. Otherwise, reading comprehension will be limited.

Effective reading instruction

One part of effective reading instruction involves (1) phonemic awareness, (2) knowledge of letters, and (3) print concepts. Variations in young children's early success with reading and spelling are not due as much to their intelligence, levels of maturity, or listening comprehension, as to their levels of phonemic awareness and knowledge of letter-sound correspondences. Children who are found to have poor development of phonemic awareness by the end of kindergarten are more likely to read poorly in later grades. Teachers can mitigate young children's risk of later failure in reading by giving them explicit instruction in identifying sounds, matching phonemes, segmenting words into phonemes, and blending phonemes into words, and associating sounds and their symbols. This type of explicit instruction also speeds up the early acquisition of reading and spelling for all young children.

Teaching reading strategies

Teachers can use a variety of approaches when teaching reading strategies. A structured approach includes:
- Modeling the strategy
- Explaining the strategy
- Describing how to apply the strategy
- Providing guided practice of the strategy

The teacher can narrate their thought processes while modeling the strategy while the students do the same while applying it. This can clarify how the strategy is used and help students understand it more clearly. As the strategy is practiced in the classroom, the teacher can provide feedback and assistance to ensure the strategy is effectively utilized.

Miscue analysis

When keeping a running record of a child's reading skill, the teacher keeps track of what words are skipped, repeated, mispronounced, or unfamiliar. The teacher then looks at the missed words and determines why the child had trouble with them. This analysis can reveal patterns in the child's reading, such as transposed letters, dropping of certain sounds, families of sounds that are not pronounced correctly, or other problems. This assessment of the child's mistakes is called a miscue analysis. Evaluating the miscues can help the teacher determine how he or she can assist the student in reading more accurately and can even help diagnose some reading disabilities, such as dyslexia or speech impediments.

Word Identification Skills and Reading Fluency

Language cues

The three major types of language cues used in decoding word pronunciation and meaning are:
1. Syntactic - This refers to the order of words, how they are placed in a sentence and how they appear to function within that sentence. A reader can often deduce whether a word is a noun or a verb based upon its placement and function in a sentence. This can also include prefixes and suffixes that affect the meaning of a word.
2. Semantic - These are clues toward the meaning of a word derived from the full context of that word. Clues could come from the individual sentence where the word is placed or from a larger section of the text such as a paragraph or the entire text.
3. Phonemes and graphemes - These provide pronunciation clues. The phoneme is the spoken sound while the grapheme is the written symbol used to represent that sound.

Decoding

Decoding is the method or strategy used to make sense of printed words and figure out how to correctly pronounce them. In order to decode, a student needs to know the relationships between letters and sounds, including letter patterns; that words are constructed from phonemes and phoneme blends; and that a printed word represents a word that can be spoken. This knowledge will help the student recognize familiar words and make informed guesses about the pronunciation of unfamiliar words. Decoding is not the same as comprehension. It does not require an understanding of the meaning of a word, only a knowledge of how to recognize and pronounce it. Decoding can also refer to the skills a student uses to determine the meaning of a sentence. These skills include applying knowledge of vocabulary, sentence structure, and context.

Structural analysis

Structural analysis refers to the ability to analyze words according to their individual parts, or syllables. A reader who understands the concepts of word structure can more easily sound out unfamiliar words. Structural analysis benefits from knowledge of phonics rules, which can affect the way each syllable is pronounced based on the structure of the rest of the word. It is also helpful to understand concepts such as prefixes and suffixes, as this element of structural analysis can not only help the reader pronounce the word, but can also give clues to the meaning of the word.

Some of the basic rules that help guide structural analysis of words include:
- Pronunciation of specific word endings
- Rules regarding where words are divided into syllables
- Pronunciation of prefixes
- Meanings of prefixes and suffixes

For young readers, these rules are most useful when they encounter words that are similar to words they already know. For example, if a child already knows a basic word, then encounters the same word with a prefix or suffix, the child will recognize the root word and, if he or she knows the rules of structural analysis, will be able to pronounce it as well as ascertain its approximate meaning.

V/cv and vc/cv rules

The v/cv and the vc/cv rules refer to how words are properly divided into syllables. In this case, v stands for vowel and c stands for consonant. In order to apply this rule a reader must know which letters are vowels and which are consonants. In the v/cv rule, the syllable division occurs between the first vowel and its following consonant. In the vc/cv rule, the division occurs between two adjacent consonants. For example, the word "afraid" is divided into syllables as "a-fraid," dividing between the leading vowel and its following consonant according to the v/cv rule. A word like "winter" follows the vc/cv rule, being divided as "win-ter." These rules can help readers break words down into syllables, making pronunciation easier.

Affixes, prefixes, and root words

Affixes are syllables attached to the beginning or end of a word to make a derivative or inflectional form of a word. Both prefixes and suffixes are affixes. A prefix is a syllable that appears at the beginning of a word that, in combination with the root or base word, creates a specific meaning. For example, the prefix "mis" means "wrong." When combined with the root word "spelling," the word "misspelling" is created, which means the "wrong spelling." A root word is the base of a word to which affixes can be added. For example, the prefix "in" or "pre" can be added to the root word "vent" to create "invent" or "prevent," respectively. The suffix "er" can be added to the root word "work" to create "worker," which means "one who works." The suffix "able," meaning "capable of," can be added to "work" to create "workable," which means "capable of working."

Suffixes

A suffix is a syllable that appears at the end of a word that, in combination with the root or base word, creates a specific meaning. There are three types of suffixes:
- Noun suffixes – There are two types of noun suffixes. One denotes the act of, state of, or quality of. For example, "ment" added to "argue" becomes "argument," which is defined as "the act of arguing." The other denotes the doer, or one who acts. For example "eer" added to "auction" becomes "auctioneer," meaning "one who auctions." Other examples include "hood," "ness," "tion," "ship," and "ism."
- Verb suffixes – These denote "to make" or "to perform the act of." For example, "en" added to "soft" makes "soften," which means "to make soft." Other verb suffixes are "ate" (perpetuate), "fy" (dignify), and "ize" (sterilize).
- Adjectival suffixes – These include suffixes such as "ful," which means "full of." When added to "care," the word "careful" is formed, which means "full of care." Other examples are "ish," "less," and "able."

Controlled vocabulary

In a controlled vocabulary situation, emerging readers are only exposed to reading materials that contain certain words. New words are gradually introduced over time, giving the reader time to learn them. Many books aimed at beginning readers use controlled vocabulary to increase exposure to certain families of words. As the texts become more advanced, more varied vocabulary is used. In this way, readers gradually build their vocabulary and comprehension.

Analysis of meanings of words and phrases in text

The meaning of words and phrases can typically be determined from the context of the sentence in which they appear, as well as the surrounding sentences. It may be necessary to read an entire text to figure out the meaning of a term, particularly a technical or legal term. While words may be used in a literal manner, phrases can be more difficult to figure out since their meaning is often not tied to the exact meaning of the words that comprise them. Phrases are often expressions that need to be interpreted. Expressions are idioms that are usually part of the vernacular of a language. They may require more effort to understand, although the meaning can often still be gleaned from the context.

Context clues

Context clues are words or phrases that help the reader figure out the meaning of an unknown word. They are built into a sentence or paragraph by the writer to help the reader develop a clear understanding of the writer's message. Context clues can be used to make intelligent guesses about the meaning of a word instead of relying on a dictionary. Context clues are the reason most vocabulary is learned through reading. There are four types of commonly used context clues:
- Synonyms – A word with the same meaning as the unknown word is placed close by for comparison.
- Antonyms – A word with the opposite meaning as the unknown word is placed close by for contrast.
- Explanations – An obvious explanation is given close to the unknown word.
- Examples – Examples of what the word means are given to help the reader define the term.

Reading strategies

Visualizing and inferences
As a reader absorbs a text, he or she visualizes the events, people and places described within it. This process of visualization helps increase the understanding of what they are reading as well as causing a higher level of engagement with the text. If they understand the text, readers make inferences naturally as they read. Prior knowledge can be combined with textual clues to allow the reader to guess what might happen next or to garner additional information about occurrences or characters that is not explicitly presented in the text.

Activating prior knowledge and asking questions
Two important reading strategies for both comprehension and engagement are:
1. Activating prior knowledge - Texts that are relevant to the student will naturally engage the student more thoroughly. Using prior knowledge, a student can relate the current text to past experiences as well as their current understanding and issues beyond his or her individual situation, adding a more personal meaning to the text overall.

2. Asking questions - A reader who is engaged in a text will ask questions about what has happened and even about what will happen next. Predicting what is coming next in a text is an important part of comprehension and involves thorough engagement with and understanding of the text.

Reflection and using parts of a book
Reflection occurs after reading is completed. The student reflects on what he or she has read, considering its meaning and what they understand in a larger context. Reflection in a journal can be a useful classroom tool to increase and evaluate comprehension.

Books often provide different sections such as maps, indices, tables of contents, charts or other tools that can help increase understanding as the student is reading. For example, a description of the Battle of the Bulge might be difficult for a student to understand unless he consults a map included in the text.

Relevance of reading speed in assessing comprehension

How fast a student reads can sometimes be relevant in assessing his or her comprehension level. Students who have difficulty with comprehension may read much more slowly or might spend extra time backtracking to reread sections, indicating difficulty with general comprehension. On the other hand, students who read very fast might not be taking the time to ensure complete understanding of details. Recording reading speeds and comparing the speed to the level of comprehension can help determine if an individual student's reading speed is related to lower comprehension scores.

Guided practice and independent practice

In guided practice, the teacher watches students as they read to ensure they are using appropriate comprehension strategies, to help when necessary, and to assess the skill levels of individual students. The teacher can correct inaccurate pronunciation or interpretation and can supply definitions or other necessary information if the student requires assistance. Guided practice helps the teacher ensure that students understand the material. In independent practice, students read on their own. The teacher can assess understanding after each reading session during a review or by having students report on what they have read.

Retelling a story to judge reading comprehension

One of the best ways to determine if a child has understood a story is to ask him to retell it. Retelling is a valuable form of informal assessment and can be performed in a casual, one-on-one approach, journaling, or more formal conversations. Children can retell stories directly to the teacher or can be asked to narrate something they have read to the classroom or study group. They could also be asked to create artwork based on the story, provide a short book report or journal entry, or retell the story in another way that will keep the student engaged and interested in the material.

Role of motivation in reading comprehension

Student motivation is vital to both their reading enough and their comprehending what they read. Students' learning to read is significantly aided by motivation, as are higher student literacy levels. The broader a student's reading experiences, the greater his/her ability to understand a broadening variety of the kinds and difficulty levels of texts. Good readers read copiously, in school and independently, choosing diverse texts for various purposes, such as for information, learning, curiosity, and entertainment. To support student motivation, teachers can: give students daily opportunities to read both texts they choose and those teachers and peers recommend; frequently afford both student-led and teacher-led discussions of their reading; arrange cooperative learning groups to discuss their reading and help one another select the best strategies for each text; encourage students to read for learning about ideas and/or subjects they find meaningful; engage them actively in reading-related pursuits; encourage independent reading; and give them opportunities to select from among texts with various reading levels and genres.

Effective literacy learning environments for young children

Young children need print-rich learning environments that facilitate and enhance their phonological awareness and supply them with ongoing reinforcement of direct instruction. Teachers should provide young children with continual, ready access to books and other literary materials, rather than simply storing them on shelves. They should expose young children to many varieties of print. A classroom library containing both fiction and non-fiction books should be located centrally, and include newspapers, magazines, telephone books, restaurant menus, etc. Teachers should also integrate literacy across the curriculum by reading and assigning texts that support their learning units in subjects such as mathematics, sciences, and social studies. For example, they can teach sequencing during science experiments by using graphic organizers. They can visually display the relevant number words and math terms during classroom calculations so the children can see these math processes represented phonetically as they work with them

Reading fluency and non-fluent reading

Reading fluency is an ability to read printed text with speed, accuracy, and (when reading aloud) appropriate expression. Fluent readers automatically recognize the words in a text when they read it silently. To derive meaning from what they are reading, they use strategies such as quickly grouping words into phrases, clauses, and sentences. When fluent readers read text out loud, they do so without effort, and they use natural-sounding vocal expression the same way as when they are speaking spontaneously. Non-fluent readers, in contrast, read slowly and laboriously, one word at a time. When reading aloud, they sound choppy rather than smooth. Fluent readers decode words effortlessly and automatically, identifying and understanding words simultaneously— freeing their attention to focus on the meaning. They form connections among the concepts presented in the text, and between these and their prior knowledge. Readers less fluent divert too much attention to decoding words, so they have little left to focus on understanding the meaning.

<u>Levels of reading fluency</u>
The three levels of reading fluency are the Frustration, Instructional, and Independent levels. At the Frustration level, the text is hard for the student to read and s/he will attain lower than 90% accuracy in decoding words. At the Instructional level, the text is challenging for the reader but not frustrating, and the reader achieves 90% word accuracy. At the Independent level, the student finds the text relatively easy to read and attains 95% accuracy in recognizing and understanding its words. Fluency instruction should utilize text that the student can read at his/her Independent reading level. This is because students can focus on practicing reading speed and expression, instead of on decoding words, at their Independent levels. Fluency is not a fixed stage where readers can read all words easily and rapidly; it varies with text and subject familiarity. For example, even students who normally read very fluently may read slowly and laboriously with

highly technical text on an unfamiliar subject, such as medical journal articles or nuclear physics textbooks.

Silent, independent reading as an instructional approach to improving reading fluency

Much research has revealed a strong correlation between a student's reading ability and the amount of time that the student spends reading. In fact, how much time they spend reading is considered one of the primary differences between poor and good readers. Because of these conclusions, experts have advised teachers for many years to encourage students to read voluntarily in classrooms. The literature in reading education and teacher education frequently offers classroom procedures, such as Silent Sustained Reading (SSR) and Drop Everything and Read (DEAR), to motivate students to read independently. However, research does not show that reading silently and independently with little or no feedback or guidance yields any improvement in reading fluency or achievement. Instead, studies find direct reading instruction to be most predictive of reading achievement. Nevertheless, teachers should not overlook the importance of providing students with time to read silently from books they can read at their Independent fluency level—i.e., they can read them with 95% word accuracy—to apply their reading skills.

Differentiating instruction in reading fluency to meet needs of individual students

When instructing students in reading fluency, experts advise dividing them into small groups based on similar reading levels and fluency rates. They recommend that teachers work with students on attending to vocal expression and following punctuation when reading aloud. Teachers should instruct students to read at a volume that is quiet without being a whisper. When all groups in a class read this way, it creates a "white noise" effect supporting individual student concentration. When using recordings, the teachers should provide headphones or have the students keep the volume reasonable. Teachers can evaluate student progress by analyzing unpracticed daily readings. While practiced readings will be faster, teachers should stress student improvement over time in unpracticed reading speeds. Experts advise teachers to make use of students they have assigned as "Fluency Leaders" of each small group for collecting and distributing materials and asking questions of the teacher on behalf of their group.

Teachers can differentiate their reading fluency instruction by dividing students into small groups with similar reading levels and fluency rates according to the results of reading and fluency assessments they have made of each student. Teachers can integrate instruction in reading comprehension with instruction in reading fluency. Because high student scores in reading fluency correlate positively with high student scores in reading comprehension, instruction in the two should naturally go together. Teachers can integrate comprehension and fluency by instructing students in "talking to the text" and author as they are reading to enhance their concentration and their understanding of the text. To model metacognition and interactive reading, teachers should periodically conduct a "Think-Aloud" with students, having them verbalize their thoughts about the text to model how students should think about text as they read, and have them practice Think-Alouds in pairs. Teachers can also instruct students in comprehension questions to help them read independently. They can integrate vocabulary development by having students write sentences with context clues for pre-taught vocabulary words.

Reading Comprehension and Assessment

Metacognition

Metacognition is thinking about thinking. For the student, this involves taking control of their own learning process, self-monitoring progress, evaluating the effectiveness of strategies, and making adjustments to strategies and learning behaviors as needed. Students who develop good metacognitive skills become more independent and confident about learning. They develop a sense of ownership about their education and realize that information is readily available to them. Metacognitive skills can be grouped into three categories:

- Awareness – This involves identifying prior knowledge; defining learning goals; inventorying resources such as textbooks, libraries, computers, and study time; identifying task requirements and evaluation standards; and recognizing motivation and anxiety levels.
- Planning – This involves doing time estimates for tasks, prioritizing, scheduling study time, making checklists of tasks, gathering needed materials, and choosing strategies for problem solving or task comprehension.
- Self-monitoring and reflection – This involves identifying which strategies or techniques work best, questioning throughout the process, considering feedback, and maintaining focus and motivation.

In terms of literacy development, metacognitive skills include taking an active role in reading, recognizing reading behaviors and changing them to employ the behaviors that are most effective, relating information to prior knowledge, and being aware of text structures. For example, if there is a problem with comprehension, the student can try to form a mental image of what is described, read the text again, adjust the rate of reading, or employ other reading strategies such as identifying unknown vocabulary and predicting meaning. Being aware of text structures is critical to being able to follow the author's ideas and relationships among ideas. Being aware of difficulties with text structure allows the student to employ strategies such as hierarchical summaries, thematic organizers, or concept maps to remedy the problem.

Literal and critical comprehension

Literal comprehension refers to the skills a reader uses to deal with the actual words in a text. It involves skills such as identifying the topic sentence, main idea, important facts, and supporting details; using context clues to determine the meaning of a word; and sequencing events. Critical comprehension involves prior knowledge and an understanding that written material, especially in nonfiction, is the author's version of the subject and not necessarily anybody else's. Critical comprehension involves analysis of meaning, evaluation, validation, questioning, and the reasoning skills a reader uses to recognize:

- Inferences and conclusions
- Purpose, tone, point of view, and themes
- The organizational pattern of a work
- Explicit and implicit relationships among words, phrases, and sentences
- Biased language, persuasive tactics, valid arguments, and the difference between fact and opinion

Using book structure and organization to increase reading comprehension

Teachers can help students increase their reading comprehension by explaining the way a book is structured and the importance of different parts of the book. This can include the table of contents, the index, chapter headings, words that are presented in bold or italic text, or other divisions such as chapter subdivisions or sidebar text. These parts of a book will not be the same in every text, so the teacher should be prepared to discuss the structure of each individual text. When students are introduced to a book's structure before they begin to read it, they are less likely to be confused when encountering a non-traditional layout and will be better able to understand what they are reading without being distracted by different organization or different typefaces.

Assessment results and instructional design for pre-reading and reading skills

Educators must collect assessment data on each of their individual students. They obtain these data by administering various standardized tests; informal assessments; progress monitoring measures included in their curricula; and daily measurements of student performance and progress, including observations and observational checklists as well as written quizzes, tests, and homework assignments. Educators must then analyze the data they gather to identify patterns in each student's learning needs. Once they have identified such patterns, teachers must focus their instruction to target their remediation. Their teaching activities must include: systematic, explicit instruction based on research evidence of effective teaching practices in skills which the students have not learned yet; how to apply those skills once they have learned them; and ample, repeated practice in applying those skills, which should be spread over sufficient periods of time. Teachers must also use assessments on an ongoing basis to monitor student progress and detect deficits in pre-reading and reading skills. They must then re-teach those skills found deficient, and reassess student learning after re-teaching.

Informal assessment methods at emergent reading level for letter knowledge

Teachers need to assess young students' pre-reading and reading skills to determine their knowledge levels to know which skills to teach and deficits to address, to identify error patterns and focus on remediating them, and even on which individual phonemes and/or letters they need to focus on learning. To assess letter knowledge, the teacher must evaluate all of its elements systematically. If the teacher has the student sing the Alphabet Song, this only shows successful memorization, not letter knowledge. Having the student list alphabet letters he or she knows is not systematic, and does not address all aspects of letter knowledge. Presenting letters visually is better, but if the teacher only has the student sound these out, this again does not assess all components of letter knowledge. The best method would be presenting letters visually and having the student name them. This addresses the student's letter recognition, knowledge of letter names, and ability to differentiate among letters, which are all elements included in letter knowledge.

Example of formal standards-based reading assessment

On a multiple-choice test, a third-grade student whose family speaks another language is given a picture of a throne and must choose the correct word from choices (A) Thrown, (B) Throne, and (C) Throan. The student selects answer (A) and his answer is marked as incorrect. The student does not understand why his answer choice was marked wrong. From an assessment result such as this, the teacher can determine that this ESL student is having difficulty in distinguishing among homophones—words that sound the same but are spelled differently. This prevents the teacher from assuming that the student's problem is with the correct spelling of English words, or with insufficient knowledge of English vocabulary words. ESL students often make this kind of error: they are likely to see the word *thrown* in print more than *throne*. The teacher can conclude more individualized instruction is indicated to help this student. The teacher should also give the student opportunities to practice telling apart words that sound the same.

Areas of instruction for comprehension, literary analysis, and literary response skills

Students need to recognize the essential features of important literary genres. These include multicultural literature; poetry, like couplets, lyrics, ballads, epics, and sonnets; drama such as plays; prose, like myths, biographies and autobiographies; and historical and realistic fiction, novels, short stories, legends, and fantasies. Students must also recognize story grammar components like settings, plots, themes, and characters; and additional important aspects of literary texts like point of view, tone, voice, and mood. They must additionally be able to respond to literary narratives and analyze them. Teachers should assess how much students know about these areas, identifying their instructional needs. Teachers should then apply explicit, systematic, research-based instructional strategies to teach students to evaluate the relevance of literary settings; identify recurrent literary themes; recognize the structural components of literary plots and evaluate their credibility and logic; compare and contrast literary characters' motivations and responses; and recognize style elements like figurative language, including metaphors, similes, personification, and hyperbole and literary devices like foreshadowing, imagery, irony, and symbolism.

Reading Applications

Prose and poetry

Prose is language as it is ordinarily spoken as opposed to verse or language with metric patterns. Prose is used for everyday communication, and is found in textbooks, memos, reports, articles, short stories, and novels. Distinguishing characteristics of prose include:
- It may have some sort of rhythm, but there is no formal arrangement.
- The common unit of organization is the sentence.
- It may include literary devices of repetition and balance.
- It must have more coherent relationships among sentences than a list would.

Poetry, or verse, is the manipulation of language with respect to meaning, meter, sound, and rhythm. A line of poetry can be any length and may or may not rhyme. Related groups of lines are called stanzas, and may also be any length. Some poems are as short as a few lines, and some are as long as a book. Poetry is a more ancient form of literature than prose.

Prose in children's literature
The majority of educational texts used in teaching are written in prose. This includes textbooks, non-fiction, and fiction. Textbooks focused specifically on reading skills might also include sections of poetry. Major types of prose include narrative, which can be either fiction or non-fiction and typically tells a story. The structure of the narrative can be linear or non-linear depending on the purpose of the author. Literature is written material generally considered to be of particularly high quality or importance. Traditional literature tends to follow established patterns of storytelling. This term is usually used to mean literature that has been passed down for many years or even

centuries. Modern literature can be more experimental and can also refer to works written more recently.

<u>Poetry in teaching children's literature</u>
Poetry can be particularly appealing to children because of its rhythmic nature. Children can make connections based on rhythm and rhyming sounds that they might not make with prose writings. Recognizing similar words and similar spellings by sight can also help early readers make connections between phonemes and graphemes. Even children who do not yet understand the spoken language can respond to the rhythms and sounds of poetry when it is read aloud. As children grow older, poetry continues to increase higher level comprehension skills by using metaphor, imagery, and other complex concepts.

Fiction and nonfiction

Fiction is a literary work usually presented in prose form that is not true. It is the product of the writer's imagination. Examples of fiction are novels, short stories, television scripts, and screenplays. Nonfiction is a literary work that is based on facts. In other words, the material is true. The purposeful inclusion of false information is considered dishonest, but the expression of opinions or suppositions is acceptable. Libraries divide their collections into works of fiction and nonfiction. Examples of nonfiction include historical materials, scientific reports, memoirs, biographies, most essays, journals, textbooks, documentaries, user manuals, and news reports.

Short stories

A short story is prose fiction that has the same elements as a novel, such as plot, characters, and point of view. Edgar Allan Poe defined the short story as a narrative that can be read in one sitting (one-half to two hours), and is limited to a single effect. In a short story, there is no time for extensive character development, large numbers of characters, in-depth analysis, complicated plot lines, or detailed backgrounds. Historically, the short story is related to the fable, the exemplum, and the folktale. Short stories have become mainly an American art form. Famous short story writers include William Faulkner, Katherine Anne Porter, Eudora Welty, Flannery O'Connor, O. Henry, and J. D. Salinger.

Fairy tales, fables, and tall tales

A fairy tale is a fictional story involving humans, magical events, and usually animals. Characters such as fairies, elves, giants, and talking animals are taken from folklore. The plot often involves impossible events (as in "Jack and the Beanstalk") and/or an enchantment (as in "Sleeping Beauty"). Other examples of fairy tales include "Cinderella," "Little Red Riding Hood," and "Rumpelstiltskin." A fable is a tale in which animals, plants, and forces of nature act like humans. A fable also teaches a moral lesson. Examples are "The Tortoise and the Hare," *The Lion King*, and *Animal Farm*. A tall tale exaggerates human abilities or describes unbelievable events as if the story were true. Often, the narrator seems to have witnessed the event described. Examples are fish stories, Paul Bunyan and Pecos Bill stories, and hyperboles about real people such as Davy Crockett, Mike Fink, and Calamity Jane.

Preadolescent and adolescent literature

Preadolescent literature is mostly concerned with the "tween" issues of changing lives, relationships, and bodies. Adolescents seeking escape from their sometimes difficult lives enjoy fantasy and science fiction. For both groups, books about modern, real people are more interesting than those about historical figures or legends. Boys especially enjoy nonfiction. Reading interests as well as reading levels for this group vary. Reading levels will usually range from 6.0 to 8.9. Examples of popular literature for this age group and reading level include:

- Series – Sweet Valley High, Bluford High, Nancy Drew, Hardy Boys, and Little House on the Prairie
- Juvenile fiction authors – Judy Blume and S. E. Hinton
- Fantasy and horror authors – Ursula LeGuin and Stephen King
- Science fiction authors – Isaac Asimov, Ray Bradbury, and H. G. Wells
- Classic books: *Lilies of the Field, Charlie and the Chocolate Factory, Pippi Longstocking, National Velvet, Call of the Wild, Anne of Green Gables, The Hobbit, The Member of the Wedding,* and *Tom Sawyer*

Expository text materials

Expository or informational text materials include such forms as websites, user manuals, research reports, news articles, and textbooks. Teachers need to apply explicit instructional strategies to further student comprehension of such expository text at the level of the word, the sentence, the paragraph, and the whole text. They need to assist students in expository text comprehension by helping them to understand the text structures commonly utilized, like cause-and-effect, comparison and contrast, chronological sequence, and problem and solution. Teachers also need to instruct students in recognizing and addressing text features related to these various text structures, such as topic sentences, transitional sentences, and concluding sentences. They also need to instruct students explicitly to help them identify various text features that support their comprehending expository texts. These include explanatory features like tables of contents, glossaries, and indexes; typographical features like color-coded text, underlining, italicized and bold-faced text; and graphical features like illustrations, diagrams, maps, and charts.

Activities and strategies to develop and reinforce comprehension
For reading expository texts with comprehension, teachers can use explicit oral language activities like introducing and explaining the key vocabulary words in text before students read it, orally previewing the content of text before reading and orally reviewing the content after reading, and engaging students in orally summarizing and paraphrasing the text they read. Teachers can also use explicit writing activities, such as having students write summaries of text, paraphrasing text in their own written words, and developing graphic organizers to show the structure and content of text visually. They should instruct students explicitly in taking notes, making outlines, and other study skills; and in techniques for the location, retrieval, and retention of information in reference materials as well as expository texts. Teachers should also explicitly instruct students in asking questions, evaluating questions, identifying research topics, conducting research, and managing information through the application of technology to develop their research skills. Teachers' instruction in these skills of comprehension, study and research should meet the needs of all learners in their classrooms.

Narrative vs. expository text

Traditional narratives depict relationships among settings, plots, and characters. They feature concluding global endings and clearly delineate elements like beginnings and endings and settings and goal accomplishment. Sociolinguistic models of narrative identify these narrative elements: abstract, orientation, complication, evaluation, result, and coda. Studies find the cognitive processes of organization, information reduction, storage, and retrieval affected by narrative structure.

Expository structure primarily employs logic, reason, and declarative statements. It is evaluated by its strength of argumentation and accuracy. It is organized into declarations whereby readers can follow the flow of text via causality and logic. Analysis of exposition typically refers to propositional structure. Authors begin with a main proposition, which organizes later propositions and connects these to the author's primary goals. One caveat with knowing such contrasts and the corresponding schemata they require is that this does not reveal their effects on comprehension, which then limits both research and practical application. To inform instruction, researchers also study the respective scopes of processing readers use for narrative versus expository text.

General research findings about elementary-age students' comprehension

Researchers and educators are both concerned about the respective significance of expository and narrative text in elementary reading curricula. Studies show strongly that children demonstrate better reading comprehension of narrative than expository texts. In fact, this is not only in the United States but in multiple nations (35 countries, NCES, 2001), where no students scored significantly higher with expository comprehension. Educational implications of this difference include that secondary and post-secondary education involve much more expository than narrative text overall, so elementary students may be inadequately prepared. Also, different narrative versus expository items and definitions of each in assessments pose problems with interpreting results. Moreover, remediation is difficult until educators know the reason (or reasons) for these differences. Some researchers believe students support comprehension using their preconceived ideas and expectations regarding text; this offers hope in that exposure could determine and thus change the disparity. Elementary literacy instruction currently favors narrative over expository text. But if disparate schemata are needed to comprehend expository versus narrative texts, then equal proficiency in each requires equal exposure.

Style, tone, and point of view

Style is the manner in which a writer uses language in prose or poetry. Style is affected by:
- Diction or word choices
- Sentence structure and syntax
- Types and extent of use of figurative language
- Patterns of rhythm or sound
- Conventional or creative use of punctuation

Tone is the attitude of the writer or narrator towards the theme of, subject of, or characters in a work. Sometimes the attitude is stated, but it is most often implied through word choices. Examples of tone are serious, humorous, satiric, stoic, cynical, flippant, and surprised.

Point of view is the angle from which a story is told. It is the perspective of the narrator, established by the author. Common points of view are:
- Third person – Third person points of view include omniscient (knows everything) and limited (confined to what is known by a single character or a limited number of characters). When the third person is used, characters are referred to as he, she, or they.
- First person – When this point of view is used, the narrator refers to himself or herself as "I."

Print-rich environment in the classroom

A teacher can provide a print-rich environment in the classroom in a number of ways. These include:
- Displaying the following in the classroom:
    o Children's names in print or cursive
    o Children's written work
    o Newspapers and magazines
    o Instructional charts
    o Written schedules
    o Signs and labels
    o Printed songs, poems, and rhymes
- Using graphic organizers such as KWL charts or story road maps to:
    o Remind students about what was read and discussed
    o Expand on the lesson topic or theme
    o Show the relationships among books, ideas, and words
- Using big books to:
    o Point out features of print, such as specific letters and punctuation
    o Track print from right to left
    o Emphasize the concept of words and the fact that they are used to communicate

Benefits of print and book awareness

Print and book awareness helps a child understand:
- That there is a connection between print and messages contained on signs, labels, and other print forms in the child's environment
- That reading and writing are ways to obtain information and communicate ideas
- That print runs from left to right and from top to bottom
- That a book has parts, such as a title, a cover, a title page, and a table of contents
- That a book has an author and contains a story
- That illustrations can carry meaning
- That letters and words are different
- That words and sentences are separated by spaces and punctuation
- That different text forms are used for different functions
- That print represents spoken language
- How to hold a book.

Critical thinking skills

It is important to teach students to use critical thinking skills when reading. Three of the critical thinking tools that engage the reader are:
- Summarization – The student reviews the main point(s) of the reading selection and identifies important details. For nonfiction, a good summary will briefly describe the main arguments and the examples that support those arguments. For fiction, a good summary will identify the main characters and events of the story.
- Question generation – A good reader will constantly ask questions while reading about comprehension, vocabulary, connections to personal knowledge or experience, predictions, etc.

- Textual marking – This skill engages the reader by having him or her interact with the text. The student should mark the text with questions or comments that are generated by the text using underlining, highlighting, or shorthand marks such as "?," "!," and "*" that indicate lack of understanding, importance, or key points, for example.

Writing a journal

Writing in a journal gives students practice in writing, which makes them more comfortable with the writing process. Journal writing also gives students the opportunity to sort out their thoughts, solve problems, examine relationships and values, and see their personal and academic growth when they revisit old entries. The advantages for the teacher are that the students become more experienced with and accustomed to writing. Through reading student journals, the teacher can also gain insight into the students' problems and attitudes, which can help the teacher tailor his or her lesson plans. A journal can be kept in a notebook or in a computer file. It shouldn't be just a record of daily events, but an expression of thoughts and feelings about everything and anything. Grammar and punctuation don't matter since journaling is a form of private communication. Teachers who review journals need to keep in mind that they should not grade journals and that comments should be encouraging and polite.

Reading strategies

Determination of important ideas and information synthesis
A reader wishing to derive essential information from a text must be able to determine which ideas in the text are most important. This skill is illustrated when a student is studying for a test; he or she must be able to sort through large quantities of information to determine which concepts are the most important. Information synthesis occurs when a reader assimilates new information, combining it with things he or she already knows. This kind of combination of information can lead to new ideas, understandings, theories or insights. Synthesizing information is essential for higher level learning and comprehension.

Repairing understanding and confirmation
If, as a student is reading, he or she experiences confusion over the text, they must take the time to backtrack and "repair" their understanding of the specific text. This can involve rereading the text, looking up unfamiliar words, or asking for assistance in understanding a specific passage. Confirmation occurs as predictions made by the reader are either confirmed or contradicted. If a reader's prediction is confirmed by the text, the student can be rewarded by knowing he or she made a correct guess. If the prediction is contradicted, he or she can be rewarded by the surprise of an unexpected conclusion or development in the text.

Analyzing a complex text

When you read a text, you need to pay attention. You need to watch for the introduction of ideas. You need to figure out how the ideas that are introduced are developed. When you read a complex text, it may be difficult to follow. Sometimes, it is hard to understand how one idea is linked to another idea. Sometimes, it helps to make an outline of a text. This will help you identify the main ideas. Then, you can figure out which ideas are supporting details. A complex text may also have vocabulary that you cannot understand. If you cannot figure out the meaning of certain words from the context, you can make a list of these words. Then, look them up in a dictionary. This will help you understand the meaning of the text.

Use of technology in differentiated literacy instruction

Much instructional software exists today. For example, KidBiz Achieve 3000 is a web-based individualized reading and writing instructional program. Students each receive KidBiz e-mails with questions designed to activate their background knowledge prior to reading current events articles. Multiple articles on the same topics are provided at different reading levels: all students in a class read similar articles, but each at his/her own reading level. After replying to answer the e-mailed question, students read the article. This software also helps teachers prepare students for high-stakes, standardized, criterion-referenced tests (CRTs). The KidBiz website provides "thought questions" that supply writing prompts related to its provided articles and require students to write constructed-response questions based on what they read, similar to CRT questions. Teachers assign small-group/whole-class discussions following these activities. Students find lists of all stories their class is reading that year on a webpage, which links to a website such as Flashcard Exchange, where teachers have entered vocabulary words for each story. Students can study/practice the words for any story they select.

Use of technology in writing instruction

In a class using technology, a teacher gives an elementary school class (4th-graders, for example) an open-ended question—e.g., about an imaginary friend—and have students IM their assigned "buddy" describing him/her/it. The teacher leads class discussion about the writing trait Ideas and Content; then has them listen for examples of this as s/he reads them a picture book about an imaginary friend. The teacher has students visit a website such as www.writingfix.com, which offers interactive writing prompts guiding students to describe the imaginary friend's specific characteristics. This prepares students for a "Quick Write" (first draft). As they write, the teacher discusses individual writing and improvements with some students. Students' Quick Writes are electronically saved for revisiting and advancing through further drafts. Students use built-in software features like spell-check, grammar-check, and thesaurus for editing, learning mindfulness when they find software is not always right. Peer review is also facilitated electronically. Students print and post finished writing on the bulletin board. Such activities show smooth transitions from traditional to new literacies.

Alternative reading and writing forms

When students read and write outside of school, they choose many alternative forms of reading and writing. To engage these students while they are in school, teachers should think about adding such alternative materials to their own instructional programs. For example, teachers might incorporate such media as graphic novels, magazines, newspapers, plays, anthologies of poetry, e-books and other digital/online content, and text that students have written themselves. Educational experts advise that just because it can be harder to determine the reading levels of such alternative text formats, teachers should not shy away from using them. Because they represent examples of text that people (including students) read in real life, they provide not only excellent practice for students' present and future reading of real-world materials, but also motivation to read and meaningful experiences in reading. Another boon of using these authentic, alternative texts is that they frequently incorporate multiple reading levels, so that nearly every student can read some portions of them.

Indications of reading problems

Parents, caregivers, and teachers should attend to how each individual child is progressing in skills areas prerequisite and related to reading. For example, with preschool-aged children, adults should observe whether a child has comparatively more difficulty than his/her age peers with pronouncing words, learning the alphabet, recognizing and producing rhymes; learning colors and/or shapes of concrete objects; learning numbers; and/or learning the days of the week. Adults can also consult many sources available online and on paper that identify common developmental milestones in language development and reading development. If a child regularly demonstrates difficulty with several developmental milestones, the adult(s) should consider having the child evaluated for potential reading and/or learning disabilities. Adults should keep in mind that children learn at different rates and in different ways. However, the majority of students with normal development can read grade-level materials, with comprehension and fluency, by the end of third grade. Preventing students from falling behind grade level in reading is important, because reading problems are best remediated at early ages.

Stimulating student motivation to read

School leaders can increase students' motivation to read by visiting classrooms and reading to students, showing their and the school's commitment to reading, demonstrating its importance and enjoyment. They should visit classes during reading group activities, praising student successes. They can let students come to their offices to read. Leaders should read some of the same books their students are reading, and discuss the books with them. This not only shows students the leaders' interest in them and their interests; it also helps leaders learn about students' interests, opinions, and reading motivations. Leaders can use programs, such as Battle of the Books or Reading Counts, to stimulate student motivations for reading. Leaders can sponsor/expedite special events reading-related for students. They should periodically participate in student progress monitoring. On occasion, they can personally teach a small student group. They can present students with goals, challenging them to read to attain these. Leaders can also do some of their own reading in classrooms during silent reading periods, so students see them reading.

Written Language - Writing Conventions

Key grammatical terms

<u>Adjective, adverb, and conjunction</u>
The definitions for these grammatical terms are as follows:
- Adjective – This is a word that modifies or describes a noun or pronoun. Examples are a *green* apple or *every* computer.
- Adverb – This is a word that modifies a verb (*instantly* reviewed), an adjective (*relatively* odd), or another adverb (*rather* suspiciously).
- Conjunctions: There are three types of conjunctions:
  - Coordinating conjunctions are used to link words, phrases, and clauses. Examples are and, or, nor, for, but, yet, and so.
  - Correlative conjunctions are paired terms used to link clauses. Examples are either/or, neither/nor, and if/then.
  - Subordinating conjunctions relate subordinate or dependent clauses to independent ones. Examples are although, because, if, since, before, after, when, even though, in order that, and while.

Gerund, infinitive, noun, direct and indirect objects
The definitions for these grammatical terms are as follows:
- Gerund – This is a verb form used as a noun. Most end in "ing." An example is: *Walking* is good exercise.
- Infinitive – This is a verbal form comprised of the word "to" followed by the root form of a verb. An infinitive may be used as a noun, adjective, adverb, or absolute. Examples include:
  - *To hold* a baby is a joy. (noun)
  - Jenna had many files *to reorganize*. (adjective)
  - Andrew tried *to remember* the dates. (adverb)
  - *To be honest*, your hair looks awful. (absolute)
- Noun – This is a word that names a person, place, thing, idea, or quality. A noun can be used as a subject, object, complement, appositive, or modifier.
- Object – This is a word or phrase that receives the action of a verb. A direct object states **to** whom/what an action was committed. It answers the question "to what?" An example is: Joan served *the meal*. An indirect object states **for** whom/what an action was committed. An example is: Joan served *us* the meal.

Preposition, prepositional phrase, pronoun, sentence, and verb
The definitions for these grammatical terms are as follows:
- Preposition – This is a word that links a noun or pronoun to other parts of a sentence. Examples include above, by, for, in, out, through, and to.
- Prepositional phrase – This is a combination of a preposition and a noun or pronoun. Examples include across the bridge, against the grain, below the horizon, and toward the sunset.
- Pronoun – This is a word that represents a specific noun in a generic way. A pronoun functions like a noun in a sentence. Examples include I, she, he, it, myself, they, these, what, all, and anybody.
- Sentence – This is a group of words that expresses a thought or conveys information as an independent unit of speech. A complete sentence must contain a noun and a verb (I ran). However, all the other parts of speech can also be represented in a sentence.
- Verb – This is a word or phrase in a sentence that expresses action (Mary played) or a state of being (Mary is).

Action verbs, linking verbs, and helping verbs
In order to understand the role of a verb and be able to identify the verb that is necessary to make a sentence, it helps to know the different types of verbs. These are:
- Action verbs – These are verbs that express an action being performed by the subject. An example is: The outfielder caught the ball (outfielder = subject and caught = action).
- Linking verbs – These are verbs that link the subject to words that describe or identify the subject. An example is: Mary is an excellent teacher (Mary = subject and "is" links Mary to her description as an excellent teacher). Common linking verbs are all forms of the verb "to be," appear, feel, look, become, and seem.
- Helping verbs – When a single verb cannot do the job by itself because of tense issues, a second, helping verb is added. Examples include: should have gone ("gone" is the main verb, while "should" and "have" are helping verbs), and was playing ("playing" is the main verb, while "was" is the helping verb).

Run-ons and comma splices

A run-on sentence is one that tries to connect two independent clauses without the needed conjunction or punctuation and makes it hard for the reader to figure out where one sentence ends and the other starts. An example is: "Meagan is three years old she goes to pre-school." Two possible ways to fix the run-on would be: "Meagan is three years old, and she goes to pre-school" or "Meagan is three years old; however, she goes to pre-school." A comma splice occurs when a comma is used to join two independent clauses without a proper conjunction. The comma should be replaced by a period or one of the methods for coordination or subordination should be used. An example of a comma splice is: "Meagan is three years old, she goes to pre-school."

Subject-verb agreement

A verb must agree in number with its subject. Therefore, a verb changes form depending on whether the subject is singular or plural. Examples include "I do," "he does," "the ball is," and "the balls are." If two subjects are joined by "and," the plural form of a verb is usually used. For example: *Jack and Jill want* to get some water (Jack wants, Jill wants, but together they want). If the compound subjects are preceded by each or every, they take the singular form of a verb. For example: *Each man and each woman brings* a special talent to the world (each brings, not bring). If one noun in a compound subject is plural and the other is singular, the verb takes the form of the subject nearest to it. For example: Neither the *students* nor their *teacher was* ready for the fire drill. Collective nouns that name a group are considered singular if they refer to the group acting as a unit. For example: The *choir is going* on a concert tour.

Capitalization and punctuation

Capitalization refers to the use of capital letters. Capital letters should be placed at the beginning of:
- Proper names (Ralph Waldo Emerson, Australia)
- Places (Mount Rushmore, Chicago)
- Historical periods and holidays (Renaissance, Christmas)
- Religious terms (Bible, Koran)
- Titles (Empress Victoria, General Smith)
- All main words in literary, art, or music titles (Grapes of Wrath, Sonata in C Major)

Punctuation consists of:
- Periods – A period is placed at the end of a sentence.
- Commas – A comma is used to separate:
  - Two adjectives modifying the same word (long, hot summer)
  - Three or more words or phrases in a list (Winken, Blinken, and Nod; life, liberty, and the pursuit of happiness)
  - Phrases that are not needed to complete a sentence (The teacher, not the students, will distribute the supplies.)

Purposes of writing

Writing always has a purpose. Two of the five reasons to write are:
- To tell a story – The story does not necessarily need to be fictional. The purposes are to explain what happened, to narrate events, and to explain how things were accomplished.

The story will need to make a point, and plenty of details will need to be provided to help the reader imagine the event or process.

- To express oneself – This type of writing is commonly found in journals, diaries, or blogs. This kind of writing is an exercise in reflection that allows writers to learn something about themselves and what they have observed, and to work out their thoughts and feelings on paper.

Beginning stages of learning to write

The following are the beginning stages of learning to write:

- Drawing pictures is the first written attempt to express thoughts and feelings. Even when the picture is unrecognizable to the adult, it means something to the child.
- The scribble stage begins when the child attempts to draw shapes. He or she may also try to imitate writing. The child may have a story or explanation to go with the shapes.
- Children have the most interest in learning to write their own names, so writing lessons usually start with that. Children will soon recognize that there are other letters too.
- Children are learning the alphabet and how to associate a sound with each letter. Reversing letters is still common, but instruction begins with teaching children to write from left to right.
- Written words may not be complete, but will likely have the correct beginning and end sounds/letters.
- Children will make some attempt to use vowels in writing.
- Children will write with more ease, although spelling will still be phonetic and only some punctuation will be used.

Written Language - Composition

Purpose and audience

Early in the writing process, the writer needs to definitively determine the purpose of the paper and then keep that purpose in mind throughout the writing process. The writer needs to ask: "Is the purpose to explain something, to tell a story, to entertain, to inform, to argue a point, or some combination of these purposes?" Also at the beginning of the writing process, the writer needs to determine the audience of the paper by asking questions such as: "Who will read this paper?," "For whom is this paper intended?," "What does the audience already know about this topic?," "How much does the audience need to know?," and "Is the audience likely to agree or disagree with my point of view?" The answers to these questions will determine the content of the paper, the tone, and the style.

Pre-writing techniques

Pre-writing techniques that help a writer find, explore, and organize a topic include:

- Brainstorming – This involves letting thoughts make every connection to the topic possible, and then spinning off ideas and making notes of them as they are generated. This is a process of using imagination, uninhibited creativity, and instincts to discover a variety of possibilities.

- Freewriting – This involves choosing items from the brainstorming list and writing about them nonstop for a short period. This unedited, uncensored process allows one thing to lead to another and permits the writer to think of additional concepts and themes.
- Clustering/mapping – This involves writing a general word or phrase related to the topic in the middle of a paper and circling it, and then quickly jotting down related words or phrases. These are circled and lines are drawn to link words and phrases to others on the page. Clustering is a visual representation of brainstorming that reveals patterns and connections.
- Listing – Similar to brainstorming, listing is writing down as many descriptive words and phrases (not whole sentences) as possible that relate to the subject. Correct spelling and grouping of these descriptive terms can come later if needed. This list is merely intended to stimulate creativity and provide a vibrant vocabulary for the description of the subject once the actual writing process begins.
- Charting – This prewriting technique works well for comparison/contrast purposes or for the examination of advantages and disadvantages (pros and cons). Any kind of chart will work, even a simple two-column list. The purpose is to draw out points and examples that can be used in the paper.

Evaluating multiple sources of information

Good information technology skills are necessary in order to sift through the enormous amount of information available on just about any topic. Before beginning any research, ask yourself how much information you think you are going to need; think about your target audience and their needs. Utilize search engines to make the task go faster. When evaluating multiple sources of information, do not rely solely on how recent they are. Consider the validity of sources as well. Do not rely on just one source. Using digital media is important because it allows you to broaden your scope beyond just words to include graphics and charts. Take the time to understand what online sources of information are available, which ones are most appropriate, and how they support one another.

Primary and secondary research information

Primary research material is material that comes from the "horse's mouth." It is a document or object that was created by the person under study or during the time period under study. Examples of primary sources are original documents such as manuscripts, diaries, interviews, autobiographies, government records, letters, news videos, and artifacts (such as Native American pottery or wall writings in Egyptian tombs). Secondary research material is anything that is not primary. Secondary sources are those things that are written or otherwise recorded about the main subject. Examples include a critical analysis of a literary work (a poem by William Blake is primary, but the analysis of the poem by T. S. Eliot is secondary), a magazine article about a person (a direct quote would be primary, but the report is secondary), histories, commentaries, and encyclopedias.

Graphic organizers

The purpose of graphic organizers is to help students classify ideas and communicate more efficiently and effectively. Graphic organizers are visual outlines or templates that help students grasp key concepts and master subject matter by simplifying them down to basic points. They also help guide students through processes related to any subject area or task. Examples of processes include brainstorming, problem solving, decision making, research and project planning, and studying. Examples of graphic organizers include:

- Reading – These can include beginning, middle, and end graphs or event maps.
- Science – These can include charts that show what animals need or how to classify living things.
- Math – These can include horizontal bar graphs or time lines.
- Language arts – These can include alphabet organizers or charts showing the components of the five-paragraph essay.
- General – These can include KWL charts or weekly planners.

Topic sentence

The topic sentence of a paragraph states the paragraph's subject. It presents the main idea. The rest of the paragraph should be related to the topic sentence, which should be explained and supported with facts, details, proofs, and examples.   The topic sentence is more general than the body sentences, and should cover all the ideas in the body of the paragraph. It may contain words such as "many," "most," or "several." The topic sentence is usually the first sentence in a paragraph, but it can appear after an introductory or background sentence, can be the last sentence in a paragraph, or may simply be implied, meaning a topic sentence is not present. Supporting sentences can often be identified by their use of transition terms such as "for example" or "that is." Supporting sentences may also be presented in numbered sequence. The topic sentence provides unity to a paragraph because it ties together the supporting details into a coherent whole.

Clear and coherent writing

Each genre of writing requires its own traits, but to attain clear and coherent writing it is necessary to plan what you will be writing. First, decide on your goal, or whether you are trying to inform, persuade, or entertain. With your goal in mind, you need to organize your material if you are writing a nonfiction piece. You need to have a clear idea of your main ideas and supporting details. If you are planning to write a narrative, you need to pay attention to developing your story in a clear and flowing manner. Then, create characters through skillful use of description, dialogue, and action. In addition in all types of writing you need to establish a tone. You also need to make sure your writing is free of grammatical or spelling errors. Close rereading and editing is part of the writing process, as well.

Drafting, revising, editing, and proofreading

When beginning to write, you should develop a plan about what you want to discuss and the points you want to make. An outline can prove helpful if you are writing a nonfiction piece. If you are writing a narrative, you might want to make a story map. Next, you should write a first draft. Drafting is creating an early version of a paper. A draft is a prototype or sketch of the finished product. A draft is a rough version of the final paper, and it is expected that there will be multiple drafts. Once you have finished the writing, you should put it aside for a time. When you come back to it, you will see it with fresh eyes and will see more easily what needs to be changed or revised.

Revising is the process of making major changes to a draft in regards to clarity of purpose, focus (thesis), audience, organization, and content. After you make the revisions and put the writing aside again, then reread the writing and begin to edit. Editing is the process of making changes in style, word choice, tone, examples, and arrangement. These are more minor than the changes made during revision. Editing can be thought of as fine tuning. The writer makes the language more precise, checks for varying paragraph lengths, and makes sure that the title, introduction, and conclusion fit well with the body of the paper. Make sure that the supporting details are clear and in a logical order in a report. Rework the dialogue to make it more precise in a story. Proofreading is performing a final check and correcting errors in punctuation, spelling, grammar, and usage. It also involves looking for parts of the paper that may be omitted. Read your work to someone else and ask for feedback. Finally, revise it again.

Considerations when revising a paper

Revising a paper involves rethinking the choices that were made while constructing the paper and then rewriting it, making any necessary changes or additions to word choices or arrangement of points. Questions to keep in mind include:

- Is the thesis clear?
- Do the body paragraphs logically flow and provide details to support the thesis?
- Is anything unnecessarily repeated?
- Is there anything not related to the topic?
- Is the language understandable?
- Does anything need to be defined?
- Is the material interesting?

Another consideration when revising is peer feedback. It is helpful during the revision process to have someone who is knowledgeable enough to be helpful and will be willing to give an honest critique read the paper.

Author's point of view

The author's point of view is not always immediately clear. It could be stated clearly in many texts, but oftentimes the author does not want the reader to know exactly how he feels so a reader needs to discover it by the choice of words that an author uses, the information he includes, and any other relevant factors. It is important to read a text closely to determine what an author thinks about an event, person, topic or issue. Always check for any emotional statements that will give an idea of what the author is feeling. Look for any judgments an author may make about his topic, and piece together what you believe is the author's point of view.

An author may use a wide array of literary techniques to discuss a topic, a character, or a situation, which could disguise the author's real feelings regarding what he or she is writing about. For instance, a writer might say that an area received a "little rain," when in fact the land might be flooded with water. Or, an author could describe a dent as "a little scratch" when there is actually an enormous dent. A reader must be able to put a writer's words into perspective to determine what has actually occurred. The same is true when a writer uses irony to make a comment. Consider the following sentence: "I have little doubt that you will receive the praise that you deserve for your hard work." Taken at face value, this would be a compliment. However, if the situation is such that the recipient of the comment has made a complete fool of himself, the comment becomes irony, because the opposite of what is being said is true. Here again, the reader has to be careful to examine a situation described by a writer before jumping to conclusions about the author's viewpoint.

Use of the Internet for individual or shared writing projects

Online sources are a wonderful tool for writers. They can get works published at little or no cost either as an e-book or a printed book. There are other options available as well, such as editing and marketing services offered on many Internet sites. Writing tools give help with everything from style to grammar. Many sites are reliable research possibilities and provide accurate and objective information. Make sure to pick reliable sources for any research. Also, be sure to cite Internet sources using an accepted format such as that from the MLA (Modern Language Association). Many sites allow people to work together on projects regardless of their physical location. Chat rooms and topic websites are other tools that allow exchanges of information and have shared writing projects.

Research writing

Primary and secondary sources

When one conducts research and then writes a research paper reporting the results of that investigation, an essential part of the paper is a literature review. In reviewing the literature, one may examine both primary and secondary sources. Primary sources contain original information, like reports other researchers have made of their findings and other first-hand accounts written by experimenters or witnesses of discoveries or events. They may be found in academic books, journals and other periodicals, and authoritative databases. Secondary sources refer to information originally given by other people or found in other places. They may be cited, quoted, or described in books, magazines, newspapers, films, audio and video materials, databases, and websites. Accounts of research and its results are always informed and directed by reviews of the pertinent literature. These depict the present research as a cumulative process integral to the scientific method. Literature reviews also test the research question one wants to answer relative to the existing knowledge about the topic.

Editing and revising a research paper in progress

After composing a rough draft of a research paper, the writer should edit and rewrite it. The purpose of the paper is to communicate the answer to one's research question in an efficient and effective manner. The writer should edit the draft to make it as concise and clear as possible. This is often easier to do after writing the first draft than during it, as writers get some distance and objectivity when reviewing their first efforts. If the paper will include an abstract and an introduction, the writer should compose these after writing the rest. Because the point is to communicate ideas and information, writing should have consistency as well as succinctness and clarity. Not all readers understand technical terminology or long words: whenever possible, writers should use these only sparingly, and otherwise replace them with shorter, simpler words that do not change the meaning. Many writing and style guides exist for researchers lacking writing experience and/or confidence to consult.

Citing sources

Formal research paper writers must cite all sources used—books, articles, interviews, conversations, and anything else that contributed to the research. One reason is to give others credit for their ideas and words. Otherwise, writers can be accused of stealing others' ideas; using others' words without quoting and citing sources is plagiarism. Another reason is to help readers find more information about the paper subject to read and research further. An additional reason is to make one's paper academically authoritative. To prepare, research writers should keep a running list of sources consulted, in an electronic file or on file cards. This prevents frantic last-minute searches for missing source information. For every source used, the writer needs the following: Author and/or editor name, title, publication date, city, and publisher name for books; author name, title, journal (or magazine or newspaper) name, volume and issue number, publication date, and page numbers for articles; and in addition to the information for articles, the URL, database name, name of the database's publisher, and the date of access for electronic resources.

Viewing and Representing

Viewing skills

Elementary/intermediate school children
Children of elementary school age should be developing or have attained the ability to understand the importance of media in people's lives. They should understand that television, radio, films, and the Internet have a role in everyday life. They should also be able to use media themselves (printing out material from the Internet or making an audio or video tape, for example). They should also be aware that the purpose of advertising is to sell. Children of intermediate school age should be developing or have attained the ability to obtain and compare information from newspapers, television, and the Internet. They should also be able to judge its reliability and accuracy to some extent. Children of this age should be able to tell the difference between fictional and non-fictional materials in media. They should also be able to use a variety of media, visuals, and sounds to make a presentation.

Instruction techniques
Viewing skills can be sharpened by having students look at a single image, such as a work of art or a cartoon, and simply asking students what they see. The teacher can ask what is happening in the image, and then elicit the details that clue the students in to what is happening. Of course, there may be more than one thing happening. The teacher should also question the students about the message of the image, its purpose, its point of view, and its intended audience. The teacher should ask for first impressions, and then provide some background or additional information to see if it changes the way students look at or interpret the image. The conclusion of the lesson should include questions about what students learned from the exercise about the topic, themselves, and others.

Developing skills
Students are exposed to multiple images every day. It is important for them to be able to effectively interpret these images. They should be able to make sense of the images and the spoken and print language that often accompany them. Learning can be enhanced with images because they allow for quicker connections to prior knowledge than verbal information. Visuals in the classroom can also be motivational, can support verbal information, and can express main points, sometimes resulting in instant recognition. Some of the common types of images that students see every day include: bulletin boards, computer graphics, diagrams, drawings, illustrations, maps, photographs, posters, book covers, advertisements, Internet sites, multimedia presentations, puppet shows, television, videos, print cartoons, models, paintings, animation, drama or dance performances, films, and online newscasts and magazines.

<u>Activities to strengthen skills</u>
Activities at school that can be used to strengthen the viewing skills of students of varying ages include:
- Picture book discussions – Students can develop an appreciation of visual text and the language that goes with it through guided discussions of picture books that focus on the style and color of the images and other details that might capture a child's attention.
- Gallery walks – Students can walk around a room or hallway viewing the posted works of other students and hear presentations about the works. They can also view a display prepared by the teacher. Students are expected to take notes as they walk around, have discussions, and perhaps do a follow-up report.
- Puppet theater and drama presentations – Students can learn about plots, dialogue, situations, characters, and the craft of performance from viewing puppet or drama presentations, which also stimulate oral communication and strengthen listening skills. Discussions or written responses should follow performances to check for detail acquisition.

Classroom viewing center

A classroom viewing center should contain magazines, CD-ROMs, books, videos, and individual pictures (photographs or drawings). Students should have a viewing guide that explains expectations related to the viewing center (before, during, and after using the center). For younger students, the teacher can ask questions that guide them through the viewing rather than expecting them to read the guidelines and write responses.
- Before viewing, students should think about what they already know about the subject and what they want to learn from the viewing.
- During the viewing, students should make notes about whatever interests them or is new to them.
- After viewing, students could discuss or individually write down what they found to be the most interesting idea or striking image and explain why it caught their attention.

Questions when viewing a narrative

A teacher should make students responsible for gaining information or insight from the viewing. Setting expectations increases student attention and critical thinking. As with any viewing, the students should consider what they already know about the topic and what they hope to gain by watching the narrative before viewing it. During the viewing, the students should take notes (perhaps to answer questions provided by the teacher).
After the viewing, students should be able to answer the following questions:
- What was the time period and setting of the story?
- Who were the main characters?
- How effective was the acting?
- What was the problem or goal in the story?
- How was the problem solved or the goal achieved?
- How would you summarize the story?
- What did you learn from the story?
- What did you like or dislike about the story or its presentation?
- Would you recommend this viewing to others?
- How would you rate it?

- 42 -

Multimedia components and visual displays in presentations

Multimedia components and visual displays not only enhance presentations, they can make information much more understandable. For instance, if you are making a presentation about a complex subject, a visual display can show the way in which the material should come together. Multimedia components including graphics, diagrams, and charts also serve to reinforce spoken information. Certainly, many people learn more quickly when a visual presentation accompanies a verbal one. They also serve to break a presentation up so that it is more interesting to the viewer. However, these multimedia components are only aids; they cannot stand on their own. The speaker must bring them everything together with his verbal presentation.

Study and Inquiry Skills

Interpreting assessment results to plan instruction in study and research skills

Once teachers have identified student needs in areas like study and research skills, they can plan their instruction accordingly to show students how to use various reference sources and materials, organize information, and relate the information they find to texts and tests in the respective subject content areas. Teacher curriculum planning should include components like the skills and behaviors they will model for students; the direct instruction strategies they will use; the resources, materials, and technology they will utilize; how they will schedule curriculum and instructional activities; and which activities they engage students in for learning. Modeling by teachers and guided practice they will give students should support the direct instruction they deliver to students. They should give students practice in finding and using information from various sources like the Internet, reference books, and other texts; and in remembering and applying information for taking tests.

Mathematics

Number Systems and Quantities

Major number concepts

Students in elementary grades must learn to relate numbers to quantities of objects. In addition to the concept that numbers refer to quantities, students will also learn:
- Counting numbers vs. whole numbers - Whole numbers are the same as counting numbers, with 0 added at the beginning of the sequence.
- Numbers vs. numerals - A number is the concept of a quantity of objects, while a numeral is a symbol representing a quantity.
- Skip counting - This includes counting by twos, threes, counting only even or odd numbers, or counting by other multiples.
- Odd vs. even numbers - Even numbers can be divided by two; odd numbers cannot.

Major concepts of sets

In mathematics, the concept of sets involves groupings of items that are similar in some way. Actions that can be performed on sets and the individual members of a set include:
- Comparing objects to each other
- Classifying objects according to a specific criteria
- Sorting objects according to a pattern (patterning)
- Sorting objects according to size (ordering)
- Students can also practice oral counting by counting the number of objects in different categories.

Base-10 and place value

Base-10 represents the system of numeration used in the US and elsewhere. The base-10 numeration system also determines the place value of numbers. In numbers with more than one digit, each digit is ten times the value of the digit to its immediate right, or one-tenth the value of the digit to its immediate left. The concept of place value is vital to understanding the value of numerals and how they are used to represent actual quantities. Students can learn place value by isolating specific digits in a number and explaining what the actual value of that numeral is according to its place value.

Mathematical operations

Mathematical operations are actions taken upon groups of numbers. The four operations are:
1. Addition
2. Subtraction
3. Multiplication
4. Division

Addition occurs when numbers are combined, producing a new numerical total. This total is referred to as a sum. The form in which addition is expressed, also called an algorithm, consists of two addends and the sum. As a binary function, addition only combines two numbers in each operation. Subtraction is the opposite, or inverse, function to addition. Also a binary operation, subtraction removes one value from another to produce the difference between those two numbers. The subtraction algorithm consists of a minuend, from which a subtrahend is subtracted to produce the difference.

Multiplication and division are also inverse functions to each other, just as addition and subtraction are. Multiplication is simply a shorthand way of performing multiple addition operations. The answer to a multiplication problem is called the product. Division is the opposite of multiplication, and functions as a shorthand method of performing multiple subtraction operations. The answer to a division problem is referred to as the quotient.

Factors, prime numbers and composite numbers

Factors - The factors of a number are those numbers that can be divided evenly into that number. Conversely, pairs of factors can be multiplied to produce the number. For example, 2 x 3 and 6 x 1 are both equal to 6. The factors of 6, then, are 1, 2, 3, and 6.

Prime numbers - Prime numbers only have two factors: the number itself and 1. For example, the only numbers that can be multiplied together to make a product of 5 are 5 and 1. This means 5 is a prime number.

Composite numbers - Composite numbers have more than two factors. In the example above, 6 is broken down into four factors; therefore 6 is a composite number.

Rational numbers, fractions, decimals and percents

Rational numbers - Numbers that can be expressed as a fraction (x/y), in which both x and y are integers and y is never 0. A rational number can also be expressed as a decimal or as a percent.

Fractions - Numbers expressed in the form x/y. Both x and y must be whole numbers. Fractions cannot always be translated into integers. However, all integers can be translated into fractions.

Decimals - Another way of representing fractions in the base ten system; each place to the right of the decimal point decreases in value by a factor of ten.

Percent - Expresses a fraction as a portion of 100. For example, 25% represents 25 out of 100 units, or 25/100.

Special properties of 0 and of 1

The numbers 0 and 1 have special properties related to multiplication and addition. These properties are:
- Identity element of addition - If 0 is added to any number, the result is that number. In other words, the number's identity or value remains the same.
- Multiplication property of 0 - If any number is multiplied by 0, the product is always 0.
- Identity element of multiplication - If any number is multiplied by 1, the result is the original number. The number's identity or value remains the same.

There is no identity element for subtraction because the commutative property does not apply to subtraction. 0 cannot be considered an identity element for division because numbers cannot be divided by 0.

Integers, prime, composite, even, and odd

Numbers are the basic building blocks of mathematics. Specific features of numbers are identified by the following terms:

Integers – The set of positive and negative numbers, including zero. Integers do not include fractions ($\frac{1}{3}$), decimals (0.56), or mixed numbers ($7\frac{3}{4}$).

Prime number – A whole number greater than 1 that has only two factors, itself and 1; that is, a number that can be divided evenly only by 1 and itself.

Composite number – A whole number greater than 1 that has more than two different factors; in other words, any whole number that is not a prime number. For example: The composite number 8 has the factors of 1, 2, 4, and 8.

Even number – Any integer that can be divided by 2 without leaving a remainder. For example: 2, 4, 6, 8, and so on.

Odd number – Any integer that cannot be divided evenly by 2. For example: 3, 5, 7, 9, and so on.

Rational, irrational, and real numbers

Rational, irrational, and real numbers can be described as follows:

Rational numbers include all integers, decimals, and fractions. Any terminating or repeating decimal number is a rational number.

Irrational numbers cannot be written as fractions or decimals because the number of decimal places is infinite and there is no recurring pattern of digits within the number. For example, pi (π) begins with 3.141592 and continues without terminating or repeating, so pi is an irrational number.

Real numbers are the set of all rational and irrational numbers.

Fractions, numerators, and denominators

A fraction is a number that is expressed as one integer written above another integer, with a dividing line between them ($\frac{x}{y}$). It represents the quotient of the two numbers "x divided by y." It can also be thought of as x out of y equal parts.

The top number of a fraction is called the numerator, and it represents the number of parts under consideration. The 1 in $\frac{1}{4}$ means that 1 part out of the whole is being considered in the calculation. The bottom number of a fraction is called the denominator, and it represents the total number of equal parts. The 4 in $\frac{1}{4}$ means that the whole consists of 4 equal parts.

A fraction cannot have a denominator of zero; this is referred to as "undefined."

Order of Operations, PEMDAS

Order of Operations is a set of rules that dictates the order in which we must perform each operation in an expression so that we will evaluate at accurately. If we have an expression that includes multiple different operations, Order of Operations tells us which operations to do first. The most common mnemonic for Order of Operations is PEMDAS, or "Please Excuse My Dear Aunt

Sally." PEMDAS stands for Parentheses, Exponents, Multiplication, Division, Addition, Subtraction. It is important to understand that multiplication and division have equal precedence, as do addition and subtraction, so those pairs of operations are simply worked from left to right in order.

Example: Evaluate the expression $5 + 20 \div 4 \times (2 + 3)^2 - 6$ using the correct order of operations.
P: Perform the operations inside the parentheses, $(2 + 3) = 5$.
E: Simplify the exponents, $(5)^2 = 25$.
The equation now looks like this: $5 + 20 \div 4 \times 25 - 6$.
MD: Perform multiplication and division from left to right, $20 \div 4 = 5$; then $5 \times 25 = 125$.
The equation now looks like this: $5 + 125 - 6$.
AS: Perform addition and subtraction from left to right, $5 + 125 = 130$; then $130 - 6 = 124$.

Percentages, fractions, and decimals

Percentages can be thought of as fractions that are based on a whole of 100; that is, one whole is equal to 100%. The word percent means "per hundred." Fractions can be expressed as percents by finding equivalent fractions with a denomination of 100. Example: $\frac{7}{10} = \frac{70}{100} = 70\%$; $\frac{1}{4} = \frac{25}{100} = 25\%$. To express a percentage as a fraction, divide the percentage number by 100 and reduce the fraction to its simplest possible terms. Example: $60\% = \frac{60}{100} = \frac{3}{5}$; $96\% = \frac{96}{100} = \frac{24}{25}$.
Converting decimals to percentages and percentages to decimals is as simple as moving the decimal point. To convert from a decimal to a percent, move the decimal point two places to the right. To convert from a percent to a decimal, move it two places to the left. Example: $0.23 = 23\%$; $5.34 = 534\%$; $0.007 = 0.7\%$; $700\% = 7.00$; $86\% = 0.86$; $0.15\% = 0.0015$.
It may be helpful to remember that the percentage number will always be larger than the equivalent decimal number.

Improper fractions and mixed numbers

A fraction whose denominator is greater than its numerator is known as a proper fraction, while a fraction whose numerator is greater than its denominator is known as an improper fraction. Proper fractions have values less than one and improper fractions have values greater than one. A mixed number is a number that contains both an integer and a fraction. Any improper fraction can be rewritten as a mixed number. Example: $\frac{8}{3} = \frac{6}{3} + \frac{2}{3} = 2 + \frac{2}{3} = 2\frac{2}{3}$. Similarly, any mixed number can be rewritten as an improper fraction. Example: $1\frac{3}{5} = 1 + \frac{3}{5} = \frac{5}{5} + \frac{3}{5} = \frac{8}{5}$.

Process of rounding

Rounding is the approximation of a number by decreasing or increasing it to the nearest possible exact value of the cutoff digit. This is done by the following steps:
1. Check the digit immediately to the right of the cutoff digit.
    a. If this digit is 5 or higher, add 1 to the cutoff digit.
    b. If this digit is 4 or lower, keep the original cutoff digit.
2. Eliminate all digits to the right of the cutoff digit.

For example, suppose we want to round the number 123.4567 to the nearest hundredth. The cutoff digit then is the 5. Immediately to the right is a 6, so we'll add 1 to the cutoff digit, making it a 6. The rounded number then is 123.46.

A number should only ever be rounded once. If we were to round our number above to the nearest tenth, the result would be 123.5. If we then tried to round it a second time, to the nearest integer, we would get 124. This is not proper rounding because rounding the original number to the nearest integer gives us 123.

A number should also not be rounded in the middle of a series of calculations; only at the end. Rounding in the middle tends to compound what is known as rounding error.

Number Operations and Algorithms

Four basic mathematical operations

There are four basic mathematical operations:
- Addition increases the value of one quantity by the value of another quantity. Example: 2 + 4 = 6; 8 + 9 = 17. The result is called the sum. With addition, the order does not matter. 4 + 2 = 2 + 4.
- Subtraction is the opposite operation to addition; it decreases the value of one quantity by the value of another quantity. Example: 6 – 4 = 2; 17 – 8 = 9. The result is called the difference. Note that with subtraction, the order does matter. $6 - 4 \neq 4 - 6$.
- Multiplication can be thought of as repeated addition. One number tells how many times to add the other number to itself. Example: 3 × 2 (three times two) = 2 + 2 + 2 = 6. With multiplication, the order does not matter. 2 × 3 (or 3 + 3) = 3 × 2 (or 2 + 2 + 2).
- Division is the opposite operation to multiplication; one number tells us how many parts to divide the other number into. Example: 20 ÷ 4 = 5; if 20 is split into 4 equal parts, each part is 5. With division, the order of the numbers does matter. $20 \div 4 \neq 4 \div 20$.

Manipulating fractions

Fractions can be manipulated by multiplying or dividing (but not adding or subtracting) both the numerator and denominator by the same number, without changing the value of the fraction. If you divide both numbers by a common factor, you are reducing or simplifying the fraction. Two fractions that have the same value, but are expressed differently are known as equivalent fractions. For example, $\frac{2}{10}, \frac{3}{15}, \frac{4}{20}$, and $\frac{5}{25}$ are all equivalent fractions. They can also all be reduced or simplified to $\frac{1}{5}$.

When two fractions are manipulated so that they have the same denominator, this is known as finding a common denominator. The number chosen to be that common denominator should be the least common multiple of the two original denominators. Example: $\frac{3}{4}$ and $\frac{5}{6}$; the least common multiple of 4 and 6 is 12. Manipulating to achieve the common denominator: $\frac{3}{4} = \frac{9}{12}$; $\frac{5}{6} = \frac{10}{12}$.

Adding, subtracting, multiplying, and dividing fractions

If two fractions have a common denominator, they can be added or subtracted simply by adding or subtracting the two numerators and retaining the same denominator. Example: $\frac{1}{2} + \frac{1}{4} = \frac{2}{4} + \frac{1}{4} = \frac{3}{4}$. If the two fractions do not already have the same denominator, one or both of them must be manipulated to achieve a common denominator before they can be added or subtracted.

Two fractions can be multiplied by multiplying the two numerators to find the new numerator and the two denominators to find the new denominator. Example: $\frac{1}{3} \times \frac{2}{3} = \frac{1 \times 2}{3 \times 3} = \frac{2}{9}$.

Two fractions can be divided flipping the numerator and denominator of the second fraction and then proceeding as though it were a multiplication. Example: $\frac{2}{3} \div \frac{3}{4} = \frac{2}{3} \times \frac{4}{3} = \frac{8}{9}$.

Problem-solving strategies for mathematics

For any problem, the following strategies can be used according to their appropriateness to the type of problem or calculation: i) Use manipulatives or act out the problem, ii) draw a picture, iii) look for a pattern, iv) guess and check, v) use logical reasoning, vi) make an organized list, vii) make a table, viii) solve a simpler problem, and ix) work backward.

In order to solve a word problem, the following steps can be used:
   a. Achieve an understanding of the problem by reading it carefully, finding and separating the information needed to solve the problem, and discerning the ultimate question in the problem.
   b. Make a plan as to what needs to be done to solve the problem.
   c. Solve the problem using the plan from step 2.
   d. Review the word problem to make sure that the answer is the correct solution to the problem and makes sense.

Algorithms and estimates

Algorithms result in an exact answer, while an estimate gives an approximation. Algorithms are systematic, problem-solving procedures used to find the solution to a mathematical computation in a finite number of steps. Algorithms are used for recurring types of problems, thus saving mental time and energy because they provide a routine, unvaried method, like a standard set of instructions or a recipe. A computer program could be considered an elaborate algorithm.

An estimate attempts only to find a value that is close to an exact answer. A multidigit multiplication problem such as 345 * 12 can be calculated on paper or with a calculator but would be difficult to do mentally. However, an estimation of the answer based on something simpler *can* be done mentally, such as 350 * 10 + 350 * 2 = 3500 + 700 = 4200. This estimate is close to the actual answer of 4140. Students can practice their number sense by computing estimations.

Number Theory

Prime Numbers and Factors, LCM and GCF

A *prime number* is a number that is only evenly divisible by 1 and itself.

A *prime factor* is a prime number that divides evenly into another number. For example, 3 is a prime factor of 21, because 3 is a prime number and 21 is evenly divisible by 3.

The *least common multiple* is the smallest number that is evenly divisible by all numbers in a given set.

The *greatest common factor* is the greatest number that all numbers in a set are evenly divisible by.

Prime Factorization

Prime Factorization is breaking a number down into a list of its prime factors. The prime factorization of 60 is $2 \times 2 \times 3 \times 5$, because 2, 3, and 5 are all prime numbers and $2 \times 2 \times 3 \times 5 = 60$. This can be found by first breaking down 60 into any two factors, perhaps 30 and 2. Since 2 is a prime number, it's already a prime factor, but 30 needs to be broken down into factors. 30 can be broken into 2 and 15, 3 and 10, or 6 and 5, but it does not matter which we use. If 3 and 10 are used, the factorization of 60 is $2 \times 3 \times 10$. Since 2 and 3 are prime but 10 is not, we have to break 10 down into 2 and 5, which now makes the factorization of $60 = 2 \times 3 \times 2 \times 5$. This is the prime factorization of 60 because these numbers are all prime. To report the answer in proper form put the numbers in order from least to greatest: the final answer for the prime factorization of 60 is $2 \times 2 \times 3 \times 5$.

Greatest common factor (GCF) and least common multiple (LCM)

The greatest common factor (GCF) is the largest number that is a factor of two or more numbers. For example, the factors of 15 are 1, 3, 5, and 15; the factors of 35 are 1, 5, 7, and 35. Therefore, the greatest common factor of 15 and 35 is 5.

The least common multiple (LCM) is the smallest number that is a multiple of two or more numbers. For example, the multiples of 3 include 3, 6, 9, 12, 15, etc.; the multiples of 5 include 5, 10, 15, 20, etc. Therefore, the least common multiple of 3 and 5 is 15.

Greatest Common Factor example
The Greatest Common Factor of 36 and 48 is 12. One way to find this is by simply listing all the factors of 36 and 48; the common factors of 36 and 48 are 1, 2, 3, 4, 6, and 12, and 12 is the greatest of these.

This can also be found using the prime factorization of both 36 and 48. The prime factorization of 36 is $2 \times 2 \times 3 \times 3$, and the prime factorization of 48 is $2 \times 2 \times 2 \times 2 \times 3$. Find how many of each prime factor these factorizations have in common: both factorizations have two 2's and one 3, so the Greatest Common Factor of 36 and 48 must be $2 \times 2 \times 3$, which equals 12.

Least Common Multiple example
The Least Common Multiple of 6 and 8 is 24. One way to find this is to list the common multiples of 6 and 8, 24, 48, 72, ...etc, and the least of these is 24.

This can also be found using the prime factorization of both 6 and 8. The prime factorization of 6 is 2×3, and the prime factorization of 8 is $2 \times 2 \times 2$. For each factor, count the number of times it occurs in each factorization. Find the greatest number of times each factor shows up, and multiply each factor that many times. Since 2 shows up three times in 8's factorization, and 3 shows up once in 6's prime factorization, multiply $2 \times 2 \times 2 \times 3$, which equals 24.

Examples of writing expressions

Write expressions to represent the following situations.
A. Turner has saved $75 toward the purchase of an iPod. How much more money does he need to save?
B. This week Marcus mowed twice the amount of lawns he mowed last week. How many lawns did Marcus mow this week?
C. Jenny earns $4 for every room she cleans in her house. How much money will she earn cleaning her whole house?

A. Turner has saved $75 toward the purchase of an iPod. The amount of money he still needs to save can be expressed by $C - 75$, representing the difference between total cost, C, of the iPod and what he already has.

B. This week Marcus mowed twice the amount of lawns he mowed last week. The number of lawns he mowed this week can be expressed as $2l$, representing two times the number of lawns mowed last week, l.

C. Jenny earns $4 for every room she cleans in her house. The amount of money she will earn cleaning her whole house can be expressed by $4r$, representing 4 times the number of rooms, r, in her whole house.

Sample Problems

At the grocery store you see two different kinds of cereal on sale for the same price. Box A has dimensions $\frac{3}{4}ft \times \frac{1}{2}ft \times \frac{2}{3}ft$ and Box B has dimensions $\frac{9}{10}ft \times \frac{1}{3}ft \times \frac{4}{5}ft$. Decide which box will give you the most cereal for your money.

Box A will give you more cereal for your money because the box can hold more volume than Box B. Find the volume of each box using the formula $V = l \times w \times h$. The volume of Box A is $\frac{3}{4} \times \frac{1}{2} \times \frac{2}{3} = \frac{6}{24} = \frac{1}{4}ft^3$, and the volume of Box B is $\frac{9}{10} \times \frac{1}{3} \times \frac{4}{5} = \frac{36}{150} = \frac{6}{25}ft^3$. Because $\frac{1}{4} = .25$ and $\frac{6}{25} = .24$, the volume of Box A is slightly larger than the volume of Box B and therefore a better deal because it will hold more cereal.

Sheila is going to make her own canvas tent for camping. She wants to make a tent that is the shape of a triangular prism. Given the dimensions below, create a net figure of the tent and determine how much canvas Sheila will need to make it.

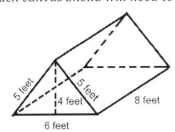

Sheila will need 152 square feet of canvas. This is found by determining the surface area of the triangular prism. In the net figure below, it is clear to see that the sum of the areas of two triangles and three rectangles will give the full surface area.

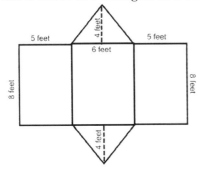

Each triangle has a base of 6 feet and height of 4 feet, so the area of each triangle is $\frac{6\times4}{2}=\frac{24}{2}=12\text{ft}^2$. Each outer rectangle in the net figure has a length of 8 feet and a width of 5 feet, so the area of each of those rectangles is $5\times8=40\text{ft}^2$. The other rectangle has a length of 8 and a width of 6, so has an area of $6\times8=48\text{ft}^2$. The total surface area is found by adding the area of all 5 of the separate shapes together: $12+12+40+40+48=152\text{ft}^2$.

Draw a net figure of the present below and determine how much wrapping paper will be needed to wrap it.

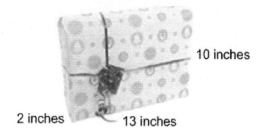

10 inches

2 inches   13 inches

352 square inches of wrapping paper will be needed to wrap the present, which is the surface area of the box. In the net figure below, it is seen that there are two rectangles with dimensions 13in × 2in which each have an area of $13\times2=26\text{in}^2$, two rectangles with dimensions 10in × 2in which each have an area of $10\times2=20\text{in}^2$, and two rectangles with dimensions 13in × 10in which each have an area of $13\times10=130\text{in}^2$. The total surface area is found by adding together the areas of the 6 rectangles: $26+26+20+20+130+130=352\text{in}^2$.

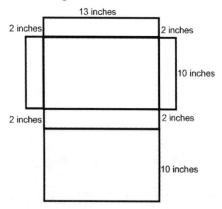

Factors, common and prime factors

Factors are numbers that are multiplied together to obtain a product. For example, in the equation $2\times3=6$, the numbers 2 and 3 are factors. A prime number has only two factors (1 and itself), but other numbers can have many factors.

A common factor is a number that divides exactly into two or more other numbers. For example, the factors of 12 are 1, 2, 3, 4, 6, and 12, while the factors of 15 are 1, 3, 5, and 15. The common factors of 12 and 15 are 1 and 3.

A prime factor is also a prime number. Therefore, the prime factors of 12 are 2 and 3. For 15, the prime factors are 3 and 5.

Decimal system and related terms

The decimal, or base 10, system is a number system that uses ten different digits (0, 1, 2, 3, 4, 5, 6, 7, 8, 9). An example of a number system that uses something other than ten digits is the binary, or base 2, number system, used by computers, which uses only the numbers 0 and 1. It is thought that the decimal system originated because people had only their 10 fingers for counting.

Decimal – a number that uses a decimal point to show the part of the number that is less than one. Example: 1.234.

Decimal point – a symbol used to separate the ones place from the tenths place in decimals or dollars from cents in currency.

Decimal place – the position of a number to the right of the decimal point. In the decimal 0.123, the 1 is in the first place to the right of the decimal point, indicating tenths; the 2 is in the second place, indicating hundredths; and the 3 is in the third place, indicating thousandths.

Charts and tables

Organization and purpose of charts and tables

Charts and *Tables* are ways of organizing information into separate rows and columns that are labeled to identify and explain the data contained in them. Some charts and tables are organized horizontally, with row lengths giving the details about the labeled information. Other charts and tables are organized vertically, with column heights giving the details about the labeled information.

Frequency Tables show how frequently each unique value appears in the set. A *Relative Frequency Table* is one that shows the proportions of each unique value compared to the entire set. Relative frequencies are given as percents; however, the total percent for a relative frequency table will not necessarily equal 100 percent due to rounding. An example of a frequency table with relative frequencies is below.

Favorite Color	Frequency	Relative Frequency
Blue	4	13%
Red	7	22%
Purple	3	9%
Green	6	19%
Cyan	12	38%

Pictograph

A *Pictograph* is a graph, generally in the horizontal orientation, that uses pictures or symbols to represent the data. Each pictograph must have a key that defines the picture or symbol and gives the quantity each picture or symbol represents. Pictures or symbols on a pictograph are not always shown as whole elements. In this case, the fraction of the picture or symbol shown represents the same fraction of the quantity a whole picture or symbol stands for. For example, a row with $3\frac{1}{2}$ ears of corn, where each ear of corn represents 100 stalks of corn in a field, would equal $3\frac{1}{2} \cdot 100 = 350$ stalks of corn in the field.

Circle graphs (pie charts)

Circle Graphs, also known as *Pie Charts*, provide a visual depiction of the relationship of each type of data compared to the whole set of data. The circle graph is divided into sections by drawing radii to create central angles whose percentage of the circle is equal to the individual data's percentage of the whole set. Each 1% of data is equal to 3.6º in the circle graph. Therefore, data represented by a 90º section of the circle graph makes up 25% of the whole. When complete, a circle graph often looks like a pie cut into uneven wedges. Below is an example of a pie chart.

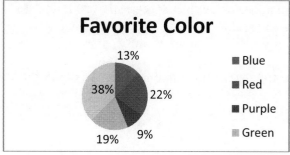

Line graph

Line Graphs have one or more lines of varying styles (solid or broken) to show the different values for a set of data. The individual data are represented as ordered pairs, much like on a Cartesian plane. In this case, the x- and y- axes are defined in terms of their units, such as dollars or time. The individual plotted points are joined by line segments to show whether the value of the data is increasing (line sloping upward), decreasing (line sloping downward) or staying the same (horizontal line). Multiple sets of data can be graphed on the same line graph to give an easy visual comparison. An example of this would be graphing achievement test scores for different groups of students over the same time period to see which group had the greatest increase or decrease in performance from year-to-year.

Bar graph

A *Bar Graph* is one of the few graphs that can be drawn correctly in two different configurations – both horizontally and vertically. A bar graph is similar to a line plot in the way the data is organized on the graph. Both axes must have their categories defined for the graph to be useful. Rather than placing a single dot to mark the point of the data's value, a bar, or thick line, is drawn from zero to the exact value of the data, whether it is a number, percentage, or other numerical value. Longer bar lengths correspond to greater data values. To read a bar graph, read the labels for the axes to find the units being reported. Then look where the bars end in relation to the scale given on the corresponding axis and determine the associated value.

Permutation

For any given set of data, the individual elements in the set may be arranged in different groups containing different numbers of elements arranged in different orders. For example, given the set of integers from one to three, inclusive, the elements of the set are 1, 2, and 3: written as {1, 2, 3}. They may be arranged as follows: 1, 2, 3, 12, 21, 13, 31, 23, 32, 123, 132, 213, 231, 312, and 321. These ordered sequences of elements from the given set of data are called **permutations**. It is important to note that in permutations, the order of the elements in the sequence is important. The sequence 123 is not the same as the sequence 213. Also, no element in the given set may be used more times as an element in a permutation than it appears as an element in the original set. For example, 223 is not a permutation in the above example because the number 2 only appears one time in the given set.

Finding the factorial of a number

The **factorial** is a function that can be performed on any **non-negative integer**. It is represented by the ! sign written after the integer on which it is being performed. The factorial of an integer is the product of all positive integers less than or equal to the number. For example, 4! (read "4 factorial") is calculated as $4 \times 3 \times 2 \times 1 = 24$.

Since 0 is not itself a positive integer, nor does it have any positive integers less than it, 0! cannot be calculated using this method. Instead, 0! is defined by convention to equal 1. This makes sense if you consider the pattern of descending factorials:

$$5! = 120$$

$$4! = \frac{5!}{5} = 24$$

$$3! = \frac{4!}{4} = 6$$

$$2! = \frac{3!}{3} = 2$$

$$1! = \frac{2!}{2} = 1$$

$$0! = \frac{1!}{1} = 1$$

Finding the number of permutations of a given set

To find the number of permutations of r items from a set of n items, use the formula $_nP_r = \frac{n!}{(n-r)!}$. When using this formula, each element of r must be unique. Also, this assumes that different arrangements of the same set of elements yields different outcomes. For example, 123 is not the same as 321; order is important.

A special case arises while finding the number of possible permutations of n items from a set of n items. Because $n = r$, the equation for the number of permutations becomes simply $P = n!$.

If a set contains one or more groups of **indistinguishable or interchangeable elements** (e.g., the set {1, 2, 3, 3}, which has a group of two indistinguishable 3's), there is a different formula for finding distinct permutations of all n elements. Use the formula $P = \frac{n!}{m_1!m_2!...m_k!}$, where P is the number of permutations, n is the total number of elements in the set, and m_1 through m_k are the number of identical elements in each group (e.g., for the set {1, 1, 2, 2, 2, 3, 3}, $m_1 = 2$, $m_2 = 3$, and $m_3 = 2$). It is important to note that each repeated number is counted as its own element for the purpose of defining n (e.g., for the set {1, 1, 2, 2, 2, 3, 3}, $n = 7$, not 3).

Finding all possible permutations of a set of unique items

To find the number of possible permutations of **any number of elements** in a set of unique elements, you must apply the permutation formulas multiple times. For example, to find the total number of possible permutations of the set {1, 2, 3} first apply the permutation formula for situations where $n = r$ as follows: $P = n! = 3! = 6$. This gives the number of permutations of the three elements when all three elements are used. To find the number of permutations when only two of the three elements are used, use the formula $_nP_r = \frac{n!}{(n-r)!}$, where n is 3 and r is 2.

$$_nP_r = \frac{n!}{(n-r)!} \Rightarrow {_3P_2} = \frac{3!}{(3-2)!} = \frac{6}{1} = 6$$

To find the number of permutations when one element is used, use the formula $_nP_r = \frac{n!}{(n-r)!}$, where n is 3 and r is 1.

$$_nP_r = \frac{n!}{(n-r)!} \Rightarrow {_3P_1} = \frac{3!}{(3-1)!} = \frac{3!}{2!} = \frac{6}{2} = 3$$

Find the sum of the three formulas: $6 + 6 + 3 = 15$ total possible permutations. Alternatively, the general formula for total possible permutations can be written as follows:

$$P_T = \sum_{i=1}^{n} \frac{n!}{(i-1)!}$$

Combinations

For any given set of data, the individual elements in the set may be arranged in different groups containing different numbers of elements arranged in different orders. For example, given the set of integers from one to three, inclusive, the elements of the set are 1, 2, and 3: written as {1, 2, 3}. If we want to select a group of numbers from the set, and it does not matter what order those numbers appear in our group, we are looking for a combination. A **combination** is a group of elements taken from a set, where the order in which they are taken or displayed does not matter. From the set {1,2,3}, the following combinations can be made: 1, 2, 3, 12, 13, 23, and 123. No element in the given set may be used more times as an element in a combination than it appears as an element in the original set. For example, 133 is not a combination in the above example because the number 3 only appears once in the set. However, if our set were {1,2,3,3}, then 133 would be an acceptable combination.

Permutations vs combinations

The biggest difference between permutations and combinations is the ordering of the sequences. In permutations, different sequences of the same group of elements create different permutations. In combinations, different sequences of the same group of elements create the same combination. It is easy to get the two terms confused, especially since the terms are misused in the English language. For example, combination locks do not require a combination, but a permutation. If you enter the correct numbers in the wrong order, you have entered a correct combination, but an incorrect permutation, and the lock will not open.

Finding the number of combinations in a set of elements

In a set containing n elements, the number of combinations of r items from the set can be found using the formula $_nC_r = \frac{n!}{r!(n-r)!}$. Notice the similarity to the formula for permutations. In effect, you are dividing the number of permutations by $r!$ to get the number of combinations, and the formula may be written $_nC_r = \frac{nP_r}{r!}$. When finding the number of combinations, it is important to remember that the elements in the set must be unique (i.e., there must not be any duplicate items), and that no item may be used more than once in any given sequence.

Using permutation and combination to calculate the number of outcomes

When trying to calculate the probability of an event using the $\frac{desired\ outcomes}{total\ outcomes}$ formula, you may frequently find that there are too many outcomes to individually count them. Permutation and combination formulas offer a shortcut to counting outcomes. A permutation is an arrangement of a specific number of a set of objects in a specific order. The number of **permutations** of r items given a set of n items can be calculated as $_nP_r = \frac{n!}{(n-r)!}$. Combinations are similar to permutations, except there are no restrictions regarding the order of the elements. While ABC is considered a different permutation than BCA, ABC and BCA are considered the same combination. The number of **combinations** of r items given a set of n items can be calculated as $_nC_r = \frac{n!}{r!(n-r)!}$ or $_nC_r = \frac{nP_r}{r!}$.

Example: Suppose you want to calculate how many different 5-card hands can be drawn from a deck of 52 cards. This is a combination since the order of the cards in a hand does not matter. There are 52 cards available, and 5 to be selected. Thus, the number of different hands is $_{52}C_5 = \frac{52!}{5! \times 47!} = 2,598,960$.

Similar triangles and congruent triangles

Similar triangles are triangles whose corresponding angles are congruent to one another. Their corresponding sides may or may not be equal, but they are proportional to one another. Since the angles in a triangle always sum to 180°, it is only necessary to determine that two pairs of corresponding angles are congruent, since the third will be also in that case.

Congruent triangles are similar triangles whose corresponding sides are all equal. Congruent triangles can be made to fit on top of one another by rotation, reflection, and/or translation. When trying to determine whether two triangles are congruent, there are several criteria that can be used. Side-side-side (SSS): if all three sides of one triangle are equal to all three sides of another triangle, they are congruent by SSS.

Side-angle-side (SAS): if two sides and the adjoining angle in one triangle are equal to two sides and the adjoining angle of another triangle, they are congruent by SAS.
Additionally, if two triangles can be shown to be similar, then there need only be one pair of corresponding equal sides to show congruence.

Pyramids, prisms, cubes, and spheres

For some of these shapes, it is necessary to find the area of the base polygon before the volume of the solid can be found. This base area is represented in the volume equations as B.

Pyramid – consists of a polygon base, and triangles connecting each side of that polygon to a vertex. The volume can be calculated as $V = \frac{1}{3}Bh$, where h is the distance between the vertex and the base polygon, measured perpendicularly.

Prism – consists of two identical polygon bases, attached to one another on corresponding sides by parallelograms. The volume can be calculated as $V = Bh$, where h is the perpendicular distance between the two bases.

Cube – a special type of prism in which the two bases are the same shape as the side faces. All faces are squares. The volume can be calculated as $V = s^3$, where s is the length of any side.

Sphere – a round solid consisting of one continuous, uniformly-curved surface. The volume can be calculated as $V = \frac{4}{3}\pi r^3$, where r is the distance from the center of the sphere to any point on the surface (radius).

Teaching strategies that can help build number sense

It is important to think flexibly to develop number sense. Therefore, it is imperative to impress upon students that there is more than one right way to solve a problem. Otherwise, students will try to learn only one method of computation, rather than think about what makes sense or contemplate the possibility of an easier way. Some strategies for helping students develop number sense include the following:

    a. Frequently asking students to make their calculations mentally and rely on their reasoning ability. Answers can be checked manually afterwards, if needed.

    b. Having a class discussion about solutions the students found using their minds only and comparing the different approaches to solving the problem. Have the students explain their reasoning in their own words.

    c. Modeling the different ideas by tracking them on the board as the discussion progresses.

    d. Presenting problems to the students that can have more than one answer.

Ordered pairs, graphs, and equations

x	y
0	6
1	2
2	−2
3	−6
4	−10

Multiple representations are shown below:

Ordered Pairs
(0, 6), (1, 2), (2, −2), (3, −6), (4, −10)

The list of ordered pairs was created by substituting each x- and y-value, into the ordered pair form, (x, y).
Graph

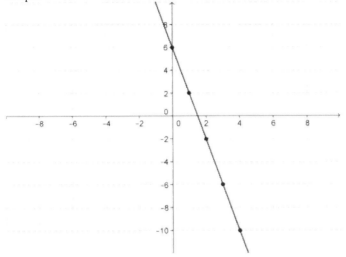

The graph was created by plotting each ordered pair and connecting the points with a line.

Equation
$y = -4x + 6$

The slope of -4 was calculated from the table. The y-intercept is shown to be 6. Substituting the slope, m, and y-intercept, b, into the slope-intercept form of $y = mx + b$ gives $y = -4x + 6$.

Mathematical Reasoning

Major elements of successful math instruction

Though mathematics instruction necessarily focuses on a certain amount of memorization, such as the multiplication tables and basic addition and subtraction facts, it also requires more complex approaches and use of higher level thinking skills. Major elements of a successful math curriculum include:
- Deductive reasoning
- Adaptive reasoning
- Inductive reasoning
- Analysis skills (upper levels of Bloom's Taxonomy)

In order to ensure students exercise all of these skills, teachers must use several approaches to instruction. Teachers must also be sure the curriculum builds upon previously learned concepts and leads logically into concepts presented in succeeding grades.

Equation example

Write the equation to represent the following table of values and graph them. Using the graph, predict the cost of mailing a 6 pound package.

The cost of mailing a package at the post office.	
Weight (in lbs)	**Cost (in dollars)**
1	1.5
2	3
3	4.5
4	6

The equation that represents the cost, C, in terms of the weight, w, of a package is $C = 1.5w$, because for each additional pound, the cost increases by $1.50 per pound. These values are graphed in the graph below:

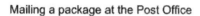

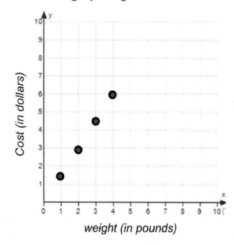

Looking at the graph, the points are going up at a constant rate of $1.50 for each pound. The next point would be at (5, 7.5), and then the next point would be at (6, 9). This means that the cost of mailing a 6 pound package would be $9.

Median of data and dot plot analysis

It appears that the median of the data is 4, as its values fall in the middle of all of the dots on the dot plot. Calculating the median is done by first listing the data in order from least to greatest. Each dot on the dot plot represents the number it is above, so therefore the data values are 1, 2, 2, 3, 3, 4, 4, 4, 4, 5, 5, 5, 6, 6, 7. To find the median the values must be crossed off until the middle number is reached: 1, 2, 2, 3, 3, 4, 4, 4, 4, 5, 5, 5, 6, 6, 7. The appearance of the median in the dot plot is accurate, as the median is 4.

Limits of functions

The limit of a function is represented by the notation $\lim_{x \to a} f(x)$. It is read as "the limit of f of x as x approaches a." In many cases, $\lim_{x \to a} f(x)$ will simply be equal to $f(a)$, but not always. Limits are important because some functions are not defined or are not easy to evaluate at certain values of x.

The limit at the point is said to exist only if the limit is the same when approached from the right side as from the left: $\lim_{x \to a^+} f(x) = \lim_{x \to a^-} f(x))$. Notice the symbol by the a in each case. When x approaches a from the right, it approaches from the positive end of the number line. When x approaches a from the left, it approaches from the negative end of the number line.

Differentiable functions

Differentiable functions are functions that have a derivative. Some basic rules for finding derivatives of functions are

$f(x) = c \Rightarrow f'(x) = 0$; where c is a constant
$f(x) = x \Rightarrow f'(x) = 1$
$(cf(x))' = cf'(x)$; where c is a constant
$f(x) = x^n \Rightarrow f'(x) = nx^{n-1}$; where n is a real number
$(f + g)'(x) = f'(x) + g'(x)$
$(fg)'(x) = f(x)g'(x) + f'(x)g(x)$
$\left(\dfrac{f}{g}\right)'(x) = \dfrac{f'(x)g(x) - f(x)g'(x)}{[g(x)]^2}$
$(f \circ g)'(x) = f'\big(g(x)\big) \cdot g'(x)$

This last formula is also known as the Chain Rule. If you are finding the derivative of a polynomial that is raised to a power, let the polynomial be represented by $g(x)$ and use the Chain Rule. The chain rule is one of the most important concepts to grasp in the early stages of learning calculus. Many other rules and shortcuts are based upon the chain rule.

These rules may also be used to take multiple derivatives of the same function. The derivative of the derivative is called the second derivative and is represented by the notation $f''(x)$. Taking one more derivative, if possible, gives the third derivative and is represented by the notation $f'''(x)$ or $f^{(3)}(x)$.

Continuity of functions

For a function to have continuity, its graph must be an unbroken curve. That is, it is a function that can be graphed without having to lift the pencil to move it to a different point. To say a function is continuous at point p, you must show the function satisfies three requirements. First, $f(p)$ must exist. If you evaluate the function at p, it must yield a real number. Second, there must exist a relationship such that $\lim_{x \to p} f(x) = f(p)$. Finally, the following relationship must be true:

$$\lim_{x \to p^+} F(x) = \lim_{x \to p^-} F(x) = F(p)$$

If all three of these requirements are met, a function is considered continuous at p. If any one of them is not true, the function is not continuous at p.

Functions

A function is an equation that has exactly one value of output variable (dependent variable) for each value of the input variable (independent variable). The set of all values for the input variable (here assumed to be x) is the domain of the function, and the set of all corresponding values of output variable (here assumed to be y) is the range of the function. When looking at a graph of an equation, the easiest way to determine if the equation is a function or not is to conduct the vertical line test. If a vertical line drawn through any value of x crosses the graph in more than one place, the equation is not a function.

Properties of functions

In functions with the notation $f(x)$, the value substituted for x in the equation is called the argument. The domain is the set of all values for x in a function. Unless otherwise given, assume the domain is the set of real numbers that will yield real numbers for the range. This is the domain of definition.

The graph of a function is the set of all ordered pairs (x, y) that satisfy the equation of the function. The points that have zero as the value for y are called the zeros of the function. These are also the x-intercepts, because that is the point at which the graph crosses, or intercepts, the x-axis. The points that have zero as the value for x are the y-intercepts because that is where the graph crosses the y-axis.

Horizontal shift and vertical shift

Horizontal and vertical shift occur when values are added to or subtracted from the x or y values, respectively.
If a constant is added to the y portion of each point, the graph shifts up. If a constant is subtracted from the y portion of each point, the graph shifts down. This is represented by the expression $f(x) \pm k$, where k is a constant.
If a constant is added to the x portion of each point, the graph shifts left. If a constant is subtracted from the x portion of each point, the graph shifts right. This is represented by the expression $f(x \pm k)$, where k is a constant.

Expected value

Expected value is a method of determining expected outcome in a random situation. It is really a sum of the weighted probabilities of the possible outcomes. Multiply the probability of an event occurring by the weight assigned to that probability (such as the amount of money won or lost). A practical application of the expected value is to determine whether a game of chance is really fair. If the sum of the weighted probabilities is greater than or equal to zero, the game is generally considered fair because the player has a fair chance to win, or at least to break even. If the expected value is less than one, then players lose more than they win. For example, a lottery drawing allows the player to choose any three-digit number, 000–999. The probability of choosing the winning number is 1:1000. If it costs \$1 to play, and a winning number receives \$500, the expected value is $\left(-\$1 \cdot \frac{999}{1,000}\right) + \left(\$500 \cdot \frac{1}{1,000}\right) = -0.499$ or $-\$0.50$. You can expect to lose on average 50 cents for every dollar you spend.

Probability

Probability is a branch of statistics that deals with the likelihood of something taking place. One classic example is a coin toss. There are only two possible results: heads or tails. The likelihood, or probability, that the coin will land as heads is 1 out of 2 (1/2, 0.5, 50%). Tails has the same probability. Another common example is a 6-sided die roll. The probability of any given number coming up is 1 out of 6.

Theoretical vs. experimental probability

Theoretical probability is the likelihood of a certain outcome occurring for a given event. It can be determined without actually performing the event. It is calculated as P (probability of success) = (desired outcomes)/(total outcomes).
Example:
There are 20 marbles in a bag: 8 blue, 5 red, 4 green, 3 yellow. The theoretical probability of randomly selecting a red marble is 5 out of 20, (5/20 = 1/4, 0.25, or 25%).

Most of the time, when we talk about probability, we mean theoretical probability. Experimental probability, or relative frequency, is the number of times an outcome occurs in a particular experiment or a certain number of observed events. While theoretical probability is based on what *should happen*, experimental probability is based on what *has happened*. Experimental probability is calculated in the same way as theoretical, except that actual outcomes are used instead of possible outcomes.
Theoretical and experimental probability do not always line up with one another. Theoretical probability says that out of 20 coin tosses, 10 should be heads. However, if we were actually to toss 20 coins, we might record just 5 heads. This doesn't mean that our theoretical probability is incorrect; it just means that this particular experiment had results that were different from what was predicted.

Using manipulative materials in the mathematics classroom

As with all classroom supplies, the students must understand that there are rules for their use, including how to store the materials when they are not in use. In addition...
   a. the teacher should discuss with the students the purpose of the manipulatives and how they will help the students to learn,
   b. the students should understand that the manipulatives are intended for use with specific problems and activities; however, time for free exploration should be made available so students are less tempted to play when assigned specific tasks,
   c. a chart posted in the classroom of the manipulatives with their names will help the students to gain familiarity with them and develop mathematical literacy skills, and
   d. loans of manipulatives for home use with a letter of explanation to the parents about the purpose and value of the manipulatives will encourage similar strategies with homework.

Algebraic expressions vs equations

An algebraic expression is a mathematical statement written in a form that uses numbers, letters, and symbols to represent a known or unknown quantity. Typically, letters from near the beginning of the alphabet (a, b, c) are used to represent known values, while letters from near the end of the alphabet are used to represent unknown values (x, y, z). An algebraic expression can contain any combination of letters or numbers, and sometimes involves arithmetic operations, such as addition, subtraction, multiplication, or division.

An equation is a mathematical statement that two expressions have the same value, or are equal to one another. An expression never contains an equals sign, but an equation always does.

Variable, dependent variable, constant, and coefficient

A variable is an unknown number or quantity represented by a letter. Sometimes the letter will be the first letter of the word it represents (for example, d for distance, h for height, t for time), but frequently the variable is indicated simply with the letter x.

A dependent variable is a variable with a value that is calculated based on the value of other quantities. For example, the area of a rectangle is dependent on the values of the base and the height; that is, $a = bh$, with a as the dependent variable. Since the area is calculated based on the values for the base and height, they are independent variables, while area is the dependent variable.

A constant is a number with a value that does not change. For example, in the algebraic expression $y = x - 5$, 5 is the constant.

A coefficient is a constant that is placed in front of a variable in an algebraic expression. For example, in the expression $3y + 1$, 3 is the coefficient of y.

Inequalities

An inequality is a mathematical statement that two algebraic expressions are not equal to one another. These are the symbols used to represent inequalities:
   a.   < means "less than"
   b.   > means "greater than"
   c.   ≠ means "not equal to."

An inequality can be solved in a way similar to an equation, though instead of a single answer (such as x = 3), the solution is a range of values, all of which make the inequality true (such as x > 5). To keep the inequality true, any term added to or subtracted from one side of the inequality must be added to or subtracted from the other side. The same is true for multiplying or dividing. The one very important exception is that if you are multiplying or dividing by a negative number, the inequality sign must be reversed.

Inductive reasoning

Inductive reasoning is a method used to make a conjecture, based on patterns and observations. The conclusion of an inductive argument may be true or false.

Mathematical Example:
A cube has 6 faces, 8 vertices, and 12 edges. A square pyramid has 5 faces, 5 vertices, and 8 edges. A triangular prism has 5 faces, 6 vertices, and 9 edges. Thus, the sum of the numbers of faces and vertices, minus the number of edges, will always equal 2, for any solid.

Non-Mathematical Example:
Almost all summer days in Tucson are hot. It is a summer day in Tucson. Therefore, it will probably be hot.

Deductive reasoning

Deductive reasoning is a method that proves a hypothesis or set of premises. The conclusion of a valid deductive argument will be true, given that the premises are true. Deductive reasoning utilizes logic to determine a conclusion.

Example:
If a ding is a dong, then a ping is a pong.
If a ping is a pong, then a ring is a ting.
A ding is a dong.
Therefore, a ring is a ting.

This example is a deductive argument. A set of premises is used to determine a valid conclusion. In this example, the chain rule is illustrated. Specifically,

$p \rightarrow q$

$q \rightarrow r$

p

_____

$\therefore q$

Rules of logic, inductive or deductive reasoning

The rules of logic are related to deductive reasoning because one conclusion must be made, given a set of premises (or statements). A truth table may be used to determine the validity of an argument. In all cases, the determination of the conclusion is based on a top-down approach, whereby a set of premises yields a certain conclusion, albeit true or false, depending on the truth values of all premises.

Mathematical induction proof and inductive reasoning

A mathematical induction proof utilizes inductive reasoning in its assumption that if $P(k)$ is true, then $P(k + 1)$ is also true. The induction hypothesis is $P(k)$. This step utilizes inductive reasoning because an observation is used to make the conjecture that $P(k + 1)$ is also true.

Example:
For all natural numbers, n, the sum is equal to $(n + 1) \left(\frac{n}{2}\right)$.
Show that $P(1)$ is true.
$1 = (1 + 1) \left(\frac{1}{2}\right)$.
Assume P(k) is true.
$1 + 2 + 3 + 4 + \cdots + k = (k + 1) \left(\frac{k}{2}\right)$.
This previous step is the inductive hypothesis. Using this hypothesis, it may be used to write the conjecture that $P(k + 1)$ is also true.

Linear Functions

Stretch, compression, and reflection

Stretch, compression, and reflection occur when different parts of a function are multiplied by different groups of constants. If the function as a whole is multiplied by a real number constant greater than 1 ($k \times f(x)$), the graph is stretched vertically. If k in the previous equation is greater than zero but less than 1, the graph is compressed vertically. If k is less than zero, the graph is reflected about the x-axis, in addition to being either stretched or compressed vertically if k is less than or greater than -1, respectively.

If instead, just the x-term is multiplied by a constant greater than 1 ($f(k \times x)$), the graph is compressed horizontally. If k in the previous equation is greater than zero but less than 1, the graph is stretched horizontally. If k is less than zero, the graph is reflected about the y-axis, in addition to being either stretched or compressed horizontally if k is greater than or less than -1, respectively.

Exponential functions and logarithmic functions

Exponential functions are equations that have the format $y = b^x$, where base $b > 0$ and $b \neq 1$. The exponential function can also be written $f(x) = b^x$. **Logarithmic functions** are equations that have the format $y = \log_b x$ or $f(x) = \log_b x$. The base b may be any number except one; however, the most common bases for logarithms are base 10 and base e. The log base e is known the natural logarithm, or ln, expressed by the function $f(x) = \ln x$. Any logarithm that does not have an assigned value of b is assumed to be base 10: $\log x = \log_{10} x$. Exponential functions and logarithmic functions are related in that one is the inverse of the other. If $f(x) = b^x$, then $f^{-1}(x) = \log_b x$. This can perhaps be expressed more clearly by the two equations: $y = b^x$ and $x = \log_b y$.

The following properties apply to logarithmic expressions:

$$\log_b 1 = 0$$
$$\log_b b = 1$$
$$\log_b b^p = p$$
$$\log_b MN = \log_b M + \log_b N$$
$$\log_b \frac{M}{N} = \log_b M - \log_b N$$
$$\log_b M^p = p \log_b M$$

Linear functions

In **linear functions**, the value of the function changes in direct proportion to x. The rate of change,represented by the slope on its graph, is constant throughout. The standard form of a linear equation is $ax + by = c$, where a, b, and c are real numbers. As a function, this equation is commonly written as $y = mx + b$ or $f(x) = mx + b$. This is known as the slope-intercept form, because the coefficients give the slope of the graphed function (m) and its y-intercept (b). Solve the equation $mx + b = 0$ for x to get $x = -\frac{b}{m}$, which is the only zero of the function. The domain and range are both the set of all real numbers.

Example function problems

The relationship between Statistics Final Exam scores and Calculus Final Exam scores, for a random sample of students, is represented by the table below.

Statistics Final Exam Scores	Calculus Final Exam Scores
74	82
78	72
84	88
89	86
93	97

A teacher models this relationship with the function, $f(x) = 0.9x + 8.4$. Describe how well this model fits the situation. Explain the process used to evaluate the model.

The linear function is a good model for the relationship between the two sets of scores, as evidenced by a correlation coefficient of approximately 0.78. Any r-value that is 0.70 or higher indicates a strong correlation. The r^2-value is approximately 0.61. A residual plot of the data would show no clear pattern, indicating that a linear model would be appropriate. The residual plot is shown below:

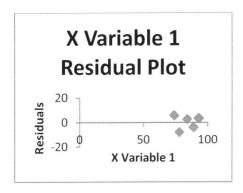

Suppose Rachel initially has $4,500. With each passing month, her account is one-half of what it was during the previous month. Show and describe the sequence, representing her balance. Write a function that may be used to model her account balance, after x months. Explain how the function was determined. Graph the function.

Sequence: 4500, 2250, 1125, 562.50, 281.25, …
The sequence is geometric, since there is a common ratio of $\frac{1}{2}$. Thus, this sequence represents an exponential function. All geometric sequences represent exponential functions. (All arithmetic sequences represent linear functions.) The general form of a geometric sequence is $a_n = a_1 \cdot r^{n-1}$, where a_n represents the value of the nth term, a_1 represents the initial value, r represents the common ratio, and n represents the number of terms. Substituting the initial value of 4500 and common ratio of $\frac{1}{2}$ into this form gives $a_n = 4500 \cdot \left(\frac{1}{2}\right)^{n-1}$.

The graph of the function is shown below:

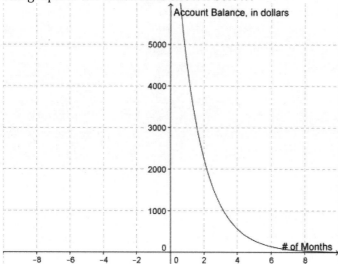

Nonlinear Functions

Constant functions and identity functions

Constant functions are given by the equation $y = b$ or $f(x) = b$, where b is a real number. There is no independent variable present in the equation, so the function has a constant value for all x. The graph of a constant function is a horizontal line of slope 0 that is positioned b units from the x-axis. If b is positive, the line is above the x-axis; if b is negative, the line is below the x-axis.

Identity functions are identified by the equation $y = x$ or $f(x) = x$, where every value of y is equal to its corresponding value of x. The only zero is the point $(0, 0)$. The graph is a diagonal line with slope 1.

Quadratic function

A **quadratic function** is a polynomial function that follows the equation pattern $y = ax^2 + bx + c$, or $f(x) = ax^2 + bx + c$, where a, b, and c are real numbers and $a \neq 0$. The domain of a quadratic function is the set of all real numbers. The range is also real numbers, but only those in the subset of the domain that satisfy the equation. The root(s) of any quadratic function can be found by plugging the values of a, b, and c into the **quadratic formula**:

$$x = \frac{-b \pm \sqrt{b^2 - 4ac}}{2a}$$

If the expression $b^2 - 4ac$ is negative, you will instead find complex roots.

Graphs of quadratic functions

A quadratic function has a parabola for its graph. In the equation $f(x) = ax^2 + bx + c$, if a is positive, the parabola will open upward. If a is negative, the parabola will open downward. The axis of symmetry is a vertical line that passes through the vertex. To determine whether or not the parabola will intersect the x-axis, check the number of real roots. An equation with two real roots

- 68 -

will cross the *x*-axis twice. An equation with one real root will have its vertex on the *x*-axis. An equation with no real roots will not contact the *x*-axis.

Theorems

Fundamental Theorem of Algebra
According to the **Fundamental Theorem of Algebra**, every non-constant, single variable polynomial has exactly as many roots as the polynomial's highest exponent. For example, if x^4 is the largest exponent of a term, the polynomial will have exactly 4 roots. However, some of these roots may have multiplicity or be non-real numbers. For instance, in the polynomial function $f(x) = x^4 - 4x + 3$, the only real roots are 1 and -1. The root 1 has multiplicity of 2 and there is one non-real root $(-1 - \sqrt{2}i)$.

Remainder Theorem
The **Remainder Theorem** is useful for determining the remainder when a polynomial is divided by a binomial. The Remainder Theorem states that if a polynomial function $f(x)$ is divided by a binomial $x - a$, where a is a real number, the remainder of the division will be the value of $f(a)$. If $f(a) = 0$, then a is a root of the polynomial.

Factor Theorem
The **Factor Theorem** is related to the Remainder Theorem and states that if $f(a) = 0$ then $(x - a)$ is a factor of the function.

Rational Root Theorem
According to the **Rational Root Theorem,** any rational root of a polynomial function $f(x) = a_n x^n + a_{n-1} x^{n-1} + \cdots + a_1 x + a_0$ with integer coefficients will, when reduced to its lowest terms, be a positive or negative fraction such that the numerator is a factor of a_0 and the denominator is a factor of a_n. For instance, if the polynomial function $f(x) = x^3 + 3x^2 - 4$ has any rational roots, the numerators of those roots can only be factors of 4 (1, 2, 4), and the denominators can only be factors of 1 (1). The function in this example has roots of 1 (or $\frac{1}{1}$) and -2 (or $-\frac{2}{1}$).

Rational functions

A **rational function** is a function that can be constructed as a ratio of two polynomial expressions: $f(x) = \frac{p(x)}{q(x)}$, where $p(x)$ and $q(x)$ are both polynomial expressions and $q(x) \neq 0$. The domain is the set of all real numbers, except any values for which $q(x) = 0$. The range is the set of real numbers that satisfies the function when the domain is applied. When you graph a rational function, you will have vertical asymptotes wherever $q(x) = 0$. If the polynomial in the numerator is of lesser degree than the polynomial in the denominator, the *x*-axis will also be a horizontal asymptote. If the numerator and denominator have equal degrees, there will be a horizontal asymptote not on the *x*-axis. If the degree of the numerator is exactly one greater than the degree of the denominator, the graph will have an oblique, or diagonal, asymptote. The asymptote will be along the line $y = \frac{p_n}{q_{n-1}} x + \frac{p_{n-1}}{q_{n-1}}$, where p_n and q_{n-1} are the coefficients of the highest degree terms in their respective polynomials.

Polynomial functions

A **polynomial function** is a function with multiple terms and multiple powers of x, such as
$$f(x) = a_n x^n + a_{n-1} x^{n-1} + a_{n-2} x^{n-2} + \cdots + a_1 x + a_0$$
where n is a non-negative integer that is the highest exponent in the polynomial, and $a_n \neq 0$. The domain of a polynomial function is the set of all real numbers. If the greatest exponent in the polynomial is even, the polynomial is said to be of even degree and the range is the set of real numbers that satisfy the function. If the greatest exponent in the polynomial is odd, the polynomial is said to be odd and the range, like the domain, is the set of all real numbers.

One-to-one functions and the horizontal line test

In a **one-to-one function**, each value of x has exactly one value for y (this is the definition of a function) *and* each value of y has exactly one value for x. While the vertical line test will determine if a graph is that of a function, the horizontal line test will determine if a function is a one-to-one function. If a horizontal line drawn at any value of y intersects the graph in more than one place, the graph is not that of a one-to-one function. Do not make the mistake of using the horizontal line test exclusively in determining if a graph is that of a one-to-one function. A one-to-one function must pass both the vertical line test and the horizontal line test. One-to-one functions are also **invertible functions**.

Sum, difference, product, or quotient of two functions

For each operation, we will use these functions as examples: $f(x) = x^2$ and $g(x) = x$.
To find the sum of two functions f and g, assuming the domains are compatible, simply add the two functions together: $(f + g)(x) = f(x) + g(x) = x^2 + x$.
To find the difference of two functions f and g, assuming the domains are compatible, simply subtract the second function from the first: $(f - g)(x) = f(x) - g(x) = x^2 - x$.
To find the product of two functions f and g, assuming the domains are compatible, multiply the two functions together: $(f \cdot g)(x) = f(x) \cdot g(x) = x^2 \cdot x = x^3$.
To find the quotient of two functions f and g, assuming the domains are compatible, divide the first function by the second: $\frac{f}{g}(x) = \frac{f(x)}{g(x)} = \frac{x^2}{x} = x \, ; x \neq 0$.

Composite of two functions

The composite of two functions f and g, written as $(f \circ g)(x)$ simply means that the output of the second function is used as the input of the first. This can also be written as $f(g(x))$. In general, this can be solved by substituting $g(x)$ for all instances of x in $f(x)$ and simplifying. Using the example functions $f(x) = x^2 - x + 2$ and $g(x) = x + 1$, we can find that $(f \circ g)(x)$ or $f(g(x))$ is equal to $f(x + 1) = (x + 1)^2 - (x + 1) + 2$, which simplifies to $x^2 + x + 2$.
It is important to note that $(f \circ g)(x)$ is not necessarily the same as $(g \circ f)(x)$. The process is not commutative like addition or multiplication expressions. If $(f \circ g)(x)$ does equal $(g \circ f)(x)$, the two functions are inverses of each other.

Foundations of Calculus

Fundamental Theorems of Calculus

The First Fundamental Theorem of Calculus shows that the process of indefinite integration can be reversed by finding the first derivative of the resulting function. It also gives the relationship between differentiation and integration over a closed interval of the function. For example, assuming a function is continuous over the interval $[m, n]$, you can find the definite integral by using the formula $\int_m^n f(x)\, dx = F(n) - F(m)$. Many times the notation $\int_m^n f(x)\, dx = F(x)\big|_m^n = F(n) - F(m)$ is also used to represent the Fundamental Theorem of Calculus. To find the average value of the function over the given interval, use the formula $\frac{1}{n-m}\int_m^n f(x)\, dx$.

The Second Fundamental Theorem of Calculus is related to the first. This theorem states that, assuming the function is continuous over the interval you are considering, taking the derivative of the integral of a function will yield the original function. The general format for this theorem is $\frac{d}{dx}\int_c^x f(x)\, dx = f(x)$ for any point having a domain value equal to c in the given interval.

Limit, converge, and diverge

Some sequences will have a limit, or a value the sequence approaches or sometimes even reaches but never passes. A sequence that has a limit is known as a convergent sequence because all the values of the sequence seemingly converge at that point. Sequences that do not converge at a particular limit are divergent sequences. The easiest way to determine whether a sequence converges or diverges is to find the limit of the sequence. If the limit is a real number, the sequence is a convergent sequence. If the limit is infinity, the sequence is a divergent sequence. Remember the following rules for finding limits:

$\lim\limits_{n\to\infty} k = k$ for all real numbers k

$\lim\limits_{n\to\infty} \frac{1}{n} = 0$

$\lim\limits_{n\to\infty} n = \infty$

$\lim\limits_{n\to\infty} \frac{k}{n^p} = 0$ for all real numbers k and positive rational numbers p.

Sequence

A sequence is a set of numbers that continues on in a define pattern. The function that defines a sequence has a domain composed of the set of positive integers. Each member of the sequence is an element, or individual term. Each element is identified by the notation a_n, where a is the term of the sequence, and n is the integer identifying which term in the sequence a is. There are two different ways to represent a sequence that contains the element a_n. The first is the simple notation $\{a_n\}$. The expanded notation of a sequence is $a_1, a_2, a_3, \ldots a_n, \ldots$. Notice that the expanded form does not end with the nth term. There is no indication that the nth term is the last term in the sequence, only that the nth term is an element of the sequence.

Equation example

Kim's savings is represented by the table below. Represent her savings, using an equation. Explain how the equation was found.

X (Number of Months)	Y (Total Savings, in Dollars)
2	1300
5	2050
9	3050
11	3550
16	4800

$$y = 250x + 800$$

The table shows a function with a constant rate of change, or slope, or 250. Given the points on the table, the slopes can be calculated as $(2050 - 1300)/(5 - 2)$, $(3050 - 2050)/(9 - 5)$, $(3550 - 3050)/(11 - 9)$, and $(4800 - 3550)/(16 - 11)$, each of which equals 250. Thus, the table shows a constant rate of change, indicating a linear function. The slope-intercept form of a linear equation is written as $y = mx + b$, where m represents the slope and b represents the y-intercept. Substituting the slope into this form gives $y = 250x + b$. Substituting corresponding x- and y-values from any point into this equation will give the y-intercept, or b. Using the point, $(2, 1300)$, gives $1300 = 250(2) + b$, which simplifies as $b = 800$. Thus, her savings may be represented by the equation, $y = 250x + 800$.

Measurement

Converting one measurement unit to another

When going from a larger unit to a smaller unit, multiply the numerical value of the known amount by the equivalent amount. When going from a smaller unit to a larger unit, divide the numerical value of the known amount by the equivalent amount. Also, you can set up conversion fractions where one fraction is the conversion fact, with the unit of the unknown amount in the numerator and the unit of the known value in the denominator. The second fraction has the known value from the problem in the numerator, and the unknown in the denominator. Multiply the two fractions to get the converted measurement.

Precision vs accuracy

Precision: How reliable and repeatable a measurement is. The more consistent the data is with repeated testing, the more precise it is. For example, hitting a target consistently in the same spot, which may or may not be the center of the target, is precision.

Accuracy: How close the data is to the correct data. For example, hitting a target consistently in the center area of the target, whether or not the hits are all in the same spot, is accuracy.

Note that it is possible for data to be precise without being accurate. If a scale is off balance, the data will be precise, but will not be accurate. For data to have precision and accuracy, it must be repeatable and correct.

Perimeter, area and volume

The perimeter is the distance around a two-dimensional object. It is determined by adding the lengths of all the sides of the object.

Area represents the space within a two-dimensional object. For example, the amount of carpet used to cover a floor is determined by calculating the area of the floor. Area is determined by multiplication and is expressed as a unit of measurement squared, such as square feet or square inches.

Volume represents the space contained within a three-dimensional object. It is also determined by multiplication and is expressed as a cubed unit, such as cubic feet or cubic inches.

Major properties of triangles and the Pythagorean Theorem

Triangles have several major properties. In any given triangle, the sum of the three angles will always equal 180°. Using this property, students can determine the value of one angle if the values of the other two angles are supplied.

The Pythagorean Theorem applies only to right triangles. A right angle consists of two lines whose vertex produces a 90° angle. A longer, third line connects these two lines to form the longest side, or hypotenuse, of the triangle. The Pythagorean Theorem states that in any right triangle, the sum of the squares of the two short sides will be the same as the square of the hypotenuse. It is expressed formulaically as $a^2 + b^2 = c^2$.

Equilateral, isosceles, and scalene triangles

An equilateral triangle is a triangle with three congruent sides. An equilateral triangle will also have three congruent angles.
An isosceles triangle is a triangle with two congruent sides. An isosceles triangle will also have two congruent angles opposite the two congruent sides.
A scalene triangle is a triangle with no congruent sides. A scalene triangle will also have three angles of different measures. The angle with the largest measure is opposite the longest side, and the angle with the smallest measure is opposite the shortest side.

Equilateral   Isosceles   Scalene

Acute, right, and obtuse triangles

An acute triangle is a triangle whose three angles are all less than 90°. If two of the angles are equal, the acute triangle is also an isosceles triangle. If the three angles are all equal, the acute triangle is also an equilateral triangle.
A right triangle is a triangle with exactly one angle equal to 90°. All right triangles follow the Pythagorean Theorem. A right triangle can never be acute or obtuse.

An obtuse triangle is a triangle with exactly one angle greater than 90°. The other two angles may or may not be equal. If the two remaining angles are equal, the obtuse triangle is also an isosceles triangle.

The sum of the measures of the interior angles of a triangle is always 180°. Therefore, a triangle can never have more than one angle greater than or equal to 90°.

Leg, hypotenuse, Pythagorean Theorem

A right triangle has exactly one right angle. (If a figure has more than one right angle, it must have more than three sides, since the sum of the three angles of a triangle must equal 180°.)

The side opposite the right angle is called the hypotenuse. The other two sides are called the legs. The Pythagorean Theorem states a unique relationship among the legs and hypotenuse of a right triangle: $a^2 + b^2 = c^2$, where a and b are the lengths of the legs of a right triangle, and c is the length of the hypotenuse. Note that this formula will only work with right triangles. Do not attempt to use it with triangles that are not right triangles.

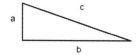

Pythagorean theorem

Named after the sixth-century Greek mathematician Pythagoras, this theorem states that, for a right triangle, the square of the hypotenuse (the longest side of the triangle, always opposite the right angle) is equal to the sum of the squares of the other two sides. Written symbolically, the Pythagorean Theorem can be expressed as $a^2 + b^2 = c^2$, where c is the hypotenuse and a and b are the remaining two sides.

The theorem is most commonly used to find the length of an unknown side of a right triangle, given the lengths of the other two sides. For example, given that the hypotenuse of a right triangle is 5 and one side is 3, the other side can be found using the formula: $a^2 + b^2 = c^2, 3^2 + b^2 = 5^2, 9 + b^2 = 25, b^2 = 25 - 9 = 16, b = \sqrt{16} = 4$.

The theorem can also be used "in reverse" to show that when the square of one side of a triangle is equal to the sum of the squares of the other two sides, the triangle must be a right triangle.

Two standard systems of measurements

There are two standard systems of measurement used for a variety of types of measurement:

US customary units – A system used in many English-speaking countries, particularly the United States, although it has been replaced by the metric system in a number of areas. The units of measurement in this system are the inch, foot, yard, mile for length; fluid ounce, cup, pint, quart, gallon for capacity; and ounce, pound, and ton for mass.

Metric system – A system used in many countries around the world that is based on decimals (e.g. tens, hundreds, thousands). The units of measurement in this system are the millimeter, centimeter, meter, kilometer for length; milligram, gram, and kilogram for mass; and milliliter and liter for capacity.

Length is the distance between two points. Mass is the amount of matter that an object contains, and capacity is the internal volume of an object or container.

Geometry

Complementary angles, supplementary angles, vertical angles, and transversals

Complimentary angles consist of two angles whose measurements add up to 90°. For example, a set of two 45° angles, or of one 30° angle and one 60° angle, would both be considered sets of complementary angles.

Supplementary angles are two angles whose measurements total 180°. If placed back to back, the bases of these angles would form a straight line.

Two intersecting lines form two sets of vertical angles. Vertical angles are situated opposite from each other, with a shared vertex, and measure the same number of degrees.

If a single line crosses two or more other lines, that line is known as a transversal. Transversals create sets of interior and exterior angles.

Polygons and regular polygons

Polygons are two-dimensional constructs formed by the intersection of at least three straight lines. Rectangles, triangles, pentagons and quadrilaterals are all polygons.

Since the intersection of lines always forms an angle, polygons enclose numerous angles. The number of angles in a polygon is determined by its number of sides. For example, a triangle encloses three angles, while a quadrilateral (four-sided polygon) encloses four angles.

A regular polygon encloses angles that are all equal to each other. A rectangle or a square consists of lines that all meet at 90° angles. An equilateral triangle is also a regular polygon, with each angle equal to 60°.

Symmetry, similarity, scaling, and translation

Symmetry refers to objects that can be divided into two identical figures with a single line. Regular polygons such as squares and rectangles are symmetrical. So are circles.

Similarity refers to objects that are shaped the same but are of different sizes. A 2 x 2 foot square is similar to a 4 x 4 foot square even though one is half the size of the other.

Transformation involves changing a geometrical object in various ways. This can include scaling, turning, sliding, or even flipping the object.

Scaling involves transforming an object by making it larger or smaller. Scaling is uniform in all directions and results in an object similar to the original, based on the geometric definition of "similar."

Ordered pairs and the coordinate plane

Ordered pairs are a way of representing the location of a specific point on a plane. The coordinate plane divides the plane into four quadrants. The coordinate plane is used to create ordered pairs by serving as a reference point from which to define the location of the point or points.

The coordinate plane consists of perpendicular lines that intersect at the origin. This intersection defines the plane's center. The horizontal line in a coordinate plane is referred to as the x-axis while the vertical line is called the y-axis. Ordered pairs represent the distance of a point from the origin of the coordinate plane, by indicating where the point is located on the x- and the y-axis of the plane.

Complementary, supplementary, and adjacent angles

Complementary: Two angles whose sum is exactly 90°. The two angles may or may not be adjacent. In a right triangle, the two acute angles are complementary.
Supplementary: Two angles whose sum is exactly 180°. The two angles may or may not be adjacent. Two intersecting lines always form two pairs of supplementary angles. Adjacent supplementary angles will always form a straight line.
Adjacent: Two angles that have the same vertex and share a side. Vertical angles are not adjacent because they share a vertex but no common side.

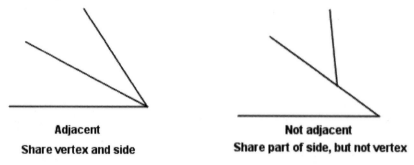

Adjacent
Share vertex and side

Not adjacent
Share part of side, but not vertex

Intersecting lines, parallel lines, vertical angles, and transversals

Intersecting Lines: Lines that have exactly one point in common.
Parallel Lines: Lines in the same plane that have no points in common and never meet. It is possible for lines to be in different planes, have no points in common, and never meet, but they are not parallel because they are in different planes.
Vertical Angles: Non-adjacent angles formed when two lines intersect. Vertical angles are congruent. In the diagram, $\angle ABD \cong \angle CBE$ and $\angle ABC \cong \angle DBE$.

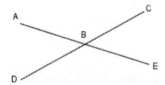

Transversal: A straight line that intersects at least two other lines, which may or may not be parallel.

Interior angles, exterior angles, and corresponding angles

Interior Angles: When two parallel lines are cut by a transversal, the angles that are between the two parallel lines are interior angles. In the diagram below, angles 3, 4, 5, and 6 are interior angles.
Exterior Angles: When two parallel lines are cut by a transversal, the angles that are outside the parallel lines are exterior angles. In the diagram below, angles 1, 2, 7, and 8 are exterior angles.

Corresponding Angles: When two parallel lines are cut by a transversal, the angles that are in the same position relative to the transversal and one of the parallel lines. The diagram below has four pairs of corresponding angles: angles 1 and 5; angles 2 and 6; angles 3 and 7; and angles 4 and 8. Corresponding angles formed by parallel lines are congruent.

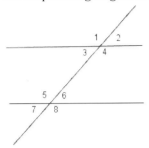

Alternate interior angles vs alternate exterior angles

Alternate Interior Angles: When two parallel lines are cut by a transversal, two interior angles that are on opposite sides of the transversal and on opposite parallel lines are congruent opposite interior angles. In the diagram below, there are two pair of alternate interior angles: angles 3 and 6, and angles 4 and 5. Alternate interior angles formed by parallel lines are congruent.

Alternate Exterior Angles: When two parallel lines are cut by a transversal, two exterior angles that are on opposite sides of the transversal and on opposite parallel lines are congruent opposite exterior angles. In the diagram below, there are two pair of alternate exterior angles: angles 1 and 8, and angles 2 and 7. Alternate exterior angles formed by parallel lines are congruent.

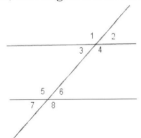

Center, radius, and diameter

Center: A single point that is equidistant from every point on a circle. (Point O in the diagram below.)
Radius: A line segment that joins the center of the circle and any one point on the circle. All radii of a circle are equal. (Segments OX, OY, and OZ in the diagram below.)
Diameter: A line segment that passes through the center of the circle and has both endpoints on the circle. The length of the diameter is exactly twice the length of the radius. (Segment XZ in the diagram below.)

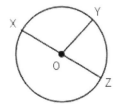

- 77 -

Geometric terms

Point – a fixed location in space; has no size or dimensions; commonly represented by a dot
Line – a set of points that extends infinitely in two opposite directions; has length, but no width or depth; a line can be defined by any two distinct points that it contains
Plane – a two dimensional surface that extends infinitely in all available directions; a plane can be defined by any three distinct points that it contains, or any line and another point not on that line
Collinear – multiple points that lie on the same line
Coplanar – multiple points or lines that lie in the same plane
Ray – a part of a line that has one endpoint and infinite length; defined by the single endpoint and a direction
Line segment – a part of a line that has two endpoints and a fixed length; defined by its two endpoints
Angle – formed by two intersecting lines (or rays or segments); defines the difference in orientation between the two; most commonly measured in degrees
Transversal – a line that crosses two or more other lines
Perpendicular – a line or plane that intersects another line or plane at a right (90°) angle
Parallel – a set of lines or planes that never intersect and are the same distance apart at every point

Polygons and related terms

A polygon is a planar shape formed from line segments called sides that are joined together at points called vertices (singular: vertex). Specific polygons are named by the number of angles or sides they have. Regular polygons are polygons whose sides are all equal and whose angles are all congruent.
An interior angle is any of the angles inside a polygon where two sides meet at a vertex. The sum of the interior angles of a polygon is dependent only on the number of sides. For example, all 5-sided polygons have interior angles that sum to 540°, regardless of the particular shape.
A diagonal is a line that joins two nonconsecutive vertices of a polygon. The number of diagonals that can be drawn on an n-sided polygon is $d = \frac{n(n-3)}{2}$.
An inscribed circle is a circle drawn within a polygon that touches each of polygon's sides exactly once. A superscribed circle is a circle drawn around a polygon such that it contains all vertices of the polygon. All triangles and all regular polygons can have an inscribed and superscribed circle.

Trapezoid, parallelogram, rhombus, rectangle, and square

A quadrilateral is a four-sided polygon.
Trapezoid – quadrilateral with exactly one pair of parallel sides (opposite one another); in an isosceles trapezoid, the two non-parallel sides have equal length and both pairs of non-opposite angles are congruent
Parallelogram – quadrilateral with two pairs of parallel sides (opposite one another), and two pairs of congruent angles (opposite one another)
Rhombus – parallelogram with four equal sides
Rectangle – parallelogram with four congruent angles (right angles)
Square – parallelogram with four equal sides and four congruent angles (right angles)

Symmetry

Symmetry is a property of a shape in which the shape can be transformed by either reflection or rotation without losing its original shape and orientation. A shape that has reflection symmetry can be reflected across a line with the result being the same shape as before the reflection. A line of symmetry divides a shape into two parts, with each part being a mirror image of the other. A shape can have more than one line of symmetry. A circle, for instance, has an infinite number of lines of symmetry. When reflection symmetry is extended to three-dimensional space, it is taken to describe a solid that can be divided into mirror image parts by a plane of symmetry. Rotational symmetry describes a shape that can be rotated about a point and achieve its original shape and orientation with less than a 360° rotation. When rotational symmetry is extended to three-dimensional space, it describes a solid that can be rotated about a line with the same conditions. Many shapes have both reflection and rotational symmetry.

Different types of polygons

The following list presents several different types of polygons:
> Triangle – 3 sides
> Quadrilateral – 4 sides
> Pentagon – 5 sides
> Hexagon – 6 sides
> Heptagon or septagon – 7 sides
> Octagon – 8 sides
> Nonagon – 9 sides
> Decagon – 10 sides
> Hendecagon – 11 sides
> Dodecagon – 12 sides

More generally, an n-gon is a polygon that has n angles and n sides.

The sum of the interior angles of an n-sided polygon is $(n – 2)180°$. For example, in a triangle n = 3, so the sum of the interior angles is $(3 – 2)180° = 180°$. In a quadrilateral, n = 4, and the sum of the angles is $(4 – 2)180° = 360°$. The sum of the interior angles of a polygon is equal to the sum of the interior angles of any other polygon with the same number of sides.

Two- and Three-Dimensional Figures

Calculating the area of planar shapes

Rectangle: $A = wl$, where w is the width and l is the length
Square: $A = s^2$, where s is the length of a side.
Triangle: $A = \frac{1}{2}bh$, where b is the length of one side (base) and h is the distance from that side to the opposite vertex measured perpendicularly (height).
Parallelogram: $A = bh$, where b is the length of one side (base) and h is the perpendicular distance between that side and its parallel side (height).
Trapezoid: $A = \frac{1}{2}(b_1 + b_2)h$, where b_1 and b_2 are the lengths of the two parallel sides (bases), and h is the perpendicular distance between them (height).

Circle: $A = \pi r^2$, where π is the mathematical constant approximately equal to 3.14 and r is the distance from the center of the circle to any point on the circle (radius).

Coordinate System and Transformations

Coordinate System examples

Label the following points and their indicated reflections in a coordinate plane and give the coordinates of the reflections:
Point A: (4, 3) reflected across the $x - axis$
Point B: (1, 2) reflected across the $y - axis$
Point C: (-2, -5) reflected across the $y - axis$
Point D: (3, 1) reflected across the $x - axis$ and then the $y - axis$

The graph below shows the points and their reflections:
The reflection of Point A is labeled as A' and has coordinates (4, -3). Because it is reflected across the $x - axis$, the $y - value$ changes in sign.
The reflection of Point B is labeled as B' and has coordinates (-1, 2). Because it is reflected across the $y - axis$, the $x - value$ changes in sign.
The reflection of Point C is labeled as C' and has coordinates (2, -5). Because it is reflected across the $y - axis$, the $x - value$ changes in sign.
The reflection of Point D is labeled as D' and has coordinates (-3, -1). Because it is reflected across both the x and $y - axes$, both the x and $y - values$ change in sign.

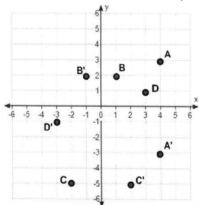

Identify the reflections that produce the second of each pair from the first of each pair:
(2, 6) and (-2, 6)
(-4, 0) and (4, 0)
(-1, -1) and (-1, 1)
(5, -7) and (-5, 7)

    A. The reflection from (2, 6) to (-2, 6) is a reflection across the $y - axis$. This is because the $x - value$ has changed in sign.
    B. The reflection from (-4, 0) to (4, 0) is a reflection across the $y - axis$. This is because the $x - value$ has changed in sign.
    C. The reflection from (-1, -1) to (-1, 1) is a reflection across the $x - axis$. This is because the $y - value$ has changed in sign.

D. The reflection from (5, -7) to (-5, 7) is a reflection across both the x and $y-$ $axis$. This is because both the x and $y - values$ have changed in sign.

Cartesian coordinate plane

The Cartesian coordinate plane consists of two number lines placed perpendicular to each other, and intersecting at the zero point, also known as the origin. The horizontal number line is known as the x-axis, with positive values to the right of the origin, and negative values to the left of the origin. The vertical number line is known as the y-axis, with positive values above the origin, and negative values below the origin. Any point on the plane can be identified by an ordered pair in the form (x,y), called coordinates. The x-value of the coordinate is called the abscissa, and the y-value of the coordinate is called the ordinate. The two number lines divide the plane into four quadrants: I, II, III, and IV.

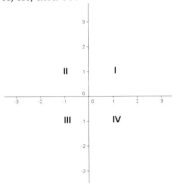

Congruent vs similar figures

Congruent figures are geometric figures that have the same size and shape. All corresponding angles are equal, and all corresponding sides are equal. It is indicated by the symbol $\cong$.
Similar figures are geometric figures that have the same shape, but do not necessarily have the same size. All corresponding angles are equal, and all corresponding sides are proportional, but they do not have to be equal. It is indicated by the symbol $\sim$.

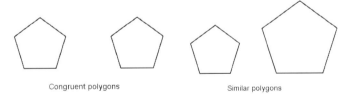

Congruent polygons   Similar polygons

Note that all congruent figures are also similar, but not all similar figures are congruent.

Symmetry, symmetric, and line of symmetry

Line of Symmetry: The line that divides a figure or object into two symmetric parts. Each symmetric half is congruent to the other. An object may have no lines of symmetry, one line of symmetry, or more than one line of symmetry.

   No lines of symmetry

One line of symmetry

More than one line of symmetry

Preimage, image, translation, reflection, rotation, and dilation

Preimage: The original unchanged image in its original position.
Image: A unique set of points
Translation: A case where a geometric image is slid, usually horizontally or vertically. The resulting image is congruent to the original image, but has been moved in a straight line.
Reflection: A case where a geometric image is flipped across a line of reflection. The resulting image is congruent to and a mirror image of the original image.
Rotation: A case where a geometric image is rotated around the center of rotation to a new position. The new image is congruent to the original image, but has been turned to a new position.
Dilation: A case where a geometric image has been expanded or contracted by a scale factor. The resulting image is similar to the original image, but not congruent.

Geometric transformations and how they relate to matrices

The four geometric transformations are translations, reflections, rotations, and dilations. When geometric transformations are expressed as matrices, the process of performing the transformations is simplified. For calculations of the geometric transformations of a planar figure, make a $2 \times n$ matrix, where n is the number of vertices in the planar figure. Each column represents the rectangular coordinates of one vertex of the figure, with the top row containing the values of the x-coordinates and the bottom row containing the values of the y-coordinates. For example, given a planar triangular figure with coordinates (x_1, y_1), (x_2, y_2), and (x_3, y_3), the corresponding matrix is $\begin{bmatrix} x_1 & x_2 & x_3 \\ y_1 & y_2 & y_3 \end{bmatrix}$. You can then perform the necessary transformations on this matrix to determine the coordinates of the resulting figure.

Cartesian product

A Cartesian product is the product of two sets of data, X and Y, such that all elements x are a member of set X, and all elements y are a member of set Y. The product of the two sets, $X \times Y$ is the set of all ordered pairs (x, y). For example, given a standard deck of 52 playing cards, there are four possible suits (hearts, diamonds, clubs, and spades) and thirteen possible card values (the numbers 2 through 10, ace, jack, queen, and king). If the card suits are set X and the card values are set Y, then there are $4 \times 13 = 52$ possible different (x, y) combinations, as seen in the 52 cards of a standard deck.

Binary relation

A binary relation, also referred to as a relation, dyadic relation, or 2-place relation, is a subset of a Cartesian product. It shows the relation between one set of objects and a second set of object, or between one set of objects and itself. The prefix *bi-* means *two*, so there are always two sets involved – either two different sets, or the same set used twice. The ordered pairs of the Cartesian

- 82 -

product are used to indicate a binary relation. Relations are possible for situations involving more than two sets, but those are not called binary relations.

Cartesian coordinate system

The Cartesian coordinate system describes the position of points on a plane or in a space in terms of their distance from lines called axes. The two lines, or axes, are the horizontal x-axis and the vertical y-axis, which are at right angles to each other and thus form a rectangular coordinate system. The point at which the two axes meet is the origin.
Points along the x-axis and to the right of the origin have a positive value, while those to the left of the origin are negative. Points along the y-axis above the origin are positive, while those below the origin are negative.

The position of a point, labeled (x,y), is described in terms of its distance from the origin. The x-coordinate is the distance of the point from the origin, parallel to the x-axis. The y-coordinate is the distance of the point from the origin, parallel to the y-axis. The x-coordinate is always written first. A quadrant is any of the four regions formed on a plane by the x-axis and the y-axis (not to be confused with the use of the term quadrant for a part of a circle). The quadrants are numbered counterclockwise, starting with the upper right quadrant (positive x and y values).

Types of angles

Each type of angle has a distinctive feature:
Congruent angle – an angle that has the same measure as another angle
Right angle – A quarter of a full turn, 90°
Straight or flat angle – half a full turn, 180°
Acute angle – Any angle smaller than a right angle (<90°)
Obtuse angle – Any angle greater than a right angle (>90°), but smaller than a straight angle (<180°)
Reflex angle – Any angle greater than a straight angle (>180°)
When angles are measured on the Cartesian coordinate system, the angle measure always begins from the positive x-axis. They can be measured in a positive (counterclockwise) or negative (clockwise) direction from the axis. Angles contained in the first quadrant are positive, and those contained in the fourth quadrant are negative.

Patterns

Line plot or dot plot

A *Line Plot*, also known as a *Dot Plot*, has plotted points that are NOT connected by line segments. In this graph, the horizontal axis lists the different possible values for the data, and the vertical axis lists the number of times the individual value occurs. A single dot is graphed for each value to show the number of times it occurs. This graph is more closely related to a bar graph than a line graph. Do not connect the dots in a line plot or it will misrepresent the data.

Stem and leaf plot

A *Stem and Leaf Plot* is useful for depicting groups of data that fall into a range of values. Each piece of data is separated into two parts: the first, or left, part is called the stem; the second, or right, part is called the leaf. Each stem is listed in a column from smallest to largest. Each leaf that has the common stem is listed in that stem's row from smallest to largest. For example, in a set of two-digit numbers, the digit in the tens place is the stem, and the digit in the ones place is the leaf. With a stem and leaf plot, you can easily see which subset of numbers (10s, 20s, 30s, etc.) is the largest. This information is also readily available by looking at a histogram, but a stem and leaf plot also allows you to look closer and see exactly which values fall in that range. Below is an example of a stem and leaf plot.

Test Scores	
7	4 8
8	2 5 7 8 8
9	0 0 1 2 2 3 5 8 9

Histogram

At first glance, a *Histogram* looks like a vertical bar graph. The difference is that a bar graph has a separate bar for each piece of data and a histogram has one continuous bar for each *Range* of data. For example, a histogram may have one bar for the range 0–9, one bar for 10–19, etc. While a bar graph has numerical values on one axis, a histogram has numerical values on both axes. Each range is of equal size, and they are ordered left to right from lowest to highest. The height of each column on a histogram represents the number of data values within that range. Like a stem and leaf plot, a histogram makes it easy to glance at the graph and quickly determine which range has the greatest quantity of values. A simple example of a histogram is below.

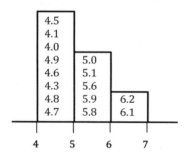

Scatter plots and bivariate data

Bivariate Data is simply data from two different variables. (The prefix *bi-* means *two*.) In a *Scatter Plot*, each value in the set of data is plotted on a grid similar to a Cartesian plane, where each axis represents one of the two variables. By looking at the pattern formed by the points on the grid, you can often determine whether or not there is a relationship between the two variables, and what that relationship is, if it exists. The variables may be directly proportionate, inversely proportionate, or show no proportion at all. It may also be possible to determine if the data is linear, and if so, to find an equation to relate the two variables.

Measure of central tendency

A *Measure of Central Tendency* is a statistical value that gives a general tendency for the center of a group of data. There are several different ways of describing the measure of central tendency. Each one has a unique way it is calculated, and each one gives a slightly different perspective on the data set. Whenever you give a measure of central tendency, always make sure the units are the same. If the data has different units, such as hours, minutes, and seconds, convert all the data to the same unit, and use the same unit in the measure of central tendency. If no units are given in the data, do not give units for the measure of central tendency.

Using the mean as the only measure of central tendency

While the mean is relatively easy to calculate and averages are understood by most people, the mean can be very misleading if used as the sole measure of central tendency. If the data set has outliers (data values that are unusually high or unusually low compared to the rest of the data values), the mean can be very distorted, especially if the data set has a small number of values. If unusually high values are countered with unusually low values, the mean is not affected as much. For example, if five of twenty students in a class get a 100 on a test, but the other 15 students have an average of 60 on the same test, the class average would appear as 70. Whenever the mean is skewed by outliers, it is always a good idea to include the median as an alternate measure of central tendency.

Measure of dispersion

A *Measure of Dispersion* is a single value that helps to "interpret" the measure of central tendency by providing more information about how the data values in the set are distributed about the measure of central tendency. The measure of dispersion helps to eliminate or reduce the disadvantages of using the mean, median, or mode as a single measure of central tendency, and give a more accurate picture of the data set as a whole. To have a measure of dispersion, you must know or calculate the range, standard deviation, or variance of the data set.

Standard deviation

Standard Deviation is a measure of dispersion that compares all the data values in the set to the mean of the set to give a more accurate picture. To find the standard deviation of a population, use the formula:

$$\sigma = \sqrt{\frac{\sum_{i=1}^{n}(x_i - \bar{x})^2}{n}}$$

where σ is the standard deviation of a population, x represents the individual values in the data set, $\bar{x}$ is the mean of the data values in the set, and n is the number of data values in the set. The higher the value of the standard deviation is, the greater the variance of the data values from the mean. The units associated with standard deviation are the same as the units of the data values.

Percentiles and quartiles

Percentiles and Quartiles are other methods of describing data within a set. *Percentiles* tell what percentage of the data in the set fall below a specific point. For example, achievement test scores are often given in percentiles. A score at the 80th percentile is one which is equal to or higher than 80 percent of the scores in the set. In other words, 80 percent of the scores were lower than that score.

Quartiles are percentile groups that make up quarter sections of the data set. The first quartile is the 25th percentile. The second quartile is the 50th percentile; this is also the median of the data set. The third quartile is the 75th percentile.

5-number summary and how it relates to a box-and-whiskers plot

The *5-Number Summary* of a set of data gives a very informative picture of the set. The five numbers in the summary include the minimum value, maximum value, and the three quartiles. This information gives the reader the range and median of the set, as well as an indication of how the data is spread about the median.

A *Box-and-Whiskers Plot* is a graphical representation of the 5-number summary. To draw a box-and-whiskers plot, plot the points of the 5-number summary on a number line. Draw a box whose ends are through the points for the first and third quartiles. Draw a vertical line in the box through the median to divide the box in half. Draw a line segment from the first quartile point to the minimum value, and from the third quartile point to the maximum value.

Skewness, including positively skewed and negatively skewed

Skewness is a way to describe the symmetry or asymmetry of the distribution of values in a data set. If the distribution of values is symmetrical, there is no skew. In general the closer the mean of a data set is to the median of the data set, the less skew there is. Generally, if the mean is to the right of the median, the data set is *Positively Skewed*, or right-skewed, and if the mean is to the left of the median, the data set is *negatively skewed*, or left-skewed.

However, this rule of thumb is not infallible. When the data values are graphed on a curve, a set with no skew will be a perfect bell curve. To estimate skew, use the formula:

$$\text{skew} = \frac{\sqrt{n(n-1)}}{n-2}\left(\frac{\frac{1}{n}\sum_{i=1}^{n}(x_i - \bar{x})^3}{\left(\frac{1}{n}\sum_{i=1}^{n}(x_i - \bar{x})^2\right)^{\frac{3}{2}}}\right)$$

where n is the number of values is the set, x_i is the ith value in the set, and $\bar{x}$ is the mean of the set.

Bar graph, line graph, and pictograph

A bar graph is a graph that uses bars to compare data, as if each bar were a ruler being used to measure the data. The graph includes a scale that identifies the units being measured.
A line graph is a graph that connects points to show how data increases or decreases over time. The time line is the horizontal axis. The connecting lines between data points on the graph are a way to more clearly show how the data changes.
A pictograph is a graph that uses pictures or symbols to show data. The pictograph will have a key to identify what each symbol represents. Generally, each symbol stands for one or more objects.

Range and quartiles

The range of a distribution is the difference between the highest and lowest values in the distribution. For example, in the data set (1, 3, 5, 7, 9, 11), the highest and lowest values are 11 and 1, respectively. The range then would be calculated as 11 – 1 = 10.
The three quartiles are the three values that divide a data set into four equal parts. Quartiles are generally only calculated for data sets with a large number of values. As a simple example, for the

data set consisting of the numbers 1 through 99, the first quartile (Q1) would be 25, the second quartile (Q2), always equal to the median, would be 50, and the third quartile (Q3) would be 75. The difference between Q1 and Q3 is known as the interquartile range.

Pie chart

A pie chart or circle graph is a diagram used to compare parts of a whole. The full pie represents the whole, and it is divided into sectors that each represent something that is a part of the whole. Each sector or slice of the pie is either labeled to indicate what it represents, or explained on a key associated with the chart. The size of each slice is determined by the percentage of the whole that the associated quantity represents. Numerically, the angle measurement of each sector can be computed by solving the proportion: x/360 = part/whole.

Histogram

A histogram is a special type of bar graph where the data are grouped in intervals (for example 20-29, 30-39, 40-49, etc.). The frequency, or number of times a value occurs in each interval, is indicated by the height of the bar. The intervals do not have to be the same amount but usually are (all data in ranges of 10 or all in ranges of 5, for example). The smaller the intervals, the more detailed the information.

Stem-and-leaf plot

A stem-and-leaf plot is a way to organize data visually so that the information is easy to understand. A stem-and-leaf plot is simple to construct because a simple line separates the stem (the part of the plot listing the tens digit, if displaying two-digit data) from the leaf (the part that shows the ones digit). Thus, the number 45 would appear as 4 | 5. The stem-and-leaf plot for test scores of a group of 11 students might look like the following:

```
9 | 5
8 | 1, 3, 8
7 | 0, 2, 4, 6, 7
6 | 2, 8
```

A stem-and-leaf plot is similar to a histogram or other frequency plot, but with a stem-and-leaf plot, all the original data is preserved. In this example, it can be seen at a glance that nearly half the students scored in the 70's, yet all the data has been maintained. These plots can be used for larger numbers as well, but they tend to work better for small sets of data as they can become unwieldy with larger sets.

Probability

Probability

Probability refers to the likelihood that a given event will take place. It is determined by the number of times the event could possibly take place divided by the number of all the possible outcomes. For example, if one buys two lottery tickets from a pool of three million tickets, the probability of that person's tickets winning is 2/3,000,000. If a bag contains four blue balls and seven green balls, the probability of pulling a blue ball from the bag is 4/11. This represents the number of blue balls divided by the total number of balls. The probability of pulling out a green ball is 7/11.

Probability and probability measure

Probability is a branch of statistics that deals with the likelihood of something taking place. One classic example is a coin toss. There are only two possible results: heads or tails. The likelihood, or probability, that the coin will land as heads is 1 out of 2 (1/2, 0.5, 50%). Tails has the same probability. Another common example is a 6-sided die roll. The probability of any given number coming up is 1 out of 6.

For every sample space, each possible event has a probability that it will occur. The probability measure, also called the distribution, is a function that assigns a real number probability, from zero to one, to each event. For a probability measure to be accurate, every event must have a real number probability measure that is greater than or equal to zero and less than or equal to one. Also, the probability measure of the sample space must equal one, and the probability measure of the union of multiple mutually exclusive events must equal the sum of the individual probability measures.

Probability of an event

Probabilities of events are expressed as real numbers from zero to one. They give a numerical value to the chance that a particular event will occur. The probability of an event occurring is the sum of the probabilities of the individual elements of that event. For example, in a standard deck of 52 playing cards as the sample space and the collection of face cards as the event, the probability of drawing a specific face card is $\frac{1}{52} = 0.019$, but the probability of drawing any one of the twelve face cards is $12(0.019) = 0.228$. Note that rounding of numbers can generate different results. If you multiplied 12 by the fraction $\frac{1}{52}$ before converting to a decimal, you would get the answer $\frac{12}{52} = 0.231$.

Likelihood of outcomes

The likelihood or probability of an outcome occurring, is given by the formula
$$P(E) = \frac{\text{Number of acceptable outcomes}}{\text{Number of possible outcomes}}$$
where $P(E)$ is the probability of an event E occurring, and each outcome is just as likely to occur as any other outcome. If each outcome has the same probability of occurring as every other possible outcome, the outcomes are said to be equally likely to occur. The total number of possible outcomes in the event must be less than or equal to the total number of possible outcomes in the sample space. If the two are equal, then the event is certain to occur and the probability is 1. If the number of outcomes that satisfy the event is zero, then the event is impossible and the probability is 0.

Addition Rule for probability

The **addition rule** for probability is used for finding the probability of a compound event. Use the formula $P(A \text{ or } B) = P(A) + P(B) - P(A \text{ and } B)$, where $P(A \text{ and } B)$ is the probability of both events occurring to find the probability of a compound event. The probability of both events occurring at the same time must be subtracted to eliminate any overlap in the first two probabilities.

Probability that at least one of something will occur

Use a combination of the multiplication rule and the rule of complements to find the probability that at least one outcome of the element will occur. This given by the general formula $P(\text{at least one event occurring}) = 1 - P(\text{no outcomes occurring})$. For example, to find the probability that at least one even number will show when a pair of dice is rolled, find the probability that two odd numbers will be rolled (no even numbers) and subtract from one. You can always use a tree diagram or make a chart to list the possible outcomes when the sample space is small, such as in the dice-rolling example, but in most cases it will be much faster to use the multiplication and complement formulas.

Statistics

Example

You have gathered data on the wait times for two different lines at the ballpark. You decide to wait in the Blue Line because it has the lower median wait time. Your friend tells you, however, that you should wait in the Red Line because it has the shortest wait time recorded. Consider the data below, decide if you should change your mind and take your friend's advice.
>   Time (in minutes):
>   <u>Red Line</u>: 5, 12, 7, 15, 11, 12, 6, 10, 9
>   <u>Blue Line</u>: 9, 9, 26, 6, 10, 8, 11, 10, 8

>   You should not take your friend's advice. You should still choose the Blue Line because the Blue Line's median is 9 minutes, while the Red Line's median is 10 minutes. The data point of 26 in the Blue Line is considered an outlier because it varies greatly from the median compared to the other data points in the set. If you ignore that outlier, the median is still 9! Even ignoring the highest wait time for each line, the mean wait time is higher for the red line, so although the Red Line had the shortest wait time and Blue Line had the longest wait time that is not the best judge of predicting wait time.

Mean, median, and mode

The quantities of mean, median, and mode are all referred to as measures of central tendency. They can each give a picture of what the whole set of data looks like with just a single number. Knowing what each of these values represents is vital to making use of the information they provide. The mean, also known as the arithmetic mean or average, of a data set is calculated by summing all of the values in the set and dividing that sum by the number of values. The mean is the average of a set of data. This is found by dividing the sum of the data values by the number of values there are. For example, if a data set has 6 numbers and the sum of those 6 numbers is 30, the mean is calculated as 30/6 = 5.

The median is the middle value of a data set. The median can be found by putting the data set in numerical order, and locating the middle value. In the data set (1, 2, 3, 4, 5), the median is 3. If there is an even number of values in the set, the median is calculated by taking the average of the two middle values. The median is the middle number in a set of data, and can be found by listing the data in order from least to greatest and crossing one off on either end until the middle is reached. If there are two middle terms the average of them is the median of the data. In the data set, (1, 2, 3, 4, 5, 6), the median would be (3 + 4)/2 = 3.5.

The mode is the value that appears most frequently in the data set. In the data set (1, 2, 3, 4, 5, 5, 5), the mode would be 5 since the value 5 appears three times. If multiple values appear the same number of times, there are multiple values for the mode. These cases are known as bimodal (2 modes) or multimodal (more than 2 modes) distributions. If no value appears more than any other value in the data set, then there is no mode. The mode is the value in a set of data that occurs the most often.

Example
Find the m*ean, median, and mode* each for the data listed below.
22, 17, 14, 15, 11, 20, 16, 15, 12, 14, 14

The mean of the given data is 15.455, which is found by dividing the sum of the data by 11 because there are 11 terms in the data: $\frac{22+17+14+15+11+20+16+15+12+14+14}{11} =$ 15.455.

The median of the given data is 15: 11, 12, 14, 14, 14, 15, 15, 16, 17, 20, 22.

In the given data the mode is 14, because that value occurs 3 times while all other values are only in the list 1 or 2 times.

Sample size and data set

Sample size is the number of people surveyed or the number of observations made in a statistical experiment. For example, if the mayor of a town surveyed 800 residents to determine the town's opinion on a new park, then the sample size is 800 and the mayor has hopefully judged that this will be a large enough sample to represent the whole population.
Data set is a list, or set, of all the numbers or values that are the results from a statistical experiment. An example would be that the following data set represents the shoe sizes of Fred's friends: {6, 7.5, 8, 8, 8.5, 9.5, 10}. That list of numbers is the data set and each number represents the shoe size of Fred's friends.

Range

The *Range* of a set of data is the difference between the greatest and lowest values of the data in the set. To calculate the range, you must first make sure the units for all data values are the same, and then identify the greatest and lowest values. Use the formula range = highest value – lowest value. If there are multiple data values that are equal for the highest or lowest, just use one of the values in the formula. Write the answer with the same units as the data values you used to do the calculations.

Experimental studies

Experimental Studies take correlational studies one step farther, in that they attempt to prove or disprove a cause-and-effect relationship. These studies are performed by conducting a series of experiments to test the hypothesis. For a study to be scientifically accurate, it must have both an experimental group that receives the specified treatment and a control group that does not get the treatment. This is the type of study pharmaceutical companies do as part of drug trials for new medications. Experimental studies are only valid when proper scientific method has been followed. In other words, the experiment must be well-planned and executed without bias in the testing process, all subjects must be selected at random, and the process of determining which subject is in which of the two groups must also be completely random.

Empirical probability

Empirical probability is based on conducting numerous repeated experiments and observations rather than by applying pre-defined formulas to determine the probability of an event occurring. To find the empirical probability of an event, conduct repeated trials (repetitions of the same experiment) and record your results. The empirical probability of an event occurring is the number of times the event occurred in the experiment divided by the total number of trials you conducted to get the number of events. Notice that the total number of trials is used, not the number of unsuccessful trials. A practical application of empirical probability is the insurance industry. There are no set functions that define life span, health, or safety. Insurance companies look at factors from hundreds of thousands of individuals to find patterns that they then use to set the formulas for insurance premiums.

Data and statistics

The term "data" is the collective name for pieces of information (the singular is datum). Statistics is the branch of mathematics that deals with collecting, recording, interpreting, illustrating, and analyzing large amounts of data. The following terms are often used in the discussion of data and statistics:
Quantitative data – measurements (such as length, mass, and speed) that provide information about quantities in numbers
Qualitative data – information (such as colors, scents, tastes, and shapes) that cannot be measured using numbers
Discrete data – information that can be expressed only by a specific value, such as whole or half numbers; For example, since people can be counted only in whole numbers, a population count would be discrete data.
Continuous data – information (such as time and temperature) that can be expressed by any value within a given range

Representation in mathematical processes

Representations are the tools of symbols and materials. They are used to help students understand mathematics by giving them visual guides in their thinking. For example, the conventional symbols that indicate addition, subtraction, equality, and so on (into the higher realms of symbols used in geometry, algebra, and calculus) tell students, at a glance, the process that is being calculated. Materials that are used as representations are called manipulatives. These can be small plastic objects or pictures for the students to count, line up, or otherwise use to solve a problem. Representations make abstract concepts become concrete. They put mathematics into the students,' hands as well as heads, and the result is improved learning. Using familiar manipulatives with new problems helps the student to make connections and feel more confident and capable of expanding their skills.

Problem Solving

Purpose of a proof

A proof serves to show the deductive or inductive process that relates the steps leading from a hypothesis to a conclusion. A proof may be direct ($p \rightarrow q$), meaning that a conclusion is shown to be true, given a hypothesis. There are also proofs by contradiction ($p \wedge \square q$), whereby the hypothesis is assumed to be true, and the negation of the conclusion is assumed to be true. (In other words, the statement is assumed to be false.) Proofs by contraposition ($\square q \rightarrow \square p$) show that the negation of the conclusion leads to the negation of the hypothesis. (In other words, the negation of the conclusion is assumed to be true, and it must be shown that the negation of the hypothesis is also true.) A mathematical induction proof seeks to show that $P(1)$ is true and that $P(k + 1)$ is true, given that $P(k)$ is true. Direct proofs, proofs by contradiction, and proofs by contraposition use deductive methods, while a mathematical induction proof uses an inductive method.

Direct and indirect proofs

Direct proofs are those that assume a statement to be true. The purpose of such a proof is to show that the conclusion is true, given that the hypothesis is true. A sample of a direct proof is shown below:
Prove "If m divides a and m divides b, then m divides a + b."
Proof: Assume m divides a and m divides b.
Thus, a equals the product of m and some integer factor, p, by the definition of division, and b equals the product of m and some integer factor, q, by the definition of division. According to substitution, a + b may be rewritten as $(m \cdot p) + (m \cdot q)$. Factoring out the m gives $m(p + q)$. Since m divides p + q, and p + q is an integer, according to the closure property, we have shown that m divides a + b, by the definition of division.

Indirect proofs (or proofs by contradiction) are those that assume a statement to be false. The purpose of such a proof is to show that a hypothesis is false, given the negation of the conclusion, indicating that the conclusion must be true. A sample of an indirect proof is shown below:
Prove "If 3x + 7 is odd, then x is even."
Proof: Assume 3x + 7 is odd and x is odd.
According to the definition of odd, x = 2a + 1, where a is an element of the integers.
Thus, by substitution, 3x + 7 = 3(2a + 1) + 7, which simplifies as 6a + 3 + 7, or 6a + 10, which may be rewritten as 2(3a + 5). Any even integer may be written as the product of 2 and some integer, k. Thus, we have shown the hypothesis to be false, meaning that the conditional statement must be true.

Proofs by contraposition and contradiction

A proof by contraposition is one written in the form, $\square q \rightarrow \square p$. In other words, a proof by contraposition seeks to show that the negation of q will yield the negation of p. A sample of a proof by contraposition is shown below:

Prove "If 5x + 7 is even, then x is odd."
Proof:
Assume that if x is even, then 5x + 7 is odd.
Assume x is even.
Thus, by the definition of an even integer, x = 2a.

By substitution, 5x + 7 may be rewritten as 5(2a) + 7, which simplifies as 10a + 7. This expression cannot be written as the product of 2 and some factor, k. Thus, 5x + 7 is odd, by definition of an odd integer. So, when 5x + 7 is even, x is odd, according to contraposition.

A proof by contradiction is one written in the form, $p \wedge \lnot q$. In other words, a proof by contradiction seeks to show the negation of q will result in a false hypothesis, indicating that the conclusion of the statement, as written, must be true. In other words, the conditional statement of $p \rightarrow q$ is true.

Proof by mathematical induction

A proof by mathematical induction must first show that $P(1)$ is true. Once that is shown, such a proof must show that $P(k + 1)$ is true when $P(k)$ is true. A sample proof by induction is shown below:

Prove "If n is a natural number, then $2 + 4 + 6 + 8 + \cdots + 2n = n(n + 1)$."
Show that $P(1)$ is true.
$2(1) = 1(1 + 1)$.
Assume P(k) is true.
$2 + 4 + 6 + 8 + \cdots + 2k = k(k + 1)$
We want to show that $2 + 4 + 6 + 8 + \cdots + 2(k + 1) = (k + 1)((k + 1) + 1)$.
$2 + 4 + 6 + 8 + \cdots + 2(k + 1) = k(k + 1) + 2(k + 1)$.
$2 + 4 + 6 + 8 + \cdots + 2(k + 1) = (k + 1)(k + 2)$.
$P(k + 1)$ is true. Thus, according to mathematical induction, $2 + 4 + 6 + 8 + \cdots + 2n = n(n + 1)$.

Sample problem

Use any proof type to prove the following: "The sum of the natural numbers is equal to n^2."

Proof by induction:
Show that $P(1)$ is true.
$1 = 1^2$.
Assume $P(k)$ is true.
$1 + 3 + 5 + 7 + \cdots + 2k + 1 = k^2$.
We want to show that $1 + 3 + 5 + 7 + \cdots + 2(k + 1) + 1 = (k + 1)^2$.
$2 + 4 + 6 + 8 + \cdots + 2(k + 1) = k^2 + 2(k + 1)$.
$2 + 4 + 6 + 8 + \cdots + 2(k + 1) = k^2 + 2k + 2$.
P(k+1) is true. Thus, according to mathematical induction,
$1 + 3 + 5 + 7 + \cdots + 2n + 1 = n^2$.

Premise

A premise is a statement that precedes a conclusion, in an argument. It is the proposition, or assumption, of an argument. An argument will have two or more premises.

Example:
If it is hot, then I will go swimming. (Premise)
It is hot. (Premise)

_____

Therefore, I will go swimming. (Conclusion)

Truth table

Use a truth table to validate the Rule of Detachment. Explain how the truth table validates the rule.

The Rule of Detachment states that given the premises, $p \rightarrow q$ and p, the valid conclusion is q.

In other words, for every case where $(p \rightarrow q) \wedge p$ is true, q will also be true. The truth table below illustrates this fact:

P	Q	$p \rightarrow q$	$(p \rightarrow q) \wedge p$
T	T	T	T
T	F	F	F
F	T	T	F
F	F	T	F

Notice the first cell under $(p \rightarrow q) \wedge p$ is true, while the first cell under q is also true. Thus, for every case where $(p \rightarrow q) \wedge p$ was true, q was also true.

Use a truth table to validate the Chain Rule. Explain how the truth table validates the rule.

The Chain Rule states that given the premises, $p \rightarrow q$ and $q \rightarrow r$, the valid conclusion is $p \rightarrow r$.

In other words, for every case where $(p \rightarrow q) \wedge (q \rightarrow r)$ is true, $p \rightarrow r$ will also be true. The truth table below illustrates this fact:

p	q	r	$p \rightarrow q$	$q \rightarrow r$	$(p \rightarrow q) \wedge (q \rightarrow r)$	$p \rightarrow r$
T	T	T	T	T	T	T
T	T	F	T	F	F	F
T	F	T	F	T	F	T
T	F	F	F	T	F	F
F	T	T	T	T	T	T
F	T	F	T	F	F	T
F	F	T	T	T	T	T
F	F	F	T	T	T	T

Notice that for every case where $(p \rightarrow q) \wedge (q \rightarrow r)$ was true, $p \rightarrow r$ was also true.

Examples of premises

If I hike a mountain, I will not eat a sandwich.
If I do not eat a sandwich, I will drink some water.
I will not drink some water.

Write a valid conclusive statement. Explain how you arrived at your answer. Be specific in your explanation

   Valid conclusive statement: I will not hike a mountain.

   Application of the chain rule and rule of contraposition give the valid conclusion of $\sim p$. According to the chain rule, given $p \rightarrow \sim q$ and $\sim q \rightarrow r$, then $p \rightarrow r$. According to the rule of contraposition, $p \rightarrow r$ and $\sim r$ yields $\sim p$. On a truth table, for every place where $(p \rightarrow r) \wedge \sim r$ is true, $\sim p$ is also true. Thus, this is a valid conclusive statement.

Formal reasoning

Formal reasoning, in mathematics, involves justification using formal steps and processes to arrive at a conclusion. Formal reasoning is utilized when writing proofs and using logic. For example, when applying logic, validity of a conclusion is determined by truth tables. A set of premises will yield a given conclusion. This type of thinking is formal reasoning. Writing a geometric proof also employs formal reasoning.

Example:
If a quadrilateral has four congruent sides, it is a rhombus.
If a shape is a rhombus, then the diagonals are perpendicular.
A shape is a quadrilateral.
Therefore, the diagonals are perpendicular.

This example employs the chain rule, shown below:
$p \rightarrow q$
$q \rightarrow r$
p
$\therefore r$

Informal reasoning

Informal reasoning, in mathematics, uses patterns and observations to make conjectures. The conjecture may be true or false. Several, or even many, examples may show a certain pattern, shedding light on a possible conclusion. However, informal reasoning does not provide a justifiable conclusion. A conjecture may certainly be deemed as likely or probable. However, informal reasoning will not reveal a certain conclusion.

Example:
Mathematical Idea – Given a sequence that starts with 1 and increases by a factor of $\frac{1}{2}$, the limit of the sum will be 2.
Informal Reasoning – The sum of 1 and $\frac{1}{2}$ is $1\frac{1}{2}$. The sum of 1, $\frac{1}{2}$, and $\frac{1}{4}$ is $1\frac{3}{4}$. The sum of 1, $\frac{1}{2}$, $\frac{1}{4}$, and $\frac{1}{8}$ is $1\frac{7}{8}$. Thus, it appears that as the sequence approaches infinity, the sum of the sequence approaches 2.

Sample Problems

Use formal reasoning to justify the statement, "If a divides b, a divides c, and a divides d, then a divides the sum of b, c, and d." Show the formal proof.

> Direct Proof:
> Assume a divides b, a divides c, a divides d.
> Given the definition of divides, a divides b indicates that there exists some integer, r, such that $b = a \cdot r$. Also, a divides c indicates that there exists some integer, s, such that $c = a \cdot s$. Finally, a divides d indicates that there exists some integer, t, such that $d = a \cdot t$. By substitution, the sum of b, c, and d may be written as $(a \cdot r) + (a \cdot s) + (a \cdot t)$. Factoring out an a gives $a(r + s + t)$. The factor $(r + s + t)$ is an integer, according to the closure property under addition. Thus, a divides the sum of b, c, and d.

Use informal reasoning to justify the statement, "If n is a whole number, then $n^2 + n + 1$ is odd." Explain the reasoning steps used.

> Given the sequence, 0, 1, 2, 3, 4, 5, 6, ..., evaluation of the expression, $n^2 + n + 1$, gives $0^2 + 0 + 1$, $1^2 + 1 + 1$, $2^2 + 2 + 1$, $3^2 + 3 + 1$, $4^2 + 4 + 1$, $5^2 + 5 + 1$, and $6^2 + 6 + 1$, or 1, 3, 7, 13, 21, 31, and 43, all of which are odd numbers. Thus, it appears that given any whole number, n, evaluation of the expression $n^2 + n + 1$ will yield an odd number.

Describe two different strategies for solving the problem, "Kevin can mow the yard in 4 hours. Mandy can mow the same yard in 5 hours. If they work together, how long will it take them to mow the yard?"

> Two possible strategies both involve the use of rational equations to solve. The first strategy involves representing the fractional part of the yard mowed by each person in one hour and setting this sum equal to the ratio of 1 to the total time needed. The appropriate equation is $1/4 + 1/5 = 1/t$, which simplifies as $9/20 = 1/t$, and finally as $t = 20/9$. So, the time it will take them to mow the yard, when working together, is a little more than 2.2 hours. A second strategy involves representing the time needed for each person as two fractions and setting the sum equal to 1 (representing 1 yard). The appropriate equation is $t/4 + t/5 = 1$, which simplifies as $9t/20 = 1$, and finally as $t = 20/9$. This strategy also shows the total time to be a little more than 2.2 hours.

Describe two different strategies for solving the problem, "A car, traveling at 65 miles per hour, leaves Flagstaff and heads east on I-40. Another car, traveling at 75 miles per hour, leaves Flagstaff 2 hours later, from the same starting point and also heads east on I-40. After how many hours will the second car catch the first car?"

One strategy might involve creating a table of values for the number of hours and distances for each car. The table may be examined to find the same distance traveled and the corresponding number of hours taken. Such a table is shown below:

Car A		Car B	
x (hours)	y (distance)	x (hours)	y (distance)
0	0	0	−150
1	65	1	−75
2	130	2	0
3	195	3	75
4	260	4	150
5	325	5	225
6	390	6	300
7	455	7	375
8	520	8	450
9	585	9	525
10	650	10	600
11	715	11	675
12	780	12	750
13	845	13	825
14	910	14	900
15	975	15	975

The table shows that after 15 hours, the distance traveled is the same. Thus, the second car catches up with the first car after a distance of 975 miles and 15 hours.

A second strategy might involve setting up and solving an algebraic equation. This situation may be modeled as $65x = 75(x − 2)$. This equation sets the distances traveled by each car equal to one another. Solving for x gives $x = 15$. Thus, once again, the second car will catch up with the first car after 15 hours.

The path of a ball, tossed into the air, from a given height, may be modeled with the function, $(x) = −2x^2 + 4x + 9$. Erica states that the ball will reach the ground after 4 seconds. Describe two different approaches for determining if her solution is, or is not, reasonable.

The ball will reach the ground when the x-value is 0. Thus, one approach involves finding a possible root for the function, by setting the equation equal to 0 and applying the quadratic formula. Doing so gives $0 = −2x^2 + 4x + 9$, where $a = -2$, $b = 4$, and $c = 9$. The positive x-value is approximately 3.3. Thus, her solution is not reasonable, since the ball would have reached ground level prior to 4 seconds. Another approach involves graphing the function and looking for the positive root. Since the root is less than 4, it can be determined that her solution is not reasonable.

Mixture word problems

Martin needs a 20% medicine solution. The pharmacy has a 5% solution and a 30% solution. He needs 50 mL of the solution. If the pharmacist must mix the two solutions, how many milliliters of 5% solution and 30% solution should be used?

To solve this problem, a table may be created to represent the variables, percentages, and total amount of solution. Such a table is shown below:

	mL solution	% medicine	Total mL medicine
5% solution	X	0.05	0.05x
30% solution	Y	0.30	0.30y
Mixture	x + y = 50	0.20	(0.20)(50) = 10

The variable, x, may be rewritten as $50 - y$, so the equation, $0.05(50 - y) + 0.30y = 10$, may be written and solved for y. Doing so gives $y = 30$. So, 30 mL of 5% solution are needed. Evaluating the expression, $50 - y$ for a y-value of 30, shows that 20 mL of 30% solution are needed.

Mathematical Connections

Triangular numbers with three different representations

The triangular numbers may be represented as follows:

List
1, 3, 6, 10, 15, 21, ...

Diagram

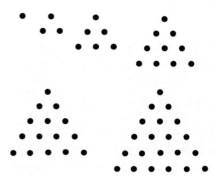

Equation
$$a_n = \frac{n(n + 1)}{2}$$

Representing the area under the normal curve, using z-scores and shading

The area under a normal curve can be represented using one or two z-scores or a mean and a z-score. A z-score represents the number of standard deviations a score falls above, or below, the mean. A normal distribution table (z-table) shows the mean to z area, small portion area, and larger portion area, for any z-score from 0 to 4. The area between a mean and z-score is simply equal to the mean to z area. The area under the normal curve, between two z-scores, may be calculated by adding or subtracting the mean to z areas. An area above, or below, a z-score is equal to the smaller or larger portion area. The area may also be calculated by subtracting the mean to z area from 0.5, when looking at the smaller area, or adding the mean to z area to 0.5, when looking at the larger area.

Example:
Suppose the class average on a final exam is 87, with a standard deviation of 2 points. Find the percentage of students who scored between 82 and 94.
Using z-scores and z-table alone:

$$z = \frac{82 - 87}{2} = -2.5$$

$$z = \frac{94 - 87}{2} = 3.5$$

The mean to z area for a z-score of −2.5 is 0.4938. The mean to z area for a z-score of 3.5 is 0.4998. The total area between these two z-scores is equal to the sum of 0.4938 and 0.4998, or 0.9936. Thus, 99.36% of the students scored between 82 and 94.

Sample problem

Represent the sine, cosine, and tangent of angles, measuring 30 degrees, 45 degrees, 60 degrees, and 90 degrees. Explain how the unit circle may be used to represent the exact values of the functions. Discuss how the unit circle may be used to find the values, when evaluating trig functions, given radian measures, as well.

The table below shows the values of each trig function:

Sine	Cosine	Tangent
$\sin(30°) = \dfrac{1}{2}$	$\cos(30°) = \dfrac{\sqrt{3}}{2}$	$\tan(30°) = \dfrac{1}{\sqrt{3}}$
$\sin(45°) = \dfrac{\sqrt{2}}{2}$	$\cos(45°) = \dfrac{\sqrt{2}}{2}$	$\tan(45°) = 1$
$\sin(60°) = \dfrac{\sqrt{3}}{2}$	$\cos(60°) = \dfrac{1}{2}$	$\tan(60°) = \sqrt{3}$
$\sin(90°) = 1$	$\cos(90°) = 0$	$\tan(90°)$ is undefined

The unit circle shows points, in the form, (x, y), on the circle, representing (cos, sin). Thus, each x-value represents the cosine of the measure, while each y-value represents the sine of the measure. The unit circle conveniently shows the degree measures and radian measures for each value. For example, in order to find the exact value of $\sin(30°)$, the degree measure may be located in Quadrant I, then the sine value will be the y-value, which is indeed $\frac{1}{2}$. Given $\sin\left(\frac{\pi}{6}\right)$, whereby theta ($\theta$) is represented in radians, the sine value will also be the y-value of the ordered pair,

- 99 -

again shown to be $\frac{1}{2}$. These values may be checked by evaluating the functions, using a graphing calculator, in both degree and radian mode.

Suppose a new bacteria, after x days, shows a growth rate of 10%. The current count for the new bacteria strain is 100. Explain how to determine the number of days that will pass before the count reaches 1 million bacteria.

The problem may be solved by writing and solving an exponential growth function, in the form, $f(x) = a(1 + r)^x$, where $f(x)$ represents the future count, a represents the current count, r represents the growth rate, and x represents the time. Once the function is evaluated for a future count of 1,000,000, a current count of 100, and a growth rate of 0.10, the exponential equation may be solved by taking the logarithm of both sides.

The problem may be modeled with the equation, $1,000,000 = 100 \cdot (1.10)^x$. Dividing both sides of the equation by 100 gives $10,000 = 1.10^x$. Taking the logarithm of both sides gives $\log(10,000) = x \log(1.10)$. Dividing both sides of this equation by $\log(1.10)$ gives $x \approx 96.6$. Thus, after approximately 97 days, the bacteria count will reach 1 million.

An object is tossed into the air. Write a function that may be used to model the height of the object, measured in feet, after x seconds have passed. Identify the number of seconds that will pass before the object reaches its maximum height. Identify the maximum height. Identify the number of seconds that will pass before the object reaches the ground. Explain how the answers were determined.

Possible function: $y = -x^2 + 6x + 6$. Three seconds will pass before the object reaches its maximum height. The function was graphed. The vertex of the graph shows an x-value of 3 and a y-value of 15. A table of values also shows a maximum y-value of 15, for a corresponding x-value of 3. Thus, after 3 seconds, the object will reach its maximum height of 15 feet. The positive x-intercept, or positive root, represents the point at which the object reaches the ground. Thus, after approximately 6.8 seconds, the object will reach the ground.

Golden Ratio

The Golden Ratio equals Phi, or 1.61803398874989484482.... The exact value of Phi is $(1 + \sqrt{5})/2$. The Golden Ratio is represented within the Fibonacci sequence. The Fibonacci sequence is 1, 1, 2, 3, 5, 8, 13, 21, 34, ..., or a sequence whereby each term is equal to the sum of the two previous terms, for $n \geq 3$. The ratio of a term to the previous term approaches Phi, or the Golden Ratio, as the sequence approaches infinity.

A diagram used to illustrate the Golden Ratio is shown below:

When the ratio of x (the longer segment) to y (the shorter segment) is equal to the ratio of the sum of x and y (the whole segment) to x (the longer segment), the ratio equals Phi or the Golden Ratio.

Thus, if a line segment is drawn, such that the ratio of the longer segment to the shorter segment equals the ratio of the whole segment to the longer segment, then the line segment illustrates the Golden Ratio, or approximately 1.618.

Positive, even numbers, using recursive and explicit formulas

Positive, even numbers:
Recursive: $a_n = a_{n-1} + 2, n \geq 2$; Explicit: $a_n = 2n$

Positive, odd numbers:
Recursive: $a_n = a_{n-1} + 2, n \geq 2$; Explicit: $a_n = 2n - 1$

Each set of numbers represents a linear function, with a constant rate of change of 2. The positive, even numbers represent a linear function that is proportional, whereas the positive, odd numbers represent a linear function that is not proportional. The set of even, positive numbers is represented by a function with a y-intercept of 0. The set of odd, positive numbers is represented by a function with a y-intercept of –1.

Sample problems

Hannah writes the following equation: $f(x) = 30{,}000 \cdot (0.25)^x$. Describe a possible real-world situation that could be modeled by the equation. Evaluate the function for the set of natural numbers, and explain what the values would represent, as related to the context.

> Since the equation is an exponential function, one possible real-world scenario would include the modeling of an initial mold spores count, a growth factor, and a current mold spores count. In this situation, it could be supposed that some bleach agent was used to eradicate the spores. Given this equation, the initial count would be 30,000, the rate of decay would be 0.25, x would represent the amount of time, perhaps in days, and f(x) would represent the current mold spores count. Evaluation of the function gives the sequence, 7500, 1875, 468.75, 117.19, 29.30, ... These values would represent the mold spores count, after 1, 2, 3, 4, and 5 days, respectively. The count for 0 days is the initial count, or y-intercept, of 30,000.

Suppose the initial population of a town was 1,200 people. The population growth is 5%. The current population is 2,400. Write a function that may be used to model the population, y, after x years. Find the number of years that have passed. Explain how the function and answer were determined and show the process used in solving.

> Correct function: $2400 = 1200e^{0.05t}$.
>
> The general form for population growth may be represented as $f(x) = ae^{rt}$, where f(x) represents the current population, a represents the initial population, r represents the growth rate, and t represents the time. Thus, substituting the initial population, current population, and rate into this form gives the equation above.
>
> The number of years that have passed were found by first dividing both sides of the equation by 1,200. Doing so gives $2 = e^{0.05t}$. Taking the natural logarithm of both sides gives $\ln(2) = ln(e^{0.05t})$. Applying the power property of logarithms, the equation may be rewritten as $\ln(2) = 0.05t \cdot \ln(e)$, which simplifies as $\ln(2) =$

$0.05t$. Dividing both sides of this equation by 0.05 gives t ≈ 13.86. Thus, approximately 13.86 years passed.

Use algebra tiles to complete the square for the expression, $x^2 + 8x$. Explain how the diagram shows the completion of the square.

Completing the square of $x^2 + 8x$ gives $x^2 + 8x + 16$, as shown by the 16 unit squares. Note. Each rod represents x. The diagram shows that $x^2 + 8x + 16$ is equal to $(x + 4)^2$. The side length of x^2 is x. The side length of each rod is 1. Thus, $(x + 4)(x + 4)$ also represents the area.

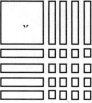

Create a small data set. Then, create a residual plot for the data. Explain why the residual plot provides more information about the linearity of the data than mere calculated residuals alone. Specifically describe what the residual plot shows and how it is interpreted.

Sample data set: $(1, 63), (2, 75), (3, 63), (4, 98), (5, 93), (6, 91), (7, 94), (8, 80), (9, 99), (10, 75), (11, 99), (12, 98), (13, 87), (14, 80), (15, 64)$

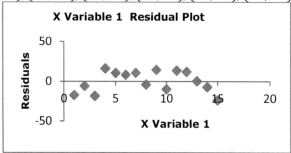

The residual plot shows a curved pattern. Thus, the plot indicates that the data are not linear and would not be appropriately modeled with a linear function. When a residual plot shows a curved or U-shaped pattern, a linear function would not be an appropriate function for modeling the data. When a residual plot shows no clear pattern or a sporadic placement of points, a linear function would be an appropriate model to use. The calculated residuals for the value at which the line of best fit is evaluated, for the given x-value.) This means that the difference in observed values minus predicted values is between 16 and −24, with the greatest difference having an absolute value of 24. These numbers alone are relative to the data set. Thus, a residual plot provides a much clearer analysis of the type of data represented.

Explain how a graphing calculator or Excel spreadsheet may be used to present the ideas of convergence and divergence. Decide if $\lim_{n \to \infty}(n^2 - 4n + 6)/(8n^2 + 2)$ represents convergence or divergence. If a limit exists, state the limit. If a limit does not exist, explain why.

The evaluation of an expression for consecutive values of n will show the pattern of the output, i.e., whether the values converge or diverge. In other words, a table of values or spreadsheet will show if the values grow without bound (diverge) or appear to converge to some single value.

This rational expression converges to a limit. This limit will approach 1/8, as n approaches infinity. Since the rational expression has the same leading powers in the numerator and denominator, the limit is simply the ratio of the coefficients of the leading terms, or 1/8.

The expression may be entered into a graphing calculator or spreadsheet. The table will show that as the x-values (or n-values) get larger and larger, the y-values (or output values) approach 0.125.

Two-way frequency table

A two-way frequency table quickly shows intersections and total frequencies. These values would have to be calculated from a manual list. The conditional probability, $P(B|A)$, read as "The probability of B, given A," is equal to $P(B \cap A)/A$. A two-way frequency table can quickly show these frequencies. Consider the table below:

	Cat	Dog	Bird	Total
Male	24	16	26	66
Female	32	12	20	64
Total	56	28	46	130

Find $P(Cat|Female)$. The two-way frequency table shows $C \cap F$ to be 32, while the total for female is 64. Thus, $P(Cat \mid Female) = 32/64 = 1/2$.

If the frequencies for male and each animal and frequencies for female and each animal had been listed, the total frequency for female would not have been as evident, at first glance.

Die roll simulator used to illustrate the concept of expected value for the roll of a die

A die roll simulator will show the results of n rolls of a die. The result of each die roll may be recorded. For example, suppose a die is rolled 100 times. All results may be recorded. The numbers of 1s, 2s, 3s, 4s, 5s, and 6s, may be counted. The experimental probability of rolling each number will equal the ratio of the frequency of the rolled number to the total number of rolls. As the number of rolls increases, or approaches infinity, the experimental probability will approach the theoretical probability of 1/6. Thus, the expected value for the roll of a die is shown to be $(1 \cdot 1/6) + (2 \cdot 1/6) + (3 \cdot 1/6) + (4 \cdot 1/6) + (5 \cdot 1/6) + (6 \cdot 1/6)$, or 3.5.

Nuances between a proper subset and a subset

A subset is simply a set that is contained within another set. The subset may or may not be equal to the set itself. If the subset is not equal to the set, the subset is said to be a proper subset. If the two sets are equal, meaning that all elements of the set are represented in the subset, the subset is simply called a subset, not a proper subset.

Given A = {4, 8, 12, 16, 20} and B = {2, 3, 4, 8, 12, 16, 20}, A is said to be a proper subset of B because the two sets are not equal. There are elements in B that are not contained in A. This would be denoted as $A \subset B$.

Now, suppose the following: A = {4, 8, 12, 16, 20} and B = {4, 8, 12, 16, 20}. A is equal to B. Thus, A is not a proper subset of B. This would be denoted as $A \subseteq B$.

How a histogram compares to a bar graph

A histogram shows frequencies for intervals of values. In other words, a histogram represents continuous data, or data that includes decimals or fractions. A bar graph simply represents frequencies for discrete values, or values that are distinct. An example of a discrete variable would be grade level. An example of a continuous variable would be weight of athletes. In order to tell if a graph is a histogram or a bar graph, the appearance of the bars and scale on the independent axis should be observed. If the bars are touching and intervals are shown, the graph is a histogram. If the bars are not touching and discrete values are given on the independent axis, the graph is a bar graph.

Differences between a t-value and a critical t-value

A t-value is the value that compares the difference in mean values to the standard deviation. The formula for t for one-sample t-test (comparing a sample mean to a population mean, when only the sample standard deviation is known) is $t = \frac{\bar{X} - \mu}{\frac{s}{\sqrt{n}}}$. It is the value that will be compared to the critical t-value, found in the t-distribution table. If the computed t-value has an absolute value that is greater than the critical t-value found in the table, for the desired level of significance and appropriate degrees of freedom, then it may be determined that a statistically significant difference exists between the groups. For example, suppose the following: a company claims to include 20 grams of beverage powder in each packet. A random sample of 30 packets shows a mean number of grams of 19.9, with a standard deviation of 0.1 grams. It may be determined if a statistically significant difference exists between the company's claim and the random sample mean by calculating a t-value and comparing it to the critical t-value for 29 degrees of freedom (n – 1). The t-value for this situation is approximately –5.4. Suppose the level of significance is 0.05. The critical t-value for 29 degrees of freedom, for a two-tailed test, would be 2.045. Since 5.4 is greater than 2.045, it may be declared that a statistically significant difference exists.

Many-to-one function vs one-to-one function

A many-to-one function is a function whereby the relation is a function, but the inverse of the function is not a function. In other words, each element in the domain is mapped to one and only one element in the range. However, one or more elements in the range may be mapped to the same element in the domain. A one-to-one function is a function, whereby the inverse is also a function. In other words, each element in the domain is mapped to one and only one element in the range, and each element in the range is mapped to one and only one element in the domain. A graph of a many-to-one function would pass the vertical line test, but not the horizontal line test. A graph of a one-to-one function would pass both tests.

Learning and Development

Cognitive theorists vs. constructivists

Constructivists believe that students may construct knowledge by themselves. In other words, students are actively engaged in the construction of their own knowledge. Students will assimilate and accommodate in order to build new knowledge, based on previous knowledge. Thus, in planning instruction based on constructivism, a teacher would focus on grouping designs, environment, problem-solving tasks, and inclusion of multiple representations. The goal in such a classroom would be for students to construct knowledge on their own. There are different levels of constructivism, including weak constructivism and radical constructivism.

Cognitivists differ from constructivists in that they believe that active exploration is important in helping students make sense of observations and experiences. However, the students are not expected to invent or construct knowledge by themselves. They are only expected to make sense of the mathematics. In planning instruction based on cognitivism, a teacher would employ similar methods to those discussed above, with the focus on active exploration. Students would do a lot of comparisons of mathematical methods in making sense of ideas.

Types of constructivism

Three types of constructivism are weak constructivism, social constructivism, and radical constructivism. Weak constructivists believe that students construct their own knowledge, but also accept certain preconceived notions or facts. Social constructivists believe that students construct knowledge by interacting with one another and holding discussions and conversations. Radical constructivists believe that all interpretations of knowledge are subjective, based on the individual learner. In other words, there is no real truth; it is all subjective. Classroom instructional planning based on a weak constructivist viewpoint might involve incorporation of some accepted theorems and definitions, while continuing to plan active explorations and discussions. Planning based on a social constructivist viewpoint might involve group activities, debates, discussion forums, etc. Planning based on a radical constructivist viewpoint would involve activities that are open-ended, where there is more than one correct answer. The problems would invite more than one correct answer.

Components of project-based learning

Project-based learning is learning that centers on the solving of a problem. Students learn many different ideas by solving one "big" problem. For example, for a unit on sine and cosine functions, a teacher may design a problem whereby the students are asked to model a real-world phenomenon using both types of functions. Students must investigate the effects of changes in amplitude, period, shifts, etc., on the graphs of the functions. Students will also be able to make connections between the types of functions when modeling the same phenomenon. Such a problem will induce high-level thinking.

Project-based learning is derived from constructivist theory, which contends that students learn by doing and constructing their own knowledge.

Control strategies for learning mathematics

"Control strategies" is another name for "metacognitive learning strategies," which indicate any strategy that promotes a learner's awareness of his or her level of learning. With such strategies, the student will work to determine what he or she knows and does not know regarding a subject. Possible control strategies are thinking, self-regulation, and discussing ideas with peers.

Example:
A student may discover his or her level of "knowing" about functions by keeping a journal of any questions he or she might have regarding the topic. The student may list everything that he or she understands, as well as aspects not understood. As the student progresses through the course, he or she may go back and reconfirm any correct knowledge and monitor progress on any previous misconceptions.

Memorization and elaboration strategies for learning mathematics

Memorization is simply a technique whereby rote repetition is used to learn information. Elaboration strategies involve the connection of new information to some previously learned information. In mathematics, for example, students may use elaboration strategies when learning how to calculate the volume of a cone, based on their understood approach for calculating the volume of a cylinder. The student would be making connections in his or her mind between this new skill and other previously acquired skills. A memorization technique would simply involve memorization of the volume of a cone formula, as well as ways to evaluate the formula.

Modifying instruction to accommodate English-language learners

In mathematics specifically, instruction may be modified to include illustrations of ideas, in addition to given words. Audio may also be included for problem tasks. English-language learners may also be grouped with other fluent English-speaking students in order to assist with learning of the mathematics topic. Students will be able to hear the conversation, in addition to seeing the topic in print. In addition, problems may be broken down into smaller pieces, which can help the student focus on one step at a time. Further, additional one-on-one time with the teacher may be needed, whereby the teacher reads aloud and illustrates examples to be learned.

Effective learning environments for ELL students

Characteristics of an effective learning environment for ELL students include creation of a low threshold for anxiety, use of pictures to teach vocabulary and mathematics ideas, implementation of graphic organizers, explicit teaching of vocabulary words, and use of active learning strategies. The latter two are extremely important, since ELL students need to learn exact terms and exact definitions while also engaging with fellow students, as opposed to sitting alone at a desk. Research completed by professors at the University of Houston and University of California list collaborative learning, use of multiple representations, and technology integration as important facets of an effective learning environment for ELL students (Waxman & Tellez, 2002).

Closed-ended mathematics questions

Closed-Ended:

Look at the graph of $y = x^2 + 2$. Decide if the graph represents a function.

Open-Ended:
Provide an example of an equation that represents a function. Provide an example of an equation that does not represent a function. Explain how the graphs of the two equations compare to one another.

The first question will elicit a simple, straightforward response, or "Yes, it is a function."

The second question prompts the student to come up with two equations and then describe how the graphs of the two equations would compare. There is more than one possible answer, and the student has to make a comparison as well.

Questioning response techniques incorporated by teachers

A few good questioning response techniques are:
1. Make sure the wait time is sufficient;
2. Do not include leading prompts within questions;
3. Ask more questions based on student answers;
4. Confirm or restate correct student comments.

The key to good questioning response techniques is to show the student that his or her comments are important and to connect those comments to other student comments. The student should feel that he or she has made a contribution to the community of learners. A teacher should always ask a meaningful, thought-provoking question and provide sufficient time for the student to provide a meaningful and well-thought-out response. Student answers should lead to more questions and ideas and not serve as an endpoint.

NCTM categories of questions that teachers should ask

The Professional Standards describe five categories of questions that teachers should ask. These categories are: 1) working together to make sense of problems; 2) individually making sense of problems; 3) reasoning about mathematics; 4) providing conjectures about mathematics; and 5) making connections within and outside of mathematics. Sample questions include "What does this mean?," "How can you prove that?," and "What does this relate to?". Categories 4 and 5 are high level and include questions that prompt students to invent ideas and make meaningful connections.

Mathematics Instruction

Activating students' prior knowledge

Three ways of activating students' prior knowledge are concept mapping, visual imagery, and comparing and contrasting. With concept mapping, a student would detail and connect all known aspects of a mathematics topic. Ideas would be grouped into subgroups. Such an approach would allow a student to see what he or she does not know, prompting the activation of any prior knowledge on the subject. Visual imagery is simply the use of any pictures or diagrams to promote activation of prior knowledge. For example, giving a picture of Pascal's triangle would likely activate students' prior knowledge regarding the Binomial Theorem. Comparing and contrasting means that the student will compare and contrast ideas or approaches. For example, a student might be given a mapping of an inverse function. He or she could then compare and contrast this mapping to a known mapping of a function, in order to decide how they are the same and different. This would activate a student's prior understanding of functions and the definition thereof.

Ascertaining students' prior knowledge

Three methods for ascertaining, or assessing, students' prior knowledge are portfolios, pre-tests, and self-inventories. Portfolios are simply a compilation of prior student activity related to mathematics topics. For example, a portfolio might show a student's work with transforming functions. Pre-tests are designed to measure a student's understanding of mathematics topics that will be taught in the course during the year. Self-inventories are just what the name implies: inventories that ask the students to name, list, describe, and explain information understood about various mathematics topics.

Modifying instruction according to prior knowledge

Once a teacher has assessed students' level of prior knowledge regarding some mathematics topic, he or she may use that information to scaffold the instruction. In other words, the teacher may decide to further break down the mathematics material into more integral parts. Exact processes or steps may be shown, including justification for using certain properties or theorems. More examples may be shown, while including examples of many different variations of problems, in order to ensure that students are not simply memorizing one approach that will be incorrectly applied to any problem of that sort. The teacher may also decide that more group work, peer cooperation, and discussion are needed.

For example, suppose a teacher determines that students have very little understanding of logic and valid arguments. The teacher may decide to re-teach the creation of truth tables, including truth values for intersections and "if p, then q" statements. The teacher may also decide to re-teach how a truth table may be used to show if an argument is valid. Students may be placed into groups and asked to determine the validity of several simple arguments. Once students understand the concept, they may move on to more rigorous arguments, including equivalence relations.

Increasing students' conceptual understanding

Understanding of how to solve one-variable equations would certainly be enhanced by using rods and counters. With this manipulative, the rod would represent the variable, or x, while the counters would represent the constants on each side of the equation. A sample diagram of the equation, $x + 4 = 8$, is shown below. Note that the vertical line represents the equals sign.

In order to solve the equation (and isolate x), four counters may be removed from each side of the mat. This process is shown below:

Now, the final illustration is:

Thus, the solution is $x = 4$. The manipulative helps students understand the meaning of the subtraction property of equality in action, without simply memorizing its meaning.

Area under the normal curve

The area under the normal curve may be found by calculating z-scores for certain endpoint values. The mean to z areas for these z-scores may be used to find the area. A graphing calculator may use the normalpdf function and ShadeNorm function in order to show the same area under the normal curve, between two values. Consider the following problem: The class average on a statistics exam is 90, with a standard deviation of 4 points. Find the percentage of students who scored above 87 on the exam.

This problem may be solved manually by first calculating the z-score.
$$z = \frac{87 - 90}{4} = \frac{-3}{4}$$

Since the score falls below the mean, the area above the score will equal the sum of 0.5 (or the area of one-half of the normal curve) and the mean to z area, which is 0.2734. Thus, the area above the z-score of −0.75 is 0.7734. The percentage of students who scored above 87 was 77.34%.

This problem may also be solved by using the graphing calculator:
1. Enter normalpdf(x, 0, 1) into the y = screen. (This represents the normal curve having a mean of 0 and standard deviation of 1.)
2. Choose 2nd Vars, ShadeNorm(.
3. Enter ShadeNorm(87,100,90,4). (This represents the lower bound, upper bound, mean, and standard deviation.)
4. Record the area of approximately 0.77.

Thus, the calculator also shows that approximately 77% of the students scored above an 87.

Understanding of derivative and anti-derivative using a graphing calculator

The derivative of an expression is the slope of a tangent line to the curve, at a specific point. The anti-derivative of an expression is the inverse operation of the derivative. Taking the derivative of the anti-derivative will give the original expression. The derivative and anti-derivative can be calculated manually as shown below:

Given $f(x) = 3x^2 + 8x + 4$, the derivative is $f(x) = 6x + 8$. The anti-derivative is $f(x) = x^3 + 4x^2 + 4x$. Thus, evaluation of the derivative and anti-derivative for an x-value of 2 gives $f(x) = 20$ and $f(x) = 32$, respectively. The student can confirm his or her derivative and anti-derivative expressions by evaluating the graphed functions for the same x-value. If the expressions were correctly determined, then evaluation of the derivative and anti-derivative for the x-value should give the same y-value, for each.

Using the graphing calculator, the derivative and anti-derivative for a given point may be evaluated by entering the expression into the y = screen, graphing the function, selecting 2nd Trace, and then choosing dy/dx and $\int f(x)dx$. After selecting the derivative or anti-derivative, the x-value may be typed. Evaluation of the derivative or anti-derivative for that x-value will appear on the screen.

Piaget's cognitive development theory

Piaget's cognitive development theory is aligned with constructivism. In fact, constructivism is built on his ideas. Piaget's cognitive development theory indicates that students actively participate in the construction of their own knowledge via assimilation and accommodation. Current cognitive theorists do not believe that students have to construct their own knowledge, but instead that they only have to make sense of what they are observing.

The four stages of learning, as developed by Piaget, are sensorimotor, preoperational, concrete operational, and formal operational. The defined stages show the progression from concrete thinking to abstract thinking. In other words, a child would need an object to understand properties, in the first stage. By the fourth stage, the child would be able to think abstractly, without some concrete form. In mathematics, this idea might be illustrated by first working with diagrams and manipulatives of numbers and then later writing symbolic forms of the numbers, including the numerals. This would illustrate the progression from 0 to 7 years. In the years of 11 to adulthood, much deeper abstraction is utilized. For example, people would be able to discuss functions and general properties, without looking at any concrete graphs or representations.

Student progression while learning mathematics

When learning mathematics, students begin with concrete representations and ideas. Later, students are able to abstract meaning and make generalizations. Students will also be asked to apply abstract ideas from one topic to another mathematics topic. In other words, students would move from concrete representations, ideas, and facts to symbolic representations and generalizations. Piaget outlined such a progression in his general four stages of cognitive learning. For example, a student may first learn about solving equations by using a balance scale. After the student understands the process, he or she can solve alone, using the symbolic equations. He or she would also be able to describe the process for solving any equation.

Direct instruction versus student-centered instruction

Direct instruction is instruction whereby the teacher delivers all content knowledge to be learned, and students, more or less, passively listen. The teacher employs a step-by-step instruction method for learning content. Student-centered instruction is learning whereby the teacher serves as a facilitator of learning and students actively participate in their own learning. Research has shown that students show a higher level of procedural and conceptual understanding when learning in a student-centered approach. Direct instruction might be more appropriate when teaching basic or fundamental theorems. Student-centered learning might be more appropriate when helping students make connections or develop higher-level thinking regarding a topic.

Cooperative learning task vs traditional task

Think-Pair-Share is an activity whereby a topic is first given for consideration on an individual basis. Next, the students are arranged in pairs and asked to discuss the topic (e.g., any questions, comments, generalizations, etc.). Finally, each pair will contribute to a whole-class discussion on the topic.

In mathematics, students would likely develop a higher level of understanding by using such an activity as Think-Pair-Share when learning about trigonometric functions. For example, students might be asked to consider different real-world situations that may be modeled with sine and cosine functions. Students could individually make a list and then share with a partner. Each partner group could then contribute to a whole class list. This list could be used as a reference sheet.

Implementing technology in mathematics classroom instruction

Technology may be implemented in the mathematics classroom in many ways. For example, Excel may be used to perform regressions, calculate lines of best fit, calculate correlation coefficients, plot residuals, show convergence or divergence of a sequence, etc. Calculators may be used to evaluate and graph functions, find area under the normal curve, calculate combinations and permutations, perform statistical tests, etc. Graphing software, such as GeoGebra, may be used to graph and explore many shapes and functions. Students may also use it to graph reflections, rotations, translations, and dilations.

Mathematics Assessment

Creating a scoring rubric

A strong rubric will include unique performance criteria for each bullet. In other words, a portion of one criteria statement should not be included in a portion of another criteria statement. Each criteria statement should be clearly delineated, describing exactly what the student must be able to do. Furthermore, a strong rubric will often have scoring options, ranging from 0 to 4. When designing the rubric, it is helpful to create a model student response that will warrant each rubric score. It is also helpful to provide a space to provide feedback to students.

Strengths of a performance task

A performance task allows the teacher to assess process as well as product, meaning that a teacher can assess students' thought processes as well as their final answer. The level of student learning will be much clearer when reviewing a performance task. A performance task goes beyond a multiple-choice format, allowing for oral and tactile-kinesthetic performances. Furthermore, a performance task may combine several mathematics concepts into one assessment instrument. This type of assessment often includes real-world problems, which helps the student connect mathematics to the outside world.

Choosing appropriate assessment tools

When a teacher needs to decide on an appropriate assessment tool, he or she needs to consider the purpose of the assessment. For example, if the purpose of an assessment is to direct the instruction, a pre-test may be a good assessment to use. If the purpose of the assessment is to determine the level of student understanding, then a whole-class discussion may be desired. If the purpose of an assessment is to assess student understanding of a unit of material, then an exam would be appropriate. If a teacher wishes to analyze student understanding and ability to abstract knowledge, then a performance assessment may be used. If a teacher wishes to check off skills mastered by students, then a checklist would be appropriate.

Test validity

A test is valid if it tests what it is supposed to test. In other words, a test is valid if it appropriately covers the material it is supposed to cover. For example, a topic not taught in class should not be included on a valid test. In order to construct a valid test, a teacher should make a list of all standards covered during that time period. The teacher should also closely mirror the design of problems examined in class, for homework, and in group discussions. Finally, the teacher should make sure that there is an even balance of questions to cover all of the material.

Selecting a valid exam

In order to select a valid exam, a teacher should make sure that the test aligns with the objectives and standards covered in the unit. The teacher should also make sure that the test problems are similar to those covered during class time. The teacher should make sure the percentages of questions devoted to each objective are balanced. In order for a test to be valid, it must be reliable, meaning that it produces similar results with different groups. A teacher may wish to check the validity and reliability results of an exam.

Components of an invalid exam

In general, an exam is considered invalid if it does not measure what it is supposed to measure. The exam may include questions from another unit. It may include questions with different wording techniques, making it much more difficult. The exam may include representations different from those covered in class. An invalid exam would not be reliable, meaning the results would not be consistent with different administrations of the exam. Biased questions and wording may also make an exam invalid.

Assessing students' thought processes

In order to assess thought processes, open-ended questions are needed. The teacher may wish to have students write an essay, write entries in a mathematics journal, undergo a performance task, or participate in a debate or discussion. The teacher may also design a pre-test that includes all constructed response questions. In particular, a performance task requires students to justify solutions, which provide the teacher with insight into students' understanding and reasoning. In general, the assessment should include questions that ask students to make abstractions and justify their thinking.

Determining exam content and level of difficulty

The teacher would need to make a list of all objectives and standards covered during the time period. The teacher would also need to compile all problems and examples covered in class and as homework. Finally, the teacher would need to do a careful analysis of the wording of the problems covered in class and as homework. If any of these items are not aligned to the exam, the teacher would need to go back and re-teach the material, using the created test as a guide for instruction.

Designing an assessment that will test mathematical misconceptions

In order to design such an assessment, the teacher should include mathematical error-type problems, whereby the student must look at a solution process or conjecture and determine if he or she agrees, of if and where an error occurred. The student would need to identify the error, correct

- 112 -

it, and explain why it was erroneous. The assessment should include a variety of mathematical misconceptions. One solution process may include more than one error. A teacher may also simply ask students to participate in a collaborative learning activity, whereby the students must share ideas and thoughts regarding a new mathematical topic.

Designing a pre-test that accurately assesses prior knowledge

Such a pre-test must not include any leading prompts. It should include open-ended and constructed-response items as well. A pre-test with solely multiple-choice items will not be sufficient, since a student has the option of guessing. The test should include higher-level questions that require connections within the field of mathematics. In other words, the questions should not all be mutually exclusive. They should build on one another. Finally, the test might include student error problems as well.

Connection between a pre-test and a post-test

A post-test should be exactly the same as an administered pre-test. If the teacher is to compare the results of a post-test to a pre-test, then the test and testing conditions should be identical. The pre-test assesses students' prior knowledge, while a post-test assesses students post knowledge. Comparing the results, side by side, allows the teacher to track student progress. The teacher may wish to add additional questions to the post-test, but the original questions should remain.

Designing an assessment that will show what students do and do not know

The teacher should include questions that are straightforward, involve errors, require justification, and require shown work. A student self-assessment is one such tool that would show misconceptions, understood material, and advanced knowledge. The assessment should include more than multiple-choice questions. Designing a performance assessment with scaffolded questions, whereby only one solution may be found based on a previous answer, will also show students' exact level of understanding. A debate format is one type of assessment whereby the teacher will be able to see a student's level of understanding, as he or she seeks to respond with a rebuttal.

Identifying error patterns in students' work

A portfolio would be an excellent assessment for monitoring any student error patterns. The teacher would be able to track student errors as the course progressed. The teacher would be given insight into how, and if, errors improved, or if some knowledge was acquired but other knowledge was still incorrect. The portfolio might include a series of similar questions related to a certain topic. For example, a portfolio may include function transformation questions. A student's ability to transform functions may be tracked, starting with simple linear functions and ending with complex sine functions.

Assessment components that support student learning

The assessment must require students to think deeper than what they have covered in class. It should prompt them to make connections between topics. It should invite different ways of thinking about problem solving. In other words, the student may think, "Okay. I have seen a similar version in class. This problem is slightly different, in that the parabola is shifted left. This is the opposite of shifting right, so I will add the constant to the x-term." The assessment will thus solidify the student's understanding of how to shift any function.

Using assessment results to modify instruction for ELL learners

The teacher would be able to see if language itself is a barrier in learning. In other words, if the group of ELL students, as a whole, show difficulty with a mathematics topic, the teacher may deduce that the content was not clear due to minimal supporting pictures, diagrams, and auditory support. The teacher may decide to reteach the lesson, using more visual cues, verbal pronunciations, explicit vocabulary usage, and peer-group placement. Collaborative learning may be employed.

Reviewing the results of an administered exam

The teacher may ask the following:
1. Did I cover the content in an explicit manner?
2. Did I show plenty of examples?
3. Did I use multiple representations when teaching the concepts?
4. Did I design instruction such as to accommodate all modes of learning?
5. Was the test valid?
6. Did students have an adequate amount of time to complete the test?
7. Why did some groups of students score lower or higher?
8. Did any biased questions affect the results?

Affects of focus on career and college readiness on assessment and instructional design

The focus on college and career-readiness standards prompts publishers and teachers to utilize more real-world problems in instruction and assessments. The focus in mathematics classrooms is shifting to more real-world, cumulative problems that require understanding of many different mathematics concepts in order to solve. Problems are related to science, finance, medicine, etc. The focus includes the ability to apply the algorithms to many different career situations. In summary, the recent focus shifts the instructional design to an application-based status.

Instructional cycle described by a learning theorist

The 5E Learning Model is based on the thinking of Jean Piaget. It is a constructivist learning model. Piaget believed that students construct their own knowledge via active participation and experiences. Problem solving is integral to student learning. The cycle is listed as engagement, exploration, explanation, elaboration, and evaluation. Thus, with active engagement and exploration, the student is able to develop his or her own explanation, use assimilation and accommodation to make sense of the information, and then evaluate the material and make conjectures, etc.

Social Studies

History

Native American Tribes in Texas

Currently, there are three federally-recognized Native American tribes that reside in Texas:
1. the Alabama-Coushatta Tribes of Texas,
2. the Kickapoo Traditional Tribe of Texas, and
3. the Ysleta Del Sur Pueblo of Texas.

There is a remnant of the Choctaw tribe in East Texas that still lives in the Mt. Tabor Community near Overton, Texas.

Spanish Texas

Spanish Texas was largely an effort by the Spanish Crown to keep its assets in the New World secure from the French in Louisiana. Texas was thus a sparsely populated buffer between the claims of these two nations. Texas was Spanish territory from 1690, the expedition of the governor of Coahuila to destroy the ruins of the French colony of Fort Saint Louis and establish a Spanish presence, until independence movements in 1821 began to shatter the Spanish Empire, resulting in the independence of Mexico. During this period, Texas was a part of four provinces in the Viceroyalty of New Spain (Colonial Mexico): New Mexico, Nueva Vizcaya, Nuevo Santander after 1749, and initially joint jurisdiction with the province of Coahuila. Slightly more than three centuries elapsed between the time the Texas shoreline was first viewed by a Spaniard in 1519 and July 21, 1821, when the flag of Castile and León was lowered for the last time at San Antonio. These three hundred years may be divided into the era of early exploration, in which there was a preliminary evaluation of the land and its resources; the period of cultural absorption, in which the Texas Indians began to acquire Hispanic cultural elements directly from the Spanish themselves; and the time of defensive occupation, in which the Spanish presence in Texas was more dictated by international considerations than caused by the momentum of an expanding empire.

Spanish efforts towards expansion during the years 1731-1762
During most of the period of Spanish Texas, the region assumed a geopolitical importance vastly disproportionate to its economic or demographic place in the Spanish Empire. Spanish civilization gained toeholds via missions and presidios. Little was known about the area outside of unsubstantiated reports from the early Conquistadore period. Spanish power was thus not geared as much toward civilizing the area than toward delineating its own extent. A system of mission-presidios were established at present day San Antonio, La Bahia, Los Adaes, El Paso, Laredo, Nagodoches, and San Louis de las Amarillas. This initial expansion, however, was met with immediate setback in the 1718 War of the Quadruple Alliance in Europe, during which France managed to briefly capture the capital of Texas, Los Adaes, in modern Northwest Louisiana. Due to Indian depredations, the Presidios of San Luis de las Amarillas had to be abandoned in 1770 after a period of economic inviability. Most Spanish efforts toward expansion in Texas during the years 1731-62 were a failure, except at La Bahía, San Antonio de Bexar, and along the lower Rio Grande. Missions and presidios, although proven frontier institutions, had clearly failed north of San Antonio.

Secondary center of Colonial power in Spanish Texas

The **secondary center of Spanish colonial power**, La Bahía (present-day Goliad), was the second oldest settlement in the province. It was originally established in 1721 at the site of La Salle's Fort St. Louis, then moved in 1749 to the San Antonio River, where the presidio and two missions had the task of guarding the Texas Gulf Coast against foreign encroachment. In 1803 the settlement's population of approximately 618 soldiers and civilians continued to live under military jurisdiction.

Texas towards the end of the 18th century

Towards the end of the 18th century Texas remained a sparsely settled territory, heavily dependent on the military and continually exposed to the depredations of Indians who resisted Spanish sovereignty in the region. Crown efforts during much of the 18th century to bolster the small population and thus improve the province's viability proved in general unsuccessful. The population remained a mixture of hispanized Indians centered on the missions, Spanish and Mexican soldiers with their families, Spanish colonial officials and their families, and various communities of French, British, Italian, German, and American settlers who had been assimilated into the Spanish system. Then in the early years of the 19th century Spain once again faced concerted efforts by rivals, now including the United States, to wrest from it important parts of its North American empire. Relations with the United States had come dangerously close to war over navigation rights on the Mississippi River and the expansion of Anglo-American frontier settlements into the Spanish Floridas. Napoleon's coerced acquisition of Louisiana in 1800 and his subsequent sale of the vast territory to the United States in 1803 left Spanish North America divided and vulnerable.

Oldest and largest colonial Texas Community

Spanish Texas had solidified upon three primary centers. The oldest and largest of colonial Texas communities was San Antonio de Béxar. In its eighty-year history the settlement had evolved from a presidio-mission complex to the first chartered municipality and finally to the provincial capital. Its population of approximately 2,000 was composed chiefly of Mexican settlers from Coahuila, Nuevo León, and other frontier provinces mixed with a small number of Canary Islanders. After the United States acquired Louisiana, reinforcement of the Spanish military presence in Texas resulted in the transfer of the Second Flying Company of San Carlos de Parras (the Álamo de Parras company) to San Antonio, where it was headquartered in 1803 at San Antonio de Valero Mission, which had been closed. Other units from Nuevo Santander and Nuevo León swelled the population to over 3,000 by 1810.

Third center of Colonial Spanish power in Texas

The third center of Spanish power and the one with the most limited amount of Spanish royal control was far to the northeast, near the Louisiana border. North-Eastern Texas had traditionally been a community of English, French, and Spanish settlers who had established the Presidio de Las Adaes as the first capital of Texas. However, North-East Texas was even further removed from Mexico City than San Antonio de Bexar. Consequently, the area was downgraded in colonial status and by Imperial edict the settlement was ordered abandoned. The viceroy eventually did permit the resettlement of East Texas, but would not consent to dwellings within 100 leagues of Natchitoches (Nacogdoches), Louisiana. Nevertheless, the refugees in San Antonio viewed any concession as encouraging. In August 1774 they founded the settlement of Bucareli on the Trinity River at a site in what is now Madison County. The town had attracted 347 inhabitants by 1777, but it was plagued by floods and Comanche raids. Without authorization, the population moved again in 1779 to Nacogdoches. The new town began to be garrisoned in 1795 by a detachment from Bexar as a means of further solidifying the interests of San Antonio over the province. By the beginning of the

19th century, the settlement was attracting increasing numbers of immigrants, legal and otherwise, from the Anglo-American frontier.

Texas history

The history of Texas (as part of the United States) began in 1845, but settlement of the region dates back to the end of the Upper Paleolithic Period, around 10,000 BC

Its history has been shaped by being part of six independent countries: Spain, France, Mexico, the Republic of Texas, the Confederacy, and the United States.

Starting in the 1820s, American and European immigrants began arriving in the area; joined by Hispanic Tejanos they revolted against a very culturally distant Mexico in 1836 in search of state freedom and defeated an invasion army led by General Antonio López de Santa Anna.

After a decade as an independent country, Texas joined the Union (the United States) in 1845.

Indigenous people

Texas lies within the regions of three North American civilizations which had reached their developmental peak prior to the arrival of European explorers. The Pueblo from the upper Rio Grande region, the Mound Builder of the Mississippi Valley region, and the civilizations of the pre-Columbian cultures of Mexico and Central America. Native American tribes that lived inside the boundaries of present-day Texas include the Alabama, Apache, Atakapan, Bidai, Caddo, Coahuiltecan, Comanche, Cherokee, Choctaw, Coushatta, Hasinai, Jumano, Karankawa, Kickapoo, Kiowa, Tonkawa, and Wichita. No one culture was dominant in the present-day Texas region and many different peoples inhabited the area.

First Europeans

The first Europeans established in the main part of Texas were the French. However, the French colonial presence was short-lived. After exploring the interior of what is now the United States, French nobleman La Salle returned with a large expedition designed to establish a French colony on the Gulf of Mexico, at the mouth of the Mississippi River. They left France in 1684 with four ships and 300 colonists. The expedition, however, was plagued by pirates, hostile Indians and poor navigation. They set up Fort Saint Louis of Texas, near Victoria, Texas. La Salle led a group eastward on foot on three occasions to try to find the shortest route from Texas to the Mississippi. During the last such search his remaining 36 followers mutinied, and he was murdered by four of them near the site of modern Navasota, Texas. The colony lasted only until 1688, when Karankawa-speaking Indians massacred the twenty remaining adults and took five children as captives. Tonti sent out search missions in 1689 when he learned of the expedition's fate, but failed to reach a fort with survivors. Despite the failure of their colony in Texas, the French continued to claim Texas, even after the Spanish had arrived and colonized it. The failure of the French colony became known throughout the world. This French period of Texan history is memorialized in the Texas state seal and as the first (or second) of the traditional "six flags over Texas."

Significance of the name Texas

The name Texas derives from táysha, a word in the Caddoan language of the Hasinai, which means "friends" or "allies".

Legacies of Spanish Texas

The Spanish occupation of Texas lasted for just 105 years. However, the legacies of Spanish Texas are lasting and significant. Perhaps most obvious, yet superficial in importance, is the use of Spanish names for hundreds of towns, cities, counties, and geographic features in Texas. San Antonio, the first formal municipality in Texas, is one of the ten largest cities in the United States. Forty-two of the 254 counties in Texas bear either Hispanic names, or an Anglicized derivation such as Galveston or a misspelling such as Uvalde. The names of physiographical features such as Llano Estacado, Guadalupe Mountains, and Padre Island serve as reminders of Spanish explorers and conquistadors who crossed portions of Texas well before the English settled the Atlantic Coast of North America. Spaniards introduced numerous European crops, irrigation at San Antonio and other mission sites, livestock, and livestock-handling techniques. Farming, initially practiced by some Indian groups in Texas, was likewise expanded and improved by Spanish missionaries and settlers. The restored missions at San Antonio and Goliad stand as enduring monuments to the Franciscans who brought the mantle of Christianity to Texas Indians. With the exception of those in California, the finest examples of Spanish mission architecture in the United States are found in Texas.

19th century Texas

The early 19th century position of Spanish Texas did not look promising. Foreign encroachments, Indian warfare, and insurrectionary activity all contributed to demographic and economic collapse. In the end, desperate Spanish authorities authorized Anglo-American colonization in an effort to bolster the province and so produced a new set of problems for the Mexican authorities who soon replaced them. In the years following the Louisiana Purchase and the acquisition of New Orleans by the U.S., American settlers had begun to move westward into Mexican claimed territory. Some settlers were active filibusters, who sought the long-term annexation of the area by the U.S. In 1812-1813; the Gutiérrez-Magee Expedition attempted to separate Texas from the Spanish Empire. In response the Spanish government in Mexico ordered a virtuall genocide of the entire Tejano-American population and any of their collaborators amongst the Tejano-Spanish population. The result was the utter devestation of Texas which left it with a population size it had at the beginning of the 18th century. Spanish Texas was a failing colonial policy.

Texas in the 1820s and 1830s

In the 1820s, the population in Texas was very sparse and the Mexican government had difficulty in attracting Mexicans to the area. Thus, in order to populate and develop the area Mexico sought settlers from Europe and especially the neighboring United States. When Mexico reached an agreement with Stephen F. Austin, it allowed several hundred families from the United States, known as Texians, to move into the region. Thousands of additional settlers soon flooded into Texas. When Mexico abolished slavery nationwide, some immigrants from the U.S. refused to comply with the law. This was coupled with complaints about the tightening political and economic control over the territory by the central government in Mexico City, which expected its citizens to be members in good standing of the Catholic Church, whereas the settlers from the United States were Protestant. In 1835, Mexican President Antonio López de Santa Anna abolished the Constitution of 1824 and sought to centralize national power in Mexico City. This caused much political unrest throughout Mexico, an example of which was the rebellion and resulting massacre in Zacatecas. As a result, the new government's efforts to tighten political and economic control over the territory of Texas would only rouse emotions in the Texian settlers and local Tejanos, leading to the Texas Revolution.

Mexican Texas

Mexican Texas is the name given by Texas historians to the brief period between 1821—1835, when Texas was part of Mexico, as a part of the State of Coahuila y Tejas. The period begins with Mexico's victory over Spain in its war of independence in 1821 and ends with Texas's Declaration of Independence from Mexico in 1836, forming the Republic of Texas. The Rio Grande and South Texas areas have a long and turbulent history of independence movements by the local Mexican population on account of unitary and perceived dictatorial and unconstitutional practices by the central Mexican government. North Texas and East Texas, meanwhile, remained largely in the hands of Native American tribes, some of whom were hostile to Spanish and then Mexican rule.

Battles of the Texas Revolution

Four days after the first declaration of independence, the two-week long Battle of the Alamo ended as Mexican General Antonio López de Santa Anna's forces defeated the nearly 200 Texans defending the small mission (which would eventually become the center of the city of San Antonio). "Remember the Alamo!" became the battle cry of the Texas Revolution. The Battle of San Jacinto was fought on April 21, 1836 (interestingly, the anniversary for the founding of the city of Rome) near the present-day city of Houston. General Santa Anna's entire force of 1,600 men was killed or captured by Texas General Sam Houston's army of 800 Texans; only nine Texans died. This decisive battle resulted in Texas's independence from Mexico. Sam Houston, a native of Virginia, was President of the Republic of Texas for two separate terms, 1836–1838 and 1841–1844. He also was Governor of the state of Texas from 1859 to 1861.

Beginning of the Republic of Texas

The first declaration of independence for modern Texas, by both Anglo-Texan settlers and local Tejanos, was signed in Goliad on December 20, 1835. The Texas Declaration of Independence was enacted at Washington-on-the-Brazos on March 2, 1836, effectively creating the Republic of Texas.

Founders of the Republic of Texas
- Stephen F. Austin (1793–1836), "Father of Texas"
- Edward Burleson (1798–1851), Texas soldier, general, and statesman
- David G. Burnet (1788–1870), interim President of the Republic of Texas
- Lorenzo de Zavala (1788–1836), first vice-president of the Republic of Texas and signer of the Texas Declaration of Independence
- Sam Houston (1793–1863), first President of Republic of Texas, later U.S. Senator from Texas and Governor of Texas
- Anson Jones (1798–1858), last President of the Republic of Texas, called the "Architect of Annexation"
- Mirabeau B. Lamar (1798–1859), second President of Republic of Texas
- Jose Antonio Navarro (1795–1871), Texas statesman, revolutionary and politician
- Thomas Jefferson Rusk (1803–1857), Secretary of War between Texas and Mexico, chief justice of the Supreme Court of Texas and Senator from Texas after admission to the Union.
- Edwin Waller (1800–1881), judge, signer of the Texas Declaration of Independence

Important people of Texas

Civil War
- Dick Dowling (1838–1867), commander at Sabine Pass and famous Houstonian
- John "Rip" Ford (1815–1897), Texas Rangers legend and commander at the Battle of Palmito Ranch
- John Bell Hood (1831–1879), commander of Hood's Texas Brigade and Confederate General
- Albert Sidney Johnston (1803–1862), Confederate General and commander of the Confederate western forces
- John B. Magruder (1807–1871), Confederate General at the Battle of Galveston
- Pleasant Tackitt (1803–1886), Confederate Officer and county official at Fort Belknap, Texas. One of the founders of Parker County, Texas.
- Charles S. West (1829–1885), Confederate officer and judge advocate general for the Trans-Mississippi Department
- Louis T. Wigfall (1816–1874), Confederate General and Senator from Texas, secured the surrender of Fort Sumter

Texas Revolution
- Jim Bowie (1796–1836), frontiersman, died at the Battle of the Alamo
- Davy Crockett (1786–1836), frontiersman and U.S. Congressman, died at the Alamo
- James Fannin (1804? –1836), key figure during the Texas Revolution
- Benjamin McCulloch (1811–1862), soldier in the Texas Revolution, Texas Ranger, U.S. Marshal and brigadier general in the army of the Confederate States during the American Civil War
- Henry Eustace McCulloch (1816–1895), soldier in the Texas Revolution, Texas Ranger, and brigadier general in the army of the Confederate States during the American Civil War
- Juan Seguin (1806–1890), Tejano hero during the Texas Revolution
- William B. Travis (1809–1836), commander of Texas forces at the Alamo
- Logan Vandeveer (1815–1855), Hero of San Jacinto

Science and medicine
- Denton Cooley (b. 1920), pioneering heart surgeon
- Michael E. DeBakey (b. 1908), pioneering heart surgeon
- Chu Ching-wu, physicist
- Robert Dennard (b. 1932), computer scientist.
- Bryce DeWitt, physicist, co-developed Wheeler-DeWitt equation ("wave function of the Universe")
- Leonard Eugene Dickson, mathematician
- G.B. Halsted, mathematician
- M. King Hubbert (1903–1989), geophysicist
- Jack Kilby, electrical engineer
- Hermann Joseph Muller, geneticist, Nobel Laureate in Physiology or Medicine
- Ilya Prigogine, physicist and chemist, Nobel Laureate in Chemistry
- John Tate, mathematician, Wolf Prize in Mathematics
- Beatrice Tinsley, astronomer
- Karen Uhlenbeck, mathematician, National Medal of Science
- Harry Vandiver, mathematician
- Steven Weinberg, Nobel Laureate in Physics

- Spencer Wells, geneticist and anthropologist
- John A. Wheeler, physicist, Wolf Prize in Physics, coined the term 'black hole'

Texas statehood

On February 28, 1845, the U.S. Congress passed a bill that would authorize the United States to annex the Republic of Texas and on March 1 U.S. President John Tyler signed the bill. The legislation set the date for annexation for December 29 of the same year. On October 13 of the same year, a majority of voters in the Republic approved a proposed constitution that specifically endorsed slavery and the slave trade. This constitution was later accepted by the U.S. Congress, making Texas a U.S. state on the same day annexation took effect (therefore bypassing a territorial phase). One of the primary motivations for annexation was that the Texas government had incurred huge debts which the United States agreed to assume upon annexation. In the Compromise of 1850, in return for this assumption of $10 million of debt, a large portion of Texas-claimed territory, now parts of Colorado, Kansas, Oklahoma, New Mexico, and Wyoming, was ceded to the Federal government.

Spindletop

Anthony F. Lucas, an experienced mining engineer, drilled the first major oil well at Spindletop on the morning of January 10, 1901 on the little hill south of Beaumont, Texas. The East Texas Oil Field, discovered on October 5, 1930 is located in east central part of the state, and is the largest and most prolific oil reservoir in the contiguous United States. Other oil fields were later discovered in West Texas and under the Gulf of Mexico. The resulting "Oil Boom" permanently transformed the economy of Texas, and led to the first significant economic expansion after the Civil War.

Secession from the United States during the Civil War

Texas seceded from the United States on February 1, 1861, and joined the Confederate States of America on March 2, 1861. Texas was mainly a "supply state" for the Confederate forces until mid 1863, when the Union capture of the Mississippi River made large movements of men, horses or cattle impossible. Texas regiments fought in every major battle throughout the war. The last battle of the Civil War, the Battle of Palmito Ranch, was fought in Texas on May 12, 1865.

Native Americans

Northwest Coast area
The main Native American tribes in the Northwest Coast are the Kwakiutl, Haida, and Nootka. These people lived in a densely forested area, with a temperate climate and heavy rainfall, and they survived mainly on salmon. The Native Americans in this region built their houses out of wood, and made canoes from cedar. These tribes built totem poles in their permanent winter villages which were elaborately carved with the faces of the tribal animal gods. They had a strict social hierarchy, with chiefs, nobles, commoners, and slaves. The Native Americans of the Pacific Northwest would be largely untouched by Europeans until the 18th century, when fur trappers began to encroach upon their territory.

Plains area
The Plains area extends from barely north of the Canadian border to Texas. Before the arrival of Columbus, the tribes in this region were either nomadic or sedentary. The sedentary tribes settled in the great river valleys and grew corn, squash, and beans. The nomads, meanwhile, moved their goods around on sleds pulled by dogs. They hunted buffalo by driving them into enclosures or by

herding them with fires. There was also a fair amount of trade with the sedentary tribes. Many Native American tribes migrated into the Plains region; among them were the Sioux, Comanche, Kiowa, Navajo, and Apache. The tribes were typically governed by a chief, who would eventually be supplanted in a violent coup.

Plateau area
The Plateau area runs from just above the Canadian border into the American southwest. Some of the larger tribes in the region were the Spokane, Nez Perce, and Shoshone. The area where these tribes dwelled was not especially hospitable, so they spent much of their time trying to eke out a living. The tribes in the south gathered fruits and nuts, and hunted small animals. The tribes in the north fished for salmon and gathered roots and berries. Later on, these tribes would begin to hunt buffalo. Many of the northern tribes had permanent winter villages, most of which were along waterways. They borrowed the architecture of the tepee from the Plains Indians, though some tribes had long houses covered with bark.

Eastern Woodlands
The Eastern Woodlands extend from the Mississippi River east to the Atlantic Ocean. The tribes of this region included the Natchez, Choctaw, Cherokee, and Creek. The people of the northeast region mostly farmed and hunted deer. They used canoes made of birch bark. The people in the Iroquois family of tribes lived either in dome-shaped wigwams or in long houses, and would typically wear clothing made from the skin of deer, often painting their faces. In the southern part of the Eastern Woodlands, there were semi-nomadic tribes who survived by hunting, fishing, and gathering. These people hunted with a bow and arrow or with a blowgun. They developed highly detailed pottery and surrounded their villages with elaborate defenses.

Region now known as Canada
The Native Americans that inhabited the region now known as Canada included the Chippewa. This region was not especially hospitable to life and therefore there was little farming. Instead, the tribes hunted, gathered, fished, and trapped in order to survive. There were many groups of nomadic hunters who moved around from season to season. Caribou was the most popular game, and people would make all kinds of products out of parts of the animal, including caribou shoes, caribou nets, and caribou bags. These people relied on snowshoes to allow them to move quickly and without falling into icy lakes. Many of the tribes in this region had a shaman, a mystic who provided spiritual guidance to the members of the tribe.

Southwest area
The Southwest area extends across Arizona, New Mexico, Colorado, and Utah. A seminomadic people known as the Basket Makers hunted with the atlatl, a device that made it possible to throw a spear accurately over a great distance. The tribes in this area lived in pit dwellings which were partly underground. Later, ancestors of the Pueblo Indians would develop community houses set into the side of cliffs and canyons. These cliff dwellings often had a ceremonial fire pit, or kiva. These people grew corn, beans, squash, cotton, and tobacco, they killed rabbits with a wooden stick, and they traded their textiles to nomadic tribes for buffalo meat. The tribes of the Southwest also had a complex mythology and religious system.

Puritanism and the Pilgrims in Massachusetts colony

Puritans believe in the idea of predestination, meaning that God has already chosen which people will get into heaven. In order to suggest to others (and to themselves) that they were among the elect, Puritans were obsessed with maintaining proper decorum in public. Those Puritans who wanted to fully separate from the Church of England were known as Pilgrims (or Separatists). The Pilgrims originally went to Holland, but after determining that they would be unable to make a good life there, they got permission from the Virginia Company to settle in the northern part of the Virginia colony in 1620. The Plymouth Company was commissioned, and the Mayflower set sail. Because of storms and poor navigation, however, they ended up in the area that would come to be known as Massachusetts. One of the early moves of the group was to agree to the Mayflower Compact, whereby all members of the group would be bound to the will of the majority.

Saratoga Campaign

The British military plan during the early stages of the Revolutionary War was known as the Saratoga campaign (or the German Plan). It called for a three-pronged attack aimed at capturing New York and thus separating the Northeast from the Southern colonies. This plan broke down because of the following reasons: One of the generals, Howe, was supposed to go up the Hudson River to Albany, but instead decided to go after Philadelphia. Another general, Burgoyne, was able to conquer Fort Ticonderoga, but then languished without supplies for months, and eventually had to surrender to colonial troops. The third general, St. Ledger, made considerable progress across New York from Lake Ontario, but lost steam after a series of small battles.

Battle of Saratoga

The colonial General Gates defeated the British General Burgoyne at the Battle of Saratoga in 1777. This defeat confirmed the failure of the British Saratoga Campaign. More importantly, perhaps, it convinced the French that the Americans could win the war. The French then signed the Treaty of Alliance in 1778, which supplied the Americans with money, men, and ships. This treaty was in part negotiated by Benjamin Franklin. The French were not necessarily motivated by a spirit of goodwill towards the Americans; they hoped to gain back the territory they had lost in the French and Indian War. Moreover, the French believed that by aiding the Americans in the Revolutionary War they could position themselves to colonize parts of North America as yet unclaimed.

Legacy of the Revolutionary War

After the conclusion of the Revolutionary War, neither the Proclamation of 1763 nor the Quebec Act applied, and thus colonists could move west across the Appalachians. A few British loyalists lost their land. After the war, many states moved to separate the church and state; in Virginia, for instance, Thomas Jefferson wrote the Virginia Statute of Religious Freedom, creating total separation in that state. States also revised the Criminal Codes, in an effort to make the punishment more closely fit the crime. Finally, whereas in 1750 most citizens did not question the institution of slavery, by 1780 many states began to examine this policy. Vermont was the first state to abolish slavery. Meanwhile, Southern states argued that the war would not have been won without slave labor.

Articles of Confederation

The Articles of Confederation were largely ineffective because they gave too much power to the states and too little to a central government. Many historians now say that the best thing about the Articles were that they showed the authors of the Constitution what to avoid. Part of the Articles was the Land Ordinance of 1785, a plan created by Jefferson for dividing the Western land into organized townships. The sale of land in these territories helped generate money for the new government. The Northwest Ordinance of 1787 divided the land above the Ohio River into five territories, which would soon become states. This ordinance would become the model for how all future states would be formed.

Constitution

On September 17, 1787, the Constitution was presented to the people of the states. This document has three parts: a preamble; 7 articles outlining the powers and responsibilities of the 3 branches of government; and a section of amendments, the first ten of which are known as the Bill of Rights. The Constitution contains no bills of attainder, meaning that individuals cannot be denied life, liberty, and property without a trial. It does contain the concept of habeas corpus, meaning that arrested individuals must be charged with a crime within 72 hours. Federal judges are to be chosen for life, and there is an electoral college to select the president. In order to be in the House of Representatives, individuals had to be land-owning white males. The Constitution is famous for its system of checks and balances whereby the president can veto Congress, but Congress can override the veto with a 2/3 vote, and the courts can call the acts of either body "unconstitutional."

Louisiana Purchase

The Louisiana Purchase was probably the high point of Jefferson's presidency; it was seen at home as a diplomatic victory that also avoided drawing the United States into conflict with the European powers. It destroyed the Federalist party. After the Louisiana Purchase was completed, explorers set out to discover just what had been bought; among these explorers were Meriwether Lewis and William Clark. Meanwhile, the United States began to make inroads into Spanish-controlled West Florida. In 1810, rebels attacked Baton Rouge and James Madison claimed that West Florida was now part of the US. Of course, the Spanish protested, but they were unable to reestablish themselves. In 1818, Andrew Jackson would lead a group of soldiers into East Florida under the pretense of taming the Seminoles. In 1819, the Spanish would reluctantly sign the Treaty of Onis, in which the US formally acquired East Florida for $5 million, which the Spanish promptly returned to pay off some of their debt to the US.

Major events of the Jackson era

In 1830, Jackson set a precedent by vetoing the funding of a road that was to be entirely within one state (Kentucky). Many believed that Jackson vetoed this bill to spite Henry Clay, but the move had some positive political consequences as well: the Southerners appreciated the idea that states should tend to their own business and northerners liked it because the road would have given people easier access to the West. Jackson's attempts at relocating Native Americans were less successful. The passage of the Indian Resettlement Act of 1830 was the first attempt by the national government to force migration. In the case of Worcester v. Georgia (1832), the Supreme Court ruled against those who sought to grab Native lands. John Marshall asserted that the Cherokee nation was sovereign, but a ward of the US. Despite Marshall's assertion of Native American rights, Jackson supported the slow and steady conquest of land in the South and West.

Expansion of the US

Role of Texas

In 1821, Mexico received its independence from Spain. Mexico sold Texan lands to Americans, yet these people were still required to live under Mexican civil law (for one thing, people had to convert to Catholicism). In 1832, however, Santa Anna led a coup in Mexico and decided to crack down on the Texans. This led to the Texas Revolution of 1836, in which Texan General William Travis' men were massacred by the forces of Santa Anna at the Alamo, in which both Davy Crockett and Jim Bowie were killed. After suffering some other defeats the Texans, led by Sam Houston, finally defeated Santa Anna at the Battle of San Jacinto in 1836 and he was forced below the Rio Grande. Nevertheless, Texas was not made part of the US, mainly because the issue of slavery was so contentious at the time.

Salt Lake City, Oregon, and California
The territory of Oregon became more important to the US government as fur-trapping became a lucrative industry. Oregon was also known to contain rich farmland. As for California, its natural bounty had been described by whalers since the 1820s. In the 1840s, whole families (including the ill-fated Donner party) began to migrate there. Around this time the Church of Jesus Christ of Latter-day Saints, otherwise known as the Mormon Church, was founded by Joseph Smith. Among the beliefs espoused by the Mormons were polygamy, communalism and the abolition of slavery. After Smith's death, the Mormons were led by Brigham Young and settled in what is now Salt Lake City. Meanwhile, in 1848 gold was discovered in a California stream, generating still more excitement over the economic potential of the West.

Road to Civil War

There was immense controversy surrounding the slavery policy in the new American territories after the war with Mexico: Polk wanted to simply extend the line of the Missouri Compromise out to the Pacific while abolitionists offered the Wilmot Proviso, which declared that none of the territories should have slaves. The Southern states felt slavery should be allowed, and a more moderate view was offered by Stephen Douglas, who declared that the people of the new states should decide whether they wanted slavery or not. In the election of 1848, the war-hero Zachary Taylor (Whig) defeated Lewis Cass (Democrat) and the former president Martin Van Buren (Free Soil party, a collection of abolitionist interests).

Election of 1852

In the election of 1852, Democrat Franklin Pierce easily defeated the Whig Winfield Scott who was hurt by his association with the abolitionist William H. Seward. At this time, despite the growing crisis of slavery, there were some positive changes in the US. One was that the introduction of California as a free state permanently upset the sectional balance. Immigration into the Northeastern cities was bringing a wealth of new ideas. The northern states resisted the fugitive slave laws by passing initiatives in support of personal liberties and by aiding the Underground Railroad. Harriet Beecher Stowe enraged the South with her novel Uncle Tom's Cabin (1852). In 1857, Hinton R. Helper published "The Impending Crisis of the South," an essay that suggested the South was becoming a slave to the North because of its reactionary view on slavery.

Reason the Civil War was fought

The Civil War was fought for a number of reasons, but the most important of these was the controversy about slavery. The issue of slavery touched on moral, economic, and political themes. Also, the differing geography of the North and South had caused the latter to develop an economy that they felt could only survive through slavery. The Civil War also sprang from the ongoing debate over states' rights; many in the South felt that states should have the power to nullify federal regulations and believed that the North had too much representation in Congress; and, indeed, the North had received much more federal aid for infrastructure. Finally, there was a general difference in culture between the North and South; the North was more of a dynamic and democratic society, while the South was more of a static oligarchy.

Battles of the Civil War

At the Battle of Fredericksburg (VA) in December of 1862, Robert E. Lee successfully repelled the attacks of the Union General Burnside. At the Battle of Chancellorsville (VA) in May of 1863, Lee scored his greatest victory of the war; it was during this battle, however, that the Confederate General Stonewall Jackson was mortally wounded by his own troops. At the Battle of Gettysburg (PA) in July of 1863, the Confederacy troops led by Lee suffered a damaging defeat. Lee had hoped to take some pressure off the South with a successful surge into the North, but instead got caught in an unfavorable tactical position and endured massive casualties. Most historians believe the Union victory at Gettysburg was the turning point in the war.

Subordination of the western Native Americans

Until 1874
The Native Americans who roamed the Great Plains were known as fierce hunters and there were a few bloody encounters between settlers heading west and the natives. In 1851, the US established the Concentration policy, which encouraged Native Americans to live close to one another. This strategy was untenable, however, and the period from 1860-90 was marked by frequent conflict. In the Sioux Wars of 1865-7, the Sioux were led by Red Cloud; they fought and lost to American troops after their sacred hunting ground was mined. For a while, the US tried to group tribes on reservations in Oklahoma and the Black Hills; from 1869-74, Generals Sherman and Sheridan engaged in a War of Extermination to kill those who refused to move.

1875-1887
According to Grant's Peace Program, each Native American tribe would be put under the control of different religious groups. In 1875, miners were allowed back into the Black Hills, prompting the Sioux War of 1875-6, during which Sitting Bull defeated Custer at the Battle of Little Big Horn. Around this time, Chief Joseph attempted to lead his Nez Perce tribe to Canada; this mission failed and the Nez Perce were sent to Oklahoma. The Apache leader Geronimo was defeated in Arizona in 1887. At the Battle of Wounded Knee, the US army massacred 300, mostly women and children. Native Americans were doomed by their inferior weapons; by the destruction by whites of their food supply, the buffalo; and by railroads which made it easier for whites to encroach on their hunting grounds.

Solutions to the Indian Problem

The US government constructed several policies in an attempt to solve the so-called "Indian Problem." The Dawes (Severalty) Act of 1887 asserted that Natives needed to be assimilated into American society; tribes were moved onto "allotments of severalty" (reservations), which they supposedly owned, although they had no control of the land. The Indian Reorganization (Howard-Wheeler) Act of 1934 encouraged a return to tribal life, and offered Natives money for college. In 1953, with the so-called "termination policy," Natives became the responsibility of the states rather than the federal government. In 1970, the new strategy was "self-determination without termination": Natives were allowed to move where they choose, and were promised money (which they did not receive).

The Nineteenth Amendment

The Nineteenth Amendment gave women the right to vote. This amendment was proposed on June 4, 1919 and was ratified on August 18, 1920. An amendment to give women the right to vote was first introduced in Congress in 1878, but it failed to pass. For the next four decades, the amendment was reintroduced in every session of Congress but was defeated each time. The involvement of women in the war effort during World War I spawned increased support for women's suffrage. Finally, in 1918, the House of Representatives approved the amendment to grant women suffrage, but the Senate defeated it. In 1919, the Senate also passed the amendment and sent it to the states for approval, where it was ratified in 1920.

International Influences on the Development of the U.S. Constitution

The U.S. Constitution was written with the influence of international sources and factors. While a number of the concepts represented in the U.S. Constitution were unique, others were taken from classical political theories and from the British model of mixed government. Specifically, the U.S. Constitution was influenced by sections of the Magna Carta, which was written in the year 1215. Another influential document in the drafting of the U.S. Constitution included the English Bill of Rights, which was established in 1689. Specifically, as in the English Bill of Rights, the U.S. Constitution mandates a trial by jury, includes the right to bear arms, and bans the application of extreme bail amounts and cruel and unusual punishments. Many of the rights provided by the Magna Carta and the 1689 English Bill of Rights were indoctrinated in state laws and in the Virginia Declaration of Rights, and subsequently were indoctrinated in the Bill of Rights and the U.S. Constitution.

Governing Principles of the Constitution

The governing principles of the United State Constitution include the principle of popular sovereignty, which is associated with a system of government is created by the people, for the people. Other governing principles of the United State Constitution include the rule of law, the Supreme Court, judicial review, the separation of powers, and the system of checks and balances. In addition, the governing principle of federalism guided the formulation of the United States Constitution, allowing for sharing of power between the federal government and the states. The governing principles of the Constitution also included individual rights, which are embodied in the Bill of Rights.

Documents that Influenced the Writing of the Constitution

There are a number of documents that influenced the writing of the United States Constitution. These include the Magna Carta, which was written in 1215 A.D. and represented the English liberty charter. In addition, the Mayflower Compact was influential; it was written in 1620 by the first settlers in the New England colony. The Virginia Declaration of Rights was written in 1776 and served as a prototype for other state constitutions and for the Bill of Rights. The Declaration of Independence was also adopted in 1776 and was influential in the writing of the Constitution. The Articles of Confederation was adopted in 1781 and served as the first constitution for the original thirteen states following the American Revolution. The Federalist Papers also served as an influence for the drafters of the U.S. Constitution; they were published in newspapers to encourage ratification of the Constitution, which was ratified in 1788.

Affect of the Treaty of Paris on Native Americans

After the Revolutionary War, the Treaty of Paris, which outlined the terms of surrender of the British to the Americans, granted large parcels of land to the U.S. that were occupied by Native Americans. The new government attempted to claim the land, treating the natives as a conquered people. This approached proved unenforceable.

Next, the government tried purchasing the land from the Indians via a series of treaties as the country expanded westward. In practice, however, these treaties were not honored, and Native Americans were simply dislocated and forced to move farther and farther west as American expansion continued, often with military action.

Indian Removal Act of 1830 and the Treaty of New Echota

The Indian Removal Act of 1830 gave the new American government power to form treaties with Native Americans. In theory, America would claim land east of the Mississippi in exchange for land west of the Mississippi, to which the natives would relocate voluntarily. In practice, many tribal leaders were forced into signing the treaties, and relocation at times occurred by force.

The Treaty of New Echota was supposedly a treaty between the US government and Cherokee tribes in Georgia. However, the treaty was not signed by tribal leaders, but rather by a small portion of the represented people. The leaders protested by refusing to be removed, but President, Martin Van Buren, enforced the treaty by sending soldiers. During their forced relocation, more than 4,000 Cherokee Indians died on what became known as the Trail of Tears.

Dred Scott Decision

Abolitionist factions coalesced around the case of Dred Scott, using his case to test the country's laws regarding slavery. Scott, a slave, had been taken by his owner from Missouri, which was a slave state. He then traveled to Illinois, a free state, then on to the Minnesota Territory, also free based on the Missouri Compromise. Then, he returned to Missouri. The owner subsequently died. Abolitionists took Scott's case to court, stating that Scott was no longer a slave but free, since he had lived in free territory. The case went to the Supreme Court.

The Supreme Court stated that, because Scott, as a slave, was not a U.S. citizen, his time in free states did not change his status. He also did not have the right to sue. In addition, the Court determined that the Missouri Compromise was unconstitutional, saying Congress had overstepped its bounds by outlawing slavery in the territories.

Adapting to environmental conditions

The environment influences the way people live. People adapt to environmental conditions in ways as simple as putting on warm clothing in a cold environment; finding means to cool their surroundings in an environment with high temperatures; building shelters from wind, rain, and temperature variations; and digging water wells if surface water is unavailable. More complex adaptations result from the physical diversity of the earth in terms of soil, climate, vegetation, and topography. Humans take advantage of opportunities and avoid or minimize limitations. Examples of environmental limitations are that rocky soils offer few opportunities for agriculture and rough terrain limits accessibility. Sometimes, technology allows humans to live in areas that were once uninhabitable or undesirable. For example, air conditioning allows people to live comfortably in hot climates; modern heating systems permit habitation in areas with extremely low temperatures, as is the case with research facilities in Antarctica; and airplanes have brought people to previously inaccessible places to establish settlements or industries.

Contributions of Sumer, Egypt, and the Indus Valley

These three ancient civilizations are distinguished by their unique contributions to the development of world civilization.

Sumer used the first known writing system, which enabled the Sumerians to leave a sizeable written record of their myths and religion; advanced the development of the wheel and irrigation; and urbanized their culture with a cluster of cities.

Egypt was united by the Nile River. Egyptians originally settled in villages on its banks; had a national religion that held their pharaohs as gods; had a central government that controlled civil and artistic affairs; and had writing and libraries.

The Indus Valley was also called Harappan after the city of Harappa. This civilization started in the 3rd and 4th centuries BC and was widely dispersed over 400,000 square miles. It had a unified culture of luxury and refinement, no known national government, an advanced civic system, and prosperous trade routes.

Traits of Mesopotamia, Egypt, Greece, and Rome

The common traits of these empires were: a strong military; a centralized government; control and standardization of commerce, money, and taxes; a weight system; and an official language.

Mesopotamia had a series of short-term empires that failed because of their oppression of subject peoples.

Egypt also had a series of governments after extending its territory beyond the Nile area. Compared to Mesopotamia, these were more stable and long-lived because they blended different peoples to create a single national identity.

Greece started as a group of city-states that were united by Alexander the Great and joined to create an empire that stretched from the Indus River to Egypt and the Mediterranean coast. Greece blended Greek values with those of the local cultures, which collectively became known as Hellenistic society.

Rome was an Italian city-state that grew into an empire extending from the British Isles across Europe to the Middle East. It lasted for 1,000 years and became the foundation of the Western world's culture, language, and laws.

Chinese and Indian empires

While the Chinese had the world's longest lasting and continuous empires, the Indians had more of a cohesive culture than an empire system. Their distinct characteristics are as follows:

China – Since the end of the Warring States period in 221 BC, China has functioned as an empire. Although the dynasties changed several times, the basic governmental structure remained the same into the 20th century. The Chinese also have an extensive written record of their culture which heavily emphasizes history, philosophy, and a common religion.

India – The subcontinent was seldom unified in terms of government until the British empire controlled the area in the 19th and 20th centuries. In terms of culture, India has had persistent institutions and religions that have loosely united the people, such as the caste system and guilds. These have regulated daily life more than any government.

Middle Ages in European history

The Middle Ages, or Medieval times, was a period that ran from approximately 500-1500 AD. During this time, the centers of European civilization moved from the Mediterranean countries to France, Germany, and England, where strong national governments were developing. Key events of this time include:
- Roman Catholicism was the cultural and religious center of medieval life, extending into politics and economics.
- Knights, with their systems of honor, combat, and chivalry, were loyal to their king. Peasants, or serfs, served a particular lord and his lands.
- Many universities were established that still function in modern times.
- The Crusades, the recurring wars between European Christians and Middle East Muslims, raged over the Holy Lands.
- One of the legendary leaders was Charles the Great, or Charlemagne, who created an empire across France and Germany around 800 AD.
- The Black Death plague swept across Europe from 1347-1350, leaving between one third and one half of the population dead.

Protestant Reformation

The dominance of the Catholic Church during the Middle Ages in Europe gave it immense power, which encouraged corrupt practices such as the selling of indulgences and clerical positions. The Protestant Reformation began as an attempt to reform the Catholic Church, but eventually led to the separation from it. In 1517, Martin Luther posted his *Ninety-Five Theses* on the door of a church in Saxony, which criticized unethical practices, various doctrines, and the authority of the pope. Other reformers such as John Calvin and John Wesley soon followed, but disagreed among themselves and divided along doctrinal lines. Consequently, the Lutheran, Reformed, Calvinist, and Presbyterian churches were founded, among others. In England, King Henry VIII was denied a divorce by the pope, so he broke away and established the Anglican Church. The Protestant reformation caused the Catholic Church to finally reform itself, but the Protestant movement continued, resulting in a proliferation of new denominations.

Renaissance

Renaissance is the French word for rebirth, and is used to describe the renewal of interest in ancient Greek and Latin art, literature, and philosophy that occurred in Europe, especially Italy, from the 14th through the 16th centuries. Historically, it was also a time of great scientific inquiry, the rise of individualism, extensive geographical exploration, and the rise of secular values.

Notable figures of the Renaissance include:
- Petrarch – An Italian scholar, writer, and key figure in northern Italy, which is where the Renaissance started and where chief patrons came from the merchant class
- Leonardo da Vinci – Artist and inventor
- Michelangelo and Raphael – Artists
- Desiderius Erasmus – Applied historical scholarship to the New Testament and laid the seeds for the Protestant Reformation
- Sir Thomas More – A lawyer and author who wrote *Utopia*
- Nicolò Machiavelli – Author of *Prince and Discourses*, which proposed a science of human nature and civil life
- William Shakespeare – A renowned playwright and poet

Industrial Revolution

The Industrial Revolution started in England with the construction of the first cotton mill in 1733. Other inventions and factories followed in rapid succession. The steel industry grew exponentially when it was realized that cheap, abundant English coal could be used instead of wood for melting metals. The steam engine, which revolutionized transportation and work power, came next. Around 1830, a factory-based, technological era was ushered into the rest of Europe. Society changed from agrarian to urban. A need for cheap, unskilled labor resulted in the extensive employment and abuse of women and children, who worked up to 14 hours a day, six days a week in deplorable conditions. Expanding populations brought crowded, unsanitary conditions to the cities, and the factories created air and water pollution. Societies had to deal with these new situations by enacting child labor laws and creating labor unions to protect the safety of workers.

Participants of World War I and World War II

World War I, which began in 1914, was fought by the Allies Britain, France, Russia, Greece, Italy, Romania, and Serbia. They fought against the Central Powers of Germany, Austria-Hungary, Bulgaria, and Turkey. In 1917, the United States joined the Allies, and Russia withdrew to pursue its own revolution. World War I ended in 1918.

World War II was truly a world war, with fighting occurring on nearly every continent. Germany occupied most of Europe and Northern Africa. It was opposed by the countries of the British Empire, free France and its colonies, Russia, and various national resistance forces. Japan, an Axis ally of Germany, had been forcefully expanding its territories in Korea, China, Indonesia, the Philippines, and the South Pacific for many years. When Japan attacked Pearl Harbor in 1941, the United States joined the Allied effort. Italy changed from the Axis to the Allied side mid-war after deposing its own dictator. The war ended in Europe in April, 1945, and in Japan in August, 1945.

Cross-cultural comparisons

It is important to make cross-cultural comparisons when studying world history so that the subject is holistic and not oriented to just Western civilization. Not only are the contributions of civilizations around the world important, but they are also interesting and more representative of the mix of cultures present in the United States. It is also critical to the understanding of world relations to study the involvement of European countries and the United States in international commerce, colonization, and development. Trade routes from ancient times linked Africa, Asia, and Europe, resulting in exchanges and migrations of people, philosophies, and religions, as well as goods. While many civilizations in the Americas thrived and some became very sophisticated, many eventually became disastrously entangled in European expansion. The historic isolation of China and the modern industrialization of Japan have had huge impacts on relations with the rest of the world. The more students understand this history and its effects on the modern world, the better they will able to function in their own spheres.

Early French explorers

The French never succeeded in attracting settlers to their territories. Those who came were more interested in the fur and fish trades than in forming colonies. Eventually, the French ceded their southern possessions and New Orleans, founded in 1718, to Spain. However, the French made major contributions to the exploration of the new continent, including:
- Giovanni da Verrazano and Jacques Cartier explored the North American coast and the St. Lawrence Seaway for France.
- Samuel de Champlain, who founded Quebec and set up a fur empire on the St. Lawrence Seaway, also explored the coasts of Massachusetts and Rhode Island between 1604 and 1607.
- Fr. Jacques Marquette, a Jesuit missionary, and Louis Joliet were the first Europeans to travel down the Mississippi in 1673.
- Rene-Robert de la Salle explored the Great Lakes and the Illinois and Mississippi Rivers from 1679-1682, claiming all the land from the Great Lakes to the Gulf of Mexico and from the Appalachians to the Rockies for France.

Early Spanish explorers

The Spanish claimed and explored huge portions of the United States after the voyages of Christopher Columbus. Among them were:
- Juan Ponce de Leon – In 1513, he became the first European in Florida; established the oldest European settlement in Puerto Rico; discovered the Gulf Stream; and searched for the fountain of youth.
- Alonso Alvarez de Pineda – He charted the Gulf Coast from Florida to Mexico in 1519. Probably the first European in Texas, he claimed it for Spain.
- Panfilo de Narvaez – He docked in Tampa Bay with Cabeza de Vaca in 1528, claimed Florida for Spain, and then sailed the Gulf Coast.
- Alvar Nuñez Cabeza de Vaca – He got lost on foot in Texas and New Mexico. Estevanico, or Esteban, a Moorish slave, was a companion who guided them to Mexico.
- Francisco Vásquez de Coronado – While searching for gold in 1540, he became the first European to explore Kansas, Oklahoma, Texas, New Mexico, and Arizona.
- Hernando De Soto – He was the first European to explore the southeastern United States from Tallahassee to Natchez.

Colonization of Virginia

In 1585, Sir Walter Raleigh landed on Roanoke Island and sent Arthur Barlow to the mainland, which they named Virginia. Two attempts to establish settlements failed. The first permanent English colony was founded by Captain John Smith in Jamestown in 1607.

The Virginia Company and the Chesapeake Bay Company successfully colonized other Virginia sites. By 1619, Virginia had a House of Burgesses. The crown was indifferent to the colony, so local government grew strong and tobacco created wealth. The First Families of Virginia dominated politics there for two centuries, and four of the first five United States presidents came from these families.

The Virginia Company sent 24 Puritan families, known as Pilgrims, to Virginia on the Mayflower. In 1620, it landed at Plymouth, Massachusetts instead. The Plymouth Plantation was established and survived with the help of natives. This is where the first Thanksgiving is believed to have occurred.

Reasons for the American Revolution

The English colonies rebelled for the following reasons:
- England was remote yet controlling. By 1775, few Americans had ever been to England. They considered themselves Americans, not English.
- During the Seven Years' War (aka French and Indian War) from 1754-1763, Americans, including George Washington, served in the British army, but were treated as inferiors.
- It was feared that the Anglican Church might try to expand in the colonies and inhibit religious freedom.
- Heavy taxation such as the Sugar and Stamp Acts, which were created solely to create revenue for the crown, and business controls such as restricting trade of certain products to England only, were burdensome.
- The colonies had no official representation in the English Parliament and wanted to govern themselves.
- There were fears that Britain would block westward expansion and independent enterprise.
- Local government, established through elections by property holders, was already functioning.

Important events and groups leading up to the American Revolution

Over several years, various events and groups contributed to the rebellion that became a revolution:
- Sons of Liberty – This was the protest group headed by Samuel Adams that incited the Revolution.
- Boston Massacre – On March 5, 1770, soldiers fired on a crowd and killed five people.
- Committees of Correspondence – These were set up throughout the colonies to transmit revolutionary ideas and create a unified response.
- The Boston Tea Party – On December 6, 1773, the Sons of Liberty, dressed as Mohawks, dumped tea into the harbor from a British ship to protest the tea tax. The harsh British response further aggravated the situation.
- First Continental Congress – This was held in 1774 to list grievances and develop a response, including boycotts. It was attended by all the colonies with the exception of Georgia.
- The Shot Heard Round the World – In April, 1775, English soldiers on their way to confiscate arms in Concord passed through Lexington, Massachusetts and met the colonial militia called the Minutemen. A fight ensued. In Concord, a larger group of Minutemen forced the British to retreat.

Original 13 colonies

The original 13 colonies were: Connecticut, Delaware, Georgia, Maryland, Massachusetts, New Hampshire, New Jersey, New York, North Carolina, Pennsylvania, Rhode Island, South Carolina, and Virginia. Delaware was the first state to ratify the constitution.

The major turning points of the American Revolution were:
- The actions of the Second Continental Congress – This body established the Continental Army and chose George Washington as its commanding general. They allowed printing of money and created government offices.
- "Common Sense" – Published in 1776 by Thomas Paine, this pamphlet calling for independence was widely distributed.
- The Declaration of Independence – Written by Thomas Jefferson, it was ratified on July 4, 1776 by the Continental Congress assembled in Philadelphia.
- Alliance with France – Benjamin Franklin negotiated an agreement with France to fight with the Americans in 1778.
- Treaty of Paris – In 1782, it signaled the official end of the war, granted independence to the colonies, and gave them generous territorial rights.

Louisiana Purchase

The Louisiana Purchase in 1803 for $15 million may be considered Thomas Jefferson's greatest achievement as president. The reasons for the purchase were to gain the vital port of New Orleans, remove the threat of French interference with trade along the Mississippi River, and double the territory of the United States. The purchase both answered and raised new questions about the use of federal power, including the constitutionality of the president making such a purchase, Jefferson asking Congress for permission, and Jefferson taking the biggest federalist action up to that time, even though he was an anti-federalist.

Jefferson sent Meriwether Lewis and William Clark to map the new territory and find a means of passage all the way to the Pacific Ocean. Although there was no river that flowed all the way west, their expedition and the richness of the land and game started the great western migration of settlers.

War of 1812

A war between France and Britain caused blockades that hurt American trade and caused the British to attack American ships and impress sailors on them. An embargo against France and Britain was imposed by Jefferson, but rescinded by Madison with a renewed demand for respect for American sovereignty. However, Britain became more aggressive and war resulted. Native Americans under the leadership of Tecumseh sided with the British. The British captured Washington, D.C., and burned the White House, but Dolly Madison had enough forethought to save priceless American treasures, such as the Gilbert Stuart portrait of George Washington. Most battles, however, came to a draw. As a result, in 1815, when the British ended the war with France, they negotiated for peace with the United States as well under the Treaty of Ghent. A benefit of the war was that it motivated Americans to become more self-sufficient due to increased manufacturing and fewer imports.

Monroe Doctrine, Manifest Destiny, and the Missouri Compromise

Three important political actions in the 19th century were:

The Monroe Doctrine – Conceived by President James Monroe in 1823, this foreign policy warned European powers to cease colonization of Central and South America or face military intervention by the United States. In return, the United States would not meddle in the political affairs or standing colonies of Europe.

The Missouri Compromise – In 1820, there were 11 free states and 11 slave states. The fear of a power imbalance between slave and free states when Missouri petitioned to become a slave state brought about this agreement. Maine was brought in as a free state; the southern border of Missouri was set as the northernmost line of any slave territory; and the western states could come in as free states, while Arkansas and Florida could be slave states.

Manifest Destiny – This was a popular belief during the 1840s that it was the right and duty of the United States to expand westward to the Pacific. The idea became a slogan for the flood of settlers and expansionist power grabs.

Andrew Jackson presidency

A number of important milestones occurred in American history during the presidency of Andrew Jackson. They included:
- Jackson's election is considered the beginning of the modern political party system and the start of the Democratic Party.
- Jeffersonian Democracy, a system governed by middle and upper class educated property holders, was replaced by Jacksonian Democracy, a system that allowed universal white male suffrage.
- The Indian Removal Act of 1830 took natives out of territories that whites wanted to settle, most notably the Trail of Tears that removed Cherokees from Georgia and relocated them to Oklahoma.
- The issue of nullification, the right of states to nullify any federal laws they thought unconstitutional, came to a head over tariffs. However, a strong majority vote in Congress supporting the Tariff Acts cemented the policy that states must comply with federal laws.

Social and religious leaders

Some of the important social and religious leaders from the 19th century were:
- Susan B. Anthony – A women's rights and abolition activist, she lectured across the nation for suffrage, property and wage rights, and labor organizations for women.
- Dorothea Dix – She created the first American asylums for the treatment of mental illness and served as the Superintendent of Army Nurses during the War Between the States.
- Frederick Douglass –An escaped slave who became an abolitionist leader, government official, and writer.
- William Lloyd Garrison –An abolitionist and the editor of the *Liberator*, the leading anti-slavery newspaper of the time.
- Joseph Smith – He founded the Latter Day Saints in 1827 and wrote the Book of Mormon.
- Horace Mann – A leader of the common school movement that made public education a right of all Americans.

- Elizabeth Cady Stanton – With Lucretia Mott, she held the Seneca Falls Convention in 1848, demanding women's suffrage and other reforms.
- Brigham Young –The leader of the Mormons when they fled religious persecution, built Salt Lake City, and settled much of the West. He was the first governor of the Utah Territory.

Historical events

The Compromise of 1850, calling upon the principle of popular sovereignty, allowed those who lived in the Mexican cession to decide for themselves whether to be a free or slave territory.

The Fugitive Slave Law of 1850 allowed slave owners to go into free states to retrieve their escaped slaves.

The Kansas-Nebraska Act of 1854 repealed the Missouri Compromise of 1820 to allow the lands from the Louisiana Purchase to settle the slavery issue by popular sovereignty. Outraged Northerners responded by defecting from the Whig Party and starting the Republican Party.

Bleeding Kansas was the name applied to the state when a civil war broke out between pro- and anti-slavery advocates while Kansas was trying to formalize its statutes before being admitted as a state.

The Dred Scott vs. Sandford case was decided by the Supreme Court in 1857. It was ruled that Congress had no authority to exclude slavery from the territories, which in effect meant that the Missouri Compromise had been unconstitutional.

States forming the Confederacy

The states that seceded from the Union to form the Confederacy were: South Carolina, North Carolina, Virginia, Florida, Mississippi, Alabama, Louisiana, Texas, and Tennessee. The slave-holding states that were kept in the Union were Delaware, Maryland, Kentucky, and Missouri.

Jefferson Davis of Mississippi, a former U. S. senator and cabinet member, was the president of the Confederacy.

Abraham Lincoln of Illinois was the President of the United States. His election triggered the secession of the south. He was assassinated shortly after winning a second term.

Robert E. Lee of Virginia was offered the position of commanding general of the Union Army, but declined because of loyalty to his home state. He led the Army of Northern Virginia and the central Confederate force, and is still considered a military mastermind.

Ulysses S. Grant of Ohio wasn't appointed to command the Union Army until 1864, after a series of other commanders were unsuccessful. He received Lee's surrender at the Appomattox Court House in Virginia in April, 1865, and went on to become President from 1869 to 1877.

Reconstruction and the 13th, 14th, and 15th Amendments

Reconstruction was the period from 1865 to 1877, during which the South was under strict control of the U.S. government. In March, 1867, all state governments of the former Confederacy were terminated, and military occupation began. Military commanders called for constitutional conventions to reconstruct the state governments, to which delegates were to be elected by universal male suffrage. After a state government was in operation and the state had ratified the 14th Amendment, its representatives were admitted to Congress. Three constitutional amendments from 1865 to 1870, which tried to rectify the problems caused by slavery, became part of the Reconstruction effort. The 13th Amendment declared slavery illegal. The 14th Amendment made all persons born or naturalized in the country U.S. citizens, and forbade any state to interfere with their fundamental civil rights. The 15th Amendment made it illegal to deny individuals the right to vote on the grounds of race.

In his 1876 election campaign, President Rutherford B. Hayes promised to withdraw the troops, and did so in 1877.

Changes in industry

Important events during this time of enormous business growth and large-scale exploitation of natural resources were:
- Industrialization – Like the rest of the world, the United States' entry into the Industrial Age was marked by many new inventions and the mechanization of factories.
- Railroad expansion – The Transcontinental Railroad was built from 1865 to 1969. Railroad tracks stretched over 35,000 miles in 1865, but that distance reached 240,000 miles by 1910. The raw materials and manufactured goods needed for the railroads kept mines and factories very busy.
- Gold and silver mining – Mines brought many prospectors to the West from 1850 to about 1875, but mining corporations soon took over.
- Cattle ranching – This was a large-scale enterprise beginning in the late 1860s, but by the 1880s open ranges were being fenced and plowed for farming and pastures. Millions of farmers moved into the high plains, establishing the "Bread Basket," which was the major wheat growing area of the country.

United States involvement in World War I

When World War I broke out in 1914, America declared neutrality. The huge demand for war goods by the Allies broke a seven-year industrial stagnation and gave American factories full-time work. The country's sympathies lay mostly with the Allies, and before long American business and banking were heavily invested in an Allied victory. In 1916, Woodrow Wilson campaigned on the slogan "He kept us out of war." However, when the British ship the Lusitania was torpedoed in 1915 by a German submarine and many Americans were killed, Wilson had already warned the Germans that the United States would enter the war if Germany interfered with neutral ships at sea. Eventually, when it was proven that Germany was trying to incite Mexico and Japan into attacking the United States, Wilson declared war in 1917, even though America was unprepared. Nonetheless, America quickly armed and transferred sufficient troops to Europe, bringing the Allies to victory in 1918.

Great Depression and the Dust Bowl

In the 1920s, the rich got richer. After World War I, however, farmers were in a depression when foreign markets started growing their own crops again. Increased credit buying, bank war debts, a huge gap between rich and poor, and a belief that the stock market would always go up got the nation into financial trouble. The Stock Market Crash in October, 1929 that destroyed fortunes dramatized the downward spiral of the whole economy. Banks failed, and customers lost all their money. By 1933, 14 million were unemployed, industrial production was down to one-third of its 1929 level, and national income had dropped by half. Adding to the misery of farmers, years of breaking sod on the prairies without adequate conservation techniques caused the topsoil to fly away in great dust storms that blackened skies for years, causing deaths from lung disease and failed crops.

United States involvement in World War II

World War II began in 1939. As with World War I, the United States tried to stay out of World War II, even though the Lend-Lease program transferred munitions to Great Britain. However, on December 7, 1941, Japan attacked Pearl Harbor in Hawaii. Since Japan was an ally of Germany, the United States declared war on all the Axis powers. Although there was fighting in both Europe and the Pacific, the decision was made to concentrate on defeating Hitler first. Since it did not have combat within its borders, the United States became the great manufacturer of goods and munitions for the war effort. Women went to work in the factories, while the men entered the military. All facets of American life were centered on the war effort, including rationing, metal collections, and buying war bonds. The benefit of this production was an end to the economic depression. The influx of American personnel and supplies eventually brought victory in Europe in April of 1945, and in Asia the following August.

Suffrage in the United States

Originally, the Constitution of 1789 provided the right to vote only to white male property owners. Through the years, suffrage was extended through the following five stages.
- In the early1800s, states began to eliminate property ownership and tax payment qualifications.
- By 1810, there were no more religious tests for voting. In the late 1800s, the 15th Amendment protected citizens from being denied the right to vote because of race or color.
- In 1920, the 19th Amendment prohibited the denial of the right to vote because of gender, and women were given the right to vote.
- Passed in 1961 and ratified in 1964, the 23rd Amendment added the voters of the District of Columbia to the presidential electorate and eliminated the poll tax as a condition for voting in federal elections. The Voting Rights Act of 1965 prohibited disenfranchisement through literacy tests and various other means of discrimination.
- In 1971, the 26th Amendment set the minimum voting age at 18 years of age.

Movement of human populations

Human populations often move from one area to another. Four major factors that lead to this movement are:
1. Physical - If a particular area does not provide the necessary resources or room for a population to thrive, that population may relocate.
2. Economic - Individuals, families, or groups might move to an area where their economic needs are better met or where the cost of living is lower. Some might move to areas with higher economic demands.
3. Political - Changes in a political system in an area can lead people to move to a different area. People might also move to an area where they perceive the political system to be better.
4. Cultural - People might move to another area where the population is more culturally similar to themselves or, in other cases, where it is different.

Geography

Plate tectonics

This theory of *plate tectonics* arose from the fusion of continental drift (first proposed in 1915 by Alfred Wegener) and seafloor spreading (first observed by Icelandic fishermen in the 1800s and later refined by Harry Hess and Robert Dietz in the early 1960s) in the late 1960s and early 1970s. Prior to this time, the generally accepted explanation for continental drift was that the continents were floating on the Earth's oceans. The discovery that mountains have "roots" (proved by George Airy in the early 1950s) did not categorically disprove the concept of floating continents; scientists were still uncertain as to where those mountainous roots were attached. It was not until the identification and study of the Mid-Atlantic Ridge and magnetic striping in the 1960s that plate tectonics became accepted as a scientific theory. Its conception was a landmark event in the field of Earth sciences—it provided an explanation for the empirical observations of continental drift and seafloor spreading.

Terms

A ***resource*** is a commodity that is useful or necessary to sustain life and/or the industries and lifestyles of global societies. ***Natural resources*** are Earth materials that can be used to further those ends. A ***renewable resource*** is one that may be replenished after use and will therefore be available in the long term. A ***nonrenewable resource*** is one that is permanently depleted after its currently available supply has been exhausted. Recovery of a ***paramarginal resource*** is feasible, given current technological capabilities, though not exceptionally profitable (the main incentive to recover any resource is an economic one). Recovery of a ***submarginal resource*** is not profitable—it would cost more in energy and financial resources to recover such a resource than such recovery would provide (the cost of recovery outweighs the potential benefits of recovery). The ***reserve*** of a resource is the estimated amount of that resource that is recoverable with current technological capabilities; this amount is usually a fraction of the total amount of the resource.

Geological processes producing natural resources

Igneous processes may result in the deposition of ore resources. For example, liquid differentiation and crystallization within magma may lead to the deposition of minerals rich in iron and titanium (relatively abundant resources) or copper (a relatively rare ore used in the construction of electrical wiring). Contact metamorphism is another geological process with the ability to produce natural resources. Limestone is a common host rock for the formation of oxides of zinc (an anticorrosive alloy) and copper through this process. The sedimentation of mineral particles in pockets along water bodies can lead to the formation of gold deposits; this was the case during the Gold Rush. Weathering processes may lead to ore deposition in humid climates, where soluble elements such as magnesium are evaporated from soil, leaving deposits of insoluble elements such as iron and nickel.

Affect of human activity on erosion rates

Human activity can affect the resistance of solid materials such as soil to erosion processes. Construction activity has the largest effect on the stability of soil—clearing trees and other vegetation makes portions of land especially susceptible to runoff. Agriculture is another industry that may adversely affect the resistance of Earth materials to erosion. Animal husbandry and urban development can also lead to increases (smaller than other activities, but still significant) in the levels of eroding materials. With increased erosion, Earth materials are more likely to shift through mass movements, changing natural landscapes and placing humans and other organisms in danger. Increased air pollution can catalyze erosive processes by increasing the speed of rock decay.

Modifying surrounding environment
The agricultural revolution led human societies to begin changing their surroundings in order to accommodate their needs for shelter and room to cultivate food and to provide for domestic animals. Clearing ground for crops, redirecting waterways for irrigation purposes, and building permanent settlements all create major changes in the environment. Large-scale agriculture can lead to loose topsoil and damaging erosion. Building large cities leads to degraded air quality, water pollution from energy consumption, and many other side effects that can severely damage the environment. Recently, many countries have taken action by passing laws to reduce human impact on the environment and reduce the potentially damaging side effects. This is called environmental policy.

Harmful interaction
Wherever humans have gone on the earth, they have made changes to their surroundings. Many are harmful or potentially harmful, depending on the extent of the alterations. Some of the changes and activities that can harm the environment include:
- Cutting into mountains by machine or blasting to build roads or construction sites
- Cutting down trees and clearing natural growth
- Building houses and cities
- Using grassland to graze herds
- Polluting water sources
- Polluting the ground with chemical and oil waste
- Wearing out fertile land and losing topsoil
- Placing communication lines cross country using poles and wires or underground cable
- Placing railway lines or paved roads cross country
- Building gas and oil pipelines cross country
- Draining wetlands
- Damming up or re-routing waterways
- Spraying fertilizers, pesticides, and defoliants
- Hunting animals to extinction or near extinction

Global warming

The natural greenhouse effect of the atmosphere is beneficial to life on Earth; it keeps temperatures on the planet 33 degrees higher than they would be without this phenomenon. Originally, this helped sustain life. However, it has been discovered in the last 20 years that this effect is being intensified by the actions of humans. In the twentieth century, certain activities of mankind, including the burning of fossils fuels like coal and oil, have resulted in an increase in the levels of greenhouse gases (such as methane and carbon dioxide) being released into the atmosphere. Also, increasing deforestation has affected the number of photosynthesis-practicing plants. The combined effect of these trends is a higher-than-normal concentration of greenhouse gases in the atmosphere. This, in turn, produces the effect of *global warming*. The average temperature at the Earth's surface has gone up 0.6 degrees Celsius in the last 100 years. Continuation of this trend is likely to have a detrimental effect on many of the planet's ecosystems, including that of human beings.

Affect of pollution on the Earth's oceans

Sewage, oil, garbage, and industrial waste are commonly disposed of in Earth's oceans. Also, the use of pesticides in agriculture can indirectly contribute to pollution—these chemicals are picked up by rainwater moving back to the oceans. Ocean pollution has many harmful effects, both within oceanic ecosystems and across the rest of the globe. For example, pesticides deposited in the ocean contaminate the normally clean water in which algae thrive. When the algae die, a number of the fish that depend on algae (or other underwater plant life) for sustenance will die as well. This can affect local economies (not to mention food supplies) that depend on fishing. Also, when toxic waste is dumped into an ocean, it may be consumed by organisms low on the food chain. If it does not kill these organisms, they can be eaten by larger predators. Pollutants can continue to move up the food chain and eventually be consumed by humans. Lead, for instance, is commonly found in seafood eaten by humans.

Wave erosion

Most coastal erosion takes place when waves crash into a shore zone during a storm. It is at this time that the height of a wave (the distance between its upper effective limit and its lower effective limit, or wave base) is the greatest. The upper and lower limits of a wave work on a coastline much like a saw moving horizontally. Like river and stream erosion, most wave erosion is accomplished through abrasion caused by eroded materials (sand and gravel, for instance) carried in the water. Fluctuations in the tide cause coastal erosion indirectly—during low tide, large portions of the shore are exposed and vulnerable to other erosive agents, such as wind and rain. The energy of waves and the strength of the material of which a coastline is composed are the main factors in the rate of wave erosion.

Landforms commonly created by wave erosion

The *sea cliff* is a landform that is often associated with coastal areas. Particularly large, high-energy waves attack coastlines during storms and abrade portions of a rock face, forming a usually steep cliff. The intensity of this effect is related to the durability of the material being eroded and the slope of the land surface. Wave erosion also produces *wave-cut platforms*, or a truncated sea cliff with a leveled surface. Sometimes these areas remain bare except for the irregularities created by the erosive process; these remnants of cliffs are called stacks. *Beaches* are created when the portion of the platform closest to the sea is covered with sand or other grainy materials. These formations are constantly being eroded away and reformed. A *marine-built terrace* (a deposit of material transported by waves) is often formed inland from a beach.

Geologic faults

A *geologic fault* is a fracture in the Earth's surface created by movement of the crust. The majority of faults are found along tectonic plate boundaries; however, smaller faults have been identified at locations far from these boundaries. There are three types of geologic faults, which are named for the original direction of movement along the active fault line. The landforms on either side of a fault are called the footwall and the hanging wall, respectively. In a *normal fault*, the hanging wall moves downward relative to the footwall. A *reverse fault* is the opposite of a normal fault: The hanging wall moves upward relative to the footwall. The dip of a reverse fault is usually quite steep; when the dip is less than 45 degrees, the fault is called a thrust fault. In the third type of geologic fault, the *strike-slip fault*, the dip is virtually nonexistent, and the footwall moves vertically left (sinistral) or right (dextral). A transform plate boundary is a specific instance of a strike-slip fault.

Terms

The rocks at Earth's surface experience physical, biological, and chemical processes that are much different from the processes ambient during their formations. The operation of these processes on Earth materials is called weathering.

Mechanical weathering causes disintegration of rocks and minerals. In this process, the affected rocks break apart into small fragments but retain their chemical compositions. This type of weathering occurs due to the presence of joints, or cracks, in rocks that allow the penetration of water and vegetative roots. Mechanical weathering occurs most often in cooler climates.

Chemical weathering refers to the processes by which rocks experience chemical changes (such as decomposition and decay) due to the influence of organic acids. Chemical weathering occurs most often in high temperature, high humidity climates. The two types of weathering are not mutually exclusive; they often occur side by side.

Erosion also occurs simultaneously with weathering. This term refers to the transportation of Earth materials by wind, water, gravity, and sometimes living organisms.

Erosion landform

An **erosion landform** is a landform created by the processes of weathering and erosion. For example, a cliff is an erosion landform. Cliffs are formed when relatively strong rocks are exposed to centuries of wind and water, weathering and erosion. Sandstone, limestone, and basalt are examples of rocks that commonly become cliffs. The canyon provides the classic instance of an erosion landform. Canyons are formed from many years of weathering and erosion processes (often water-based), usually operating on a plateau (a mountain which has been eroded down to a flat but elevated surface). Strata of rocks that resisted the destructive processes remain visible in the canyon walls.

Climate

Climate is usually defined as the "average weather" in a particular area on Earth. The timespan over which climate is measured is variable, but it is generally accepted that the climate of an area does not vary during a human life span (though climate is extremely various in geologic time). This may change, however, due to the increasing greenhouse effect. Meteorologists measure climate by averaging certain quantifiable elements such as rainfall or temperature. Climate may be studied on several different scales:

Local climate refers to the climate of small geographic areas (generally up to tens of miles wide). The local climate of an area is affected by things such as its location relative to an ocean and the presence of mountains near the location.

A regional climate is the climate of a larger geographic area, such as a country. A regional climate may also be delineated due to climate features that are distinctive from the surrounding climate. Global climate refers to the average weather experienced across the Earth.

Environmental effects of burning fossil fuels

Burning fossil fuels (naturally-occurring hydrocarbon compounds that may be used by humans for fuel), especially coal, releases harmful elements into the atmosphere. The chemical reaction of coal combustion produces, for example, large amounts of carbon dioxide. When these gases reach the atmosphere, they inhibit the release of infrared photons into space—carbon dioxide molecules absorb the photons and may reflect them inward, back toward the Earth. This phenomenon is called the greenhouse effect. While the greenhouse effect is desirable, to a certain degree, to maintain a comfortable climate on the planet, increased levels of carbon dioxide can change the balance of energy in the atmosphere. This is termed global warming. Coal burning can also cause acid rain. Sulfur dioxide, a byproduct of burning coal, rises to the atmosphere and combines with water molecules to form sulfuric acid. This acid rain falls back to Earth, where it can cause harm to plants, animals, water bodies, and exposed structures. Burning gasoline can also contribute to the formation of acid rain.

Human systems

Human systems affect geography in the way in which they settle, form groups that grow into large-scale habitations, and even create permanent changes in the landscape. Geographers study movements of people, how they distribute goods among each other and to other settlements or cultures, and how ideas grow and spread. Migrations, wars, forced relocations, and trade all can spread cultural ideas, language, goods and other practices to wide-spread areas. Some major migrations or the conquering of one people by another have significantly changed cultures throughout history. In addition, human systems can lead to various conflicts or alliances to control access to and the use of natural resources.

Erosion, weathering, transportation and deposition

a. Erosion involves movement of any loose material on the earth's surface. This can include soil, sand, or rock fragments. These loose fragments can be displaced by natural forces such as wind, water, ice, plant cover, and human factors. Mechanical erosion occurs due to natural forces. Chemical erosion occurs as a result of human intervention and activities.
b. Weathering occurs when atmospheric elements affect the earth's surface. Water, heat, ice, and pressure all lead to weathering.
c. Transportation refers to loose material being moved by wind, water or ice. Glacial movement, for example, carries everything from pebbles to boulders, sometimes over long distances.
d. Deposition is the result of transportation. When material is transported, it is eventually deposited, and builds up to form formations like moraines and sand dunes.

Cartography

Cartography is the art and science of mapmaking. Maps of local areas were drawn by the Egyptians as early as 1300 BC, and the Greeks began making maps of the known world in the 6th century BC. Cartography eventually grew into the field of geography.

The first step in modern mapmaking is a survey. This involves designating a few key sites of known elevation as benchmarks to allow for measurement of other sites. Aerial photography is then used to chart the area by taking photos in sequence. Overlapping photos show the same area from different positions along the flight line. When paired and examined through a stereoscope, the cartographer gets a three-dimensional view that can be made into a topographical map. In addition, a field survey (on the ground) is made to determine municipal borders and place names.

The second step is to compile the information and computer-draft a map based on the collected data. The map is then reproduced or printed.

Types of maps

There are three basic types of maps:

- Base maps – Created from aerial and field surveys, base maps serve as the starting point for topographic and thematic maps.
- Thematic maps – These use a base or topographic map as the foundation for showing data based on a theme, such as population density, wildlife distribution, hill-slope stability, economic trends, etc.
- A physical map is one that shows natural features such as mountains, rivers, lakes, deserts, and plains. Color is used to designate the different features.
- A topographic map is a type of physical map that shows the relief and configuration of a landscape, such as hills, valleys, fields, forest, roads, and settlements. It includes natural and human-made features.
- A topological map is one on which lines are stretched or straightened for the sake of clarity, but retain their essential geometric relationship. This type of map is used, for example, to show the routes of a subway system.
- A political map uses lines for state, county, and country boundaries; points or dots for cities and towns; and various other symbols for features such as airports and roads.

Scale is the size of a map expressed as a ratio of the actual size of the land (for example, 1 inch on a map represents 1 mile on land). In other words, it is the proportion between a distance on the map and its corresponding distance on earth. The scale determines the level of detail on a map. Small-scale maps depict larger areas, but include fewer details. Large-scale maps depict smaller areas, but include more details.

Map terms

The most important terms used when describing items on a map or globe are:

- Latitude and longitude – Latitude and longitude are the imaginary lines (horizontal and vertical, respectively) that divide the globe into a grid. Both are measured using the 360 degrees of a circle.
- Coordinates – These are the latitude and longitude measures for a place.
- Absolute location – This is the exact spot where coordinates meet. The grid system allows the location of every place on the planet to be identified.
- Equator – This is the line at 0° latitude that divides the earth into two equal halves called hemispheres.
- Parallels – This is another name for lines of latitude because they circle the earth in parallel lines that never meet.
- Meridians – This is another name for lines of longitude. The Prime Meridian is located at 0° longitude, and is the starting point for measuring distance (both east and west) around the globe. Meridians circle the earth and connect at the Poles.

Terms

Northern Hemisphere – This is the area above, or north, of the equator.
Southern Hemisphere – This is the area below, or south, of the equator.
Western Hemisphere – This is the area between the North and South Poles. It extends west from the Prime Meridian to the International Date Line.
Eastern Hemisphere – This is the area between the North and South Poles. It extends east from the Prime Meridian to the International Date Line.

North and South Poles – Latitude is measured in terms of the number of degrees north and south from the equator. The North Pole is located at 90°N latitude, while the South Pole is located at 90°S latitude.

Tropic of Cancer – This is the parallel, or latitude, 23½° north of the equator.

Tropic of Capricorn – This is the parallel, or latitude, 23½° south of the equator. The region between these two parallels is the tropics. The subtropics is the area located between 23½° and 40° north and south of the equator.

Arctic Circle – This is the parallel, or latitude, 66½° north of the equator.

Antarctic Circle – This is the parallel, or latitude, 66½° south of the equator.

Physical and cultural features studied

Physical features:
- Vegetation zones, or biomes – Forests, grasslands, deserts, and tundra are the four main types of vegetation zones.
- Climate zones – Tropical, dry, temperate, continental, and polar are the five different types of climate zones. Climate is the long-term average weather conditions of a place.

Cultural features:
- Population density – This is the number of people living in each square mile or kilometer of a place. It is calculated by dividing population by area.
- Religion – This is the identification of the dominant religions of a place, whether Christianity, Hinduism, Judaism, Buddhism, Islam, Shinto, Taoism, or Confucianism. All of these originated in Asia.
- Languages – This is the identification of the dominant or official language of a place. There are 12 major language families. The Indo-European family (which includes English, Russian, German, French, and Spanish) is spoken over the widest geographic area, but Mandarin Chinese is spoken by the most people.

Ways that mountains form

Mountains are formed by the movement of geologic plates, which are rigid slabs of rocks beneath the earth's crust that float on a layer of partially molten rock in the earth's upper mantle. As the plates collide, they push up the crust to form mountains. This process is called orogeny. There are three basic forms of orogeny:
- If the collision of continental plates causes the crust to buckle and fold, a chain of folded mountains, such as the Appalachians, the Alps, or the Himalayas, is formed.
- If the collision of the plates causes a denser oceanic plate to go under a continental plate, a process called subduction; strong horizontal forces lift and fold the margin of the continent. A mountain range like the Andes is the result.
- If an oceanic plate is driven under another oceanic plate, volcanic mountains such as those in Japan and the Philippines are formed.

Carrying capacity and natural hazards

Carrying capacity is the maximum, sustained level of use of an environment can incur without sustaining significant environmental deterioration that would eventually lead to environmental destruction. Environments vary in terms of their carrying capacity, a concept humans need to learn to measure and respect before harm is done. Proper assessment of environmental conditions enables responsible decision making with respect to how much and in what ways the resources of a particular environment should be consumed. Energy and water conservation as well as recycling can extend an area's carrying capacity.

In addition to carrying capacity limitations, the physical environment can also have occasional extremes that are costly to humans. Natural hazards such as hurricanes, tornadoes, earthquakes, volcanoes, floods, tsunamis, and some forest fires and insect infestations are processes or events that are not caused by humans, but may have serious consequences for humans and the environment. These events are not preventable, and their precise timing, location, and magnitude are not predictable. However, some precautions can be taken to reduce the damage.

Applying geography to interpret the past

Space, environment, and chronology are three different points of view that can be used to study history. Events take place within geographic contexts. If the world is flat, then transportation choices are vastly different from those that would be made in a round world, for example. Invasions of Russia from the west have normally failed because of the harsh winter conditions, the vast distances that inhibit steady supply lines, and the number of rivers and marshes to be crossed, among other factors. Any invading or defending force anywhere must make choices based on consideration of space and environmental factors. For instance, lands may be too muddy or passages too narrow for certain equipment. Geography played a role in the building of the Panama Canal because the value of a shorter transportation route had to outweigh the costs of labor, disease, political negotiations, and equipment, not to mention a myriad of other effects from cutting a canal through an isthmus and changing a natural land structure as a result.

Applying geography to interpret the present and plans for the future

The decisions that individual people as well as nations make that may affect the environment have to be made with an understanding of spatial patterns and concepts, cultural and transportation connections, physical processes and patterns, ecosystems, and the impact, or "footprint," of people on the physical environment. Sample issues that fit into these considerations are recycling programs, loss of agricultural land to further urban expansion, air and water pollution, deforestation, and ease of transportation and communication. In each of these areas, present and future uses have to be balanced against possible harmful effects. For example, wind is a clean and readily available resource for electric power, but the access roads to and noise of wind turbines can make some areas unsuitable for livestock pasture. Voting citizens need to have an understanding of geographical and environmental connections to make responsible decisions.

Spatial organization

Spatial organization in geography refers to how things or people are grouped in a given space anywhere on earth. Spatial organization applies to the placement of settlements, whether hamlets, towns, or cities. These settlements are located to make the distribution of goods and services convenient. For example, in farm communities, people come to town to get groceries, to attend church and school, and to access medical services. It is more practical to provide these things to groups than to individuals. These settlements, historically, have been built close to water sources and agricultural areas. Lands that are topographically difficult, have few resources, or experience extreme temperatures do not have as many people as temperate zones and flat plains, where it is easier to live. Within settlements, a town or city will be organized into commercial and residential neighborhoods, with hospitals, fire stations, and shopping centers centrally located. All of these organizational considerations are spatial in nature.

Themes of geography

The five themes of geography are:
- Location – This includes relative location (described in terms of surrounding geography such as a river, sea coast, or mountain) and absolute location (the specific point of latitude and longitude).
- Place – This includes physical characteristics (deserts, plains, mountains, and waterways) and human characteristics (features created by humans, such as architecture, roads, religion, industries, and food and folk practices).
- Human-environmental interaction – This includes human adaptation to the environment (using an umbrella when it rains), human modification of the environment (building terraces to prevent soil erosion), and human dependence on the environment for food, water, and natural resources.
- Movement –Interaction through trade, migration, communications, political boundaries, ideas, and fashions.
- Regions – This includes formal regions (a city, state, country, or other geographical organization as defined by political boundaries), functional regions (defined by a common function or connection, such as a school district), and vernacular regions (informal divisions determined by perceptions or one's mental image, such as the "Far East").

Geomorphology

The study of landforms is call geomorphology or physiography, a science that considers the relationships between geological structures and surface landscape features. It is also concerned with the processes that change these features, such as erosion, deposition, and plate tectonics. Biological factors can also affect landforms. Examples are when corals build a coral reef or when plants contribute to the development of a salt marsh or a sand dune. Rivers, coastlines, rock types, slope formation, ice, erosion, and weathering are all part of geomorphology.

A landform is a landscape feature or geomorphological unit. These include hills, plateaus, mountains, deserts, deltas, canyons, mesas, marshes, swamps, and valleys. These units are categorized according to elevation, slope, orientation, stratification, rock exposure, and soil type. Landform elements include pits, peaks, channels, ridges, passes, pools, and plains.

The highest order landforms are continents and oceans. Elementary landforms such as segments, facets, and relief units are the smallest homogenous divisions of a land surface at a given scale or resolution.

Oceans, seas, lakes, rivers, and canals

Oceans are the largest bodies of water on earth and cover nearly 71% of the earth's surface. There are five major oceans: Atlantic, Pacific (largest and deepest), Indian, Arctic, and Southern (surrounds Antarctica).

Seas are smaller than oceans and are somewhat surrounded by land like a lake, but lakes are fresh water and seas are salt water. Seas include the Mediterranean, Baltic, Caspian, Caribbean, and Coral.

Lakes are bodies of water in a depression on the earth's surface. Examples of lakes are the Great Lakes and Lake Victoria.

Rivers are a channeled flow of water that start out as a spring or stream formed by runoff from rain or snow. Rivers flow from higher to lower ground, and usually empty into a sea or ocean. Great rivers of the world include the Amazon, Nile, Rhine, Mississippi, Ganges, Mekong, and Yangtze.

Canals are artificial waterways constructed by humans to connect two larger water bodies. Examples of canals are the Panama and the Suez.

Mountains, hills, foothills, valleys, plateaus, and mesas

The definitions for these geographical features are as follows:
- Mountains are elevated landforms that rise fairly steeply from the earth's surface to a summit of at least 1,000-2,000 feet (definitions vary) above sea level.
- Hills are elevated landforms that rise 500-2,000 feet above sea level.
- Foothills are a low series of hills found between a plain and a mountain range.
- Valleys are a long depression located between hills or mountains. They are usually products of river erosion. Valleys can vary in terms of width and depth, ranging from a few feet to thousands of feet.
- Plateaus are elevated landforms that are fairly flat on top. They may be as high as 10,000 feet above sea level and are usually next to mountains.
- Mesas are flat areas of upland. Their name is derived from the Spanish word for table. They are smaller than plateaus and often found in arid or semi-arid areas.

Plains, deserts, deltas, and basins

Plains are extensive areas of low-lying, flat, or gently undulating land, and are usually lower than the landforms around them. Plains near the seacoast are called lowlands.

Deserts are large, dry areas that receive less than 10 inches of rain per year. They are almost barren, containing only a few patches of vegetation.

Deltas are accumulations of silt deposited at river mouths into the seabed. They are eventually converted into very fertile, stable ground by vegetation, becoming important crop-growing areas. Examples include the deltas of the Nile, Ganges, and Mississippi River.

Basins come in various types. They may be low areas that catch water from rivers; large hollows that dip to a central point and are surrounded by higher ground, as in the Donets and Kuznetsk basins in Russia; or areas of inland drainage in a desert when the water can't reach the sea and flows into lakes or evaporates in salt flats as a result. An example is the Great Salt Lake in Utah.

Physical vs. cultural geography

Physical geography is the study of climate, water, and land and their relationships with each other and humans. Physical geography locates and identifies the earth's surface features and explores how humans thrive in various locations according to crop and goods production.

Cultural geography is the study of the influence of the environment on human behaviors as well as the effect of human activities such as farming, building settlements, and grazing livestock on the environment. Cultural geography also identifies and compares the features of different cultures and how they influence interactions with other cultures and the earth.

Physical vs. political locations

Physical location refers to the placement of the hemispheres and the continents.

Political location refers to the divisions within continents that designate various countries. These divisions are made with borders, which are set according to boundary lines arrived at by legal agreements.

Both physical and political locations can be precisely determined by geographical surveys and by latitude and longitude.

Types of resources

Natural resources are things provided by nature that have commercial value to humans, such as minerals, energy, timber, fish, wildlife, and the landscape.

Renewable resources are those that can be replenished, such as wind, solar radiation, tides, and water (with proper conservation and clean-up). Soil is renewable with proper conservation and management techniques, and timber can be replenished with replanting. Living resources such as fish and wildlife can replenish themselves if they are not over-harvested.

Nonrenewable resources are those that cannot be replenished. These include fossil fuels such as oil and coal and metal ores. These cannot be replaced or reused once they have been burned, although some of their products can be recycled.

Commodities are natural resources that have to be extracted and purified rather than created, such as mineral ores.

Uses of geography

Geography involves learning about the world's primary physical and cultural patterns to help understand how the world functions as an interconnected and dynamic system. Combining information from different sources, geography teaches the basic patterns of climate, geology, vegetation, human settlement, migration, and commerce. Thus, geography is an interdisciplinary study of history, anthropology, and sociology. History incorporates geography in discussions of battle strategies, slavery (trade routes), ecological disasters (the Dust Bowl of the 1930s), and mass migrations. Geographic principles are useful when reading literature to help identify and visualize the setting, and also when studying earth science, mathematics (latitude, longitude, sun angle, and population statistics), and fine arts (song, art, and dance often reflect different cultures). Consequently, a good background in geography can help students succeed in other subjects as well.

Areas covered by geography

Geography is connected to many issues and provides answers to many everyday questions. Some of the areas covered by geography include:
- Geography investigates global climates, landforms, economies, political systems, human cultures, and migration patterns.
- Geography answers questions not only about where something is located, but also why it is there, how it got there, and how it is related to other things around it.
- Geography explains why people move to certain regions (climate, availability of natural resources, arable land, etc.).
- Geography explains world trade routes and modes of transportation.
- Geography identifies where various animals live and where various crops and forests grow.
- Geography identifies and locates populations that follow certain religions.
- Geography provides statistics on population numbers and growth, which aids in economic and infrastructure planning for cities and countries.

Globe and map projections

A globe is the only accurate representation of the earth's size, shape, distance, and direction since it, like the earth, is spherical. The flat surface of a map distorts these elements. To counter this problem, mapmakers use a variety of "map projections," a system for representing the earth's curvatures on a flat surface through the use of a grid that corresponds to lines of latitude and longitude. Some distortions are still inevitable, though, so mapmakers make choices based on the map scale, the size of the area to be mapped, and what they want the map to show. Some projections can represent a true shape or area, while others may be based on the equator and therefore become less accurate as they near the poles. In summary, all maps have some distortion in terms of the shape or size of features of the spherical earth.

Physical geographical features of the earth

Organizing place names into categories of physical features helps students learn the type of information they need to know to compete in the National Geographic Bee. The physical features students need to be knowledgeable about are:
- The continents (Although everyone has been taught that there are seven continents, some geographers combine Europe and Asia into a single continent called Eurasia.)
- The five major oceans
- The highest and lowest points on each continent (Mt. Everest is the highest point in the world; the Dead Sea is the lowest point.)
- The 10 largest seas (The Coral Sea is the largest.)
- The 10 largest lakes (The Caspian Sea is actually the largest lake.)
- The 10 largest islands (Greenland is the largest island.)
- The longest rivers (The Nile is the longest river.)
- Major mountain ranges
- Earth's extremes such as the hottest (Ethiopia), the coldest (Antarctica), the wettest (India), and the driest (Atacama Desert) places; the highest waterfall (Angel Falls); the largest desert (Sahara); the largest canyon (Grand Canyon); the longest reef (Great Barrier Reef); and the highest tides.

Immigration trends in the late 1800s

The population of the United States doubled between 1860 and 1890, the period that saw 10 million immigrants arrive. Most lived in the north. Cities and their slums grew tremendously because of immigration and industrialization. While previous immigrants had come from Germany, Scandinavia, and Ireland, the 1880s saw a new wave of immigrants from Italy, Poland, Hungary, Bohemia, and Greece, as well as Jewish groups from central and eastern Europe, especially Russia. The Roman Catholic population grew from 1.6 million in 1850 to 12 million in 1900, a growth that ignited an anti-Catholic backlash from the anti-Catholic Know-Nothing Party of the 1880s and the Ku Klux Klan.

Exploited immigrant workers started labor protests in the 1870s, and the Knights of Labor was formed in 1878, calling for sweeping social and economic reform. Its membership reached 700,000 by 1886. Eventually, this organization was replaced by the American Federation of Labor, headed by Samuel Gompers.

Themes of geography

Geography is the study of places on the earth. It covers five main themes:

1. Location - Absolute vs. relative location used to identify where a specific landmark is found
2. Place - Names of states, cities, towns, countries and regions; includes political science
3. Movement and connections - How transportation and communication connect people all over the world and how these connections have grown and changed
4. Regions, processes and patterns - Includes variations in economy, climate, politics, and culture within specific regions, making each one unique; includes sociology, politics and economics
5. Human interaction with the environment - How human beings make use of, change, and are limited by the environment; includes ecology.

Physical geography

Physical geography refers to the study of Earth's physical attributes. This can include landforms like mountains, rivers, deserts and plateaus; types of soil; climate, altitude and rainfall; and types and quantity of vegetation. It also includes the movement and position of the earth itself, as well as the makeup of its atmosphere. Physical geography can tell students a great deal about how the earth is made up and how various factors lead to the development of physical features on the earth, but it does not include how humans interact with these physical features.

Geographical concepts relating past events and conditions to the present

The past has a profound effect on the present, and determines the human component of an area develops and grows. The three major concepts involving this idea are:
- Human populations will modify an environment to meet their needs. This can lead either to improvement of the environment, or environmental destruction.
- Cultural factors are influenced by physical factors. The type of clothes, food, and shelter a particular group of people uses is determined largely by what is available in their environment.
- Changes occur constantly. Populations change the environment and the environment itself changes due to human and geological factors.

Cultural geography

Cultural geography discusses how humans and animals interact with their environment. Physical properties of the environment can affect various factors including:
- Types of vegetation available
- Types of animals that can survive
- How accessible an area is
- What kind of shelter is available
- What kinds of physical resources are available

The availability of important resources such as food, water, and shelter can determine whether or not a large human population can be sustained in a specific area. Physical geography that restricts growth of a population can keep certain settlements from growing. All of these factors are important to an understanding of a particular area or region and why it developed in the way it has.

Populations adapting to the environment

The physical environment determines what types of activities are most suitable to a specific area. However, human populations can adapt to prosper in most environments by using clothing and shelter and by developing ways of procuring or producing food. In many cases, these activities lead to changes in the environment. For example, a human population might redirect a water source to enable them to grow food. This could lead to a reduction in water supplied to another area, causing local vegetation and animal populations to fluctuate or die out. More recently, humans have become more aware of the negative impacts of changing their environment and work harder to ensure that modifying the environment produces a less negative impact on existing animals, plants and physical structures.

Advance of technology with tools

Even in the earliest stages of human development, humans have used tools to modify their environment. They killed animals for food, cleared out and even decorated caves for shelter, and gathered food from plants in the surrounding area. Although these tools were used to improve the human condition, as tools became more sophisticated they tended to lead to destruction of the environment. As tools advanced in technology, the ability of humans to modify their environment became even more powerful. The more complex technology becomes, the more potential it has to change the environment.

Major regions of the world

The world can be divided into regions in a number of ways; one common way is the seven continents: Africa, Asia, Europe, North America, South America, Australia, and Antarctica. Another way is to discuss the Northern and Southern Hemispheres or the Eastern and Western Hemispheres. A discussion could also involve climatic regions, latitude or political divisions.

In the elementary classroom, students can compare and contrast these various regions by researching the areas and discovering ways in which they are similar and different. They can also compare social studies concepts to familiar concepts from other study areas, such as science, for higher-level thinking and analysis.

Economics

Monetary System

As in other markets, the same elements of analysis may be used for the money market. The laws of demand and supply apply to the money market and result in market equilibrium for the price of money. The quantity of money in the system is also a product of these forces. Money in circulation includes actual paper money and coins. Paper money may be banknotes or Federal Reserve notes that are physically produced by the United State's mint but represent money created by the Federal Reserve based on the credit of the federal government. This credit is electronically created by the government to influence the economy. In reality, since all paper money is based on the promise of the government to honor the currency, all notes are electronically produced. Coins may be produced outside of the Federal Reserve system by legislation. The total money supply is within the scope of the Federal reserve system.

Currency

Currency may be defined technically as any legal tender with which debts may be settled. Currency's major use is to facilitate the exchange of goods and services in the marketplace. the world is divided into "currency zones" which determine what currency may be used in trade. Rates of exchange are a market where different currencies may be bought and sold. Both bank notes and coins are considered currency. The country that issues the currency owns a monopoly in that market. Central banks of countries are the institutions that control currency (and the money supply) through monetary and fiscal policy. These central banks or other monetary authorities (set up as an agency by the government) control and implement monetary policy and activity. Such authorities differ in their power from country to country. For example, in the United States the Federal Reserve is a wholly independent agency free of political controls. Although Congress legislated the Federal Reserve into existence it remains completely independent in its activity.

Gold standard

A monetary system linked to the value of gold is said to be on the gold standard. Those who issue currency agree to exchange bank notes and coins for gold based on a fixed exchange rate. Thus gold becomes the basic unit of account to measure all wealth against. Gold standards were originally created to stabilize currencies by making it impossible for governments to create money at their pleasure. The gold standard also protects against hyper-inflation and the over -expansion of debt in an economy. Originally, when the major form of money was coins (usually silver or gold) there was a logic to the gold standard. The gold standard was once a common phenomena among nations, but has now been replaced by systems giving the central banks of countries the power to create money and manipulate monetary policy for the good of the economy. No modern country would return to the gold standard despite the protection it affords.

Inflation

Inflation strikes when there is an general price increase of goods and services against one currency. Using a price index such as the Consumer Price Index as a measuring tool to compare prices at different times. A fictional "market basket" of commonly consumed staples is measured and charted over a period of time (usually one year). If the price of the representative market basket has gone up, inflation has occurred. For example if a typical basket costs $500 this year as compared to $400 last year for the same basket inflation has risen over a year. Inflation reduces the buying power of money, and if uncontrolled can threaten the entire economy. An example of runaway inflation occurred in Germany in the 1930's. Inflation was rampant and people literally had to take barrels of money to markets to exchange for goods and services. This rampant inflation helped bring the Nazis to power. Deflation, the general lowering of prices and the subsequent increase in purchasing power of money is a much less frequent phenomena.

History of money

Money has been defined as any store of value which has intrinsic value or is a representation of a store of value (bank notes). Money is the lifeblood of market transactions, serving as a measure of value, a medium of exchange, and as an accounting convention. As a means to exchange value for goods and services money has no peer. But for this to be the case, money must have a guaranteed and obvious value of its own. Historically, commodities including crops and livestock were the first forms of money. When money became accepted as a representation of commodities, the market system was revolutionized. It made simple trading and quickly became an accepted medium of exchange. In earlier times, money represented the commodities of precious metals, notably gold and silver. In modern economies, money depends on the guarantee of the government to honor its value. These guarantees permit international trade without risk about the value of the money involved.

Qualities of money

All money or forms of exchange share common characteristics which define the store of value of the currency used. Money must be a generally accepted medium for trading and settling debts. Acceptance of money depends on trust in the issuing institution or nation. To be useful as a deferred payment instrument, money must serve as a basic unit of account in an economic system. This requisite is fulfilled if money is seen to be a standard of value through which other goods may be given comparative value. The relative cost of any good or service must be measured against a standard which is the value of money. Perhaps most importantly, money must be accepted a store of value by everyone in an economy. In this manner money is a representation of the essential worth of any traded good or service. The system of deferred payment under which most markets operate make it imperative that money has its own essential store of value resting on the promise of a central bank or nation to honor the currency.

Effects of money in economics

Money is an essential element in economics and forms the basis for individual, business, and government markets. Both the quality and the quantity of money affects the economy in fundamental ways. Central banks manipulate money quantities in order to influence the economy by expanding or contracting available funds. Monetary policies of nations have an important impact on the economies of those countries. It can be used to stimulate growth or to slow an overheated economy. Monetary failure in a economy produces uncertainty and chaotic markets. When the USSR dissolved in the early 1990's a financial crisis occurred that still impacts nations. Defining money in the modern world can be difficult due to the myriad forms of credit available globally. The revolution started by credit cards in the last 50 years has completely changed the nature of exchange in most markets. Money has many substitutes, including demand deposits, savings accounts, credit and debit cards which serve as a store of value that is generally accepted.

Forms of money

The first "money" were commodities that were traded under a barter system. The next advance in the form of money was the minting of coins of precious metals, usually silver and gold. This form of money had intrinsic value but was a very limited resource. It could be transported fairly easily in moderate amounts, and was difficult to forge. The next leap in the form of money was the advent of paper notes, issued and guaranteed by governments. In modern economies money has taken on a variety of new forms, some a result of increasing technological advances. Modern economies feature paper notes backed by the central bank and government who issues them. Coins with a small percentage of silver or gold are also assets honored by central banks. The intrinsic value of precious metals in most coins is negligible. By far the most revolutionary change in the form of money has occurred in the last 100 years. Demand deposits, credit cards, commercial paper, certificates of deposit, mortgages, and public and private promissory notes are all a form of money today.

Wealth

The definition of wealth is both an objective and subjective one. In normal parlance, wealth is understood to consist primarily of money, land, and investments of an individual. However, wealth includes many subjective factors that cannot be measured by strictly economic values. Additionally, concepts of wealth differ between cultures and societies. Economic wealth must be measured in relation to all other individuals in the same economic systems. The income of an average middle-class American would make a third world citizen very wealthy. Within the United States, cost-of-living, income, and taxes vary widely. A wealthy person in Iowa may not be considered wealthy is Los Angeles because of differentials in the economic situations of the two places. Additionally, intangibles such as environmental health, health of the individual, quality of life and dozens of other less objective factors all must be accounted for in considering real wealth.

Limits to Growth debate

Economic growth carries with it substantial costs, both measurable and intangible. Given a world of limited resources, economic growth includes the more rapid depletion of such resources. the combined effects of economic growth on air and water pollution is too great to be measured. The destruction of rainforests and extinction of plant and animal species at an unprecedented rate are added and sometimes hidden costs of economic growth. The combination of rapid growth and resource depletion may eventually stop economic growth completely. The introduction of new technology has fueled the rate of economic growth in the world. This technology may also be able to allow growth without many of the negative results. There are many social scientists and economists who contend growth must slow or stop in order to maintain a level of well being that is acceptable. Other put faith in the ability of mankind to innovate and adjust to allow growth without devastating consequences.

Labor economics

As in all the factors of production, labor has a separate market based on supply and demand. The interaction between employers and workers is the frame of reference of labor economics. The result of these interactions effect labor economics and determine income, employment, and wage levels. Labor economics is a vital field since most countries include maximized employment as an economic priority. When labor economics is studied through the individuals and their role in labor markets, microeconomic methods are used. The larger interactions between labor markets and the demand for goods and services, production, consumption, and investment fall under macroeconomic analysis. Both are necessary and useful methods for evaluating the role that labor plays in economic activity. Most of us are more aware of the macroeconomics of labor which tends to be in the news more often as trends of unemployment and productivity.

High technology economics

Many economists and investors feel the sector of the economy using cutting edge high technological methods is the most promising for economic growth. This conclusion has promoted increased and sometimes speculative investment in high tech fields. But as we learned from the anticipated boom in information technology, reality does not always meet expectations. The so called "dot-com" boom in the last 20 years saw the making of great fortunes but also the loss of investments when companies failed to meet their expected growth. High technology economics still offers uncommon rewards for the astute investor, but must also be regarded as very high risk for investors. Areas usually associated with high technology advances include nanotechnology, information technology, and biotechnology, among many others. High technology industries flourish across the world, making constant progress in developing new techniques and applications for multiple growth industries.

Economic policy

Economic policy refers to the broad planning and implementation of economic measures of the government in regulating and effecting economic activity. It includes wide areas of monetary and fiscal policy, and effects virtually every aspect of an economic system. Politics and social pressures play a major role in influencing economic policy. International agencies and institutions such as the World Bank may also play a part in determining economic policy.

Several general areas of economic policy may be identified:
1. Fiscal policy and stance refers to the government deficit or surplus and the methods of financing government operations.
2. Policies on taxation include changing tax regulations, enforcing tax codes, and the methodology of tax collection.
3. Government spending for usual operations of the government and special allocations for natural disasters and war.
4. Determining the amount of money in circulation.
5. The determination of interest rates that fall under government control.
6. International trade policy including tariffs, reciprocal trade arrangements, and trade treaties.
7. The rules and regulations that apply to the banking system.

Economic policy goals and tools
Governments and economies usually set goals for their economic plans and policy decisions. Goals are short-tern and long-term ones, and focus on big picture elements such as inflation control, employment levels, and economic growth rates. These policy goals are implemented with economic tools that include monetary and fiscal policy, increases or decreases in government spending, international trade practices, regulation of labor markets, and many additional methods. Often goals are not exclusively economic, as with defense and other areas of the general welfare. A government must determine which short term goals are most important to its policy. It may be impossible to reduce inflation while promoting more employment at the same time. Governments are usually more successful with a few short term goals that work with each other to affect long

- 156 -

term goals. A consistent policy approach to economic problems is essential to achieve economic goals.

Opportunity cost

The opportunity cost of an economic decision is always the cost of what opportunity is sacrificed by making that decision.

For example, a person may have enough money for a vacation in Europe, or enough to purchase a new automobile, but not both. The opportunity cost of buying the automobile will be the trip to Europe. These decisions are made usually on the utility of each choice - which would provide the most pleasure to the consumer. In a complex economy, there are many competing factors that provide utility. An individual, firm, or government will always choose what they perceive to be the choice that will be most beneficial given limited resources.

These choices are usually not clear-cut and many factors go into some economic decisions. This is more common when companies or governments have to choose between a number of needed and attractive choices. Different parts of society or firms will have much different ideas about the best way in which to utilize their resources.

Theories of value

Placing value on goods and services has been a problem concerning economists for centuries. Many scholastic and scientific arguments of the reformation period focused on the definition of value. The classical argument of value is illustrated in the "diamond-water paradox". It is pointed out that in comparisons of these goods, water is essential to life and either free or available at a low price. Diamonds, on the other hand are an unnecessary luxury and are very expensive.

Classical economic thinkers claimed that value could only be measured as the cost of production of the product. The difficulty and expense of making a good available imputed it with intrinsic value. Both Adam Smith and David Ricardo promulgated this theory of value.

Another school of thought on determining value stated that the value of anything was completely subjective. Nothing is valuable in and of itself, and only the perceived value imputed by the consumer is valid. This school, called the subjective theory of value, asserted itself in through the 20th century.

Income

Income, in common parlance, is the compensation received by economic units during the normal activities of business. This includes monies received from multiple sources including employers, investments, and gifts.

In the business world, gross income is the amount a company earns before expenses. Net income is the money the company has earned after paying the costs of doing business. A company's revenue flow starts with monies received from goods and services sold to consumers. From this amount must be subtracted all monies spent in the operations of the business. This includes employees salaries, costs of production, fixed and variable costs of doing business, and any intangible costs. The resulting figure is the firm's income (or loss). If a profit is made, this may be paid as additional compensation to owners, appropriate tax levies, or reinvested to improve the company's position in some respect. Publicly held corporations may choose to pay their stockholders a dividend.

Per capita income vs. personal income

The calculation of per capita income is made by taking the total of all monies earned by residents of a particular area divided by the number of inhabitants of the region. Note that per capita income is based on where the individuals live, rather than where they actually physically work. The aggregate of all monies is called Total Personal Income. This figure includes all earnings paid to individuals, transfer payments (social security for example), and investment income from all sources. the relative economic health of a particular area can be measured in part by per capita income and Total Personal Income.

Passive income is also accounted for in Total Personal Income. These are monies derived from rents, private portfolios of stocks and bonds, earned interest from any source, and various payments from pension funds and other employee retirement programs.

Another class of income is derived from government transfer payments. These include various social and disability benefits, as well as compensation for the unemployed.

Perfect competition vs. monopolistic competition

There is no such thing as perfect competition in the real world. It exists only as an economic model, describing a theoretical market where the base of producers and consumers is so large that they are unable to influence prices. Ideally this would lead to a textbook definition of economic efficiency. For perfect competition to exist, products are essentially the same, each type being an equal substitute for another. Prices are set by the market, and firms must accept this determination. All businesses must have equal access to existing information, raw materials, and the latest technology.

Monopolistic competition has a different set of standards. Usually there are numerous producers and a great number of consumers in any market. No regulations exist to entering or leaving the market, and consumers have more product knowledge and have definite choices between products. These markets give individual companies more influence over their markets. They may raise or lower prices and make adjustments based on the response of the market.

Taxation

Any assessment or charge to an individual economic unit by a government or quasi-government may be termed a tax.

Some taxes are direct, such as a sales tax on goods and services sold. Other taxes may be indirect, property taxes being a prime example.

Taxation has a long history dating back to biblical times. It is often mentioned in the Old and New Testaments. Earlier economic systems received "taxes" as goods and services rendered to a ruling authority. In contemporary economics, we usually think of taxes in terms of legal currency.

Taxes have caused revolutions, "No taxation without representation," overturned governments, and have become a social and political issue of controversy and debate. Who should pay taxes, how much should be paid, and the use of tax revenue are all critical issues in the fabric of society.

The branch of formal economics most concerned with taxes is public finance.

History of taxes
Nations, states, and local governments use taxes to finance their operations and for special purposes. Typical uses of tax revenue are for public utilities, promotion of public safety and defense, reinvesting in capital improvement and replacement projects for the public, general operating expenses of the state, and to fund public and welfare services.

Other uses for tax revenues include social benefits for retired and disabled citizens, public transportation systems, compensation for those unable to work, educational uses, public health and healthcare systems, and waste removal operations.

Governments also use taxes to stimulate or contract the economy, alter resource allocations in the economic system, insure an equitable tax burden on all citizens, and to change patterns of income distribution for members of a society.

Taxation and its revenues have become an important proactive tool for economists attempting to fine tune macroeconomic activities.

Tax rates

Tax rates are a percentage figure levied on the tax base to raise revenues. When the tax base is a good, service, or property, the tax is called an ad valorem tax. Examples of ad valorem taxes are common, including most property and sales taxes. Value added taxes, common in Western Europe, add a "hidden" tax to all goods and services, (with a few exceptions) computed on the added value at each stage of the manufacturing process. An excise tax is a tax levied on a tax base of a determined figure. Excess profit taxes are an example of an excise tax. Tax rates may be either marginal rates or average rates. To compute the average tax rate, the total tax revenue is compared to the total tax base as a ratio. Marginal tax rates are those imposed on the next unit of currency earned. For example, in a progressive income taxation system the marginal tax rate will differ from person to person, depending on their income. Typically tax brackets are the framework for determining marginal rates of taxes at various income levels.

Business competition

Competition is the driving force that is the life blood of capitalism. It tends to motivate innovations, and promotes efficient use of resources and profits. Microeconomic theory holds that competition is the most important factor in determining resource allocation.

Competition forces companies to develop new products and improve existing ones. It spurs technology, refines production capability, and thus provides consumers with an abundance of superior products and services. Competition tends to stabilize prices and insures no one major supplier can dominate an industry.

Competition may find two products competing head-to-head in direct competition. Sometimes firms develop similar products that may be used instead of existing ones, an example of substitute competition. Most competition is seen in pricing, production costs, product mixes, marketing, channels of distribution and consumer satisfaction. These elements fall under the umbrella of budget competition.

Direct vs. indirect taxation

Direct taxes are defined as those that are imposed and collected directly from the economic units being taxed.

For example, income taxes are levied and collected from the individual or business that actually receives monies as income.

Indirect taxes, by contrast, are collected from a third party who is not the being actually taxed. Value added taxes are indirect taxes, hidden from the consumer who pays an increased retail or wholesale price that includes the value added tax.

Statutes determine for whom the tax is being collected. The individual who ends up paying the tax is another matter. For example, a tax may be placed on alcoholic beverages of all kinds. Only those who choose to consume these products will actually be subject to the tax. Laws of supply and demand in the marketplace will determine the individuals that will pay this tax. if an individual chooses not to buy wine, beer, or liquor, they will be, in effect, exempt from that tax. the more a person consumes the taxed items, the more tax will be paid by that individual.

Scarcity and choice

Economics could rightfully be called the study of scarcity. Limited resources are available to satisfy the wants and needs of both individuals and states. Economics involves the choices made by an economy to satisfy these wants and needs. Every economy must choose what goods and services to produce, how to produce them, and for whom they are intended. Limitations of the factors of production - land, labor, and capital, sometimes make these choices difficult.

When an economic choice is made, there is an "opportunity cost" implicit in the choice. The opportunity cost is what is given up by making a choice. If a country chooses to manufacture automobiles, it may not have the industrial capacity to produce tanks or aircraft. Thus, the economic choice to make automobiles involves the opportunity cost of not making tanks or aircraft. Individuals and countries continually make economic choices and sacrifice opportunist costs in the process. An individual may choose to attend a film rather than go out to dinner. Choices are driven by what people and countries feel is in their best interest.

Principles of supply and demand

A competitive market is composed of buyers and sellers engaged in trade in an organized manner. Price and the amount of products sold are determined by the supply of and demand for the goods or services. Microeconomics is the study of these market factors to understand and predict market activity.

A central tenet of the market is when demand exceeds supply of a good or service, the price will rise. However, when supply exceeds demand for a good or service the price will fall. The constant flux of demand, supply, and price always tends toward equilibrium - when supply and demand equal each other. In real economic systems, this point is rarely reached, and if so, only briefly. In a complex economy, where there are endless choices to be made, demand and supply only occasionally reach an equilibrium. Elements of economic choice and the opportunity cost of such choices make it very difficult for demand and supply to be equal for a particular good or service.

Causes of the Great Depression

The Great Depression, which began in 1929 with the Stock Market Crash, grew out of several factors that had developed over the previous years including:

- Growing economic disparity between the rich and middle-class, with the rich amassing wealth much more quickly than the lower classes
- Disparity in economic distribution in industries
- Growing use of credit, leading to an inflated demand for some goods
- Government support of new industries rather than providing additional support for agriculture
- Risky stock market investments, leading to the stock market crash

Additional factors contributing to the Depression also included the Labor Day Hurricane in the Florida Keys (1935) and the Great Hurricane of 1938, in Long Island, along with the Dust Bowl in the Great Plains, which destroyed crops and resulted in the displacement of as many as 2.5 million people.

The Great Depression was the result of a number of converging factors. For one thing, there was an agricultural depression in the 1920s brought on by tremendous post-war surpluses. The automobile and housing industries both experienced diminished demand in the 20s. One major problem was that wealth was so unevenly distributed: one-third of the nation's wealth was controlled by 5% of the population. There was not much in the way of international trade, in part because of Hoover's high tariff. Overproduction on assembly lines led to factory surpluses and unemployment. Finally, there was persistent unsound speculation in the stock markets. By 1929, many stocks were considered to be overvalued and thus no one was buying them. This caused the catastrophic market crashes of Black Thursday and Black Tuesday (October 24 and 29, 1929), in which 40% of the market value (about $30 billion) was lost.

Hoover and the Great Depression

Hoover's first strategy for combating the Great Depression was to balance the budget, reduce federal spending, keep the US on the gold standard, and just wait it out. Later, he developed some work-relief programs, employing people on public work projects. The Hoover Dam was one of those projects. Hoover also created the Reconstruction Finance Group, which loaned money directly to state and local governments as well as to railroads and banks. Hoover's aid projects were unprecedented; still, he resisted giving direct aid to the people in the form of welfare. World War I veterans descended on Washington in 1932 when they were told that their pensions would not be paid until 1945. These so-called "Bonus Marchers" eventually had to be dispersed with force, leading many citizens to believe that the country was descending into anarchy. The 20th amendment, known as the anti-Hoover amendment, actually brought the date of the next inauguration forward.

Capitalism

Capitalism is an economic system in which the means of production are privately owned, in which the investment of capital, and the production, distribution and prices of goods and services are determined in a free market, and in which the goal of production is to generate profits. The features of a capitalist economic system include a private sector, private property, free enterprise, and profit. Other features of a capitalist economic system include unequal distribution of wealth, competition, self-organization, the existence of markets, the existence of both a bourgeoisie class and a proletariat class, and the pursuit of self-interest.

Basics of a market economy

A market economy is based on supply and demand. Demand has to do with what customers want and need, as well as how quantity those consumers are able to purchase based on other economic factors. Supply refers to how much can be produced to meet demand, or how much suppliers are willing and able to sell. Where the needs of consumers meet the needs of suppliers is referred to as a market equilibrium price. This price varies depending on many factors, including the overall health of a society's economy, overall beliefs and considerations of individuals in society, and other factors.

Planned economy vs. market economy

In a market economy, supply and demand are determined by consumers.

In a planned economy, a public entity or planning authority makes the decisions about what resources will be produced, how they will be produced, and who will be able to benefit from them. The means of production, such as factories, are also owned by a public entity rather than by private interests.

In market socialism, the economic structure falls somewhere between the market economy and the planned economy. Planning authorities determine allocation of resources at higher economic levels, while consumer goods are driven by a market economy.

Unemployment and inflation

When demand outstrips supply, prices are driven artificially high, or inflated. This occurs when too much spending causes an imbalance in the economy. In general, inflation occurs because an economy is growing too quickly.

When there is too little spending and supply has moved far beyond demand, a surplus of product results. Companies cut back on production, reduce the number of workers they employ, and unemployment rises as people lose their jobs. This imbalance occurs when an economy becomes sluggish.

In general, both these economic instability situations are caused by an imbalance between supply and demand. Government intervention is often necessary to stabilize an economy when either inflation or unemployment becomes too serious.

E-commerce

The growth of the Internet has brought many changes to our society, not the least of which is the ways we do business. Where supply channels used to have to move in certain ways, many of these channels are now bypassed as e-commerce makes it possible for nearly any individual to set up a direct market to consumers, as well as direct interaction with suppliers. Competition is fierce. In many instances e-commerce can provide nearly instantaneous gratification, with a wide variety of products. Whoever provides the best product most quickly often rises to the top of a marketplace. How this added element to the marketplace will affect the economy in the near and not-so-near future remains to be seen. Many industries are still struggling with the best ways to adapt to the rapid, continuous changes.

Effects of the Industrial Revolution

The Industrial Revolution led to widespread education, a wider franchise, and the development of mass communication in the political arena.

Economically, conflicts arose between companies and their employees, as struggles for fair treatment and fair wages increased. Unions gained power and became more active. Government regulation over industries increased, but at the same time, growing businesses fought for the right to free enterprise.

In the social sphere, populations increased and began to concentrate around centers of industry. Cities became larger and more densely populated. Scientific advancements led to more efficient agriculture, greater supply of goods, and increased knowledge of medicine and sanitation, leading to better overall health.

Globalism

In the modern era, globalism has emerged as a popular political ideology. Globalism is based in the idea that all people and all nations are interdependent. Each nation is dependent on one or more other nations for production of and markets for goods, and for income generation. Today's ease of international travel and communication, including technological advances such as the airplane, has heightened this sense of interdependence.

The global economy, and the general idea of globalism, has shaped many economic and political choices since the beginning of the twentieth century. Many of today's issues, including environmental awareness, economic struggles, and continued warfare, often require the cooperation of many countries if they are to be dealt with effectively.

Affect of globalization on the way countries interact with each other

With countries worldwide often seeking the same resources, some, particularly nonrenewable resources, have experienced high demand. At times this has resulted in wild price fluctuations. One major example is the demand for petroleum products such as oil and natural gas.

Increased travel and communication make it possible to deal with diseases in remote locations; however, it also allows diseases to be spread via travelers, as well.

A major factor contributing to increased globalization over the past few decades has been the Internet. By allowing instantaneous communication with anyone nearly anywhere on the globe, the Internet has led to interaction between far-flung individuals and countries, and an ever increasing awareness of happenings all over the world.

United States currency system

The Constitution of 1787 gave the United States Congress the central authority to print or coin money and to regulate its value. Before this time, states were permitted to maintain separate currencies.

The currency system is based on a modified gold standard. There is an enormous store of gold to back up United States currency housed at Fort Knox, Kentucky.

Paper money is actually Federal Reserve notes and coins. It is the job of the Bureau of Engraving and Printing in the Treasury Department to design plates, special types of paper, and other security measures for bills and bonds. This money is put into general circulation by the Treasury and Federal Reserve Banks, and is taken out of circulation when worn out. Coins are made at the Bureau of the Mint in Philadelphia, Denver, and San Francisco.

Economic principles of supply and demand

Supply is the amount of a product or service available to consumers. Demand is how much consumers are willing to pay for the product or service. These two facets of the market determine the price of goods and services. The higher the demand, the higher the price the supplier will charge; the lower the demand, the lower the price.

Scarcity is a measure of supply in that demand is high when there is a scarcity, or low supply, of an item. Choice is related to scarcity and demand in that when an item in demand is scarce, consumers have to make difficult choices. They can pay more for an item, go without it, or go elsewhere for the item.

Money is the cash or currency available for payment. Resources are the items one can barter in exchange for goods. Money is also the cash reserves of a nation, while resources are the minerals, labor force, armaments, and other raw materials or assets a nation has available for trade.

Abundant natural resources can result in negative effects

The positive economic aspects of abundant natural resources are an increase in revenue and new jobs where those resources have not been previously accessed. For example, the growing demand for oil, gas, and minerals has led companies to venture into new regions.

The negative economic aspects of abundant natural resources are:
- Environmental degradation, if sufficient regulations are not in place to counter strip mining, deforestation, and contamination.
- Corruption, if sufficient regulations are not in place to counter bribery, political favoritism, and exploitation of workers as greedy companies try to maximize their profits.
- Social tension, if the resources are privately owned such that the rich become richer and the poor do not reap the benefits of their national resources. Class divisions become wider, resulting in social unrest.
- Dependence, if the income from the natural resources is not used to develop other industries as well. In this situation, the economy becomes dependent on one source, and faces potential crises if natural disasters or depletion take away that income source.

Kinds of economies

Economics is the study of the buying choices that people make, the production of goods and services, and how our market system works.

The two kinds of economies are command and market. In a command economy, the government controls what and how much is produced, the methods used for production, and the distribution of goods and services. In a market economy, producers make decisions about methods and distribution on their own. These choices are based on what will sell and bring a profit in the marketplace. In a market economy, consumers ultimately affect these decisions by choosing whether or not to buy certain goods and services. The United States has a market economy.

Characteristics of a market economy

The five characteristics of a market economy are:
- Economic freedom – There is freedom of choice with respect to jobs, salaries, production, and price.
- Economic incentives – A positive incentive is to make a profit. However, if the producer tries to make too high a profit, the consequences might be that no one will purchase the item at that price. A negative incentive would be a drop in profits, causing the producer to decrease or discontinue production. A boycott, which might cause the producer to change business practices or policies, is also a negative economic incentive.
- Competition – There is more than one producer for any given product. Consumers thereby have choices about what to buy, which are usually made based on quality and price. Competition is an incentive for a producer to make the best product at the best price. Otherwise, producers will lose business to the competition.
- Private ownership – Production and profits belong to an individual or to a private company, not to the government.
- Limited government – Government plays no role in the economic decisions of its individual citizens.

Factors of production and economic flow

The factors of production are:
- Land – This includes not only actual land, but also forests, minerals, water, etc.
- Labor – This is the work force required to produce goods and services, including factors such as talent, skills, and physical labor.
- Capital – This is the cash and material equipment needed to produce goods and services, including buildings, property, tools, office equipment, roads, etc.
- Entrepreneurship – Persons with initiative can capitalize on the free market system by producing goods and services.

The two types of markets are factor and product markets. The factor market consists of the people who exchange their services for wages. The people are sellers and companies are buyers. The product market is the selling of products to the people who want to buy them. The people are the buyers and the companies are the sellers. This exchange creates a circular economic flow in which money goes from the producers to workers as wages, and then flows back to producers in the form of payment for products.

Economic impact of technology

At the start of the 21st century, the role of information and communications technologies (ICT) grew rapidly as the economy shifted to a knowledge-based one. Output is increasing in areas where ICT is used intensively, which are service areas and knowledge-intensive industries such as finance; insurance; real estate; business services, health care, and environmental goods and services; and community, social, and personal services. Meanwhile, the economic share for manufacturers is declining in medium- and low-technology industries such as chemicals, food products, textiles, gas, water, electricity, construction, and transport and communication services. Industries that have traditionally been high-tech, such as aerospace, computers, electronics, and pharmaceuticals are remaining steady in terms of their economic share.

Technology has become the strongest factor in determining per capita income for many countries. The ease of technology investments as compared to industries that involve factories and large labor forces has resulted in more foreign investments in countries that do not have natural resources to call upon.

Government and Citizenship

Roe v. Wade

Roe v. Wade was a controversial 1973 U.S. Supreme Court case. The case originated in 1970 in Texas, which had an anti-abortion law. The plaintiff was an unmarried pregnant woman who was assigned the name "Jane Roe" to protect her identity. Texas anti-abortion law characterized the acts of having or attempting to perform an abortion as crimes, with the exception of cases in which an abortion could save the life of a mother. The lawsuit argued that the Texas law was unconstitutionally vague and was not consistent with the rights guaranteed by the First, Fourth, Fifth, Ninth, and Fourteenth Amendments. While the Texas court ruled in favor of Roe, it did not rule that Texas had to discontinue the enforcement of its anti-abortion law. Roe appealed to the Supreme Court in 1971, and the court's decision in 1973 struck down Texas's abortion laws. The case overturned most state laws prohibiting abortion.

Brown v. Board of Education

Brown versus the Board of Education of Topeka was a Supreme Court case that was decided in 1954. The case made it illegal for racial segregation to exist within public education facilities. This decision was based on the finding that separate but equal public educational facilities would not provide black and white students with the same standard of facilities. The case originated in 1951, when a lawsuit was filed by Topeka parents, who were recruited by the NAACP, against the Board of Education of the City of Topeka, Kansas in a U.S. District Court. The parents, one of whom was named Oliver Brown, wanted the Topeka Board of Education to eliminate racial segregation. The District Court agreed that segregation had negative effects, but did not force the schools to desegregate because it found that black and white school facilities in the District were generally equal in standards. The case was appealed to the Supreme Court, where the finding was that separate educational facilities are unequal.

Plessy v. Ferguson

Plessy v. Ferguson was an 1896 Supreme Court case. The case resulted in the decision that de jure racial segregation in public facilities was legal in the United States, and permitted states to restrict blacks from using public facilities. The case originated when, in 1890, a black man named Homer Plessy decided to challenge a Louisiana law that segregated blacks and whites on trains by sitting in the white section of a train. Plessy was convicted of breaking the law in a Louisiana court, and the case was appealed to the U.S. Supreme Court, where the Supreme Court upheld the Louisiana decision. The case established the legality of the doctrine of separate but equal, thereby allowing racial segregation. The decision was later overturned by Brown versus the Board of Education of Topeka.

Process of Making Amendments to the U.S. Constitution

The process for making amendments to the U.S. Constitution are outlined in Article Five of the Constitution. Amendments can be proposed by either two thirds of both chambers of the United States Congress or by a convention of at least two thirds of the legislatures of the states. Before an amendment can be included in the Constitution, it must be ratified by three fourths of the legislatures of the states, or by three fourths of special conventions that have been assembled in each of the states for the purpose of ratifying the Constitutional amendment. The President of the United States plays no official part in the process of making constitutional amendments. To date, twenty-seven amendments have been ratified and included in the Constitution.

Making of laws

Laws can originate in either the House of Representatives or the Senate. When a Congressman wants to propose a new law, that person sponsors the bill and introduces it to the respective Congressional chamber by either giving it to the clerk or placing it in a special box known as the hopper. A legislative number is assigned to the bill, designated by H.R. for bills originating in the House of Representatives or S. for bills originating in the Senate. The bill is printed and given to all members of the house. The bill is assigned to a committee for investigation and discussion, which often involves hearings.

Following an investigation into a proposed bill the committee either releases the bill and recommends that it be passed, recommends that the bill be revised prior to being released, or sets it aside so that it cannot be voted on. If a bill is released it is added to a calendar of bills waiting to be voted on. On the floor of the chamber the bill is read and if it passes by a simple majority it goes to the other Congressional house. In order for the bill to be introduced in the other house, a member of that house must announce the introduction of it. The same process of being assigned to a committee and investigation is repeated in the second house. If the bill also passes by a simple majority in the second house, it goes to a conference committee comprised of members of both houses.

The conference committee reconciles any differences between the two houses with regard to the bill and if any alterations are made the committee sends the bill back to each house for final approval. After the bill has been approved it is printed, or enrolled, and certified. The enrolled bill is the signed by both the Speaker of the House and the Vice President, who is the leader of the Senate. After the bill has received the necessary signatures, it is sent to the President of the United States, where he must sign it within ten days or veto it. If the President signs the bill it becomes law. If the President chooses to veto the bill, it is sent back to Congress, and if two-thirds of both houses vote to pass the bill, it becomes law without the President's signature.

State versus Federal Government

Initially, government systems in the United States were characterized as state governments that were essentially self-governed. These circumstances in the early days of the United States represented an aversion to the centralized government that was present in England, the colonial power that first controlled America. The state government system proved to be insufficient and therefore the Constitution was written to delineate the powers afforded to a federal government. The Constitution also delineates the relationship between the federal and state governments. The system instituted in the Constitution is a known as a federalist system, in which powers are shared between the federal and state governments. Specific powers are allocated to the federal government, while other powers remain in the hands of state governments.

Powers of State Governments

Each state government reserves the power to issue state licenses, the power to regulate business and commerce within the boundaries of the state, the power to hold elections, the power to create local governments, the power to ratify Constitutional amendments, and the power to regulate public health and safety. The state governments may also exercise powers that are not explicitly stipulated in the United States Constitution as being held by the federal government. Similarly, the state governments may exercise powers that the Constitution does not explicitly restrict the states from exercising.

Powers denied to State Governments
There are a number of powers that are denied to state governments within the United States of America. These restrictions are stipulated by the Constitution of the United States. States are restricted from doing anything that the federal government is restricted from doing. States are also restricted from forming alliances or confederations. States are restricted from declaring war and maintaining navies. State governments are restricted from making and entering into treaties with foreign countries. In addition state governments are restricted from making money. State governments are also restricted from placing taxes on imports and exports from or to other states, respectively. States are restricted from preventing the requirements of a contract from being met as well. Finally, states are restricted from taking away an individual's rights without due process of law.

Powers of the Federal Government

The national, or federal, government reserves powers that are not afforded to the states. The national government has the power to print money, the power to regulate business and commerce between states, the power to regulate business and commerce between the United States and other countries, the power to create treaties and to carry our foreign policies, the power to declare war, the power to maintain military forces, and the power to create post offices. The national government also has the power to create laws that are deemed essential to carrying out all of the other powers that are constitutionally granted to the national government.

Powers denied to the Federal Government
There are a number of powers that are denied to the national, or federal, government of the United States of America. These restrictions are stipulated by the Constitution of the United States. The

federal government is restricted from breaking or abusing the Bill of Rights. The federal government is also restricted from placing taxes on exports from one state to another state. In addition, the federal government is restricted from using funds from the United States Treasury unless an appropriations bill is passed and approved. Finally, the federal government is restricted from altering state borders.

Concurrent Powers

While both the national and state governments reserve specific powers that the other does not have, there are certain powers that are shared between the national and state governments. These shared powers are known as concurrent powers. The concurrent powers that are shared by both the national government and the state governments include the power to collect taxes, the power to build roads, the power to borrow money, the power to create courts, the power to create and enforce laws, the power to establish banks and corporations, the power to spend funds in the interest of the general welfare of the United States and its citizens, and the power to take private property for purposes that benefit the public so long as just compensation is provided.

Powers denied to both the federal and state governments

There are a number of powers that are denied to both the federal government and state governments in the United States of America. These restrictions are stipulated by the Constitution of the United States. The federal government and state governments are restricted from conferring titles of nobility. Both levels of government are also restricted from allowing slavery to take place; this restriction is specifically stated in the thirteenth amendment of the United States Constitution. The federal and state governments are also restricted from prohibiting citizens of the United States from exercising their right to vote based on race, color, or based on previous conditions of servitude; this restriction is specifically stated in the fifteenth amendment of the United States Constitution. Finally, both the federal and state governments are also restricted from prohibiting citizens of the United States from exercising their right to vote based on gender; this restriction is explicitly stated in the nineteenth amendment of the United States Constitution.

State Constitutions

In the United States, state governments each have a unique state constitution. State constitutions resemble the federal Constitution in many ways. However, state constitutions may not be in disaccord with the federal Constitution. State governments have control over affairs that occur within state boundaries, such as communications within state boundaries, regulations concerning property, industry, business, and public utilities, criminal codes, and labor conditions. There are also numerous matters over which state and federal government shares jurisdiction. State constitutions differ from one another with regard to some issues, but typically they all are laid out similarly to the federal Constitution. All state constitutions contain a section on people's rights and a section that outlines how government should be organized. Every state constitution also stipulates that ultimate authority rests with the people and establishes specific standards and values as the basis of government.

State Executive and Legislative Branches

State governments are divided into executive, legislative, and judicial branches, just as in the federal government. In a state government, the governor serves as the head of the executive branch. The governor is elected by popular vote for a term of either two or four years depending on the state. Every state in the U.S. has a bicameral legislature except Nebraska, which has a single legislative body. The bicameral legislature is divided into an upper house and a lower house. The upper house is typically referred to as the Senate, as in the federal government, and the lower house can be referred to by a number of names, including the House of Representatives, the House of Delegates, or the General Assembly. State senators typically serve for a term of four years, while members of the House of Representatives, House of Delegates or the General Assembly serve for a term of two years.

State and Local Courts

Every state has a court system that is independent and distinct from the federal court system. The hierarchy of the state court system includes trial courts at the lowest level; appellate courts are the highest courts in the state court system. The great majority, over ninety-five percent, of the court cases in the United States are heard and decided in state courts and local courts, which also fall under the jurisdiction of the states. Depending on the state, there may be one or two appellate courts within the state. States organize and name their courts differently. Typically, lower courts are assigned specific names and authority to hear specific types of cases, such as family courts and probate courts. Beneath the specialized trial courts are more informal trial courts, including magistrate courts and justice of the peace courts, which typically do not involve a jury.

Separation of powers

Government at both the federal and state levels is characterized by a separation of powers. At the local level, the organization of government is different. State and local government often distinguishes between executive powers and law enforcement powers by allowing citizens to choose public prosecutors through elections. In some states citizens elect judges as well. In local governments, the election of individuals who represent special authority, such as police chiefs and members of school boards, serves to separate such individuals from the executive and legislative branches of government. At the local level, juries also have a significant role in maintaining the system of checks and balances, as they have the sole authority to determine the facts in most criminal and civil cases, restricting the power of the executive and judicial branches in enforcement of laws.

Democratic Party

The Democratic Party was founded in 1792. In the United States, it is one of the two dominant political parties, along with the Republican Party. The Democratic Party is to the left of the Republican Party. The Democratic Party began as a conservative party in the mid-1800s, shifting to the left during the 1900s. There are many factions within the Democratic Party in the United States. The Democratic National Committee (DNC) is the official organization of the Democratic Party, and it develops and promotes the party's platform and coordinates fundraising and election strategies. There are Democratic committees in every U.S. state and most U.S. counties. The official symbol of the Democratic Party is the donkey.

Republican Party

The Republican Party is often referred to as the GOP, which stands for Grand Old Party. The Republican Party is considered socially conservative and economically neoliberal relative to the Democratic Party. Like the Democratic Party, there are factions within the Republic Party that agree with the party's overall ideology, but disagree with the party's positions on specific issues.

The official symbol of the Republican Party is the elephant. The Republican National Committee (RNC) is the official organization of the Republican Party, and it develops and promotes the party's platform and coordinates fundraising and election strategies. There are Republican committees in every U.S. state and most U.S. counties.

Presidential Elections

The President of the United States is elected indirectly, by members of an electoral college. Members of the electoral college nearly always vote along the lines of the popular vote of their respective states. The winner of a presidential election is the candidate with at least 270 Electoral College votes. It is possible for a candidate to win the electoral vote, and lose the popular vote. Incumbent Presidents and challengers typically prefer a balanced ticket, where the President and Vice President are elected together and generally balance one another with regard to geography, ideology, or experience working in government. The nominated Vice Presidential candidate is referred to as the President's running mate.

State and local elections

State elections are regulated by state laws and constitutions. In keeping with the ideal of separation of powers, the legislature and the executive are elected separately at the state level, as they are at the federal level. In each state, a Governor and a Lieutenant Governor are elected. In some states, the Governor and Lieutenant Governor are elected on a joint ticket, while in other states they are elected separately from one another. In some states, executive positions such as Attorney General and Secretary of State are also elected offices. All members of state legislatures are elected, including state senators and state representatives. Depending on the state, members of the state supreme court and other members of the state judiciary may be chosen in elections. Local government can include the governments of counties and cities. At this level, nearly all government offices are filled through an election process. Elected local offices may include sheriffs, county school boards, and city mayors.

Representative Democracy

In a system of government characterized as a representative democracy, voters elect representatives to act in their interests. Typically, a representative is elected by and responsible to a specific subset of the total population of eligible voters; this subset of the electorate is referred to as a representative's constituency. A representative democracy may foster a more powerful legislature than other forms of government systems; to compensate for a strong legislature, most constitutions stipulate that measures must be taken to balance the powers within government, such as the creation of a separate judicial branch. Representative democracy became popular in post-industrial nations where increasing numbers of people expressed an interest in politics, but where technology and census counts remained incompatible with systems of direct democracy. Today, the majority of the world's population resides in representative democracies, including constitutional monarchies that possess a strong representative branch.

Authoritarianism

Authoritarian regimes enforce strong, even oppressive, measures against individuals that fall within their sphere of influence; they often arise when a governing body presumes that it knows what is right for a nation and enforces it. They are typically led by an elite group that employs repressive measures to maintain power, and they do not generally make efforts to gain the consent of individuals or permit feedback on their policies. Under an authoritarian government, people are often subject to government control over aspects of their lives that in many other systems would be considered personal matters. There is a spectrum of authoritarian ideologies. Examples of authoritarian regimes include absolute monarchies and dictatorships. Democracies can also exhibit authoritarian characteristics in some situations, such as efforts to promote national security. Authoritarian governments typically extend broad-reaching powers to law enforcement bodies, sometimes resulting in a police state, they may or may not have a rule of law, and are often corrupt.

Totalitarianism

Totalitarianism is a form of authoritarian political system in which the government regulates practically every aspect of public and private conduct. Under totalitarianism, individuals and institutions are enveloped into the state's ideology, and the government imposes its political authority by exercising absolute and centralized control over all aspects of life. Individuals are subordinate to the state, and opposition to political and cultural expression is suppressed. Totalitarian regimes do not tolerate activities by individuals or groups that are not geared toward achieving the state's goals and maintaining the state's ideology. A totalitarian regime maintains power via the use of secret police, propaganda disseminated through government controlled media, regulation and restriction of free speech, and use of terror tactics.

Communism

Communism is a form of an authoritarian, or in some cases totalitarian, political system. A communist country is governed by a single political party that upholds the principles of Marxism-Leninism. The goal of communism is to dissolve the state into a classless society. According to Marxism, a communist state is one in which the resources and means of production are communally owned rather than individually owned and which provides for equal sharing of all freedoms, work and benefits. Marxism argues that socialism is a necessary intermediate phase in achieving communism. Therefore, states that are governed by a communist party are actually socialist states, and not true communist states, since a true communist state could not exist given the goal of elimination of the state. Historically, communist states have often arisen during political instability. Within communist states there have rarely been restrictions on state power, resulting in state structures which are totalitarian or authoritarian. Marxist-Leninist ideology views any restriction on state power as an interference in the goal of reaching communism.

Fascism

Fascism is an authoritarian political ideology and defined the form of rule in Italy from 1922 to 1943 under the leadership under Mussolini. Fascism is characterized by efforts to exert state control over all aspects of life, to hold the nation and political party above the individual, and to hold the state as supreme. Fascism also emphasizes loyalty to a single leader, and submission to a single nationalistic culture. Fascists support corporatism as an economic system, in which economic and social interests of diverse individuals are combined with the interests of the state.

Monarchy

Monarchy, or rule by a single individual, is one of the oldest forms of government and is defined as an autocratic system in which a monarch serves as Head of State. In such a system, the monarch holds office for life. Also included in a monarchy are the individuals and institutions that comprise the royal establishment. In elective monarchies, monarchs are appointed to their position for life;

in most instances, elective monarchies been succeeded by hereditary monarchies. In a hereditary monarchy, the title of monarch is inherited according to a line of succession; typically one family can trace its origin along a dynasty or bloodline. Most monarchs represent merely a symbol of continuity and statehood, rather than actually serving as a participant in partisan politics. The practice of choosing a monarch varies between countries. A constitutional monarchy is one in which the rule of succession is typically established by a law passed by a representative body.

Democracy

Democracy, or rule by the people, is a form of government in which power is vested in the people and in which policy decisions are made by the majority in a decision-making process such as an election that is open to all or most citizens. Definitions of democracy have become more generalized and include aspects of society and political culture in democratic societies that do not necessarily represent a form of government. What defines a democracy varies, but some of the characteristics of a democracy could include the presence of a middle class, the presence of a civil society, a free market, political pluralism, universal suffrage, and specific rights and freedoms. In practice however, democracies do have limits on specific freedoms, which are justified as being necessary to maintain democracy and ensure democratic freedoms. For example, freedom of association is limited in democracies for individuals and groups that pose a threat to government or to society.

A Republic

A republic is a state in which supreme power rests with citizens who vote to elect representatives to be responsible to them. The organization of government in a republic can vary. In most republics the head of state is referred to as the President, and in a democratic republic the head of state is chosen in an election. In some countries the constitution restricts the number of terms that an individual can serve as president. In the United States, where the head of state is also the head of government, the system is known as a presidential system.

Influences of philosophers on political study

Ancient Greek philosophers Aristotle and Plato believed political science would lead to order in political matters, and that this scientifically organized order would create stable, just societies. Thomas Aquinas adapted the ideas of Aristotle to a Christian perspective. His ideas stated that individuals should have certain rights, but also certain duties, and that these rights and duties should determine the type and extent of government rule. In stating that laws should limit the role of government, he laid the groundwork for ideas that would eventually become modern constitutionalism.

Niccolò Machiavelli, author of *The Prince*, was a proponent of politics based solely on power.

Principles of government outlined in the United States Constitution

1. Federalism—the power of the government does not belong entirely to the national government, but is divided between national and state governments.
2. Popular sovereignty—the government is determined by the people, and gains its authority and power from the people.
3. Separation of powers—the government is divided into three branches, executive, legislative and judicial, with each branch having its own set of powers.

4. Judicial review—courts at all levels of government can declare laws invalid if they contradict the constitutions of individual states, or the US Constitution, with the Supreme Court serving as the final judicial authority on decisions of this kind.
5. Checks and balances—no single branch can act without input from another, and each branch has the power to "check" any other, as well as balance other branches' powers.
6. Limited government—governmental powers are limited and certain individual rights are defined as inviolable by the government.

Types of powers delegated to the national government by the US Constitution

The structure of the US government divides powers between national and state governments. Powers delegated to the national government by the Constitution are:
1. Expressed powers—powers directly defined in the Constitution, including power to declare war, regulate commerce, make money, and collect taxes.
2. Implied powers—powers the national government must have in order to carry out the expressed powers.
3. Inherent powers—powers inherent to any government. These powers are not expressly defined in the constitution.

Some of these powers, such as collection and levying of taxes, are also granted to the individual state governments.

Federalism

How federalism functions as a government
Debate on how federalism should function in practice has gone on since the period when the Constitution was being written. There were—and still are—two main factions regarding this issue:
1. States' rights—those favoring the states' rights position feel that the state governments should take the lead in performing local actions to manage various problems.
2. Nationalist—those favoring a nationalist position feel the national government should take the lead to deal with those same matters.

The flexibility of the Constitution has allowed US government to shift and adapt as the needs of the country have changed. Power has often shifted from the state governments to the national government and back again, and both levels of government have developed various ways to influence each other.

How federalism affects policy-making
Federalism has three major effects on public policy in the US.
1. Determining whether the local, state or national government originates policy
2. Affecting how policies are made
3. Ensuring policy-making functions under a set of limitations

Federalism also influences the political balance of power in the US by:
1. making it difficult if not impossible for a single political party to seize total power.
2. ensuring that individuals can participate in the political system at various levels.
3. making it possible for individuals working within the system to be able to affect policy at some level, whether local or more widespread.

- 174 -

Branches of the US Federal government

1. Legislative Branch—consists of the two Houses of Congress: the House of Representatives and the Senate. All members of the Legislative Branch are elected officials.
2. Executive Branch—consists of the President, Vice President, presidential advisors, and other various cabinet members. These advisors are appointed by the President, but must be approved by Congress.
3. Judicial Branch—is made up of the federal court system, headed by the Supreme Court.

Responsibilities
1. The Legislative Branch is largely concerned with law-making. All laws must be approved by Congress before they go into effect. They are also responsible for regulating money and trade, approving presidential appointments, and establishing organizations like the postal service and federal courts. Congress can also propose amendments to the Constitution, and can impeach, or bring charges against, the president. Only Congress can declare war.
2. The Executive Branch carries out laws, treaties, and war declarations enacted by Congress. The President can also veto bills approved by Congress, and serves as commander-in-chief of the US military. The president appoints cabinet members, ambassadors to foreign countries, and federal judges.
3. The Judicial Branch makes decisions on challenges as to whether laws passed by Congress meet the requirements of the US Constitution. The Supreme Court may also choose to review decisions made by lower courts to determine their constitutionality.

Civil liberties vs. civil rights

While the terms civil liberties and civil rights are often used synonymously, in actuality their definitions are slightly different. The two concepts work together, however, to define the basics of a free state.
1. "Civil liberties" defines the role of the state in providing equal rights and opportunities to individuals within that state. An example is non-discrimination policies with regards to granting citizenship.
2. "Civil rights" defines the limitations of state rights, describing those rights that belong to individuals and which cannot be infringed upon by the government. Examples of these rights include freedom of religion, political freedom, and overall freedom to live how we choose.

Voting process

The first elections in the US were held by public ballot. However, election abuses soon became common, since public ballot made it easy to intimidate, threaten, or otherwise influence the votes of individuals or groups of individuals. New practices were put into play, including registering voters before elections took place, and using a secret or Australian ballot.

In 1892, the introduction of the voting machine further privatized the voting process, since it allowed voters to vote in complete privacy. Even today debate continues about the accuracy of various voting methods, including high-tech voting machines and even low tech punch cards.

Contributions of ancient Greece existing today

Ancient Greece made numerous major contributions to cultural development, including:
- Theater—Aristophanes and other Greek playwrights laid the groundwork for modern theatrical performance.
- Alphabet—the Greek alphabet, derived from the Phoenician alphabet, developed into the Roman alphabet, and then into our modern-day alphabet.
- Geometry—Pythagoras and Euclid pioneered much of the system of geometry still taught today. Archimedes made various mathematical discoveries, including the value of pi.
- Historical writing—much of ancient history doubles as mythology or religious texts. Herodotus and Thucydides made use of research and interpretation to record historical events.
- Philosophy—Socrates, Plato, and Aristotle served as the fathers of Western philosophy. Their work is still required reading for philosophy students.

Basic principles of the Constitution

The six basic principles of the Constitution are:
- Popular Sovereignty – The people establish government and give power to it; the government can function only with the consent of the people.
- Limited Government – The Constitution specifies limits on government authority, and no official or entity is above the law.
- Separation of Powers – Power is divided among three government branches: the legislative (Congress), the executive (President), and the judicial (federal courts).
- Checks and Balances – This is a system that enforces the separation of powers and ensures that each branch has the authority and ability to restrain the powers of the other two branches, thus preventing tyranny.
- Judicial Review – Judges in the federal courts ensure that no act of government is in violation of the Constitution. If an act is unconstitutional, the judicial branch has the power to nullify it.
- Federalism – This is the division of power between the central government and local governments, which limits the power of the federal government and allows states to deal with local problems.

Classic forms of government

Forms of government that have appeared throughout history include:
- Feudalism – This is based on the rule of local lords who are loyal to the king and control the lives and production of those who work on their land.
- Classical republic – This form is a representative democracy. Small groups of elected leaders represent the interests of the electorate.
- Absolute monarchy – A king or queen has complete control of the military and government.
- Authoritarianism – An individual or group has unlimited authority. There is no system in place to restrain the power of the government.
- Dictatorship – Those in power are not held responsible to the people.
- Autocracy – This is rule by one person (despot), not necessarily a monarch, who uses power tyrannically.
- Oligarchy – A small, usually self-appointed elite rules a region.

- Liberal democracy – This is a government based on the consent of the people that protects individual rights and freedoms from any intolerance by the majority.
- Totalitarianism – All facets of the citizens' lives are controlled by the government.

Historical background to the Bill of Rights

The United States Bill of Rights was based on principles established by the Magna Carta in 1215, the 1688 English Bill of Rights, and the 1776 Virginia Bill of Rights. In 1791, the federal government added 10 amendments to the United States Constitution that provided the following protections:
1. Freedom of speech, religion, peaceful assembly, petition of the government, and petition of the press
2. The right to keep and bear arms
3. No quartering of soldiers on private property without the consent of the owner
4. Regulations on government search and seizure
5. Provisions concerning prosecution
6. The right to a speedy, public trial and the calling of witnesses
7. The right to trial by jury
8. Freedom from excessive bail or cruel punishment
9. These rights are not necessarily the only rights
10. Powers not prohibited by the Constitution are reserved to the states.

Making a formal amendment to the Constitution

So far, there have been only 27 amendments to the federal Constitution. There are four different ways to change the wording of the constitution: two methods for proposal and two methods for ratification:
- An amendment is proposed by a two-thirds vote in each house of Congress and ratified by three-fourths of the state legislatures.
- An amendment is proposed by a two-thirds vote in each house of Congress and ratified by three-fourths of the states in special conventions called for that purpose.
- An amendment is proposed by a national convention that is called by Congress at the request of two-thirds of the state legislatures and ratified by three-fourths of the state legislatures.
- An amendment is proposed by a national convention that is called by Congress at the request of two-thirds of the state legislatures and ratified by three-fourths of the states in special conventions called for that purpose.

National, concurrent, and state powers of government

The division of powers in the federal government system is as follows: National – This level can coin money, regulate interstate and foreign trade, raise and maintain armed forces, declare war, govern United States territories and admit new states, and conduct foreign relations.
Concurrent – This level can levy and collect taxes, borrow money, establish courts, define crimes and set punishments, and claim private property for public use.
State – This level can regulate trade and business within the state, establish public schools, pass license requirements for professionals, regulate alcoholic beverages, conduct elections, and establish local governments.

There are three types of delegated powers granted by the Constitution:
Expressed or enumerated powers – These are specifically spelled out in the Constitution. Implied –
These are not expressly stated, but are reasonably suggested by the expressed powers.
Inherent – These are powers not expressed by the Constitution but ones that national governments
have historically possessed, such as granting diplomatic recognition.
Powers can also be classified or reserved or exclusive. Reserved powers are not granted to the
national government, but not denied to the states. Exclusive powers are those reserved to the
national government, including concurrent powers.

Types of federal taxes

The four types of federal taxes are:
- Income taxes on individuals – This is a complex system because of demands for various
  exemptions and rates. Further, the schedule of rates can be lowered or raised according to
  economic conditions in order to stimulate or restrain economic activity. For example, a tax
  cut can provide an economic stimulus, while a tax increase can slow down the rate of
  inflation. Personal income tax generates about five times as much as corporate taxes. Rates
  are based on an individual's income, and range from 10 to 35 percent.
- Income taxes on corporations – The same complexity of exemptions and rates exists for
  corporations as individuals. Taxes can be raised or lowered according to the need to
  stimulate or restrain the economy.
- Excise taxes – These are taxes on specific goods such as tobacco, liquor, automobiles,
  gasoline, air travel, and luxury items, or on activities such as highway usage by trucks.
- Customs duties – These are taxes imposed on imported goods. They serve to regulate trade
  between the United States and other countries.

Purpose of government its organization

Originally, governments were created to protect citizens and their property. Although government
systems have evolved a great deal since these origins, the basic intent is the same. There are
governments representing all types of human groups. Even the smallest tribe has some sort of
organization and leadership structure. In most cases, a national government is predicated upon a
populace with a shared language and culture as well as a large and powerful middle class. This is
not always the case, however, as evidenced by Canada, which has English and French Canadian as
its official languages. There are several different organizational structures for governments,
including communism, socialism, theocracy, confederation, hereditary monarchy, constitutional
monarchy, democracy, and tribal council.

Socialism, communism, capitalism, and mixed economies

In a socialist system, both the means of production and the land are owned by the state, which
means that the wealth generated by economic activity is also distributed by the state. Nevertheless,
a socialist state may have regular elections and a functional legislative body. The following northern
European countries are considered socialist: Romania, Poland, Hungary, Bulgaria, Sweden, Ukraine,
Belarus, Russia, and Armenia. The communist system is similar insofar as the means of production
and the land are owned by the state, but it is typical for political life to be dominated by one party,
often in a totalitarian manner. North Korea, Vietnam, Cuba, and China are all communist countries,
though China has successfully introduced some elements of capitalism. The capitalist system places
control of the means of production and the land in the hands of private interests. Finally, in a mixed

economy, control over the economy is divided between private citizens and the government. In other words, the government controls some functions and leaves others to citizens.

International factors influencing a country's public policy

Public policy can also be influenced by international factors. For instance, economic treaties will adjust the incentives for various public policy actions. They will also determine the extent to which a country regulates its imports, exports, and tariffs. Many nations have military treaties as well. For instance, the United States has declared that it will support Taiwan should the island nation be invaded by China. In some countries, political instability leads to inaction. One example would be Nigeria before 1999; uncertainty about the military government made it difficult for the nation to engage in international trade. Some nations, like Iran, become pariahs internationally and have a hard time cooperating on trade agreements for that reason. Finally, many nations decide public policy issues based on their perceived effects on the value of that nation's own currency relative to the currencies of other nations.

Culture; Science, Technology and Society

Culture

"Culture" refers to all learned human behaviors and behavioral patterns. Culture is made up of:
- Cultural universals—traits shared by all human beings such as language.
- Culture—all traditions that define a society.
- Subculture—groups within a culture that share specific traits.

While culture serves as a survival mechanism by bringing people together in groups and helping individuals identify with each other, it also undergoes frequent and sometimes profound change as groups respond to new technologies, knowledge, or contact with other cultures.

Processes bringing about cultural change

Three major processes bring about the majority of changes in a culture:
1. Discovery—finding things that already exist, such as fire, a major cultural transformer.
2. Invention—Creating new equipment, machinery, etc. that changes the way tasks are accomplished.
3. Diffusion—borrowing elements from other cultures.

Over 70 traits have been identified that are found in nearly every culture to some level. These traits can be divided into five categories that determine the basic structure, mores, norms, and other characteristics of a culture.
1. Arts
2. Language
3. Environment
4. Recreation
5. Economy
6. Institution
7. Beliefs

Gender and age and discrimination

In spite of legislation, education, and other attempts to bring about a higher level of equality, discrimination still exists against women and the elderly, particularly as involves law, politics and economic standing. Discrimination against women is particularly profound in most developing countries. It is believed that increasing the standing of women in a society is a major element in increasing the overall livelihood of that society.

While some societies value the elderly for their knowledge and experience, others discriminate against older people because of their decreased physical ability and ability to contribute economically. In the US, the poverty level for the elderly still stands at about ten percent. As lifespan increases, all societies must find a way to accommodate the needs of the elderly population.

Subsistence patterns

The term subsistence patterns are a reference to ways in which societies obtain the necessities of life such as food and shelter. The subsistence pattern of a society often is directly correlated to its economy, population size, political systems, and overall technological development. Certain subsistence patterns can only support lower levels of societal development, while others can support a much more developed culture.

The four major subsistence patterns are:
- Foraging, or hunter-gatherer
- Pastoralism—herding
- Horticulture—small-scale farming
- Intensive agriculture—large-scale farming

Hunter-gatherer societies by nature are nomadic and do not tend to support highly developed cultures. Intensive agriculture, by contrast, can support a large population to a high subsistence level, allowing for the development of a sophisticated, modern culture.

Characteristics and importance of religion

Strictly defined, religion consists of a belief system and usually a set of rituals involving worship of a supernatural force or forces that have some effect upon both everyday life and the overall structure and functioning of the world around us. Religion provides meaning and explanation for various life events and profoundly affects a cultures worldviews. Religion provides emotional support for individuals and a sense of community within a group that has shared religious views. Religious organization also provides structured sets of moral norms and motivation to abide by these norms and rules. Increased secularization, particularly in developed countries, has reduced the role of religion in everyday life, leading individuals to find other systems to fill these basic human needs.

Inventors from the 1800s

1. Alexander Graham Bell—the telephone
2. Orville and Wilbur Wright—the airplane
3. Richard Gatling—the machine gun
4. Walter Hunt, Elias Howe and Isaac Singer—the sewing machine
5. Nikola Tesla—alternating current

6. George Eastman—the camera
7. Thomas Edison—light bulbs, motion pictures, the phonograph
8. Samuel Morse—the telegraph
9. Charles Goodyear—vulcanized rubber
10. Cyrus McCormick—the reaper
11. George Westinghouse—the transformer, the air brake

This was an active period for invention, with about 700,000 patents registered between 1860 and 1900.

Requirements for civilization

Civilizations are defined as having the following characteristics:
- Use of metal to make weapons and tools
- Written language
- A defined territorial state
- A calendar

The earliest civilizations developed in river valleys where reliable, fertile land was easily found, including:
- Nile River valley in Egypt
- Mesopotamia
- Indus River
- Hwang Ho in China

The very earliest civilizations developed in the Tigris-Euphrates valley in Mesopotamia, which is now part of Iraq, and in Egypt's Nile valley. These civilizations arose between 4,000 and 3,000 BCE. The area where these civilizations grew is known as the Fertile Crescent. There, geography and the availability of water made large-scale human habitation possible.

Areas being selected for specific activities

The growth of cities and even nations is based on the choice of specific areas for activities such as habitation, agriculture, transportation, and other activities. Several factors determine whether locations are suitable for these activities:
- Climate
- Altitude
- Presence of water
- Types of plants present
- Density of population
- Type of government
- Existing landforms

Any of these factors, or a combination thereof, will determine if a location is suitable for habitation or population expansion. As technology advances in an area, these factors can determine whether certain industries will be successful there.

Science of sociology

The social interaction of human beings is quite complex. The science of sociology seeks to study the wide variety of social interaction that exists in human populations. Groups observed by sociologists include:
- Populations of cities or towns
- Families of various sizes
- Organizations
- Groups of the same gender
- Groups of similar ages
- Groups with specific characteristics such as similar occupations or racial characteristics

Sociologists also observe the way individuals interact with institutions, such as governments. These studies can help determine differences and similarities between individual groups and can help improve how these groups interact and communicate with each other.

Science of anthropology

Anthropology studies human culture, both modern and prehistoric. Anthropology tells us about how ancient cultures lived, worked, and communicated; examines how different existing cultures function; analyzes languages and their use in individual and social contexts; and the behavior of our closest relatives, the primates, including chimpanzees and gorillas.

There are five major divisions in the field of anthropology:
1. Physical anthropology - Focuses on living humans and primates as well as fossil remains.
2. Primatology - Studies behavior of non-human primates.
3. Archaeology - Studies items and fossils left behind by prehistoric cultures and individuals.
4. Ethnography - Studies specific cultures by interacting with those cultures.
5. Linguistic anthropology - Studies various human languages.

Science of psychology

Psychology is the study of human behavior, especially as it applies to individuals and small groups. Psychologists try to determine reasons why people act the way they do, and help them to overcome specific problems.

The science of psychology is most often associated with the figures of Sigmund Freud and Karl Jung. In the education field, prominent psychologists include B. F. Skinner and Jean Piaget, who developed theories of learning. The three main types of psychologists are:
1. Cognitive psychologists - Focus on the process of thinking and learning and how it occurs
2. Clinical psychologists – Focus on abnormal behaviors
3. Social psychologists - Focus on behaviors of small groups of people

Social Studies Foundations and Skills

Appropriate graphic format for conveying information in social science

The type of information being conveyed guides the choice of format. Textual information and numeric information must be displayed with different techniques. Text-only information may be most easily summarized in a diagram or a timeline. If text includes numeric information, it may be converted into a chart that shows the size of groups, connects ideas in a table or graphic, or shows information in a hybridized format. Ideas or opinions can be effectively conveyed in political cartoons. Numeric information is often most helpfully presented in tables or graphs. When information will be referred to and looked up again and again, tables are often most helpful for the reader. When the trends in the numeric information are more important than the numbers themselves, graphs are often the best choice. Information that is linked to the land and has a spatial component is best conveyed using maps.

Appropriate situations for using electronic resources and periodicals for reference

Electronic resources are often the quickest, most convenient way to get background information on a topic. One of the particular strengths of electronic resources is that they can also provide primary-source multimedia video, audio, or other visual information on a topic that would not be accessible in print. Information available on the Internet is not often carefully screened for accuracy or for bias, so choosing the source of electronic information is often very important. Electronic encyclopedias can provide excellent overview information, but publicly edited resources like Wikipedia are open to error, rapid change, incompleteness, or bias. Students should be made aware of the different types and reliabilities of electronic resources, and they should be taught how to distinguish between them. Electronic resources can often be too detailed and overwhelm students with irrelevant information. Periodicals provide current information on social science events, but they too must be screened for bias. Some amount of identifiable bias can actually be an important source of information, because it indicates prevailing culture and standards. Periodicals generally have tighter editorial standards than electronic resources, so completeness and overt errors are not usually as problematic. Periodicals can also provide primary-source information with interviews and photographs.

Using encyclopedias, bibliographies, and almanacs

Encyclopedias are ideal for getting background information on a topic. They provide an overview of the topic, and link it to other concepts that can provide additional keywords, information, or subjects. They can help students narrow their topic by showing the sub-topics within the overall topic, and by relating it to other topics. Encyclopedias are often more useful than the Internet because they provide a clearly organized, concise overview of material. Bibliographies are bound collections of references to periodicals and books, organized by topic. Students can begin researching more efficiently after they identify a topic, look it up in a bibliography, and look up the references listed there. This provides a branching network of information a student can follow. A pitfall of bibliographies is that when in textbooks or other journal articles, the references in them are chosen to support the author's point of view, and so may be limited in scope. Almanacs are volumes of facts published annually. They provide numerical information on just about every topic, and are organized by subject or geographic region. They are often helpful for supporting arguments made using other resources, and do not provide any interpretation of their own.

Primary vs. secondary resources

Primary resources provide information about an event from the perspective of people who were present at the event. They might be letters, autobiographies, interviews, speeches, artworks, or anything created by people with first-hand experience. Primary resources are valuable because they provide not only facts about the event, but also information about the surrounding circumstances; for example, a letter might provide commentary about how a political speech was received. The Internet is a source of primary information, but care must be taken to evaluate the perspective of the website providing that information. Websites hosted by individuals or special-interest organizations are more likely to be biased than those hosted by public organizations, governments, educational institutions, or news associations. Secondary resources provide information about an event, but were not written at the time the event occurred. They draw information from primary sources. Because secondary sources were written later, they have the added advantage of historical perspective, multiple points of view, or resultant outcomes. Newsmagazines that write about an event even a week after it occurred count as secondary sources. Secondary sources tend to analyze events more effectively or thoroughly than primary sources.

Interpreting a map

The map legend is an area that provides interpretation information such as the key, the scale, and how to interpret the map. The key is the area that defines symbols, abbreviations, and color schemes used on the map. Any feature identified on the map should be defined in the key. The scale is a feature of the map legend that tells how distance on the map relates to distance on the ground. It can either be presented mathematically in a ratio or visually with a line segment. For example, it could say that one inch on the map equals one foot on the ground, or it could show a line segment and tell how much distance on the map the line symbolizes. Latitude and longitude are often shown on maps to relate their area to the world. Latitude shows how far a location is north or south from the earth's equator, and longitude shows how far a location is east or west from the earth's prime meridian. Latitude runs from 90 N (North Pole) – 0 (equator) – 90 S (South Pole), and longitude runs 180 E (international date line) – 0 (prime meridian) – 180 W (international date line).

Formulating research questions or hypotheses

Formulating research questions or hypotheses is the process of finding questions to answer that have not yet been asked. The first step in the process is reading background information. Knowing about a general topic and reading about how other people have addressed it helps identify areas that are well understood. Areas that are not as well understood may either be lightly addressed in the available literature, or distinctly identified as a topic that is not well understood and deserves further study. Research questions or hypotheses may address such an unknown aspect, or they may focus on drawing parallels between similar, well-researched topics that have not been connected before. Students usually need practice in developing research questions that are of the appropriate scope so that they will find enough information to answer the question, yet not so much that they become overwhelmed. Hypotheses tend to be more specific than research questions.

Collecting information and organizing and reporting it

The first step of writing a research paper involves narrowing down on a topic. The student should first read background information to identify areas that are interesting or need further study and that the student does not have a strong opinion about. The research question should be identified, and the student should refer to general sources that can point to more specific information. When he begins to take notes, his information must be organized with a clear system to identify the source. Any information from outside sources must be acknowledged with footnotes or a bibliography. To gain more specific information about his topic, the student can then research bibliographies of the general sources to narrow down on information pertinent to his topic. He should draft a thesis statement that summarizes the main point of the research. This should lead to a working outline that incorporates all the ideas needed to support the main point in a logical order. A rough draft should incorporate the results of the research in the outlined order, with all citations clearly inserted. The paper should then be edited for clarity, style, flow, and content.

Analyzing artifacts

Artifacts, or everyday objects used by previous cultures, are useful for understanding life in those cultures. Students should first discover, or be provided with, a description of the item. This description should tell during what period the artifact was used and what culture used it. From that description and/or from examination of the artifact, students should be able to discuss what the artifact is, what it is made of, its potential uses, and the people who likely used it. They should then be able to draw conclusions from all these pieces of evidence about life in that culture. For example, analysis of coins from an early American archaeological site might show that settlers brought coins with them, or that some classes of residents were wealthy, or that trade occurred with many different nations. The interpretation will vary depending on the circumstances surrounding the artifact. Students should consider these circumstances when drawing conclusions.

Organizing information chronologically and analyzing the sequence of events

To organize information chronologically, each piece of information must be associated with a time or a date. Events are ordered according to the time or date at which they happened. In social sciences, chronological organization is the most straightforward way to arrange information, because it relies on a uniform, fixed scale – the passage of time. Information can also be organized based on any of the "who, what, when, where, why?" principles.

Analyzing the sequence of chronological events involves not only examining the event itself, but the preceding and following events. This can put the event in question into perspective, showing how a certain thing might have happened based on preceding history. One large disadvantage of chronological organization is that it may not highlight important events clearly relative to less important events. Determining the relative importance of events depends more strongly on interpreting their relationships to neighboring events.

Distinguishing between fact and opinion

Students easily recognize that facts are true statements that everyone agrees on, such as an object's name or a statement about a historical event. Students also recognize that opinions vary about matters of taste, such as preferences in food or music, that rely on people's interpretation of facts. Simple examples are easy to spot. Fact-based passages include certainty-grounded words like is, did, or saw. On the other hand, passages containing opinions often include words that indicate possibility rather than certainty, such as would, should or believe. First-person verbs also indicate opinions, showing that one person is talking about his experience.

Less clear are examples found in higher-level texts. For example, primary-source accounts of a Civil War battle might include facts ("X battle was fought today") and also opinions ("Union soldiers are not as brave as Confederate soldiers") that are not clearly written as such ("I believe Union soldiers..."). At the same time as students learn to interpret sources critically (Was the battle account written by a Southerner?), they should practice sifting fact from these types of opinion. Other examples where fact and opinion blend together are self-authored internet websites.

Determining the adequacy, relevance, and consistency of information

Before information is sought, a list of guiding questions should be developed to help determine whether information found is adequate, relevant, and consistent. These questions should be based on the research goals, which should be laid out in an outline or concept map. For example, a student writing a report on Navajo social structure might begin with questions concerning the general lifestyle and location of Navajos, and follow with questions about how Navajo society was organized. While researching his questions, he will come up with pieces of information. This information can be compared to his research questions to determine whether it is relevant to his report. Information from several sources should be compared to determine whether information is consistent. Information that is adequate helps answer specific questions that are part of the research goals. Inadequate information for this particular student might be a statement such as "Navajos had a strong societal structure," because the student is probably seeking more specific information.

Drawing conclusions and making generalizations about a topic

Students reading about a topic will encounter different facts and opinions that contribute to their overall impression of the material. The student can critically examine the material by thinking about what facts have been included, how they have been presented, what they show, what they relate to outside the written material, and what the author's conclusion is. Students may agree or disagree with the author's conclusion, based on the student's interpretation of the facts the author presented. When working on a research project, a student's research questions will help him gather details that will enable him to draw a conclusion about the research material. Generalizations are blanket statements that apply to a wide number of examples. They are similar to conclusions, but do not have to summarize the information as completely as conclusions. Generalizations in reading material may be flagged by words such as all, most, none, many, several, sometimes, often, never, overall, or in general. Generalizations are often followed by supporting information consisting of a list of facts. Generalizations can refer to facts or the author's opinions, and they provide a valuable summary of the text overall.

Comparing maps, drawing conclusions and making generalizations

Maps can provide a great deal of information about an area by showing specific locations where certain types of settlement, land use, or population growth occurred. Datasets and texts can provide more specific information about events that can be hypothesized from maps. This specific information may provide dates of significant events (for example, the date of a fire that gutted a downtown region, forcing suburban development) or important numerical data (e.g., population growth by year). Written datasets and texts enable map interpretation to become concrete and allow observed trends to be linked with specific causes ("Real estate prices rose in 2004, causing

- 186 -

middle-class citizens to move northwest of the city"). Without specific information from additional sources, inferences drawn from maps cannot be put in context and interpreted in more than a vague way.

Interpreting charts and tables

Charts used in social science are a visual representation of data. They combine graphic and textual elements to convey information in a concise format. Often, charts divide the space up in blocks, which are filled with text and/or pictures to convey a point. Charts are often organized in tabular form, where blocks below a heading all have information in common. Charts also divide information into conceptual, non-numeric groups (for example, "favorite color"), which are then plotted against a numerical axis (e.g., "number of students"). Charts should be labeled in such a way that a reader can locate a point on the chart and then consult the surrounding axes or table headings to understand how it compares to other points. Tables are a type of chart that divides textual information into rows and columns. Each row and column represents a characteristic of the information. For example, a table might be used to convey demographic information. The first column would provide "year," and the second would provide "population." Reading across the rows, one could see that in the year 1966, the population of Middletown was 53,847. Tracking the columns would show how frequently the population was counted.

Interpreting graphs and diagrams

Graphs are similar to charts, except that they graphically show numeric information on both axes. For example, a graph might show population through the years, with years on the X-axis and population on the Y-axis. One advantage of graphs is that population during the time in between censuses can be estimated by locating that point on the graph. Each axis should be labeled to allow the information to be interpreted correctly, and the graph should have an informative title. Diagrams are usually drawings that show the progression of events. The drawings can be fairly schematic, as in a flow chart, or they can be quite detailed, as in a depiction of scenes from a battle. Diagrams usually have arrows connecting the events or boxes shown. Each event or box should be labeled to show what it represents. Diagrams are interpreted by following the progression along the arrows through all events.

Using timelines

Timelines are used to show the relationships between people, places, and events. They are ordered chronologically, and usually are shown left-to-right or top-to-bottom. Each event on the timeline is associated with a date, which determines its location on the timeline. On electronic resources, timelines often contain hyperlinks associated with each event. Clicking on the event's hyperlink will open a page with more information about the event. Cause-and-effect relationships can be observed on timelines, which often show a key event and then resulting events following in close succession. These can be helpful for showing the order of events in time or the relationships between similar events. They help make the passage of time a concrete concept, and show that large periods pass between some events, and other events cluster very closely.

Gathering and testing data

The three major methods of gathering data for sociological studies are:
- Surveys—gathering information via direct questioning of members of the social group being studied.

- Controlled experiments—performing experiments that change an element of society.
- Field observations—living among members of a particular group or culture and observing how they interact and how they live their everyday lives.

Patterns used by sociologists to define relationships involving race and ethnicity

In general, relationships within cultures involving race and ethnicity are defined by either assimilation or conflict.

Assimilation can involve:
a. Anglo-conformity—immigrants and racial minorities conform to the expectations of Anglo-American society, whether by choice, necessity or force.
b. Cultural pluralism—acceptance of varieties of racial and ethnic groups.
c. Accommodation—mutual adaptation between majority and minority groups.
d. Melting pot—the mixing together of various ethnic groups will bring about a new cultural group.

Patterns of conflict include:
a. Population transfer—one group is required or forced to leave by another group.
b. Subjugation—one group exercises control over the other.
c. Genocide—one group slaughters another.

Skills and materials necessary to be successful in a social studies course

For classes in history, geography, civics/government, anthropology, sociology, and economics, the goal is for students to explore issues and learn key concepts. Social studies help improve communication skills in reading and writing, but students need sufficient literacy skills to be able to understand specialized vocabulary, identify key points in text, differentiate between fact and opinion, relate information across texts, connect prior knowledge and new information, and synthesize information into meaningful knowledge. These literacy skills will be enhanced in the process, and will extend into higher order thinking skills that enable students to compare and contrast, hypothesize, draw inferences, explain, analyze, predict, construct, and interpret. Social studies classes also depend on a number of different types of materials beyond the textbook, such as nonfiction books, biographies, journals, maps, newspapers (paper or online), photographs, and primary documents.

Benefits of social studies for students

Social studies cover the political, economic, cultural, and environmental aspects of societies not only in the past, as in the study of history, but also in the present and future. Students gain an understanding of current conditions and learn how to prepare for the future and cope with change through studying geography, economics, anthropology, government, and sociology. Social studies classes teach assessment, problem solving, evaluation, and decision making skills in the context of good citizenship. Students learn about scope and sequence, designing investigations, and following up with research to collect, organize, and present information and data. In the process, students learn how to search for patterns and their meanings in society and in their own lives. Social studies build a positive self-concept within the context of understanding the similarities and differences of people. Students begin to understand that they are unique, but also share many feelings and concerns with others. As students learn that each individual can contribute to society, their self-awareness builds self-esteem.

Knowledge gained from disciplines

Anthropology and sociology provide an understanding of how the world's many cultures have developed and what these cultures and their values have to contribute to society.

Sociology, economics, and political science provide an understanding of the institutions in society and each person's role within social groups. These topics teach the use of charts, graphs, and statistics.

Political science, civics, and government teach how to see another person's point of view, accept responsibility, and deal with conflict. They also provide students with an understanding of democratic norms and values, such as justice and equality. Students learn how to apply these norms and values in their community, school, and family.

Economics teaches concepts such as work, exchange (buying, selling, and other trade transactions), production of goods and services, the origins of materials and products, and consumption.

Geography teaches students how to use maps, globes, and locational and directional terms. It also provides them with an understanding of spatial environments, landforms, climate, world trade and transportation, ecological systems, and world cultures.

Inquiry-based learning

Facilitated by the teacher who models, guides, and poses a starter question, inquiry-based learning is a process in which students are involved in their learning. This process involves formulating questions, investigating widely, and building new understanding and meaning. This combination of steps asks students to think independently, and enables them to answer their questions with new knowledge, develop solutions, or support a position or point of view. In inquiry-based learning activities, teachers engage students, ask for authentic assessments, require research using a variety of resources (books, interviews, Internet information, etc.), and involve students in cooperative interaction. All of these require the application of processes and skills. Consequently, new knowledge is usually shared with others, and may result in some type of action. Inquiry-based learning focuses on finding a solution to a question or a problem, whether it is a matter of curiosity, a puzzle, a challenge, or a disturbing confusion.

Characteristics of the essential questions

Essential questions for learning include those that:
- Ask for evaluation, synthesis, and analysis – the highest levels of Bloom's Taxonomy
- Seek information that is important to know
- Are worth the student's awareness
- Will result in enduring understanding
- Tend to focus on the questions "why?" or "how do we know this information?"
- Are more open-ended and reflective in nature
- Often address interrelationships or lend themselves to multi-disciplinary investigations
- Spark curiosity and a sense of wonder, and invite investigation and activity
- Can be asked over and over and in a variety of instances
- Encourage related questions

- Have answers that may be extended over time
- Seek to identify key understandings
- Engage students in real-life, applied problem solving
- May not be answerable without a lifetime of investigation, and maybe not even then

Verifying the credibility of research sources

Some sources are not reliable, so the student must have a means to evaluate the credibility of a source when doing research, particularly on the Internet. The value of a source depends on its intended use and whether it fits the subject. For example, students researching election campaigns in the 19th century would need to go to historical documents, but students researching current election practices could use candidate brochures, television advertisements, and web sites.

A checklist for examining sources might include:
- Check the authority and reputation of the author, sponsoring group, or publication
- Examine the language and illustrations for bias
- Look for a clear, logical arrangement of information
- If online, check out the associated links, archives, contact ability, and the date of last update

Research methods

Social science research relies heavily on empirical research, which is original data gathering and analysis through direct observation or experiment. It also involves using the library and Internet to obtain raw data, locate information, or review expert opinion. Because social science projects are often interdisciplinary, students may need assistance from the librarian to find related search terms.

While arguments still exist about the superiority of quantitative versus qualitative research, most social scientists understand that research is an eclectic mix of the two methods. Quantitative research involves using techniques to gather data, which is information dealing with numbers and measurable values. Statistics, tables, and graphs are often the products. Qualitative research involves non-measurable factors, and looks for meaning in the numbers produced by quantitative research. Qualitative research takes data from observations and analyzes it to find underlying meanings and patterns of relationships.

Community relations knowledge acquired from social studies

An important part of social studies, whether anthropology, sociology, history, geography, or political science, is the study of local and world cultures, as well as individual community dynamics. Students should be able to:
- Identify values held by their own culture and community
- Identify values held by other cultures and communities
- Recognize the influences of other cultures on their own culture
- Identify major social institutions and their roles in the students' communities
- Understand how individuals and groups interact to obtain food, clothing, and shelter
- Understand the role of language, literature, the arts, and traditions in a culture
- Recognize the role of media and technology in cultures, particularly in the students' own cultures

- Recognize the influence of various types of government, economics, the environment, and technology on social systems and cultures
- Evaluate the effectiveness of social institutions in solving problems in a community or culture
- Examine changes in population, climate, and production, and evaluate their effects on the community or culture

Systematic inquiry

Systematic inquiry requires students to gather information from several sources, organize it, and analyze it. Students can independently design and carry out their own inquiries or investigations to bring together information regarding specific issues in the field of social studies. Sources that can be employed in these investigations include:
- Primary sources - Sources written in the historical period being studied or by the historical figure being studied.
- Secondary sources - Sources written about the historical period or figure; including biographies, encyclopedias and historical texts.

Both types of sources are readily available in libraries, online, or other outlets. Students and teachers can use these sources to conduct investigations or set up lesson plans. Teachers should help students evaluate the validity of secondary sources.

Primary source documents

Primary source documents are among the most relevant and useful tools in social studies instruction. Using primary sources allows a student to obtain an intimate look into the thoughts and activities of people who were alive during the time being studied. Documents can include court records, census data, letters, diaries, music, or legal documents.

Primary source documents are more accessible than ever thanks to the Internet. The Library of Congress maintains a number of primary source documents online. In addition, many historical societies or organizations dedicated to a particular historical period also maintain online archives of primary source documents. Local museums or historical societies might have primary source documents available where students can actually look at them or, in some cases, read or handle them.

Study of maps and major concepts

Maps create a graphical representation of various portions of the Earth or, in the case of global maps, of the entire Earth. Map study generally begins with studying the globe to give students an understanding of the makeup of the Earth and where different regions are located. Other concepts included in map study are:
- Types of maps - Geologic, political, environmental, resource, topographical, themed, etc.
- Map key - Includes the compass rose, map scale, and legends that explain each of the symbols used on a particular map
- Measurement grids - Applicable mostly to globes, this includes latitude and longitude, the Equator, the Tropics of Cancer and Capricorn, parallels and meridians.

Social Studies Instruction and Assessment

Scope and sequence for elementary school level social studies curriculum

The scope and sequence for social studies at the elementary level can differ from state to state, but the overall progression remains similar. A typical scope and sequence from Kindergarten through eighth grade is:

- Kindergarten — Immediate environment; topics cover home, family, and school
- First grade — Continued exploration of the immediate environment
- Second grade — Includes the local community
- Third grade — History and geography of the local state; can also include the history of the US and US holidays.
- Fourth grade — World regions and/or the history and geography of their state
- Fifth grade — Extended American history and geography
- Sixth grade — World history and world geography
- Seventh grade — More in-depth study of American history and/or state history
- Eighth grade — Continued exploration of American history and introduction of civics.

Purpose of assessment

As in other subjects, assessment in the social studies classroom involves three major goals:

1. Keep track of student progress to be sure they are meeting learning goals
2. Stay aware of specific needs of individual students and classrooms
3. Make changes to instruction or teaching methods if necessary to meet individual students' needs

Ideally, assessment should be performed both formally and informally to provide a more complete view of a student's understanding and progress. Formal assessment includes:

- Standardized tests
- Exams required at the district level
- Tests designed by the teacher

Informal assessment includes:

- Journals
- Portfolios
- Informal discussions
- Observation in the classroom

Science

Safety

Basic safety procedures in the science laboratory

The most important safety precaution is to be prepared. Be acquainted with all potential hazards of any procedure, as well as all equipment, its associated safety procedures, and all lab manuals before beginning an experiment. Calibrate all equipment properly and handle it with care and only for its intended purpose. Read all safety data sheets before beginning a procedure. Perform all procedures yourself before assigning them to students.

Secure and label all biological, chemical, and carcinogenic materials, away from heat and food, not on a high surface or on the floor, and segregated by reactivity. Follow all local disposal procedures for used lab materials, labeling all chemical and biological waste. Make sure all storage and waste containers are leakproof.

Avoid contamination. Use distilled water in the lab, not tap water, as tap water contains impurities. Clean and rinse all glassware after use.

Secure items with clamps as necessary. Use, and have students use, goggles, gloves, and lab coats. Take extra caution with knives, glass rods, weights, and any potentially injurious materials.

Safety precautions

Performing light- and laser-based procedures
Light: Do not use broken mirrors, prisms, or glass; grind or tape those with sharp edges. Periodically check all connections for spectroscopic light voltage. Shield all people from ultraviolet and infrared light sources. Be aware of students with neurological conditions (for instance, epilepsy) that make them susceptible to strobe lights. Never allow students to look directly into the sun; design viewfinders for solar-eclipse viewing.

Lasers: Be aware of the laser classification system, and know which type you are using. Shield all people from direct exposure to a laser; contain people's movements when using lasers to avoid inadvertent exposure. Project lasers only onto non-reflective surfaces, maintain a sufficient light level to prevent pupil dilation, and make sure to shield all prisms and reflective objects. Use the minimum effective optical power. Terminate the beam at a point beyond the furthest point of interest, in a non-reflective material. Be familiar with the safety features of a laser projector, and use beam stops when the laser is not actively being used. Equip the laser with a key switch if possible.

Performing sound-, radiation-, and radioactivity-based procedures
Sound: Never exceed 110 decibels, which causes hearing damage. When using a high-speed siren disk, make sure to use the safety disk.

Radiation: Shield all people properly when using X-rays, and keep them at least 10 feet from any radiation experiment. Periodically check all tubes, including vacuum, heat effect, magnetic, and deflection tubes. Enclose cathode rays in a frame, never allow students to use them themselves, and operate them for the shortest possible time and at the lowest practical voltage.

Radioactivity: Ensure you have access to a radiation survey meter before doing any radioactivity experiment, and make sure you have been trained properly in equipment handling, demonstration, and disposal procedures. Never use bare hands to handle radioactive materials. Shield all people from all radioactive material as required, by paper, glass, or lead. Store all radioactive material securely, and dispose of it properly.

Setting up a science laboratory for student use

The most important safety guideline in setting up a laboratory is to plan well and become familiar with all equipment and materials. Understand theoretically as well as practically the risks and effects of all materials you are using; know how to neutralize the effects of all materials. Set up all equipment so that it is in no danger of falling. Verify the locations and functionality of all safety equipment. Regularly monitor the condition and stock of all materials, including safety materials. Always choose the least hazardous effective materials for all procedures.

Perform all experiments yourself before doing them with students. Provide clear instructions on all procedures, including waste-disposal procedures, to students before having them perform them. Reinforce students' knowledge of safety procedures throughout the term.

Keep the laboratory locked at all times when not in use.

Basic safety rules
It is critical to plan for all eventualities when it comes to laboratory safety. Maintain all safety equipment and know how to use it. Understand first-aid procedures and re-familiarize yourself with the relevant ones when planning student experiments.

Distribute safety rules to students, and keep instructions for all safety procedures readily available for all parties. Post multiple and clear signs warning of any dangers associated with hazardous chemicals or delicate equipment. Post copies of all laboratory rules and spell out appropriate material-handling procedures.

Be prepared and willing to seek help in the event of an emergency. Students should never clean chemical or biological spills; only the teacher should, using appropriate chemical spill kits or bleach as appropriate. Large spills must be reported to the school administration and the fire department as soon as possible. You must also immediately report any injuries or accidents to the school administration and a health provider.

Students must wear safety goggles during heating, dissecting, and using acids and bases. Long hair should be tied back, and hands washed before and after experiments. Food must be forbidden in the lab.

Basic safety equipment
All labs should contain the following items:
- Bucket of sand for absorption of spills and smothering of alkali fires
- Fire blanket
- First-aid kit, containing bandages and antiseptic
- One GFCI within two feet of all water supplies

- Exit signs
- Emergency shower and eyewash station
- Splashproof eye protection for all parties, and a means to sanitize it
- Face shields
- Emergency exhaust fans that vent to the outside of the building
- Gloves, both rubber and nitrile
- Master cutoff switches for gas, electricity, and compressed air
- ABC fire extinguisher
- Storage cabinets for flammable items
- Chemical spill-control kit
- Fume hood with a spark-proof motor
- Flame-retardant lab aprons
- Mercury clean-up kit
- Neutralizing agents, including acetic acid and sodium bicarbonate
- Signs drawing attention to potential hazards
- Segregated, clearly labeled containers for storing broken glassware, flammable items, solid chemicals, corrosive items, and waste.

Major safety procedures that should be observed

Safety procedures are particularly important in a science lab or classroom. Among the procedures that should be observed are:
- Proper and regular use of safety equipment
- Proper and regular monitoring of chemicals
- Proper use and disposal of chemicals
- Proper storage of chemicals
- Fire prevention strategies and equipment
- Guidelines for handling living things

All these procedures should be implemented in the classroom. All students should also be aware of the proper procedures in case of any kind of accident. For example, if a student spills a chemical, he or she should know the proper procedure for cleanup. An important part of teaching science curriculum includes teaching, reviewing and enforcing safety procedures.

Legal responsibilities of a science teacher

At all levels of the legal system, it is the responsibility of a teacher to provide a safe environment for students. Never leave the room accessible to unsupervised students; if you must leave the room, provide students with proper alternative supervision. Familiarize students with safety procedures, and review them regularly. Posting the rules is insufficient; you must continually review them with students. If a procedure cannot be safely carried out, it must not be performed.

Avoid negligence. Always consider all possible outcomes before performing a procedure, and exercise care to minimize any danger to students and property. State Departments of Education have encoded the specific legal responsibilities of science teachers; familiarize yourself with state laws.

Appropriate safety and emergency procedures for science classrooms and laboratories

Laboratory safety rules should include the following. Never perform unauthorized experiments. Read all Safety Data Sheets (SDSs) before each lab. Always pour acids into water. Avoid skin contact with chemicals. If chemicals come in contact with skin or eyes, flush immediately. Never use a carbon dioxide fire extinguisher on a person. Use a fire blanket. Wear appropriate apparel in the laboratory including safety goggles, aprons, and gloves when necessary. Rules for behavior include the following. No horseplay. No eating, drinking, or chewing gum. Always wash your hands when done in the laboratory. In addition to the above rules, these standard emergency procedures should be followed. Notify the instructor in case of an emergency. Be aware of fire evacuation routes and the locations of fire blankets and fire extinguishers. In the event of a fire, pull the fire alarm. In cases of ingestion of chemicals, call a poison control center.

Correct Use of Tools, Materials, Equipment and Technology

Proper handling and calibration guidelines for electrical equipment

Know the location of the main cutoff switch for the laboratory. Regularly check all electrical connections, live wires, and batteries before turning the power on. All outlets should be GFCI, and extension cords should only be used extremely judiciously.

Keep all electrical current away from flammable materials and water. Use only 6- or 12-volt direct current, and double-insulate or ground all power equipment.

In all procedures, the insertion of the plug should be the last step in setup; when disassembling, remove the plug first. Use only one hand in all procedures involving an electrical current. Never allow oneself or a student to become part of an electrical circuit.

Proper handling and calibration guidelines for heat- and pressure-related equipment

Heat: Periodically check the gas connections and burners in the laboratory. Unless the gas is actively being used, keep the master gas valve off at all times. Never heat anything in a closed container, where pressure can build, and use only glassware approved for lab use. Use gloves, goggles, and fire-retardant pads as needed around hot materials. Never place a heat source in a location where it can be knocked over accidentally. Keep all flames and gas water heaters far from the vapors of flammable liquids.

Pressure: When using a pressure cooker, never exceed 20 pounds per square inch of pressure. Never open a hot pressure cooker. Always make sure the safety valve is in working order.

Laboratory equipment best suited to a specific use in the science classroom

Science classrooms have several types of equipment available to perform experiments and to facilitate various learning experiences. Students can evaluate an experiment based on the desired results in order to determine the best equipment to use to measure those results. Some guidance will be required at first to help students determine the suitability of certain equipment. They will also require guidance in how to use the equipment. After students acquire an understanding of how the equipment works and how to use it, they will be able to use equipment to confirm their own hypotheses and to independently develop questions and find the answers.

Ways in which technology can be used in the science classroom

Technology such as microscopes, telescopes and other measuring equipment is vital to the science classroom because they are used in scientific experimentation. Technology can also help with presenting science concepts, gathering and organizing data, assessing student performance, and keeping track of class records as well as results of experiments. Students can use computers for research, to keep track of experiments, and to compose papers and other materials. Major types of software that can be integrated into the classroom include:

- Databases
- Spreadsheets
- Word processing programs
- Desktop publishing
- Online databases or cloud computing elements
- Internet browsers for research and/or communication
- Practice lessons or drills
- Tutorials

Connection between science and technology

Technology and science go hand in hand. Technology is the practical application of science. Science leads to the improvement of technology and more advanced technology allows us as a society to make additional discoveries in the field of science. Knowledge of science helps individuals understand and apply technology in ways that can improve their individual quality of life and even help improve conditions for the world population as a whole.

Some technology, however, can be detrimental to the environment, individuals, or communities. In these cases, science can help determine how the technology can be improved to reduce these detrimental effects.

Internet safety in the classroom

The Internet is an excellent resource for research and learning, but it can also present problems in a classroom. These problems can include:

- Viruses or spyware infiltrating the system
- Vulnerability of the school computer systems to hacking
- Exposure of students to inappropriate material
- Research that uncovers inaccurate information

In order to prevent issues from developing, the teacher should institute a set of rules regarding Internet use including:

- Ensure classroom use of material from the Internet is not in violation of copyright
- Install firewalls and virus protection in all computers
- Only allow specific, qualified personnel to install or uninstall software
- Install filters to prevent students from accessing inappropriate material
- Help students learn to judge the accuracy and reliability of various Internet sources

Appropriate metric and International System of Units (SI) units

Quantity	Unit Name	Symbol
Volume	Liter	L
Length	Meter	M
Time	Second	S
Amount of a substance	Mole	Mol
Mass	Kilogram	Kg
Absolute temperature	Kelvin	K
Force	Newton	N
Energy	Joule	J
Pressure	Pascal	Pa
Electric current	Ampere	A
Frequency	Hertz	Hz

Performing unit conversions

A convenient way to perform unit conversions is dimensional analysis. In this method, conversion unit factors are used to obtain the needed unit. For example, because 1 kilogram is equal to 1,000 grams, and 1 gram equals 1,000 milligrams, the possible conversion factors are $\left(\frac{1 \text{ kg}}{1,000 \text{ g}}\right)$ and $\left(\frac{1 \text{ g}}{1,000 \text{ mg}}\right)$. The reciprocals of these factors may also be used. To convert 2,800 mg to kg, multiply $(2,800 \text{ mg})\left(\frac{1 \text{ g}}{1,000 \text{ mg}}\right)\left(\frac{1 \text{kg}}{1,000 \text{ g}}\right) = 2.8 \times 10^{-3}$ kg. To convert 3,900 kg to mg, multiply $(3,900 \text{ kg})\left(\frac{1,000 \text{ g}}{\text{kg}}\right)\left(\frac{1,000 \text{ mg}}{\text{g}}\right) = 3.9 \times 10^{9}$ mg.

Choosing appropriate types of graphs or charts

Pie charts are best used when comparing parts to the whole. For example, a pie chart could be used to show the components of blood and their respective percentages. Line graphs are best used when showing small or large changes over time. For example, a line chart could be used to record the weekly rainfall of a region. Bar graphs can be used to compare groups or track large changes over time. For example, a bar graph could be used to compare the average plant height of three groups of plants used in an experiment. Scatter plots are used to determine if there is a correlation between two sets of data. For example, hours of sleep could be plotted against waking blood pressure to determine a possible correlation.

History and Nature of Science

Labels given to scientific statements

Hypotheses are educated guesses about what is likely to occur, and are made to provide a starting point from which to begin design of the experiment. They may be based on results of previously observed experiments or knowledge of theory, and follow logically forth from these. Assumptions are statements that are taken to be fact without proof for the purpose of performing a given experiment. They may be entirely true, or they may be true only for a given set of conditions under which the experiment will be conducted. Assumptions are necessary to simplify experiments;

indeed, many experiments would be impossible without them. Scientific models are mathematical statements that describe a physical behavior. Models are only as good as our knowledge of the actual system. Often models will be discarded when new discoveries are made that show the model to be inaccurate. While a model can never perfectly represent an actual system, they are useful for simplifying a system to allow for better understanding of its behavior. Scientific laws are statements of natural behavior that have stood the test of time and have been found to produce accurate and repeatable results in all testing. A theory is a statement of behavior that consolidates all current observations. Theories are similar to laws in that they describe natural behavior, but are more recently developed andare more susceptible to being proved wrong. Theories may eventually become laws if they stand up to scrutiny and testing.

Basics of experimental design

Designing relevant experiments that allow for meaningful results is not a simple task. Every stage of the experiment must be carefully planned to ensure that the right data can be safely and accurately taken. Ideally, an experiment should be controlled so that all of the conditions except the ones being manipulated are held constant. This helps to ensure that the results are not skewed by unintended consequences of shifting conditions. A good example of this is a placebo group in a drug trial. All other conditions are the same, but that group is not given the medication. In addition to proper control, it is important that the experiment be designed with data collection in mind. For instance, if the quantity to be measured is temperature, there must be a temperature device such as a thermocouple integrated into the experimental setup. While the data are being collected, they should periodically be checked for obvious errors. If there are data points that are orders of magnitude from the expected value, then it might be a good idea to make sure that no experimental errors are being made, either in data collection or condition control. Once all the data have been gathered, they must be analyzed. The way in which this should be done depends on the type of data and the type of trends observed. It may be useful to fit curves to the data to determine if the trends follow a common mathematical form. It may also be necessary to perform a statistical analysis of the results to determine what effects are significant. Data should be clearly presented.

Contributions to physics

Marie Curie (Polish/French, 19th century): Curie was the foremost pioneer of radioactivity. She isolated the radioactive elements polonium and radium, and established that radioactivity was a property of an atom itself rather than of the relationship between multiple molecules.

Michael Faraday (English, 18th/19th century): Faraday's most important work was in the fields of electromagnetism and electrochemistry. His work led directly to some of the most important breakthroughs in electrical technology of the twentieth century. Faraday introduced the concept of fields to the study of magnetism and electricity. He discovered what would become known as the Faraday Effect, the effect of a strong magnetic field on the behavior of light rays. The Farad (the SI unit of capacitance) and the Faraday constant (the amount of charge on one mole of electrons) are both named for him.

Wilhelm Ostwald (Latvian, 19th/20th century): One of the founders of classical physical chemistry, Ostwald did important work on the properties of atomic particles, and defined a mole as the molecular weight, in grams, of a given substance.

Sir Isaac Newton (English, 17th/18th century): Newton, one of the most important scientists of all time, made critical breakthroughs in the understanding of scientific methods, motion, and optics.

Newton described universal gravitation, observed that white light contains the entire spectrum of colors, and discovered the calculus independently of Leibniz (who is credited with it). The three Newtonian laws of motion are:
- An object in motion (or at rest) remains in motion (or at rest) unless acted upon by an external force.
- Force equals mass times acceleration.
- For every action, there is an equal and opposite reaction.

Galileo Galilei (Italian, 17th century): Galileo determined that all bodies, regardless of mass, fall at the same rate. He argued that motion is continuous, changed only when an external force is applied to it (later incorporated in Newton's laws of motion). His work in astronomy was important in confirming Copernicus' heliocentric model of the solar system. His principle of relativity states that the laws of physics are constant within a constantly moving system, a theory that became central to Einstein's work on relativity.

J. Robert Oppenheimer (American, 20th century): Oppenheimer's scientific contributions are in astrophysics, nuclear physics, and quantum field theory. He served as scientific director of the Manhattan Project, which constructed the first atomic bomb.

Linus Pauling (American, 20th century): Pauling applied new discoveries in quantum mechanics to the field of chemistry, pioneering the study of molecular medicine. He researched the biochemical origins of genetic diseases like sickle-cell anemia.

Enrico Fermi (Italian/American, 20th century): Fermi discovered the process of making elements artificially radioactive by bombarding them with neutrons. He divided elements into the two groups of fermions and bosons. His work on nuclear reactions led him to participate in the Manhattan Project.

Niels Bohr (Danish, 20th century): Bohr established that the number of electrons determined the atom's chemical properties. He articulated the organization of electrons, in discrete orbits around an atom's nucleus, and that electrons could move orbits, thereby emitting radiation—the basis for quantum theory. Bohr worked on the Manhattan Project along with Oppenheimer and Fermi.

Albert Einstein (German, 20th century): Einstein, the most famous twentieth-century scientist, was a theoretical physicist whose special theory of relativity describes the relationship of time and space, and mass and gravity. In it, he declared that gravity is a consequence of the properties of space-time and that the speed of light is constant. He hypothesized that electromagnetic energy can be absorbed or expelled by matter in quanta, and discovered the photoelectric effect.

Stephen Hawking (English, 20th/21st century): Hawking's principal fields of research are theoretical cosmology and quantum gravity. Expanding on Einstein's work, he has hypothesized about the physical properties of black holes, described conditions necessary for a singularity, and made important contributions in string theory, in an attempt to generalize Einstein's special theory of relativity.

Changing nature of scientific knowledge

Perhaps the greatest peculiarity of scientific knowledge is that, at the same time that it is taken as fact, it may be disproved. Current scientific knowledge is the basis from which new discoveries are made. Yet even knowledge that has stood for hundreds of years is not considered too infallible to be challenged. If someone can create an experiment whose results consistently and reproducibly defy a law that has been in place for generations, that law will be nullified. It is absolutely essential, however, that these reproductions of the experiment be conducted by many different scientists who are in isolation from one another so there is no bias or interacting effects on the results.

Inquiry-based science in the classroom

If learning in the science classroom is inquiry based, children should see themselves as being involved in the process of learning. They should feel free to express curiosity and skepticism, change ideas and procedures, take risks, and exchange information with their classmates. Inquiry-based learning in science begins with observations of details, sequences, events, changes, similarities and differences, etc. Observations are followed by investigations based on scientific standards and safety that are designed by students. Designs should allow for verification, extension, or dismissal of ideas. Investigations should involve choosing tools, handling materials, measuring, observing, and recording data. The results of an investigation can take the form of a journal, report, drawing, graph, or chart. The summary of the observations and investigation should include explanations, solutions, and connections to other ideas, as well as further questions, an assessment of the quality of the work, a description of any problems encountered, and a description of the strengths and weaknesses of the investigation. Finally, students should reflect together about the lessons learned from the investigation.

Components of scientific experimentation

A hypothesis is a tentative supposition about a phenomenon (or a fact or set of facts) made in order to examine and test its logical or empirical consequences through investigation or methodological experimentation.
A theory is a scientifically proven, general principle offered to explain phenomena. A theory is derived from a hypothesis and verified by experimentation and research.
A scientific law is a generally accepted conclusion about a body of observations to which no exceptions have been found. Scientific laws explain things, but do not describe them.
A control is a normal, unchanged situation used for comparison against experimental data.
Constants are factors in an experiment that remain the same.
Independent variables are factors, traits, or conditions that are changed in an experiment. A good experiment has only one independent variable so that the scientist can track one thing at a time. The independent variable changes from experiment to experiment.
Dependent variables are changes that result from variations in the independent variable.

Science as a series of processes

Science is not just the steps of experimentation. While the process of posing a question, forming a hypothesis, testing the hypothesis, recording data, and drawing a conclusion is at the heart of scientific inquiry, there are other processes that are important as well. Once the scientist has completed the testing of a hypothesis and possibly come up with a theory, the scientist should then go through the process of getting feedback from colleagues, publishing an article about the work in a peer-reviewed journal, or otherwise reporting the results to the scientific community, replicating the experiment for verification of results (by the original scientist or others), and developing new questions. Science is not just a means of satisfying curiosity, but is also a process for developing technology, addressing social issues, building knowledge, and solving everyday problems.

Drawing conclusions after an experiment

Conclusions are based on data analysis and background research. The scientist has to take a hard look at the results of an experiment and check the accuracy of the data to draw preliminary conclusions. These should be compared to the background research to find out if the preliminary conclusion can be supported by previous research experiments. If the results do not support the hypothesis, or if they are contrary to what the background research predicted, then further research is needed. The focus should be on finding a reason for the different results. Finally, the scientist provides a discussion of findings that includes a summary of the results of the experiment, a statement as to whether the hypothesis was proven or disproven, a statement of the relationship between the independent and dependent variable, a summary and evaluation of the procedures of the experiment (including comments about successes and effectiveness), and suggestions for changes/modifications in procedures for further studies.

Scientific method

The scientific method provides a framework by which theories can be tested through prediction, hypotheses, experimentation, and interpretation of resulting data. It should be presented, taught and practiced as a process that can change from one situation to another, but that still follows certain guidelines to preserve the accuracy and relevance of results. Performing scientific inquiry according to the scientific method also enables different scientists to communicate with each other using a shared vocabulary so that they can understand each other's results and build upon each other's work.

Using the scientific method requires students to articulate their understanding of scientific concepts. Adherence and understanding of the scientific method can be used as a means of assessing how well a student has understood a specific concept.

Elements of scientific observation and experimentation

Five steps vital to the scientific method and to any experimentation performed in a science classroom are as follows:
1. Observe - Determining an occurrence that can be measured via experimentation
2. Organize - Placing data in a cohesive form
3. Predict - Stating the expected result of an experiment before performing that experiment
4. Infer - Use existing information to infer additional information
5. Experiment - Test a single variable in a controlled experimental environment where only that variable is independent

Using these five elements helps students adhere to the scientific method in order to produce relevant results in the classroom. How a student predicts the outcome of an experiment can also serve as an assessment of his or her understanding of scientific concepts.

Tools used in scientific experiments, observation, and inquiry

Major tools used in the science classroom enable students to make observations beyond what they can observe with the naked eye. These tools include:
- Microscope - Used to observe objects too small to see with the naked eye
- Telescope - Used to observe objects too distant to see in detail with the naked eye
- Spectroscope - Breaks beams of light down into individual colors

- Spectrophotometer - Determines how much of each color is absorbed and uses this information to determine what substance is being observed.

In addition to these tools, mathematics is an important tool in scientific observation and inquiry. Mathematics allows students to evaluate results and determine their relevance. Math is also often employed in making predictions about the outcome of an experiment.

Inquiry method of teaching science concepts

The inquiry method is another way to present scientific concepts to an elementary classroom. The inquiry method can be presented in one of two ways:
1. Inductive method - Students perform research and gather data from which they form generalizations and rules.
2. Deductive method - Students are presented with generalizations and rules, and then find specific examples of these rules through research.

The inquiry method encourages students to employ higher level thinking skills. In inquiry lessons, the teacher facilitates learning, but students must do their own research and projects in order to learn the specific concepts being presented. Inquiry lessons require preparation and work on the part of the teacher, who must ensure the goals of the lesson are clearly defined and that sufficient resources are available.

Hypothesis and steps in planning an experiment

A hypothesis is a type of prediction. Before performing an experiment, the student considers the variables that are to be tested and makes a prediction about how these variables will relate to each other. The experiment is then designed to determine the validity of the hypothesis. A hypothesis must be clearly defined and testable in order to result in a successful experiment. The four major steps in planning a scientific experiment are:
1. Identify variables relevant to the experiment
2. Decide what tools will work best to measure these variables and record results
3. Remove any variables that could adversely affect the outcome of the experiment
4. Determine the best way to evaluate the resulting data

Teachable questions in both assessment and planning scientific experiments

Teachable questions are those which can be easily demonstrated and which a student can easily prove he or she understands. In assessment, a teachable question has a clear-cut answer that the student can provide in order to demonstrate his knowledge of the subject. In planning scientific experiments, a teachable question is one that can be easily answered through experimentation. It also must present variables that can be measured accurately and adequately controlled during the course of the experiment.

Teachable questions are straightforward, well-defined, and have a single answer. If too many variables or too many possible answers are introduced, the experiment will not be successful or the student will not be able to demonstrate his knowledge of the subject being tested.

Contribution to heredity made by Mendel

Johann Gregor Mendel is known as the father of genetics. Mendel was an Austrian monk who performed thousands of experiments involving the breeding of the common pea plant in the monastery garden. Mendel kept detailed records including seed color, pod color, seed type, flower color, and plant height for eight years and published his work in 1865. Unfortunately, his work was largely ignored until the early 1900s. Mendel's work showed that genes come in pairs and that dominant and recessive traits are inherited independently of each other. His work established the law of segregation, the law of independent assortment, and the law of dominance.

Contribution to evolution made by Darwin

Charles Darwin's theory of evolution is the unifying concept in biology today. From 1831 to 1836, Darwin traveled as a naturalist on a five-year voyage on the *H.M.S. Beagle* around the tip of South America and to the Galápagos Islands. He studied finches, took copious amounts of meticulous notes, and collected thousands of plant and animal specimens. He collected 13 species of finches each with a unique bill for a distinct food source, which led him to believe that due to similarities between the finches, that the finches shared a common ancestor. The similarities and differences of fossils of extinct rodents and modern mammal fossils led him to believe that the mammals had changed over time. Darwin believed that these changes were the result from random genetic changes called mutations. He believed that mutations could be beneficial and eventually result in a different organism over time. In 1859, in his first book, *On the Origin of Species*, Darwin proposed that natural selection was the means by which adaptations would arise over time. He coined the term "natural selection" and said that natural selection is the mechanism of evolution. Because variety exists among individuals of a species, he stated that those individuals most compete for the same limited resources. Some would die, and others would survive. According to Darwin, evolution is a slow, gradual process. In 1871, Darwin published his second book, *Descent of Man, and Selection in Relation to Sex*, in which he discussed the evolution of man.

Drawing conclusions and making predictions from data

In order to more easily draw conclusions and make predictions, data must be graphed. Next, the scientist looks for patterns and trends in the data to identify correlations between the independent variable and the dependent variable. Then, the scientist checks to determine if the trends and correlations observed from experimentation support or reject the hypothesis. The conclusion should state whether or not the trends in the data support the hypothesis. Predictions can often be made if the data support the hypothesis. If the data have a linear correlation, a line of best fit enables the scientist to make predictions.

Limitations of models

Models are visual representations or replicas of natural phenomena such as objects or processes that are based on scientific evidence. Models can be used to make predictions. Models help scientists explain natural phenomena that are difficult to understand. Models usually have specific limits. Models usually make approximations when describing natural phenomena. Models should be as simple as possible while still maintaining their accuracy. Many models cannot incorporate all the details of the phenomena being studied due to the complexity of the phenomena. Models have to be simple enough to use to make predictions. Models should make visualizing a process easier, not more difficult, but simplicity may be sacrificed at the expense of accuracy.

Ethical concerns

Use of embryonic stem cells for research
Research involving the use of embryonic stem cells offers hope for genetically related health issues. However, ethical issues are seriously debated. New therapies could be developed using embryonic stem cells that would greatly alleviate suffering for many people. However, that benefit comes at the cost of human embryos. Proponents of embryonic stem cell research argue that an early embryo is not yet a person because the embryo cannot survive without being implanted in the uterus. Proponents argue that the embryo's status as a human being with full moral rights increases as the embryo develops. Many believe that the embryo should have no moral status. Fertilized eggs should be treated as the property of the parents who should have the right to donate that property to research. Opponents of embryonic stem cell research argue that the embryo is a human life at fertilization and should have full moral status at fertilization, and that a human embryo is a human being. Opponents argue that judgments determining when an embryo is viable or when an embryo is fully human cannot be made. Some opponents of stem cell research do not believe that the fertilized egg is a human being, but they still argue that by removing the stem cells from the early embryo, the embryo is prevented from becoming a human being. They argue that embryonic stem cell research destroys potential life.

Human cloning and animal cloning
Many issues are raised with the topic of human cloning and animal cloning. Disagreements arise over who would be allowed to produce human clones. Many are concerned about how clones would integrate into families and societies. Some believe that human cloning for procreation purposes should be regulated based on motivation. For example, individuals interested in raising a genetically related child should be granted approval, but those seeking immortality or viewing cloning as a novelty should be denied. Many believe that mandatory counseling and a waiting period should be enforced. Others argue that individuals do not have a right to a genetically related child that cloning is not safe, and that cloning is not medically necessary. Proponents argue that cloning is needed to generate tissues and whole organs that eliminate the need for immunosuppressive drugs. Cloned tissues and organs could be used to counter the effects of aging. Others fear that this will lead to the generation of humans solely for the purpose of harvesting tissues and organs. Animal rights activists are opposed to the cloning of animals. Animals are being cloned in laboratories and in livestock production. Activists argue that many cloned animals suffer from defects before they die. Some believe that animals have moral rights and should be treated with the same ethical consideration given to humans.

Impact of Science

Controversies surrounding the use of nuclear power

Nuclear fission power, while sustainable, has a host of attendant controversial problems. Among them is the incredibly dangerous transportation and long-term storage of its radioactive waste products, for which there is still no safe long-term solution. Its effects on those environments and creatures that come in contact with nuclear waste are still largely unknown. In addition, nuclear materials can be used in weaponry, and accidents at nuclear power plants like the one at Chernobyl can be devastating for thousands of years.

Scientists continue their study of the process of nuclear fusion, hoping that if humans can learn to harness the energy produced by smashing atoms rather than splitting them, the attendant problems of nuclear waste storage will be minimized.

Issues concerning management of renewable resources

Natural resources can be divided into two types, renewable and non-renewable. Renewable resources include plants and animals, along with water, air, and soil.

A pre-industrial earth was a self-sustaining system, maintaining a natural balance among plants, animals, and non-living elements in which waste products from one natural process were the fuel for another. Modern humans have intervened in this process in a way that upsets the natural balance of life. Humans have introduced non-native species from one part of the world to another, resulting in the devastation of local populations. Industrial-scale buildings can create disasters for local ecosystems, ruining habitats for animal populations.

Humans remove an increasing amount of the world's resources for industrial use, too quickly for nature to recover from easily. Renewable resources must be carefully managed to maintain a balanced ecosystem; over-harvesting of forests or over-hunting of animal populations can be devastating. Pollution of the air and water with chemical pollutants has far-reaching effects on the ecosystems of the earth, including the depletion of the ozone layer that protects earth life from ultraviolet rays, as does the removal of forests that produce the earth's oxygen.

Issues concerning management of non-renewable resources

Non-renewable resources include minerals, which are created naturally over millions of years. The industrialized world extracts minerals for fuel as well as for use in electronic equipment and medicine. Increased human extraction of non-renewable resources has endangered their availability, and over-mining has created other ecological problems, including runoff and water pollution. The use of fossil fuels for energy and transportation causes air pollution and is unsustainable. Fossil fuels cannot be replaced once depleted, and they are being depleted at an increasing rate. The need to find a sustainable alternative to the use of non-renewable fossil fuels is imperative.

Interactions among humans, natural hazards, and the environment

In science class, students will learn that the human population on earth can be affected by various factors from both their natural environments and from the technologies they use in their daily lives. These factors can be positive or negative, so students need to learn how to prepare for, respond to, and evaluate the consequences of environmental occurrences over a long period of time.

Natural disasters are a negative experience, but so are human-made disasters such as pollution and deforestation. Students need to understand that science is involved in the interactions between the human population, natural hazards, and the environment. They should know that the aim of science is to make these interactions balanced and positive. Science is a discipline that can help find ways to increase safety during and remediate after natural disasters, advance technology and transportation in an environmentally safe manner, prevent and cure diseases, and remediate the environmental damage that has already been done.

Studying science in the context of personal and social perspectives

Learning must be relevant, so when students study science in the context of personal and social perspectives, they see the practical application of the textbook knowledge. They are given an understanding of the issues around them that can be solved by science and the means to act on those issues.

Science should be taught within the social context of history so that students can see where society has been and how far it has come thanks to scientific advancements related to tools, medicine, transportation, and communication. Students should also understand how these advances developed in response to resources, needs, and values.

Students need to review the process of scientific inquiry through the centuries to get a sense of the benefits of intellectual curiosity, the inter-relatedness of science, and the development of civilization. Students should question the role science has played in the development of various cultures by considering how computers, refrigeration, vaccines, microscopes, fertilizers, etc. have improved the lives of people.

Interactions of science and technology with society

The interactions of science and technology with society include:
- Scientific knowledge and the procedures used by scientists influence the way many people think about themselves, others, and the environment.
- Technology influences society through its products and processes. It influences quality of life and the ways people act and interact. Technological changes are often accompanied by social, political, and economic changes. Science and technology contribute enormously to economic growth and productivity. The introduction of the cell phone into society is a perfect example of technology influencing society, quality of life, human interaction, and the economy.
- Societal challenges often inspire questions for scientific research, and social priorities often influence research priorities through the availability of research funding.

Science and technology have been advanced through the contributions of many different people in a variety of cultures during different time periods in history. Scientists and engineers work in colleges, businesses and industries, research institutes, and government agencies, touching many lives in a variety of settings.

Affect of habitat destruction on ecological systems and biodiversity

Many habitats have been altered or destroyed by humans. In fact, habitat destruction brought about by human endeavors has been the most significant cause of species extinctions resulting in the decrease in biodiversity throughout the world. As the human population has increased exponentially, the extinction rate has also increased exponentially. This is largely due to habitat destruction by humans. Humans use many resources in their various enterprises including agriculture, industry, mining, logging, and recreation. Humans have cleared much land for agriculture and urban developments. As habitats are destroyed, species are either destroyed or displaced. Often, habitats are fragmented into smaller areas, which only allow for small populations that are under threat by predators, diseases, weather, and limited resources. Especially hard hit are areas near the coastline, estuaries, and coral reefs. Nearly half of all mangrove ecosystems have been destroyed by human activity. Coral reefs have nearly been decimated from pollution such as oil spills and exploitation from the aquarium fish market and coral market.

Impact on the environment

Pollution mitigation
Pollution greatly affects the environment, but pollution mitigation has greatly reduced pollution and its effects during the past 40 years. New pollution-control technology has greatly reduced the amount of pollution from new power plants and factories. The Clean Air Act has greatly reduced the amount of pollution. With this legislation, new industrial sites are designed and built with pollution-control technology fully integrated into the facility. These technologies avoid or minimize the negative effects on the environment. New coal-fired power plants are fitted with pollution-control devices that greatly reduce and nearly eliminate sulfur dioxide and nitrogen oxide emissions. This greatly reduces acid rain, improves water quality, and improves the overall health of ecosystems. Reducing acid rain improves soil quality, which in turn improves the health of producers, which consequently improves the health of consumers, essentially strengthening the entire ecosystem. Reduced greenhouse gas emissions have lessened the impact of global warming such as rising sea levels due to melting glaciers and the resulting loss of habitats and biodiversity. Reduced smog and haze improves the intensity of sunlight required for photosynthesis.

Resource management
Resource management such as waste management and recycling greatly impacts the environment. Waste management is the monitoring, collection, transportation, and recycling of waste products. Methods of waste disposal include landfills and incineration. Well-managed landfills include burying wastes, but using clay or another lining material to prevent liquid leachate and layers of soil on top to reduce odors and vermin. Methane gas produced during decomposition can be extracted and burned to generate electricity. Landfills can be used as temporary storage for recyclable materials before transportation to a recycling plant. Wastes can be incinerated to reduce waste volume. Hazardous biomedical waste can be incinerated. However, incineration does emit pollutants and greenhouse gases. Proper waste management always includes recycling. Recycling is a method to recover resources. Recycled materials can be reprocessed into new products. Metals such as aluminum, copper, and steel are recycled. Plastics, glass, and paper products can be recycled. Organic materials such as plant materials and food scraps can be composted. The current trend is to shift from waste management to resource recovery. Wastes should be minimized and reduced to minimize the need for disposal. Unavoidable nonrecyclable wastes should be converted to energy by combustion if at all possible.

Renewable and sustainable resources
The management of natural resources and the renewability or sustainability of those natural resources greatly impact society. Sustainable agriculture involves growing foods in economical ways that do not harm resources. If left unchecked, farming can deplete the soil of valuable nutrients. Crops grown in these depleted soils are less healthy and more susceptible to disease. Sustainable agriculture uses more effective pest control such as insect-resistant corn, which reduces runoff and water pollution in the surrounding area. Sustainable forestry involves replenishing trees as trees are being harvested, which maintains the environment. Energy sources such as wind, solar power, and biomass energy are all renewable. Wind power is clean with no pollution and no greenhouse gas emissions. Cons of wind power include the use of land for wind farms, threats to birds, and the expense to build. Solar power has no greenhouse gas emissions, but some toxic metal wastes result in the production of photovoltaic cells, and solar power requires large areas of land. Biomass energy is sustainable, but its combustion produces greenhouse

emissions. Farming biomass requires large areas of land. Fossil fuels, which are nonrenewable, cause substantially more air pollution and greenhouse gas emissions, contributing to habitat loss and global warming.

Ethical and societal concerns regarding genetically modified food

Genetically modified (GM) foods are transgenic crops that have had their genes altered by technology. For example, herbicide-tolerant soybeans and insect-resistant corn have been grown for years in the United States. Several issues have been raised concerning GM foods. Some people do not want to go against Mother Nature. Even scientists may feel that because the genes in organisms have evolved over millions of years that man should not interfere. Others would argue that man has been selectively breeding plants and animals for hundreds of years, and genetic modification is just an extension of that concept. Scientists are concerned about introducing new allergens into the food supply. For example, if a gene from a peanut plant is introduced into a soybean plant, there may be a potential for allergic reactions. Proteins from microorganisms may have never been tested as allergens. Many are concerned that the genetic modifications will not be contained. Pollen from fields of genetically modified crops may be carried by insects or wind to other fields. In some cases, traits such as herbicide resistance might pass from the cultivated plants to the wild populations of those plants. Insect-resistant plants may harm insects other than those that were being targeted. For example, studies show that pollinators such as the monarch butterfly may be harmed from GM corn.

Force and Motion

Kinematic equations resulting from the case of constant acceleration

The phenomenon of constant acceleration allows physicists to construct a number of helpful equations. Perhaps the most fundamental equation of an object's motion is the position equation: $x = at^2/2 + v_it + x_i$. If the object is starting from rest at the origin, this equation reduces to $x = at^2/2$. The position equation can be rearranged to give the displacement equation: $\Delta x = at^2/2 + v_it$. If the object's acceleration is unknown, the position or displacement may be found by the equation $\Delta x = (v_f + v_i)t/2$. If the position of an object is unknown, the velocity may be found by the equation $v = v_i + at$. Similarly, if the time is unknown, the velocity after a given displacement may be found by the equation $v = \text{sqrt}(v_i^2 + 2a\Delta x)$.

Basics of relative motion and inertial reference frames

When we describe motion as being *relative*, we mean that it can only be measured in relation to something else. If a moving object is considered as it relates to some stationary object or arbitrary location, it will have a different measured velocity than it would if it were compared to some other object that is itself in motion. In other words, the measure of an object's velocity depends entirely on the reference frame from which the measurement is taken. When performing measurements of this kind, we may use any reference point we like. However, once we have decided on a reference point, we must be consistent in using it as the basis for all of our measurements, or else we will go astray. Additionally, if we want to be able to apply Newton's laws of motion or Galilean principles of relativity, we must select an inertial reference frame: that is, a reference frame that is not accelerating or rotating. A car traveling at a constant speed in a straight line is an inertial reference frame. A car moving in uniform circular motion is not.An object's velocity with respect to a frame fixed to the earth can be computed by measuring its velocity from any inertial reference frame and combining that velocity by vector addition with the velocity of the inertial frame with respect to the earth. For instance, if a man is traveling in the x-direction at 20 m/s, and he throws a rock out the window at a relative velocity of 15 m/s in the y-direction, the rock's velocity with respect to the earth is found by adding the two vectors: $\mathbf{v_r} = 20\mathbf{i} + 15\mathbf{j}$ m/s.

Newton's first law

Before Newton formulated his laws of mechanics, it was generally assumed that some force had to act on an object continuously in order to make the object move at a constant velocity. Newton, however, determined that unless some other force acted on the object (most notably friction or air resistance), it would continue in the direction it was pushed at the same velocity forever. In this light, a body at rest and a body in motion are not all that different, and Newton's first law makes little distinction. It states that a body at rest will tend to remain at rest, while a body in motion will tend to remain in motion. This phenomenon is commonly referred to as inertia, the tendency of a body to remain in its present state of motion. In order for the body's state of motion to change, it must be acted on by a non-zero net force. Net force is the vector sum of all forces acting on a body. If this vector sum is zero, then there is no unbalanced force, and the body will remain in its present state of motion. It is important to remember that this law only holds in inertial reference frames.

Newton's second law

Newton's second law states that an object's acceleration is directly proportional to the net force acting on the object, and inversely proportional to the object's mass. It is generally written in equation form $\mathbf{F} = m\mathbf{a}$, where $\mathbf{F}$ is the net force acting on a body, m is the mass of the body, and $\mathbf{a}$ is its acceleration. It is important to note from this equation that since the mass is always a positive quantity, the acceleration vector is always pointed in the same direction as the net force vector. Of course, in order to apply this equation correctly, one must clearly identify the body to which it is being applied. Once this is done, we may say that $\mathbf{F}$ is the vector sum of all forces acting on that body, or the net force. This measure includes only those forces that are external to the body; any internal forces, in which one part of the body exerts force on another, are discounted. Newton's second law somewhat encapsulates his first, because it includes the principle that if no net force is acting on a body, the body will not accelerate. As was the case with his first law, Newton's second law may only be applied in inertial reference frames.

Newton's third law

Newton's third law of motion is quite simple: for every force, there is an equal and opposite force. When a hammer strikes a nail, the nail hits the hammer just as hard. If we consider two objects, A and B, then we may express any contact between these two bodies with the equation $F_{AB} = -F_{BA}$. It is important to note in this kind of equation that the order of the subscripts denotes which body is exerting the force. Although the two forces are often referred to as the *action* and *reaction* forces, in physics there is really no such thing. There is no implication of cause and effect in the equation for Newton's third law. At first glance, this law might seem to forbid any movement at all. We must remember, however, that these equal, opposite forces are exerted on different bodies with different masses, so they will not cancel each other out.

Static and kinetic frictional forces, kinetic rolling frictional force

In order to illustrate the concept of friction, let us imagine a book resting on a table. As it sits there, the force of its weight (W) is equal and opposite to the normal force (N). If, however, we were to exert a force (F) on the book, attempting to push it to one side, a frictional force (f) would arise, equal and opposite to our force. This kind of frictional force is known as *static frictional force*. As we increase our force on the book, however, we will eventually cause it to accelerate in the direction of our force. At this point, the frictional force opposing us will be known as *kinetic frictional force*. For the most part, kinetic frictional force is lower than static frictional force, and so the amount of force needed to maintain the movement of the book will be less than that needed to initiate movement. For wheels and spherical objects on a surface, static friction at the point of contact allows them to roll, but there is a frictional force that resists the rolling motion as well, due primarily to deformation effects in the rolling material. This is known as rolling friction, and tends to be much smaller than either static or kinetic friction.

Basic properties of friction

The first property of friction is that, if the body does not move when horizontal force F is applied, then the static frictional force is exactly equal and opposite to F. Static frictional force has a maximum value, however, which is expressed as $f_{s,max} = \mu_s N$, in which μ_s is the coefficient of static friction, and N is the magnitude of the normal force. If the magnitude of F should exceed the maximum value of static friction, the body will begin to move. Once the body has begun to slide, the frictional force will generally decrease. The value to which the frictional force will diminish is expressed as $f_k = \mu_k N$, in which μ_k is the coefficient of kinetic friction. For objects inclined to roll, such as balls or wheels, there is a rolling frictional force that resists the continued rolling of such an object. This force is expressed by $f_r = \mu_r N$, in which μ_r is the coefficient of rolling friction. All of these frictional coefficients are dimensionless. Since the value of the frictional force depends on the interaction of the body and the surface, it is usually described as friction between the two.

Conservative and non-conservative forces

Forces that change the state of a system by changing kinetic energy into potential energy, or vice versa, are called conservative forces. This name arises because these forces conserve the total amount of kinetic and potential energy. Every other kind of force is considered non-conservative. One example of a conservative force is gravity. Consider the path of a ball thrown straight up into the air. Since the ball has the same amount of kinetic energy when it is thrown as it does when it returns to its original location (known as completing a closed path), gravity can be said to be a conservative force. More generally, a force can be said to be conservative if the work it does on an object through a closed path is zero. Frictional force would not meet this standard, of course, because it is only capable of performing negative work.

Potential energy

Potential energy is the amount of energy that can be ascribed to a body or bodies based on configuration. There are a couple of different kinds of potential energy. Gravitational potential energy is the energy associated with the separation of bodies that are attracted to one another gravitationally. Any time you lift an object, you are increasing its gravitational potential energy. Gravitational potential energy can be found by the equation PE = mgh, where m is the mass of an object, g is the gravitational acceleration, and h is its height above a reference point, most often the ground. Another kind of potential energy is elastic potential energy; elastic potential energy is associated with the compression or expansion of an elastic, or spring-like, object. Physicists will often refer to potential energy as being stored within a body, the implication being that it could emerge in the future.

Work performed by a spring

The work performed by a spring is one of the classic examples of work performed by variable force. When a spring is neither compressed nor extended, we may say that it is in a relaxed state. Any time the spring is taken out of this state, whether by being stretched or compressed, it will exert what is called a restoring force, as it attempts to return to its relaxed state. In most cases, we can say that the force, F, exerted by the spring is proportional to the displacement of the free end from its position during the relaxed state. This is known as Hooke's law, and is expressed $F = -kx$, where k is the spring constant or stiffness. The x-coordinate in this equation corresponds to an axis where $x = 0$ is the coordinate of the relaxed position. The negative sign in this equation indicates that the force is always opposite to the displacement.

Mass-energy relationship

Because mass consists of atoms, which are themselves formed of subatomic particles, there is an energy inherent in the composition of all mass. If all the atoms in a given mass were formed from their most basic particles, it would require a significant input of energy. This rest energy is the energy that Einstein refers to in his famous mass-energy relation $E = mc^2$, where c is the speed of light in a vacuum. In theory, if all the subatomic particles in a given mass were to spontaneously split apart, it would give off energy $E = mc^2$. For example, if this were to happen to a single gram of mass, the resulting outburst of energy would be $E = 9 \times 10^{13}$ J, enough energy to heat more than 200,000 cubic meters of water from the freezing point to the boiling point. In some nuclear reactions, small amounts of mass are converted to energy. The amount of energy released can be calculated through the same relation, $E = mc^2$. Most such reactions involve mass losses on the order of 10^{-30} kg.

Newton's law of gravitation

One of Newton's major insights into the behavior of physical objects was that every object in the universe exerts an attractive force on every other body. In quantitative terms, we may say that the gravitational force with which particles attract one another is given by $F = Gm_1m_2/r^2$, in which r is the distance between the particles and G is the gravitational constant, $G = 6.672 \times 10^{-11}$ N-m^2/kg^2. Although this equation is usually applied to particles, it may also be applied to objects, assuming that they are small relative to the distance between them. Newton expressed this relation by saying that a uniform spherical shell of matter attracts a particle outside the shell as if all the shell's matter were concentrated at its center. In the case of gravitation on earth, for instance, objects behave as if the earth were a single particle located at its center, and with the mass of the entire earth. Thus, regardless of an object's distance from the surface of the earth, it can be approximated as a particle due to the effective distance from the earth's center of mass. The difference in the gravitational pull on an object at sea level and that same object at the highest point on the earth's surface is about a quarter of a percent. Thus, the gravitational acceleration anywhere on the earth's surface is considered to be a constant, $g = 9.81$ m/s^2. For an object orbiting the earth, its period of orbit can be found by equating the gravitational force to the centripetal force, giving the equation $Gm_em/r^2 = mr\omega^2 = mr(2pi/T)^2$. Solving for the period yields $T = sqrt(4pi^2r^3/Gm_e)$.

- 212 -

Four basic laws of thermodynamics

The laws of thermodynamics are generalized principles dealing with energy and heat.
- The zeroth law of thermodynamics states that two objects in thermodynamic equilibrium with a third object are also in equilibrium with each other. Being in thermodynamic equilibrium basically means that different objects are at the same temperature.
- The first law deals with conservation of energy. It states that neither mass nor energy can be destroyed; only converted from one form to another.
- The second law states that the entropy (the amount of energy in a system that is no longer available for work or the amount of disorder in a system) of an isolated system can only increase. The second law also states that heat is not transferred from a lower-temperature system to a higher-temperature one unless additional work is done.
- The third law of thermodynamics states that as temperature approaches absolute zero, entropy approaches a constant minimum. It also states that a system cannot be cooled to absolute zero.

Different types of energy

Some discussions of energy consider only two types of energy: kinetic energy (the energy of motion) and potential energy (which depends on relative position or orientation). There are, however, other types of energy. Electromagnetic waves, for example, are a type of energy contained by a field. Another type of potential energy is electrical energy, which is the energy it takes to pull apart positive and negative electrical charges. Chemical energy refers to the manner in which atoms form into molecules, and this energy can be released or absorbed when molecules regroup. Solar energy comes in the form of visible light and non-visible light, such as infrared and ultraviolet rays. Sound energy refers to the energy in sound waves.

Motion and displacement

Motion is a change in the location of an object, and is the result of an unbalanced net force acting on the object. Understanding motion requires the understanding of three basic quantities: displacement, velocity, and acceleration.

When something moves from one place to another, it has undergone *displacement*. Displacement along a straight line is a very simple example of a vector quantity. If an object travels from position $x = -5$ cm to $x = 5$ cm, it has undergone a displacement of 10 cm. If it traverses the same path in the opposite direction, its displacement is -10 cm. A vector that spans the object's displacement in the direction of travel is known as a displacement vector.

Gravitational force

Gravitational force is a universal force that causes every object to exert a force on every other object. The gravitational force between two objects can be described by the formula, $F = Gm_1m_2/r^2$, where m_1 and m_2 are the masses of two objects, r is the distance between them, and G is the gravitational constant, $G = 6.672 \times 10^{-11}$ N-m^2/kg^2. In order for this force to have a noticeable effect, one or both of the objects must be extremely large, so the equation is generally only used in problems involving planetary bodies. For problems involving objects on the earth being affected by earth's gravitational pull, the force of gravity is simply calculated as $F = mg$, where g is 9.81 m/s^2 toward the ground.

Newton's first two laws of motion

Newton's first law
An object at rest or in motion will remain at rest or in motion unless acted upon by an external force.

This phenomenon is commonly referred to as inertia, the tendency of a body to remain in its present state of motion. In order for the body's state of motion to change, it must be acted on by an unbalanced force.

Newton's second law
An object's acceleration is directly proportional to the net force acting on the object, and inversely proportional to the object's mass.

It is generally written in equation form $F = ma$, where F is the net force acting on a body, m is the mass of the body, and a is its acceleration. Note that since the mass is always a positive quantity, the acceleration is always in the same direction as the force.

Simple machines

Simple machines include the inclined plane, lever, wheel and axle, and pulley. These simple machines have no internal source of energy. More complex or compound machines can be formed from them. Simple machines provide a force known as a mechanical advantage and make it easier to accomplish a task. The inclined plane enables a force less than the object's weight to be used to push an object to a greater height. A lever enables a multiplication of force. The wheel and axle allows for movement with less resistance. Single or double pulleys allows for easier direction of force. The wedge and screw are forms of the inclined plane. A wedge turns a smaller force working over a greater distance into a larger force. The screw is similar to an incline that is wrapped around a shaft.

Friction

Friction is a force that arises as a resistance to motion where two surfaces are in contact. The maximum magnitude of the frictional force (f) can be calculated as $f = F_c\mu$, where F_c is the contact force between the two objects and μ is a coefficient of friction based on the surfaces' material composition. Two types of friction are static and kinetic. To illustrate these concepts, imagine a book resting on a table. The force of its weight (W) is equal and opposite to the force of the table on the book, or the normal force (N). If we exert a small force (F) on the book, attempting to push it to one side, a frictional force (f) would arise, equal and opposite to our force. At this point, it is a *static frictional force* because the book is not moving. If we increase our force on the book, we will eventually cause it to move. At this point, the frictional force opposing us will be a *kinetic frictional force*. Generally, the kinetic frictional force is lower than static frictional force (because the frictional coefficient for static friction is larger), which means that the amount of force needed to maintain the movement of the book will be less than what was needed to start it moving.

Physical Properties of Matter

Hydrolysis, oxidation, catalysis and polymerization

Hydrolysis is a chemical reaction of a molecule with water in which a molecule is broken into parts, forming one or more new compounds. This process is present in the metabolism of, for example, carbohydrates and proteins. *Oxidation* is a chemical reaction, usually of an atom or molecule with an oxygen atom, in which a compound gains one or more electrons. Reduction is the process that complements oxidation.

Catalysis is a process in which the rate of a chemical reaction is affected by the introduction of a substance called a catalyst. A catalyst contributes to a chemical reaction but remains unaffected by it. Enzymes are essential natural catalysts for chemical reactions that enable life in Earth's organisms. The chemical process of creating polymers (a chain of small molecules called monomers linked through covalent bonding) is called **polymerization**. Some polymers, such as proteins, are formed naturally. Other polymers, such as plastic and rubber, can be artificially produced through the provision of a catalyst or increased heat.

Fluid density and pressure

The density of a fluid is generally expressed with the symbol ρ. The density may be found with the simple equation $\rho = m/V$, mass per unit volume. Density is a scalar property, meaning that it has no direction component. It is typically measured in SI units of kilograms per cubic meter. While the density of a gas will tend to fluctuate considerably depending on the level of pressure, the density of a liquid is comparatively stable. The density of water is most often taken to be 1000 kg/m^3.
The pressure of a fluid is calculated as $P = F/A$, force per unit area. To find the pressure at a given depth in a fluid, or the hydrostatic pressure, the pressure can be calculated as $P = \rho g h$, where h is the fluid depth. Pressure, like fluid density, is a scalar, and does not have a direction. The equation for pressure is concerned only with the magnitude of that force, not with the direction in which it is pointing. The SI unit of pressure is the Newton per square meter, or pascal.

States of matter

The three states in which matter can exist are solid, liquid, and gas. They differ from each other in the motion of and attraction between individual molecules. In a solid, the molecules have little or no motion and are heavily attracted to neighboring molecules, giving them a definite structure. This structure may be ordered/crystalline or random/amorphous. Liquids also have considerable attraction between molecules, but the molecules are much more mobile, having no set structure. In a gas, the molecules have little or no attraction to one another and are constantly in motion. They are separated by distances that are very large in comparison to the size of the molecules. Gases easily expand to fill whatever space is available. Unlike solids and liquids, gases are easily compressible. The three states of matter can be traversed by the addition or removal of heat. For example, when a solid is heated to its melting point, it can begin to form a liquid. However, in order to transition from solid to liquid, additional heat must be added at the melting point to overcome the latent heat of fusion. Upon further heating to its boiling point, the liquid can begin to form a gas, but again, additional heat must be added at the boiling point to overcome the latent heat of vaporization.

Solutions

A solution is a homogeneous mixture. A mixture is two or more different substances that are mixed together, but not combined chemically. Homogeneous mixtures are those that are uniform in their composition. Solutions consist of a solute (the substance that is dissolved) and a solvent (the substance that does the dissolving). An example is sugar water. The solvent is the water and the solute is the sugar. The intermolecular attraction between the solvent and the solute is called solvation. Hydration refers to solutions in which water is the solvent. Solutions are formed when the forces of the molecules of the solute and the solvent are as strong as the individual molecular forces of the solute and the solvent. An example is that salt ($NaCl$) dissolves in water to create a solution. The Na^+ and the Cl^- ions in salt interact with the molecules of water and vice versa to overcome the individual molecular forces of the solute and the solvent.

Mixtures, suspensions, colloids, emulsions, and foams

A mixture is a combination of two or more substances that are not bonded. Suspensions are mixtures of heterogeneous materials. Particles are usually larger than those found in true solutions. Dirt mixed vigorously with water is an example of a suspension. The dirt is temporarily suspended in water, but the two separate once the mixing is ceased. A mixture of large (1 nm to 500 nm) particles is called a colloidal suspension. The particles are termed dispersants and the dispersing medium is similar to the solvent in a solution. Sol refers to a liquid or a solid that also has solids dispersed through it, such as milk or gelatin. An aerosol spray is a colloid suspension of gas and the solid or liquid being dispersed. An emulsion refers to a liquid or a solid that has a liquid dispersed through it. A foam is a liquid that has gas dispersed through it.

Chemical and physical properties

Matter has both physical and chemical properties. Physical properties can be seen or observed without changing the identity or composition of matter. For example, the mass, volume, and density of a substance can be determined without permanently changing the sample. Other physical properties include color, boiling point, freezing point, solubility, odor, hardness, electrical conductivity, thermal conductivity, ductility, and malleability. Chemical properties cannot be measured without changing the identity or composition of matter. Chemical properties describe how a substance reacts or changes to form a new substance. Examples of chemical properties include flammability, corrosivity, oxidation states, enthalpy of formation, and reactivity with other chemicals.

Properties of water

Water exhibits numerous properties. Water has a high surface tension due to the cohesion between water molecules from the hydrogen bonds between the molecules. The capillary action of water is also due to this cohesion, and the adhesion of water is due to its polarity. Water is an excellent solvent due to its polarity and is considered the universal solvent. Water exists naturally as a solid, liquid, and gas. The density of water is unusual as it moves between the liquid and solid phases. The density of water decreases as ice freezes and forms crystals in the solid phase. Water is most dense at 4°C. Water can act as an acid or base in chemical reactions. Pure water is an insulator because it has virtually no ions. Water has a high specific heat capacity due to its low molecular mass and bent molecular shape.

Chemical Properties of Matter

Forms of fossil fuels

Coal, *natural gas*, and *petroleum* are all fossil fuels. Each of these energy sources contains potential energy received from the Sun. To release the stored energy, the fuel must be burned. This process changes the stored energy into heat energy. That heat energy, in turn, can be used to create electrical power or to produce heat for indoor climate control. One problem with the use of fossil fuels lies in the fact that fuel combustion creates by-products, such as carbon dioxide, that adversely affect Earth's atmosphere. Another problem with fossils fuels lies in their limited availability.

Forms of renewable energy

Wind, hydroelectric, and geothermal power are renewable energy sources. In *wind* and *hydroelectric* power, the motion of wind and water, respectively, are used to turn rotors called turbines. The motion of the turbines is converted by generators into electric power. *Geothermal* power is created by nuclear reactions in the Earth's core. Those reactions create heat, which travels below the Earth's surface in the form of water or magma. This heat energy is sometimes released through hot springs or geysers on the Earth's surface. Geothermal power can be used for indoor climate control or, like water and wind, to power electric generators.

Organization of matter

An element is the most basic type of matter. It has unique properties and cannot be broken down into other elements. The smallest unit of an element is the atom. A chemical combination of two or more types of elements is called a compound. Compounds often have properties that are very different from those of their constituent elements. The smallest independent unit of an element or compound is known as a molecule. Most elements are found somewhere in nature in single-atom form, but a few elements only exist naturally in pairs. These are called diatomic elements, of which some of the most common are hydrogen, nitrogen, and oxygen. Elements and compounds are represented by chemical symbols, one or two letters, most often the first in the element name. More than one atom of the same element in a compound is represented with a subscript number designating how many atoms of that element are present. Water, for instance, contains two hydrogen atoms and one oxygen atom. Thus, the chemical formula is H_2O. Methane contains one carbon atom and four hydrogen atoms, so its formula is CH_4.

Mixtures vs compounds

Mixtures are similar to compounds in that they are produced when two or more substances are combined. However, there are some key differences as well. Compounds require a chemical combination of the constituent particles, while mixtures are simply the interspersion of particles. Unlike compounds, mixtures may be separated without a chemical change. A mixture retains the chemical properties of its constituent particles, while a compound acquires a new set of properties. Given compounds can exist only in specific ratios, while mixtures may be any ratio of the involved substances.

Periodic table

The periodic table groups elements with similar chemical properties together. The grouping of elements is based on atomic structure. It shows periodic trends of physical and chemical properties and identifies families of elements with similar properties. It is a common model for organizing and understanding elements. In the periodic table, each element has its own cell that includes varying amounts of information presented in symbol form about the properties of the element. Cells in the table are arranged in rows (periods) and columns (groups or families). At minimum, a cell includes the symbol for the element and its atomic number. The cell for hydrogen, for example, which appears first in the upper left corner, includes an "H" and a "1" above the letter. Elements are ordered by atomic number, left to right, top to bottom.

Chemical reactions

Chemical reactions measured in human time can take place quickly or slowly. They can take fractions of a second or billions of years. The rates of chemical reactions are determined by how frequently reacting atoms and molecules interact. Rates are also influenced by the temperature and various properties (such as shape) of the reacting materials. Catalysts accelerate chemical reactions, while inhibitors decrease reaction rates. Some types of reactions release energy in the form of heat and light. Some types of reactions involve the transfer of either electrons or hydrogen ions between reacting ions, molecules, or atoms. In other reactions, chemical bonds are broken down by heat or light to form reactive radicals with electrons that will readily form new bonds. Processes such as the formation of ozone and greenhouse gases in the atmosphere and the burning and processing of fossil fuels are controlled by radical reactions.

Structure of atoms

All matter consists of atoms. Atoms consist of a nucleus and electrons. The nucleus consists of protons and neutrons. The properties of these are measurable; they have mass and an electrical charge. The nucleus is positively charged due to the presence of protons. Electrons are negatively charged and orbit the nucleus. The nucleus has considerably more mass than the surrounding electrons. Atoms can bond together to make molecules. Atoms that have an equal number of protons and electrons are electrically neutral. If the number of protons and electrons in an atom is not equal, the atom has a positive or negative charge and is an ion.

Models of atoms

Atoms are extremely small. A hydrogen atom is about 5×10^{-8} mm in diameter. According to some estimates, five trillion hydrogen atoms could fit on the head of a pin. Atomic radius refers to the average distance between the nucleus and the outermost electron. Models of atoms that include the proton, nucleus, and electrons typically show the electrons very close to the nucleus and revolving around it, similar to how the Earth orbits the sun. However, another model relates the Earth as the nucleus and its atmosphere as electrons, which is the basis of the term "electron cloud." Another description is that electrons swarm around the nucleus. It should be noted that these atomic models are not to scale. A more accurate representation would be a nucleus with a diameter of about 2 cm in a stadium. The electrons would be in the bleachers. This model is similar to the not-to-scale solar system model.

Physical and chemical properties

Both physical changes and chemical reactions are everyday occurrences. Physical changes do not result in different substances. For example, when water becomes ice it has undergone a physical change, but not a chemical change. It has changed its form, but not its composition. It is still H_2O. Chemical properties are concerned with the constituent particles that make up the physicality of a substance. Chemical properties are apparent when chemical changes occur. The chemical properties of a substance are influenced by its electron configuration, which is determined in part by the number of protons in the nucleus (the atomic number). Carbon, for example, has 6 protons and 6 electrons. It is an element's outermost valence electrons that mainly determine its chemical properties. Chemical reactions may release or consume energy.

Elements, compounds, solutions, and mixtures

Elements: These are substances that consist of only one type of atom.
Compounds: These are substances containing two or more elements. Compounds are formed by chemical reactions and frequently have different properties than the original elements. Compounds are decomposed by a chemical reaction rather than separated by a physical one.
Solutions: These are homogeneous mixtures composed of two or more substances that have become one.
Mixtures: Mixtures contain two or more substances that are combined but have not reacted chemically with each other. Mixtures can be separated using physical methods, while compounds cannot.

Chemical vs physical changes

Physical changes do not produce new substances. The atoms or molecules may be rearranged, but no new substances are formed. Phase changes or changes of state such as melting, freezing, and sublimation are physical changes. For example, physical changes include the melting of ice, the boiling of water, sugar dissolving into water, and the crushing of a piece of chalk into a fine powder. Chemical changes involve a chemical reaction and do produce new substances. When iron rusts, iron oxide is formed, indicating a chemical change. Other examples of chemical changes include baking a cake, burning wood, digesting a cracker, and mixing an acid and a base.

Ionic bonding

Ionic bonding results from the transfer of electrons between atoms. A cation or positive ion is formed when an atom loses one or more electrons. An anion or negative ion is formed when an atom gains one or more electrons. An ionic bond results from the electrostatic attraction between a cation and an anion.

One example of a compound formed by ionic bonds is sodium chloride or NaCl. Sodium (Na) is an alkali metal and tends to form Na^+ ions. Chlorine is a halogen and tends to form Cl^- ions. The Na^+ ion and the Cl^- ion are attracted to each other. This electrostatic attraction between these oppositely charged ions is what results in the ionic bond between them.

electron transer from sodium to chlorine

Covalent bonding

Covalent bonding results from the sharing of electrons between atoms. Atoms seek to fill their valence shell and will share electrons with another atom in order to have a full octet (except hydrogen and helium, which only hold two electrons in their valence shells). Molecular compounds have covalent bonds. Organic compounds such as proteins, carbohydrates, lipids, and nucleic acids are molecular compounds formed by covalent bonds. Methane (CH_4) is a molecular compound in which one carbon atom is covalently bonded to four hydrogen atoms as shown below.

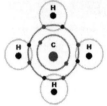

Oxidation, reduction, oxidizing agent, reducing agent, oxidation states

Oxidation can be defined as any process involving a loss of one or more electrons.
Reduction can be defined as any process involving a gain of one or more electrons.
Oxidizing agent can be defined as the reactant in an oxidation-reduction reaction that causes oxidation. The *oxidizing agent* is reduced.
Reducing agent can be defined as the reactant in an oxidation-reduction reaction that causes reduction. The *reducing agent* is oxidized.
Oxidation states, also known as oxidation numbers, represent the charge that an atom has in a molecule or ion.

General chemical equation for a neutralization reaction

Neutralization is a reaction of an acid and a base that yields a salt and water. The salt is formed from the cation of the base and the anion of the acid. The water is formed from the cation of the acid and the anion of the base: acid + base → salt + water.

An example is the neutralization reaction of hydrochloric acid and sodium hydroxide to form sodium chloride and water:
HCl (aq) + NaOH (aq) → NaCl (s) + H_2O (l).

Chemical properties of several common household products

Table sugar, or sucrose, is a disaccharide of glucose molecules and fructose molecules. Sugar dissolves in water. When heated, as sugar nears its melting point, it will darken or caramelize as the sucrose breaks into glucose and fructose. Upon further heating, the sugar will continue to break down and leave a carbon residue. Salt, or sodium chloride, is an ionic compound of sodium ions and chlorine ions. Salt crystals form a face-centered cubic structure. Adding salt lowers the freezing point of water and raises its boiling point. Vinegar is a dilute (typically 5%) acetic (ethanoic) acid solution. Acetic acid is a weak acid. A 5% solution of acetic acid has a pH of approximately 2.4. Baking soda is the common name for the compound sodium bicarbonate. Sodium bicarbonate neutralizes acids.

Matter and Energy

Matter and its properties

Matter refers to substances that have mass and occupy space (or volume). The traditional definition of matter describes it as having three states: solid, liquid, and gas. These different states are caused by differences in the distances and angles between molecules or atoms, which result in differences in the energy that binds them. Solid structures are rigid or nearly rigid and have strong bonds. Molecules or atoms of liquids move around and have weak bonds, although they are not weak enough to readily break. Molecules or atoms of gases move almost independently of each other, are typically far apart, and do not form bonds. The current definition of matter describes it as having four states. The fourth is plasma, which is an ionized gas that has some electrons that are described as free because they are not bound to an atom or molecule.

Energy transformations

Electric to mechanical: Ceiling fan
Chemical to heat: A familiar example of a chemical to heat energy transformation is the internal combustion engine, which transforms the chemical energy (a type of potential energy) of gas and oxygen into heat. This heat is transformed into propulsive energy, which is kinetic. Lighting a match and burning coal are also examples of chemical to heat energy transformations.
Chemical to light: Phosphorescence and luminescence (which allow objects to glow in the dark) occur because energy is absorbed by a substance (charged) and light is re-emitted comparatively slowly. This process is different from the one involved with glow sticks. They glow due to chemiluminescence, in which an excited state is created by a chemical reaction and transferred to another molecule.
Heat to electricity: Examples include thermoelectric, geothermal, and ocean thermal.
Nuclear to heat: Examples include nuclear reactors and power plants.
Mechanical to sound: Playing a violin or almost any instrument
Sound to electric: Microphone
Light to electric: Solar panels
Electric to light: Light bulbs

Relationship between conservation of matter and atomic theory

Atomic theory is concerned with the characteristics and properties of atoms that make up matter. It deals with matter on a microscopic level as opposed to a macroscopic level. Atomic theory, for instance, discusses the kinetic motion of atoms in order to explain the properties of macroscopic quantities of matter. John Dalton (1766-1844) is credited with making many contributions to the field of atomic theory that are still considered valid. This includes the notion that all matter consists of atoms and that atoms are indestructible. In other words, atoms can be neither created nor destroyed. This is also the theory behind the conservation of matter, which explains why chemical reactions do not result in any detectable gains or losses in matter. This holds true for chemical reactions and smaller scale processes. When dealing with large amounts of energy, however, atoms can be destroyed by nuclear reactions. This can happen in particle colliders or atom smashers.

Models for the flow of electric charge

Models that can be used to explain the flow of electric current, potential, and circuits include water, gravity, and roller coasters. For example, just as gravity is a force and a mass can have a potential for energy based on its location, so can a charge within an electrical field. Just as a force is required to move an object uphill, a force is also required to move a charge from a low to high potential. Another example is water. Water does not flow when it is level. If it is lifted to a point and then placed on a downward path, it will flow. A roller coaster car requires work to be performed to transport it to a point where it has potential energy (the top of a hill). Once there, gravity provides the force for it to flow (move) downward. If either path is broken, the flow or movement stops or is not completed.

Magnetic fields

The motions of subatomic structures (nuclei and electrons) produce a magnetic field. It is the direction of the spin and orbit that indicate the direction of the field. The strength of a magnetic field is known as the magnetic moment. As electrons spin and orbit a nucleus, they produce a magnetic field. Pairs of electrons that spin and orbit in opposite directions cancel each other out, creating a net magnetic field of zero. Materials that have an unpaired electron are magnetic. Those with a weak attractive force are referred to as paramagnetic materials, while ferromagnetic materials have a strong attractive force. A diamagnetic material has electrons that are paired, and therefore does not typically have a magnetic moment. There are, however, some diamagnetic materials that have a weak magnetic field.

Phenomenon of sound

Sound is a pressure disturbance that moves through a medium in the form of mechanical waves, which transfer energy from one particle to the next. Sound requires a medium to travel through, such as air, water, or other matter since it is the vibrations that transfer energy to adjacent particles, not the actual movement of particles over a great distance. Sound is transferred through the movement of atomic particles, which can be atoms or molecules. Waves of sound energy move outward in all directions from the source. Sound waves consist of compressions (particles are forced together) and rarefactions (particles move farther apart and their density decreases). A wavelength consists of one compression and one rarefaction. Different sounds have different wavelengths. Sound is a form of kinetic energy.

Pitch, loudness, sound intensity, timbre, and oscillation

Pitch: Pitch is the quality of sound determined by frequency. For example, a musical note can be tuned to a specific frequency. A, for instance, has a frequency of 440 Hz, which is a higher frequency than middle C. Humans can detect frequencies between about 20 Hz to 20,000 Hz.
Loudness: Loudness is a human's perception of sound intensity.
Sound intensity: Sound intensity is measured as the sound power per unit area, and can be expressed in decibels.
Timbre: This is a human's perception of the type or quality of sound.
Oscillation: This is a measurement, usually of time, against a basic value, equilibrium, or rest point.

Doppler effect

The Doppler effect refers to the effect the relative motion of the source of the wave and the location of the observer has on waves. The Doppler effect is easily observable in sound waves. What a person hears when a train approaches or a car honking its horn passes by are examples of the Doppler effect. The pitch of the sound is different not because the emitted frequency has changed, but because the received frequency has changed. The frequency is higher (as is the pitch) as the train approaches, the same as emitted just as it passes, and lower as the train moves away. This is because the wavelength changes. The Doppler effect can occur when an observer is stationary, and can also occur when two trains approach and pass each other. Electromagnetic waves are also affected in this manner. The motion of the medium can also affect the wave. For waves that do not travel in a medium, such as light waves, it is the difference in velocity that determines the outcome.

Heat, energy, work, and thermal energy

Heat: Heat is the transfer of energy from a body or system as a result of thermal contact. Heat consists of random motion and the vibration of atoms, molecules, and ions. The higher the temperature is, the greater the atomic or molecular motion will be.
Energy: Energy is the capacity to do work.
Work: Work is the quantity of energy transferred by one system to another due to changes in a system that is the result of external forces, or macroscopic variables. Another way to put this is that work is the amount of energy that must be transferred to overcome a force. Lifting an object in the air is an example of work. The opposing force that must be overcome is gravity. Work is measured in joules (J). The rate at which work is performed is known as power.
Thermal energy: Thermal energy is the energy present in a system due to temperature.

Thermal contact

Thermal contact refers to energy transferred to a body by a means other than work. A system in thermal contact with another can exchange energy with it through the process of heat transfer. Thermal contact does not necessarily involve direct physical contact. Heat is energy that can be transferred from one body or system to another without work being done. Everything tends to become less organized and less useful over time (entropy). In all energy transfers, therefore, the overall result is that the heat is spread out so that objects are in thermodynamic equilibrium and the heat can no longer be transferred without additional work.

Heat and temperature

Heat is energy transfer (other than direct work) from one body or system to another due to thermal contact. Everything tends to become less organized and less orderly over time (entropy). In all energy transfers, therefore, the overall result is that the energy is spread out uniformly. This transfer of heat energy from hotter to cooler objects is accomplished by conduction, radiation, or convection. Temperature is a measurement of an object's stored heat energy. More specifically, temperature is the average kinetic energy of an object's particles. When the temperature of an object increases and its atoms move faster, kinetic energy also increases. Temperature is not energy since it changes and is not conserved. Thermometers are used to measure temperature.

Electric charges

The attractive force between the electrons and the nucleus is called the electric force. A positive (+) charge or a negative (-) charge creates a field of sorts in the empty space around it, which is known as an electric field. The direction of a positive charge is away from it and the direction of a negative charge is towards it. An electron within the force of the field is pulled towards a positive charge because an electron has a negative charge. A particle with a positive charge is pushed away, or repelled, by another positive charge. Like charges repel each other and opposite charges attract. Lines of force show the paths of charges. Electric force between two objects is directly proportional to the product of the charge magnitudes and inversely proportional to the square of the distance between the two objects. Electric charge is measured with the unit Coulomb (C). It is the amount of charge moved in one second by a steady current of one ampere ($1C = 1A \times 1s$).

Electric current movement through circuits

Electric current is the sustained flow of electrons that are part of an electric charge moving along a path in a circuit. This differs from a static electric charge, which is a constant non-moving charge rather than a continuous flow. The rate of flow of electric charge is expressed using the ampere (amp or A) and can be measured using an ammeter. A current of 1 ampere means that 1 coulomb of charge passes through a given area every second. Electric charges typically only move from areas of high electric potential to areas of low electric potential. To get charges to flow into a high potential area, you must to connect it to an area of higher potential, by introducing a battery or other voltage source.

Simple circuits

Movement of electric charge along a path between areas of high electric potential and low electric potential, with a resistor or load device between them, is the definition of a simple circuit. It is a closed conducting path between the high and low potential points, such as the positive and negative terminals on a battery. One example of a circuit is the flow from one terminal of a car battery to the other. The electrolyte solution of water and sulfuric acid provides work in chemical form to start the flow. A frequently used classroom example of circuits involves using a D cell (1.5 V) battery, a small light bulb, and a piece of copper wire to create a circuit to light the bulb.

Basics of a magnet, including composition, poles, and permanence

A magnet is a piece of metal, such as iron, steel, or magnetite (lodestone) that can affect another substance within its field of force that has like characteristics. Magnets can either attract or repel other substances. Magnets have two poles: north and south. Like poles repel and opposite poles (pairs of north and south) attract. The magnetic field is a set of invisible lines representing the paths of attraction and repulsion. Magnetism can occur naturally, or ferromagnetic materials can be magnetized. Certain matter that is magnetized can retain its magnetic properties indefinitely and become a permanent magnet. Other matter can lose its magnetic properties. For example, an iron nail can be temporarily magnetized by stroking it repeatedly in the same direction using one pole of another magnet. Once magnetized, it can attract or repel other magnetically inclined materials, such as paper clips. Dropping the nail repeatedly will cause it to lose its charge.

Magnetic fields and current and magnetic domains

A magnetic field can be formed not only by a magnetic material, but also by electric current flowing through a wire. When a coiled wire is attached to the two ends of a battery, for example, an electromagnet can be formed by inserting a ferromagnetic material such as an iron bar within the coil. When electric current flows through the wire, the bar becomes a magnet. If there is no current, the magnetism is lost. A magnetic domain occurs when the magnetic fields of atoms are grouped and aligned. These groups form what can be thought of as miniature magnets within a material. This is what happens when an object like an iron nail is temporarily magnetized. Prior to magnetization, the organization of atoms and their various polarities are somewhat random with respect to where the north and south poles are pointing. After magnetization, a significant percentage of the poles are lined up in one direction, which is what causes the magnetic force exerted by the material.

- 224 -

Waves

Waves have energy and can transfer energy when they interact with matter. Although waves transfer energy, they do not transport matter. They are a disturbance of matter that transfers energy from one particle to an adjacent particle. There are many types of waves, including sound, seismic, water, light, micro, and radio waves. The two basic categories of waves are mechanical and electromagnetic. Mechanical waves are those that transmit energy through matter. Electromagnetic waves can transmit energy through a vacuum. A transverse wave provides a good illustration of the features of a wave, which include crests, troughs, amplitude, and wavelength.

Electromagnetic spectrum

The electromagnetic spectrum is defined by frequency (f) and wavelength (λ). Frequency is typically measured in hertz and wavelength is usually measured in meters. Because light travels at a fairly constant speed, frequency is inversely proportional to wavelength, a relationship expressed by the formula $f = c/\lambda$, where c is the speed of light (about 300 million meters per second). Frequency multiplied by wavelength equals the speed of the wave; for electromagnetic waves, this is the speed of light, with some variance for the medium in which it is traveling. Electromagnetic waves include (from largest to smallest wavelength) radio waves, microwaves, infrared radiation (radiant heat), visible light, ultraviolet radiation, x-rays, and gamma rays. The energy of electromagnetic waves is carried in packets that have a magnitude inversely proportional to the wavelength. Radio waves have a range of wavelengths, from about 10^{-3} to 10^5 meters, while their frequencies range from about 10^3 to 10^{11} Hz.

Visible light as part of the electromagnetic spectrum

Light is the portion of the electromagnetic spectrum that is visible because of its ability to stimulate the retina. It is absorbed and emitted by electrons, atoms, and molecules that move from one energy level to another. Visible light interacts with matter through molecular electron excitation (which occurs in the human retina) and through plasma oscillations (which occur in metals). Visible light is between ultraviolet and infrared light on the spectrum. The wavelengths of visible light cover a range from 380 nm (violet) to 760 nm (red). Different wavelengths correspond to different colors.

Kinetic and potential energy

The internal energy of a system may be categorized as kinetic energy or potential energy. Kinetic energy is the energy of a system associated with movement. In chemical systems, this movement is predicted by the kinetic theory of matter and is due to the random movement of the particles that make up the system. The kinetic energy of a particle may be calculated by the following formula: $KE = \frac{1}{2}mv^2$, where KE is the kinetic energy in joules, m is the mass of the particle in kilograms, and v is the velocity of the particle in meters per second. Potential energy is the stored energy in a system associated with position or configuration. In chemical systems, this energy is the energy associated with the chemical bonds and intermolecular forces of the matter contained in the system.

Temperature and temperature scales

Temperature is a measure of the average kinetic energy of the atoms or molecules in a system. The Celsius scale is the most commonly used scale with the freezing point of water at 0 °C and the boiling point of water at 100 °C. Normal body temperature is 37 °C. On the Fahrenheit scale, water freezes at 32 °F and boils at 212 °F. Normal body temperature is 98.6 °F. In chemistry, the Kelvin scale is frequently used. Water freezes at 273.15 K and boils at 373.15 K. The Celsius scale and the Kelvin scale have exactly 100 ° between the freezing point and boiling point of water. The Fahrenheit scale has 180 ° between the freezing point and the boiling point of water. The value of 1 °F is 100/180 or 5/9 of the size of 1 °C. The formulas to convert between the temperature scales are as follows: $T_C = \frac{5}{9}(T_F - 32)$; $T_F = \frac{9}{5}T_C + 32$; $T_K = T_C + 273.15$.

<u>Temperature conversion examples</u>
Perform the following temperature conversions
    a. *Convert 200.0 °F to the Celsius scale.*
    b. *Convert 24.0 °C to the Fahrenheit scale.*
    c. *Convert 21.5 °C to the Kelvin scale.*

    a. To convert from 200.0 °F to °C, use the equation $T_C = \frac{5}{9}(T_F - 32)$. Substituting 200.0 in for T_F yields $T_C = \frac{5}{9}(200.0 - 32) = \frac{5}{9}(168.0) = 93.33$ °C.

    b. To convert from 24.0 °C to °F, use the equation $T_F = \frac{9}{5}T_C + 32$. Substituting 24.0 in for T_C yields $T_F = \frac{9}{5}(24.0) + 32 = 43.2 + 32 = 75.2$ °F.

    c. To convert from 21.5 °C to K, use the equation $T_K = T_C + 273.15$. Substituting 21.5 in for T_C yields $T_K = 21.5 + 273.15 = 294.7$ K.

Process of heat transfer

Heat transfer is the flow of thermal energy, which is measured by temperature. Heat will flow from warmer objects to cooler objects until an equilibrium is reached in which both objects are at the same temperature. Because the particles of warmer objects possess a higher kinetic energy than the particles of cooler objects, the particles of the warmer objects are vibrating more quickly and collide more often, transferring energy to the cooler objects in which the particles have less kinetic energy and are moving more slowly. Heat may be transferred by conduction, convection, or radiation. In conduction, heat is transferred by direct contact between two objects. In convection, heat is transferred by moving currents. In radiation, heat is transferred by electromagnetic waves.

Energy Transformations and Conservation

Light energy and Earth's ecosystems

Light energy, necessary to sustain life on Earth, reaches our planet in the form of sunlight. Photosynthesis, a process that occurs in plants, converts light energy into chemical energy. By consuming plants, animals acquire some of the potential energy stored in those plants. Through digestion, the animals obtain the energy they need to survive. Smaller animals are then eaten by larger predators, which are consumed by other animals, including humans. Such a progression is called a food chain. Some of the transferred energy is recycled into the environment through processes such as respiration and nitrification. A portion of energy is lost with each transfer from organism to organism. The carbon and nitrogen cycles involve similar processes of chemical energy transfer.

Nuclear fusion

Nuclear fusion, unlike fission, occurs often in nature: This process generates the massive amounts of vital light and heat energy Earth receives from the Sun. In fusion reactions (also called thermonuclear reactions) two nuclei are joined (fused) to form one heavier nucleus. This combination requires extreme amounts of energy (usually in the form of heat energy) to overcome the natural electrostatic force that drives nuclei (positively charged due to the presence of protons) apart. When the nuclei are close enough to each other, the strong force that holds them together binds the two. The resultant molecule is unstable; it splits into new stable elements and free neutrons. The change from instability to stability includes a release of potential energy. Fusion reactions involve hydrogen or one of its heavier isotopes, such as deuterium or tritium.

The law of conservation of mass

The law of conservation of mass is also known as the law of conservation of matter. This basically means that in a closed system, the total mass of the products must equal the total mass of the reactants. This could also be stated that in a closed system, mass never changes. A consequence of this law is that matter is never created or destroyed during a typical chemical reaction. The atoms of the reactants are simply rearranged to form the products. The number and type of each specific atom involved in the reactants is identical to the number and type of atoms in the products. This is the key principle used when balancing chemical equations. In a balanced chemical equation, the number of moles of each element on the reactant side equals the number of moles of each element on the product side.

Exothermic and endothermic reactions

Exothermic reactions release heat energy, whereas endothermic reactions absorb energy. Exothermic reactions can be represented by reactants → products + heat. Endothermic reactions can be represented by reactants + heat → products. The change in enthalpy for exothermic reactions is negative, whereas the change in enthalpy for endothermic reactions is positive. An example of an exothermic reaction is the burning of propane. An example of an endothermic reaction is the reaction that takes place in a first-aid cold pack.

Renewable and nonrenewable energy

Types of nonrenewable energy include fossil fuels and nuclear fuels. Advantages of nonrenewable energy include low fuel costs and available technologies. Disadvantages of nonrenewable energy include harmful gaseous emissions and radioactive waste disposal. Types of renewable energy include solar, wind, water (hydroelectricity), hydrogen alternative energy, geothermal, and biofuels. Advantages to renewable energy include a never-ending supply of fuel and no harmful effects on the environment. Disadvantages to renewable energy sources include the need for specific locations and the need for development of technologies to better use these energy resources.

Importance of conservation and recycling

Conserving means saving important resources from loss or waste. Conservation helps the demand for natural resources to be met. Conservation helps maintain the health of the environment, which in turn protects biodiversity, agriculture (soil erosion), and the fishing industry. Conservation helps protect the climate, and the climate impacts every area of life. Recycling reduces the depletion of limited resources, and it reduces the need for waste disposal. Recycling saves energy and reduces gaseous emissions that contribute to global warming and air pollution.

Pros and cons of fossil fuel and nuclear fuel

Fossil fuels and nuclear fuels are considered nonrenewable fuels. Pros of using fossil fuels such as coal, oil, and natural gas include excellent fuel availability, low costs, available technology, and easy transportation. New, clean-burning coal technologies reduce air pollution significantly. Cons of using fossil fuels include the emission of harmful gases, which contribute to acid rain, the greenhouse effect, and ozone-layer depletion. Drilling and mining irreparably damage habitats and the environment. Pros of using nuclear fuels include low fuel costs, available technology, no pollution, reliability, and overall safety. Cons of using nuclear fuels include the possibility of meltdowns, possible radiation exposure, and radioactive waste disposal.

Pros and cons of hydropower, wind power, solar power, and geothermal power

Hydropower, wind power, solar power, and geothermal power are types of renewable energy. A major pro of renewable energy is that it is clean with no harmful emissions that contribute to the greenhouse effect, air pollution, acid rain, or ozone-layer depletion. Also, water, wind, sunlight, and heat from the Earth are never-ending sources of energy. A con of these renewable energy sources is that they are often location specific. For example, solar panels need to be placed in locations with good exposure to sunlight. Hydropower needs to be located near an ample supply of running water.

Structure and Function of Living Things

Subfields of biology

There are a number of subfields of biology:
- Zoology – The study of animals
- Botany – The study of plants
- Biophysics – The application of the laws of physics to the processes of organisms and the application of the facts about living things to human processes and inventions
- Biochemistry – The study of the chemistry of living organisms, including diseases and the pharmaceutical drugs used to cure them
- Cytology – The study of cells
- Histology – The study of the tissues of plants and animals
- Organology – The study of tissues organized into organs
- Physiology – The study of the way organisms function, including metabolism, the exchange of matter and energy in nutrition, the senses, reproduction and development, and the work of the nervous system and brain

- Genetics – The study of heredity as it relates to the transmission of genes
- Ethology – The study of animal behavior
- Ecology – The study of the relationship of living organisms to their environments

Kingdoms of life forms

All living creatures can be classified into one of these kingdoms:
1. **The Moneran Kingdom** – This group contains the simplest known organisms (prokaryotes). Members have just one chromosome, reproduce asexually, may have flagella, and are very simple in form. Members are either bacteria or blue-green algae.
2. **The Protist Kingdom** – This group contains the simplest eukaryotes. They have a true nucleus surrounded by a membrane that separates it from the cytoplasm. Most are one-celled and have no complex tissues like plants. Members include protozoa and algae.
3. **The Fungi Kingdom** – Members have no chlorophyll, so they don't make their own food like plants. They reproduce using spores. Fungi are made up of filaments called hyphae that, in larger fungi, can interlace to form a tissue called mycelium. Fungi include mushrooms and microscopic organisms that may be parasitic.
4. **The Plant Kingdom** – This group consists of all multi-celled organisms that have chlorophyll and make their own food. Plants have differentiated tissues and reproduce either sexually or asexually.
5. **The Animal Kingdom** – This group consists of all multi-celled organisms that have no chlorophyll and have to feed on existing organic material. Animals have the most complex tissues and can move about.

Hunters and prey animals

The interaction between predators and their prey is important to controlling the balance of an ecosystem.

Hunters are carnivorous animals at the top of the ecological pyramid that eat other animals. Hunters tend to be territorial, leaving signs to warn others to stay out or risk a fight. Hunters are equipped to capture with claws, curved beaks, spurs, fangs, etc. They try to use a minimum amount of energy for each capture, so they prey upon the more vulnerable (the old, ill, or very young) when given a choice. Predators never kill more than they can eat. Some hunters have great speed, some stalk, and some hunt in groups.

Prey animals are those that are captured by predators for food. They are usually herbivores further down the ecological pyramid. Prey animals have special characteristics to help them flee from predators. They may hide in nests or caves, become totally immobile to escape detection, have protective coloration or camouflage, have warning coloration to indicate being poisonous, or have shells or quills for protection.

Life processes that all living things have in common

Living things share many processes that are necessary to survival, but the ways these processes and interactions occur is highly diverse. Processes include those related to:
- Nutrition – the process of obtaining, ingesting, and digesting foods; excreting unused or excess substances; and extracting energy from the foods to maintain structure.
- Transport (circulation) – the process of circulating essential materials such as nutrients, cells, hormones, and gases (oxygen and hydrogen) to the places they are needed by moving

them through veins, arteries, and capillaries. Needed materials do not travel alone, but are "piggybacked" on transporting molecules.

- Respiration – the process of breathing, which is exchanging gases between the interior and exterior using gills, trachea (insects), or lungs.
- Regulation – the process of coordinating life activities through the nervous and endocrine systems.
- Reproduction and growth – the process of producing more of one's own kind and growing from birth to adulthood. The more highly evolved an animal is, the longer its growth time is.
- Locomotion (in animals) – the process of moving from place to place in the environment by using legs, flight, or body motions.

Organisms that interfere with cell activity

Viruses, bacteria, fungi, and other parasites may infect plants and animals and interfere with normal life functions, create imbalances, or disrupt the operations of cells.

Viruses – These enter the body by inhalation (airborne) or through contact with contaminated food, water, or infected tissues. They affect the body by taking over the cell's protein synthesis mechanism to make more viruses. They kill the host cell and impact tissue and organ operations. Examples of viruses include measles, rabies, pneumonia, and AIDS.
Bacteria – These enter the body through breaks in the skin or contaminated food or water, or by inhalation. They reproduce rapidly and produce toxins that kill healthy host tissues. Examples include diphtheria, bubonic plague, tuberculosis, and syphilis.
Fungi – These feed on healthy tissues of the body by sending rootlike tendrils into the tissues to digest them extracellularly. Examples include athlete's foot and ringworm.
Parasites – These enter the body through the skin, via insect bites, or through contaminated food or water. Examples include tapeworms, malaria, or typhus.

How plants manufacture food

Plants are the only organisms capable of transforming inorganic material from the environment into organic matter by using water and solar energy. This transformation is made possible by chloroplasts, flat structures inside plant cells. Chloroplasts, located primarily in the leaves, contain chlorophyll (the pigment capable of absorbing light and storing it in chemical compounds), DNA, ribosomes, and numerous enzymes. Chloroplasts are surrounded by a membrane. The leaves of plants are the main producers of oxygen, which helps purify the air.

The chlorophyll in chloroplasts is responsible for the light, or luminous, phase of photosynthesis. The energy it absorbs breaks down water absorbed through the roots into hydrogen and oxygen to form ATP molecules that store energy. In the dark phase, when the plant has no light, the energy molecules are used to attach carbon dioxide to water and form glucose, a sugar.

Role of a cell

The cell is the basic organizational unit of all living things. Each piece within a cell has a function that helps organisms grow and survive. There are many different types of cells, but cells are unique to each type of organism. The one thing that all cells have in common is a membrane, which is comparable to a semi-permeable plastic bag. The membrane is composed of phospholipids. There are also some transport holes, which are proteins that help certain molecules and ions move in and out of the cell. The cell is filled with a fluid called cytoplasm or cytosol.

Within the cell are a variety of organelles, groups of complex molecules that help a cell survive, each with its own unique membrane that has a different chemical makeup from the cell membrane. The larger the cell, the more organelles it will need to live.

Chloroplasts of plant cells

Chloroplasts, which make plants green, are the food producers of a plant cell. They differ from an animal cell's mitochondria, which break down sugars and nutrients. Photosynthesis occurs when the energy from the sun hits a chloroplast and the chlorophyll uses that energy to combine carbon dioxide and water to make sugars and oxygen. The nutrition and oxygen obtained from plants makes them the basis of all life on earth. A chloroplast has two membranes to contain and protect the inner parts. The stroma is an area inside the chloroplast where reactions occur and starches are created. A thylakoid has chlorophyll molecules on its surface, and a stack of thylakoids is called a granum. The stacks of sacs are connected by stromal lamellae, which act like the skeleton of the chloroplast, keeping all the sacs a safe distance from each other and maximizing the efficiency of the organelle.

Passive and active transport

Passive transport within a cell does not require energy and work. For example, when there is a large concentration difference between the outside and the inside of a cell, the pressure of the greater concentration, not energy, will move molecules across the lipid bilayer into the cell. Another example of passive transport is osmosis, which is the movement of water across a membrane. Too much water in a cell can cause it to burst, so the cell moves ions in and out to help equalize the amount of water.

Active transport is when a cell uses energy to move individual molecules across the cell membrane to maintain a proper balance. Proteins embedded in the lipid bilayer do most of the transport work. There are hundreds of different types of proteins because they are specific. For instance, a protein that moves glucose will not move calcium. The activity of these proteins can be stopped by inhibitors or poisons, which can destroy or plug up a protein.

Functions of roots, stems, and leaves

Roots are structures designed to pull water and minerals from soil or water. In large plants such as trees, the roots usually go deep into the ground to not only reach the water, but also to support and stabilize the tree. There are some plant species that have roots above ground, and there are also plants called epiphytes that live in trees with their roots clinging to the branches. Some roots, like carrots and turnips, serve as food. Roots are classified as primary and lateral (like a trunk and branches). The apical meristem is the tip of a root or shoot that helps the plant increase in length. Root hairs are fuzzy root extensions that help with the absorption of water and nutrients.

The majority of the plant above ground is made up of the stems (trunk and branches) and leaves. Stems transport food and water and act as support structures. Leaves are the site for photosynthesis, and are connected to the rest of the plant by a vascular system.

Characteristics of gymnosperms, cycads, and conifers

Gymnosperms are plants with vascular systems and seeds but no flowers (flowers are an evolutionary advancement). The function of the seed is to ensure offspring can be produced by the plant by providing a protective coating that lets the plant survive for long periods until it germinates. It also stores food for the new plant to use until it can make its own. Seeds can be spread over a wide area.

Cycads are sturdy plants with big, waxy fronds that make them look like ferns or palms. They can survive in harsh conditions if there is warm weather. For reproduction, they have big cones located in the center of the plant. The female plant grows a fruit in the middle of the stem.

Conifers are trees that thrive in northern latitudes and have cones. Examples of conifers are pine, cedar, redwood, and spruce. Conifers are evergreens because they have needles that take full advantage of the sun year round. They are also very tall and strong because of the chemical substance xylem in their systems.

Characteristics of angiosperms

Angiosperms are plants that have flowers. This is advantageous because the plant's seeds and pollen can be spread not only by gravity and wind, but also by insects and animals. Flowers are able to attract organisms that can help pollinate the plant and distribute seeds. Some flowering plants also produce fruit. When an animal eats the fruit, the plant seeds within will be spread far and wide in the animal's excrement.

There are two kinds of angiosperm seeds: monocotyledons (monocots) and dicotyledons (dicots). A cotyledon is the seed leaf or food package for the developing plant. Monocots are the simple flowering plants such as grasses, corn, palm trees, and lilies. They always have three petals on their flowers, and their leaves are long strands (like a palm frond). A dicot has seeds with two cotyledons, or two seed leaves of food. Most everyday flowers are dicots with four or five petals and extremely complex leaves with veins. Examples include roses, sunflowers, cacti, and cherry trees.

Characteristics of arthropods

Arthropods have a number of unique characteristics:
- They have an exoskeleton (outside instead of inside).
- They molt. As the arthropod grows, it must shed its old shell and grow a new one.
- They have several legs, which are jointed.
- Their advanced nervous systems allow for hunting, moving around, finding a mate, and learning new behaviors for adaptation.
- They develop through metamorphosis. As arthropods develop, they change body shape. There are two types of metamorphosis:
  - Complete – The entire body shape changes. An example is butterflies, which change from worm-like larvae to insects with wings.
  - Gradual – The arthropod starts off small with no wings, and then molts and grows wings. Example: Grasshoppers.

Arthropods include spiders, crustaceans, and the enormous insect species (26 orders) called uniramians. Ranging from fleas to mosquitoes, beetles, dragonflies, aphids, bees, flies, and many more, uniramians have exoskeletons made of chitin, compound eyes, complex digestive systems, and usually six legs. This group is extremely diverse. Some can fly, some have toxins or antennae, and some can make wax, silk, or honey.

Characteristics of the reptiles

One group of vertebrates is the reptile. This group includes:
- Crocodilia – This is a group of reptiles that can grow quite large, and includes alligators and crocodiles. Normally found near the water in warmer climates, Crocodilia might be more closely related to birds than other reptiles.
- Squamata – This is the order of reptiles that includes snakes and lizards. Snakes are special because they have no legs and no ears. They feel vibrations, smell with their tongues, have specialized scales, and can unhinge their jaws to swallow prey that is larger than they are. Like snakes, lizards have scales, but they differ in that they have legs, can dig, can climb trees, and can grab things.
- Chelonia – This is the order of reptiles that includes turtles and tortoises. It is a special group because its members have shells. Different varieties live in forests, water, and deserts, or anywhere the climate is warm enough. They also live a long time, even hundreds of years. Turtles are typically found near water and tortoises on land, even dry areas.

Respiratory system

The respiratory system exchanges gases with the environment. Amphibians exchange gases through their moist skin and fish use gills, but mammals, birds, and reptiles have lungs. The human respiratory system is made up of the nose, mouth, pharynx, trachea, and two lungs. The purpose of the respiratory system is to bring oxygen into the body and expel carbon dioxide.

The respiratory system can inhale viruses, bacteria, and dangerous chemicals, so it is vulnerable to toxins and diseases such as pneumonia, which causes the lungs to fill with fluid until they cannot take in enough oxygen to support the body. Emphysema, often caused by smoking tobacco, destroys the tissues in the lungs, which cannot be regenerated.

The respiratory system interacts with the digestive system in that the mouth and pharynx are used to swallow food and drink, as well as to breathe. It interacts with the circulatory system in that it provides fresh oxygen through blood vessels that pass through the lungs. This oxygen is then carried by the circulatory system throughout the body.

Skeletal system

The human body has an endoskeleton, meaning it is inside the body. It is made up of bones instead of the hard plate of exoskeletons or fluids in tubes, which comprise the hydrostatic system of the starfish. The purpose of the skeleton is to support the body, provide a framework to which the muscles and organs can connect, and protect the inner organs. The skull protects the all-important brain and the ribs protect the internal organs from impact. The skeletal system interacts with the muscular system to help the body move, and softer cartilage works with the calcified bone to allow smooth movement of the body. The skeletal system also interacts with the circulatory system in that the marrow inside the bones helps produce both white and red blood cells.

Nervous system

The nervous system is divided into two parts: the central nervous system (brain and spinal cord) and the peripheral nervous system (a network of billions of neurons of different types throughout the entire body). The neurons are connected end to end, and transmit electrical impulses to each other. Efferent neurons send impulses from the central system to the limbs and organs. Afferent neurons receive sensory information and transmit it back to the central system.

The nervous system is concerned with senses and action. In other words, it senses something and then acts upon it. An example is a predator sensing prey and attacking it. The nervous system also automatically senses activity inside the body and reacts to stimuli. For example, the first bite of a meal sets the whole digestive system into motion.

The nervous system interacts with every other system in the body because all the tissues and organs need instruction, even when individuals are not aware of any activity occurring. For instance, the endocrine system is constantly working to produce hormones or adrenalin as needed.

System of classification for living organisms

The main characteristic by which living organisms are classified is the degree to which they are related, not the degree to which they resemble each other. The science of classification is called taxonomy, a difficult science since the division lines between groups is not always clear. Some animals have characteristics of two separate groups.

The basic system of taxonomy involves placing an organism into a major kingdom (Moneran, Protist, Fungi, Plants, and Animals), and then dividing those kingdoms into phyla, then classes, then orders, then families, and finally genuses. For example, the family cat is in the kingdom of animals, the phylum of chordates, the class of mammals, the order of carnivores, the family of felidae, and the genus of felis. All species of living beings can be identified with Latin scientific names that are assigned by the worldwide binomial system. The genus name comes first, and is followed by the name of the species. The family cat is *felis domesticus*.

Although not part of taxonomy, behavior is also considered in identifying living beings. For example, birds are identified according to their songs or means of flight.

Major structures and systems of animals

Animals are made up of specialized cells that group together to form tissues; these tissues group together to form organs; these groups of organs form a system; and each system within an animal performs a specific function. The systems that make up animals are:
- Skeletal - Supports the body; made of bones as well as ligaments and cartilage
- Muscular - Controls bodily movement, both voluntary and involuntary
- Nervous - Sends signals that stimulate bodily movement, both voluntary and involuntary; includes the brain, which evaluates and interprets these signals.
- Respiratory - Brings air and oxygen into the body
- Circulatory - Transports blood, which contains oxygen along with different nutrients and lymph, throughout the body

- Immune - Removes foreign bodies, such as viruses, from the body
- Digestive - Converts food into energy
- Excretory - Removes waste from the body

Importance of cells and structural organization associated with living things

All organisms, whether plants, animals, fungi, protists, or bacteria, exhibit structural organization on the cellular and organism level. All cells contain DNA and RNA and can synthesize proteins. Cells are the basic structural units of all organisms. All organisms have a highly organized cellular structure. Each cell consists of nucleic acids, cytoplasm, and a cell membrane. Specialized organelles such as mitochondria and chloroplasts have specific functions within the cell. In single-celled organisms, that single cell contains all of the components necessary for life. In multicellular organisms, cells can become specialized. Different types of cells can have different functions. Life begins as a single cell whether by asexual or sexual reproduction. Cells are grouped together in tissues. Tissues are grouped together in organs. Organs are grouped together in systems. An organism is a complete individual.

Structure, organization, modes of nutrition, and reproduction of plants

Plants are multicellular organisms with eukaryotic cells containing cellulose in their cell walls. Plant cells have chlorophyll and perform photosynthesis. Plants can be vascular or nonvascular. Vascular plants have true leaves, stems, and roots that contain xylem and phloem. Nonvascular plants lack true leaves, stems and roots and do not have any true vascular tissue but instead rely on diffusion and osmosis for most transport of materials. Almost all plants are autotrophic, relying on photosynthesis for food. A small number do not have chlorophyll and are parasitic, but these are extremely rare. Plants can reproduce sexually or asexually. Many plants reproduce by seeds produced in the fruits of the plants. Some plants reproduce by seeds on cones. Ferns reproduce by spores. Some plants can reproduce asexually by vegetative reproduction.

Cells

Cells are the basic structural units of all living things. Cells are composed of various molecules including proteins, carbohydrates, lipids, and nucleic acids. All animal cells are eukaryotic. All animal cells have a nucleus, cytoplasm, and a cell membrane. Organelles include mitochondria, ribosomes, endoplasmic reticulum, Golgi apparatuses, and vacuoles. Specialized cells are numerous including but not limited to various muscle cells, nerve cells, epithelial cells, bone cells, blood cells, and cartilage cells. Cells are grouped to together in tissues to perform specific functions.

Tissues

Tissues are groups of cells that work together to perform a specific function. Tissues can be grouped into four broad categories: muscle tissue, nerve tissue, epithelial tissue, and connective tissue. Muscle tissue is involved in body movement. Muscle tissues can be composed of skeletal muscle cells, cardiac muscle cells, or smooth muscle cells. Skeletal muscles include the muscles commonly called biceps, triceps, hamstrings, and quadriceps. Cardiac muscle tissue is found only in the heart. Smooth muscle tissue provides tension in the blood vessels, control pupil dilation, and aid in peristalsis. Nerve tissue is located in the brain, spinal cord, and nerves. Epithelial tissue makes up the layers of the skin and various membranes. Connective tissues include bone tissue, cartilage, tendons, ligaments, fat, blood, and lymph. Tissues are grouped together as organs to form specific functions.

Organs

Organs are groups of tissues that work together to perform specific functions. Complex animals have several organs that are grouped together in multiple systems. For example, the heart is specifically designed to pump blood throughout an organism's body. The heart is composed mostly of muscle tissue in the myocardium, but it also contains connective tissue in the blood and membranes, nervous tissue that controls the heart rate, and epithelial tissue in the membranes. Gills in fish and lungs in reptiles, birds, and mammals are specifically designed to exchange gases. In birds, crops are designed to store food and gizzards are designed to grind food.

Organ systems

Organ systems are groups of organs that work together to perform specific functions. In mammals, there are 11 major organ systems: integumentary system, respiratory system, cardiovascular system, endocrine system, nervous system, immune system, digestive system, excretory system, muscular system, skeletal system, and reproductive system. For example, in mammals, the cardiovascular system that transports materials throughout the body consists of the heart, blood vessels, and blood. The respiratory system, which provides for the exchange of gases, consists of the nasal passages, pharynx, larynx, trachea, bronchial tubes, lungs, alveoli, and diaphragm. The digestive system, which processes consumed food, consists of the alimentary canal and additional organs including the liver, gallbladder, and pancreas.

Cardiovascular system

The cardiovascular system consists primarily of the heart, blood, and blood vessels. The heart is a pump that pushes blood through the arteries. Arteries are blood vessels that carry blood away from the heart, and veins are blood vessels that carry blood back to the heart. The exchange of materials between blood and cells occur in the capillaries, which are the tiniest of the blood vessels. Blood is the fluid that carries materials to and from each cell of an organism. The main function of the cardiovascular system is to provide for gas exchange, the delivery of nutrients and hormones, and waste removal. All vertebrates and a few invertebrates including annelids, squids, and octopuses have a closed circulatory system. Blood is pumped through a series of vessels and does not fill body cavities. Mammals, birds and crocodilians have a four-chambered heart. Most amphibians and reptiles have a three-chambered heart. Fish have only a two-chambered heart. Arthropods and most mollusks have open circulatory systems. Usually blood is pumped by a heart into the body cavities and bathes the tissues in blood. Muscle movement moves the blood through the body. Blood then diffuses back to the heart through the cells. Many invertebrates do not have a cardiovascular system. For example, echinoderms have a water vascular system.

Respiratory system

The function of the respiratory system is to move air in and out of the body in order to facilitate the exchange of oxygen and carbon dioxide. The respiratory system consists of the nasal passages, pharynx, larynx, trachea, bronchial tubes, lungs, and diaphragm. When the diaphragm contracts, the volume of the chest increases, which reduces the pressure in the lungs. The intercostal muscles also aid in breathing. Then, air is inhaled through the nose or mouth and passes through the pharynx, larynx, trachea, and bronchial tubes into the lungs. Bronchial tubes branch into bronchioles, which end in clusters of alveoli. The alveoli are tiny sacs inside the lungs where gas exchange takes place.

When the diaphragm relaxes, the volume in the chest cavity decreases, forcing the air out of the lungs.

Digestive system

The main function of the digestive system is to process the food that is consumed by the animal. This includes mechanical and chemical processing. Depending on the animal, mechanical processes can happen in various ways. Mammals have teeth to chew their food. Saliva is secreted, which contains enzymes to begin the breakdown of starches. Many animals such as birds, earthworms, crocodilians, and crustaceans have a gizzard or gizzard-like organ that grinds the food. Many animals such as mammals, birds, reptiles, amphibians, and fish have a stomach that stores and absorbs food. Gastric juice containing enzymes and hydrochloric acid is mixed with the food. The intestine or intestines absorb nutrients and reabsorb water from the undigested material. Many animals have a liver, gallbladder, and pancreas, which aid in digestion of proteins and fats although not being part of the muscular tube through which the waste passes. Undigested wasted are eliminated from the body through an anus or cloaca.

Excretory system

All animals have some type of excretory system that has the main function of processing and eliminating metabolic wastes. In complex animals such as mammals, the excretory system consists of the kidneys, ureters, urinary bladder, and urethra. Urea and other toxic wastes must be eliminated from the body. The kidneys constantly filter the blood. The nephron is the working unit of the kidney. Each nephron functions like a tiny filter. Nephrons not only filter the blood, but they also facilitate reabsorption and secretion. Basically, the glomerulus filters the blood. Water and dissolved materials such as glucose and amino acids pass on into the Bowman's capsule. Depending on concentration gradients, water and dissolved materials can pass back into the blood primarily through the proximal convoluted tubule. Additional water can be removed at the loop of Henle. Antidiuretic hormone regulates the water that is lost or reabsorbed. Urine passes from the kidneys through the ureters to the urinary bladder where it is stored before it is expelled from the body through the urethra.

Endocrine system

The endocrine system consists of several ductless glands, which secrete hormones directly into the bloodstream. The pituitary gland is the master gland, which controls the functions of the other glands. The pituitary gland regulates skeletal growth and the development of the reproductive organs. The pineal gland regulates sleep cycles. The thyroid gland regulates metabolism and helps regulate the calcium level in the blood. The parathyroid glands also help regulate the blood calcium level. The adrenal glands secrete the emergency hormone epinephrine, stimulate body repairs, and regulate sodium and potassium levels in the blood. The islets of Langerhans located in the pancreas secrete insulin and glucagon to regulate the blood sugar level. In females, ovaries produce estrogen, which stimulates sexual development, and progesterone, which functions during pregnancy. In males, the testes secrete testosterone, which stimulates sexual development and sperm production.

Immune system

The immune system in animals defends the body against infection and disease. The immune system can be divided into two broad categories: innate immunity and adaptive immunity. Innate immunity includes the skin and mucous membranes, which provide a physical barrier to prevent pathogens from entering the body. Special chemicals including enzymes and proteins in mucus, tears, sweat, and stomach juices destroy pathogens. Numerous white blood cells such as neutrophils and macrophages protect the body from invading pathogens. Adaptive immunity involves the body responding to a specific antigen. Typically, B-lymphocytes or B cells produce antibodies against a specific antigen, and T-lymphocytes or T-cells take special roles as helpers, regulators, or killers. Some T-cells function as memory cells.

Products of photosynthesis

Plants produce glucose during photosynthesis. That glucose then enters reactions to form sucrose, starch, and cellulose. Glucose is a simple carbohydrate or monosaccharide. Plants do not transport glucose molecules. Instead, the glucose is joined to a fructose to form a sucrose, which is transported in sap. Sucrose is a disaccharide. Glucose and sucrose are simple carbohydrates. Starches and cellulose are long chains of glucose molecules called polysaccharides. Plants store glucose as starch, and plants use cellulose for rigidity in their cell walls. Both starch and cellulose are complex carbohydrates.

Structure and function of the nucleus

Typically, a eukaryote has only one nucleus that takes up approximately 10% of the volume of the cell. Components of the nucleus include the nuclear envelope, nucleoplasm, chromatin, and nucleolus. The nuclear envelope is a double-layer membrane with the outer layer connected to the endoplasmic reticulum. The nucleus can communicate with the rest of the cell through several nuclear pores. The chromatin consists of deoxyribonucleic acid (DNA) and histones that are packaged into chromosomes during mitosis. The nucleolus, which is the dense central portion of the nucleus, manufactures ribosomes. Functions of the nucleus include the storage of genetic material, production of ribosomes, and transcription of ribonucleic acid (RNA).

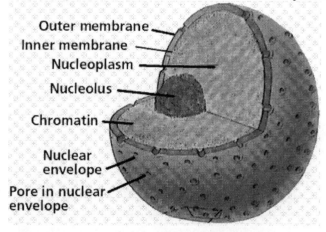

Outer membrane
Inner membrane
Nucleoplasm
Nucleolus
Chromatin
Nuclear envelope
Pore in nuclear envelope

Stages of mitosis

Mitosis is the asexual process of cell division. During mitosis, one parent cell divides into two identical daughter cells. Mitosis is used for growth, repair, and replacement of cells. Some unicellular organisms reproduce asexually by mitosis. Some multicellular organisms can reproduce by fragmentation or budding, which involves mitosis. Mitosis consists of four phases: prophase, metaphase, anaphase, and telophase. During prophase, the spindle fibers appear, and the DNA is condensed and packaged as chromosomes that become visible. The nuclear membrane breaks down, and the nucleolus disappears. During metaphase, the spindle apparatus is formed and the centromeres of the chromosomes line up on the equatorial plane. During anaphase, the centromeres divide and the two chromatids separate and are pulled toward the opposite poles of the cell. During telophase, the spindle fibers disappear, the nuclear membrane reforms, and the DNA in the chromatids is decondensed.

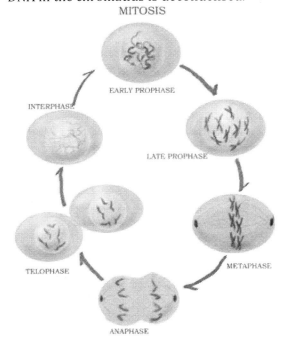

MITOSIS

EARLY PROPHASE

INTERPHASE

LATE PROPHASE

TELOPHASE

METAPHASE

ANAPHASE

Stages of meiosis

Meiosis is a type of cell division in which the number of chromosomes is reduced by half. Meiosis produces gametes, or egg and sperm cells. Meiosis occurs into two successive stages, which consist of a first mitotic division followed by a second mitotic division. During meiosis I, or the first meiotic division, the cell replicates its DNA in interphase and then continues through prophase I, metaphase I, anaphase I, and telophase I. At the end of meiosis I, there are two daughter cells that have the same number of chromosomes as the parent cell. During meiosis II, the cell enters a brief interphase but does not replicate its DNA. Then, the cell continues through prophase II, metaphase II, anaphase II, and telophase II. During prophase II, the unduplicated chromosomes split. At the end of telophase II, there are four daughter cells that have half the number of chromosomes as the parent cell.

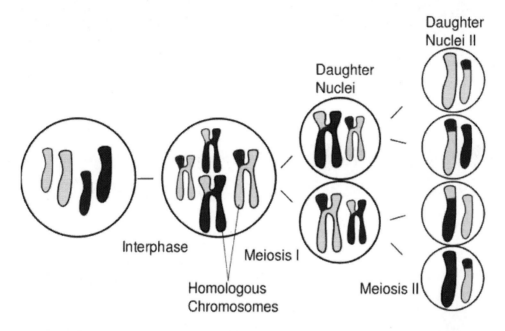

Reproduction and the Mechanisms of Heredity

Types of reproduction in mammals

When classified according to how they reproduce, there are three types of mammals:

Monotremes are rare mammals that lay eggs. These were the first mammals, and are more closely related to reptiles than other mammals. Examples include the duck-billed platypus and the spiny anteater.

Marsupials are special mammals. They give birth to live young, but the babies mature in pouches, where they are carried and can feed on milk. Many are found in Australia. The isolation of this island continent prevented placental mammals from taking hold. Examples of marsupials include kangaroos, possums, and koalas.

Placental mammals give birth from the females' placenta to live young. The young may be able to walk immediately, or they may need to be carried. They are still dependent on parental care for at least a short time. Placental mammals are the dominant form of mammals. Members of this group include cetaceans such as whales and dolphins, which are mammals that evolved but returned to the ocean.

Genetics, genes, and chromosomes

Genetics is the science devoted to the study of how characteristics are transmitted from one generation to another. In the 1800s, Gregor Mendel discovered the three laws of heredity that explain how genetics works.

Genes are the hereditary units of material that are transmitted from one generation to the next. They are capable of undergoing mutations, can be recombined with other genes, and can determine the nature of an organism, including its color, shape, and size. Genotype is the genetic makeup of an individual based on one or more characteristics, while phenotype is the external manifestation of the genotype. For example, genotype can determine hair color, and phenotype is the actual color of the hair.

Chromosomes are the structures inside the nucleus of a cell made up primarily of deoxyribonucleic acid (DNA) and proteins. The chromosomes carry the genes. The numbers vary according to the species, but they are always the same for each species. For example, the human has 46 chromosomes, and the water lily has 112.

Genetic variation

Mutations as sources of genetic variation
Mutations are one of the main sources of genetic variation. Mutations are changes in DNA. The changes can be gene mutations such as the point mutations of substitution, addition, or deletion, or the changes can be on the chromosomal level such as the chromosomal aberrations of translocations, deletions, inversions, and duplications. Mutations are random and can benefit, harm, or have no effect on the individual. Somatic mutations do not affect inheritance and therefore do not affect genetic variation with regard to evolution. Germline mutations that occur in gametes (eggs and sperm) can be passed to offspring and therefore are very important to genetic variation and evolution. Mutations introduce new genetic information into the genome.

Crossing over as a source of genetic variation
Crossing over is a major source of genetic variation. Crossing over is the exchange of equivalent segments of DNA between homologous chromosomes. Crossing over occurs during meiosis in prophase I. During synapsis, a tetrad is formed when homologous chromosomes pair up. Also during synapsis, the chromatids are extremely close together and sometimes the chromatids swap genes. Because genes have more than one allele, this allows for an exchange of genetic information. Crossing over is that exchange of genes. Crossing over can occur several times along the length of the chromosomes. Although crossing over does not introduce new information, it does introduce new combinations of the information that is available. Without crossing over during meiosis, only two genetically different gametes can be formed. With just one instance of crossing over, four genetically different gametes can be formed. With crossing over, each gamete contains genes from both the father and the mother. Crossing over leads to variation in traits among gametes, which leads to variation in traits among offspring.

Sources of genetic variation

Genetic exchange, or the transfer of DNA from one organism to another, is a source of genetic variation. Three general types of genetic exchange are transduction, transformation, and conjugation. Transduction occurs when genetic material is transferred from one bacterium to another by a bacteriophage. A bacteriophage is a virus that infects a bacterium. As the new bacteriophages are replicated, some of the host bacteria DNA can be added to the virus particles. Transformation occurs when a cell obtains new genetic information from its environment or surroundings. Many bacteria take up DNA fragments such as plasmids from their surroundings to obtain new genes. Conjugation occurs when bacteria or single-celled organisms are in direct contact with each other. Genes can be transferred from one into the other while the two cells are joined.

Independent assortment during sexual reproduction

Independent assortment during sexual reproduction is a source of genetic variation. Mutations originally brought about changes in DNA leading to alleles or different forms of the same gene. During sexual reproduction, these allele are "shuffled" or "independently sorted," producing individuals with unique combinations of traits. Gametes are produced during meiosis, which consists of two cell divisions: meiosis I and meiosis II. Meiosis I is a reduction division in which the diploid parent cell divides into two haploid daughter cells. During the metaphase of meiosis I, the homologous pairs (one from the mother and one from the father) align on the equatorial plane. The orientation of the homologous pairs is random, and each placement is independent of another's placement. The number of possible arrangements increases exponentially as the number of chromosomes increases. The independent assortment of chromosomes during metaphase in meiosis I provides a variety of gametes with tremendous differences in their combinations of chromosomes.

Growth and reproduction associated with living things

All organisms must be capable of growth and reproduction. Growth is necessary for each organism individually for multicellular organisms to develop and mature and to increase in size. Growth allows cells to be replaced or repaired. All cells eventually die. Without growth from cell division, tissues could not be maintained or repaired. Through mitosis, most cells routinely replace themselves with identical daughter cells. All organisms eventually die. Reproduction is necessary to increase the number of individuals in a population. Reproduction is either sexual by the joining of gametes or asexual by binary fission or some other related method. Not all organisms reproduce, but all must grow or they will die. Even single-celled organisms grow a small amount.

Modes of reproduction of the major animal phyla

Animals can reproduce sexually or asexually. Most animals reproduce sexually. In sexual reproduction, males and females have different reproductive organs that produce gametes. Males have testes that produce sperm, and females have ovaries that produce eggs. During fertilization, a sperm cell unites with an egg cell, forming a zygote. Fertilization can occur internally such as in most mammals and birds or externally such as aquatic animals such as fish and frogs. The zygote undergoes cell division, which develops into an embryo and eventually develops into an adult organism. Some embryos develop in eggs such as in most fish, amphibians, reptiles, and birds. Some mammals are oviparous and lay eggs. Most mammals are viviparous and have a uterus in which the embryo develops. Some mammals are marsupials and give birth to an immature fetus that finishes developing in a pouch. Some animals reproduce asexually. For example, hydras reproduce by

- 242 -

budding, and starfish and planarians can reproduce by fragmentation and regeneration. Some fish, frogs, and insects reproduce by parthenogenesis.

Advantages and disadvantages of asexual reproduction in animals

Very few species of animals reproduce by asexual reproduction, and nearly all of those species also have the ability to reproduce sexually. While not common, asexual reproduction is useful for animals that tend to stay in one place and may not find mates. Asexual reproduction takes considerably less effort and energy than sexual reproduction. In asexual reproduction, all of the offspring are genetically identical to the parent. This can be a disadvantage of asexual reproduction because of the lack of genetic variation. Although asexual reproduction is advantageous in a stable environment, if the environment changes, the organisms may lack the genetic variability to survive or selectively adapt.

Adaptations and Evolution

Theory of evolution

Evolution is the process whereby organisms pass certain acquired traits to successive generations, affecting the attributes of later organisms and even leading to the creation of new species. Charles Darwin is the name often associated with the formulation of natural selection, a vital component of evolution as it is known today. Natural selection states that members of a species are not identical—due to their respective genetic make-ups, each individual will possess traits which make it stronger or weaker and more or less able to adapt. The other tenet of natural selection is that members of a species will always have to compete for scarce resources to survive. Therefore, organisms with traits which will help them survive are more likely to do so and produce offspring, passing along the "desirable" traits. Darwin suggested that this process, by creating groups of a species with increasingly different characteristics, would eventually lead to the formation of a new species. The fossil record has provided support for this theory.

Natural and artificial selection as mechanisms of evolution

Natural selection and artificial selection are both mechanisms of evolution. Natural selection is a process of nature. Natural selection is the way in which a population can change over generations. Every population has variations in individual heritable traits. Not all individuals of a population reproduce. The organisms best suited for survival typically reproduce and pass on their genetic traits. Typically, the more advantageous a trait is, the more common that trait becomes in a population. Natural selection brings about evolutionary adaptations and is responsible for biological diversity. Artificial selection is another mechanism of evolution. Artificial selection is a process brought about by humans. Artificial selection is the selective breeding of domesticated animals and plants such as when farmers choose animals or plants with desirable traits to reproduce. Artificial selection has led to the evolution of farm stock and crops. For example, cauliflower, broccoli, and cabbage all evolved due to artificial selection of the wild mustard plant.

Adaptive radiation as a mechanism of evolution

Adaptive radiation is an evolutionary process in which a species branches out and adapts and fills numerous unoccupied ecological niches. The adaptations occur relatively quickly, driven by natural selection and resulting in new phenotypes and possibly new species eventually. An example of adaptive radiation is the finches that Darwin studied on the Galápagos Islands. Darwin recorded 13 different varieties of finches, which differed in the size and shape of their beaks. Through the process of natural selection, each type of finch adapted to the specific environment and specifically the food sources of the island to which it belonged. On newly formed islands with many unoccupied ecological niches, the adaptive radiation process occurred quickly due to the lack of competing species and predators.

Molecular evidence that supports evolution

Because all organisms are made up of cells, all organisms are alike on a fundamental level. Cells share similar components, which are made up of molecules. Specifically, all cells contain DNA and RNA. This should indicate that all species descended from a common ancestor. Humans and chimpanzees share approximately 98% of their genes in common, and humans and bacteria share approximately 7% of their genes in common. Humans and zebra fish share approximately 85% of their genes in common. Humans and mustard greens share approximately 15% of their genes in common. Biologists have been able to use DNA sequence comparisons of modern organisms to reconstruct the "root" of the tree of life. Recent discoveries indicate that RNA can both store information and cause itself to be copied, which means that it could produce proteins. Therefore, RNA could have could have evolved first, followed by DNA.

Convergent vs divergent evolution

Convergent evolution is the evolutionary process in which two or more unrelated species become increasingly similar in appearance. In convergent evolution, natural selection leads to adaptation in these unrelated species belonging to the same kind of environment. For example, the mammals shown below, although found in different parts of the world, developed similar appearances due to their similar environments.

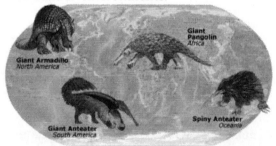

Divergent evolution is the evolutionary process in which organisms of one species become increasingly dissimilar in appearance. As several small adaptations occur due to natural selection, the organisms will finally reach a point at which two new species are formed. Then, these two species will further diverge from each other as they continue to evolve. Adaptive radiation is an example of divergent evolution. Another example is the divergent evolution of the wooly mammoth and the modern elephant from a common ancestor.

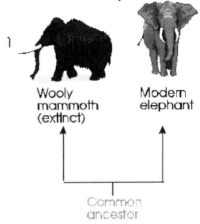

Gradualism as a model of evolutionary rates

Gradualism is a model of evolutionary rates that states that evolutionary changes occurred slowly or gradually by a divergence of lineages due largely to natural selection. These accumulated changes occurred over millions of years. Many transitional forms occurred between ancestors and modern descendants. Although not all of these transitional forms were preserved in the fossil record, the fossil record clearly supports gradualism. Many transition fossils show adaptations as organisms evolve. The geologic time scale describes this gradual change from simple to complex organisms over millions of years.

DNA replication

DNA replication begins when the double strands of the parent DNA molecule are unwound and unzipped. The enzyme helicase separates the two strands by breaking the hydrogen bonds between the base pairs that make up the rungs of the twisted ladder. These two single strands of DNA are called the replication fork. Each separate DNA strand provides a template for the complementary DNA bases, G with C and A with T. The enzyme DNA polymerase aids in binding the new base pairs together. Short segments of DNA called Okazaki fragments are synthesized with the lagging strand with the aid of RNA primase. At the end of this process, part of the telomere is removed. Then, enzymes check for any errors in the code and make repairs. This results in two daughter DNA molecules each with half of the original DNA molecule that was used as a template.

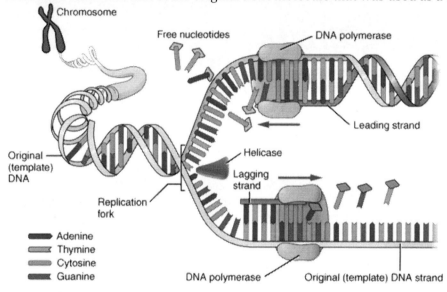

Regulatory Mechanisms and Behavior

Organisms must be able to adapt to their environment in order to thrive or survive. Individual organisms must be able to recognize stimuli in their surroundings and adapt quickly. For example, an individual euglena can sense light and respond by moving toward the light. Individual organisms must also be able to adapt to changes in the environment on a larger scale. For example, plants must be able to respond to the change in the length of the day to flower at the correct time. Populations must also be able to adapt to a changing environment. Evolution by natural selection is the process by which populations change over many generations. For example, wooly mammoths were unable to adapt to a warming climate and are now extinct, but many species of deer did adapt and are abundant today.

Feedback mechanisms play a major role in the homeostasis in organisms. Each feedback mechanism consists of receptors, an integrator, and effectors. Receptors such as mechanoreceptors or thermoreceptors in the skin detect the stimuli. The integrator such as the brain or spinal cord receives the information concerning the stimuli and sends out signals to other parts of the body. The effectors such as muscles or glands respond to the stimulus. Basically, the receptors receive the stimuli and notify the integrator, which signals the effectors to respond. Feedback mechanisms can

- 246 -

be negative or positive. Negative-feedback mechanisms are mechanisms that provide a decrease in response with an increase in stimulus that inhibits the stimulus, which in turn decreases the response. Positive-feedback mechanisms are mechanisms that provide an increase in response with an increase in stimulus, which actually increases the stimulus, which in turn increases the response.

Organisms and the Environment

Difference of living entities from nonliving matter

The elemental components most commonly found in living organisms (hydrogen, oxygen, carbon, nitrogen, sulfur, and phosphorus) are common throughout the universe. However, the chemistry of carbon displayed in living beings is unique. Also, the organic compounds (proteins, certain sugars, and nucleic acids necessary in protein synthesis and the storage and transmission of genetic information) found in live organisms are not found in inorganic matter. Presently on earth, there are no observable instances of the spontaneous generation of these compounds in nonliving matter. Another important factor which distinguishes live organisms from those which are not alive is the ability of life to reproduce itself. Also, organic beings possess the unique ability to react to external stimuli.

Autotrophs, producers, herbivores, carnivores, omnivores, and decomposers

Energy flows in one direction: from the sun, through photosynthetic organisms such as green plants (producers) and algae (autotrophs), and then to herbivores, carnivores, and decomposers. Autotrophs are organisms capable of producing their own food. The organic molecules they produce are food for all other organisms (heterotrophs).
Producers are green plants that manufacture food by photosynthesis.
Herbivores are animals that eat only plants (deer, rabbits, etc.). Since they are the first animals to receive the energy captured by producers, herbivores are called primary consumers.
Carnivores, or secondary consumers, are animals that eat the bodies of other animals for food. Predators (wolves, lions, etc.) kill other animals, while scavengers consume animals that are already dead from predation or natural causes (buzzards).
Omnivores are animals that eat both plants and other animals (humans).
Decomposers include saprophytic fungi and bacteria that break down the complex structures of the bodies of living things into simpler forms that can be used by other living things. This recycling process releases energy from organic molecules.

Microbes

Microbes are the smallest, simplest, and most abundant organisms on earth. Their numbers are incalculable, and a microscope is required to see them. There is a huge variety of microbes, including bacteria, fungi, some algae, and protozoa. Microbes can be harmful or helpful.

Microbes can be heterotrophic (eat other things) or autotrophic (make food for themselves). They can be solitary or colonial, sexual or asexual. Examples include mold, a multi-cellular type of fungus, and yeasts, which are single-celled (but may live in colonies).

A mushroom is a fungus that lives as a group of strands underground called hyphae that decompose leaves or bark on the ground. When it reproduces, it develops a mushroom whose cap contains spores. Mold is a type of zygote fungi that reproduces with a stalk, but releases zygospores.

Good bacteria can be those that help plants absorb the nitrogen needed for growth or help grazing animals break down the cellulose in plants. Some bad bacteria are killed by the penicillin developed from a fungus.

Roles in the food chain

The food chain, or food web, is a series of events that happens when one organism consumes another to survive. Every organism is involved in dozens of connections with others, so what happens to one affects the environment of the others. In the food chain, there are three main categories:

- Producers – Plants and vegetables are at the beginning of the food chain because they take energy from the sun and make food for themselves through photosynthesis. They are food sources for other organisms.
- Consumers – There are three levels of consumers: the organisms that eat plants (primary consumers, or herbivores); the organisms that eat the primary consumers (secondary consumers, or carnivores); and, in some ecosystems, the organisms that eat both plants and animals (tertiary consumers, or omnivores).
- Decomposers – These are the organisms that eat dead things or waste matter and return the nutrients to the soil, thus returning essential molecules to the producers and completing the cycle.

Physical laws and principles governing biological systems

Biological systems are governed by the same physical laws and principles that govern the rest of the universe. For example, biological systems must obey the laws of thermodynamics. These laws govern energy and the transformations of energy. The first law of thermodynamics is the law of conservation of energy, which states that energy is neither created nor destroyed but can change forms. The energy needed for life on Earth comes from the Sun. Sunlight reaches the Earth and is transformed by green plants and cyanobacteria during photosynthesis into the chemical bonds of ATP molecules, which can be used by these organisms for energy. Consumers eat the producers or other consumers in order to obtain energy. The second law of thermodynamics states that systems tend toward more disorder or entropy and less energy. This is evident in the fact that organisms must continually acquire energy to sustain life. Energy is continuously entering the biosphere from the sun, and that energy is continuously being dissipated as stated in the second law of thermodynamics.

How living things obtain and use energy

All cells must obtain and use energy in order to grow, make repairs, and reproduce. Cells use energy to take in food, process that food, and eliminate wastes from this process. Cells obtain the energy they need by the breaking of bonds of molecules. The energy is stored in the chemical bonds of the nutrient molecules. This process of converting this stored energy into usable adenosine triphosphate (ATP) is known as cellular respiration. Organisms differ in how they obtain food. Plants and other autotrophs produce energy through photosynthesis or chemosynthesis. Animals and other heterotrophs obtain their energy from consuming autotrophs or other heterotrophs.

Copyright © Mometrix Media. You have been licensed one copy of this document for personal use only. Any other reproduction or redistribution is strictly prohibited. All rights reserved.

Structure, organization, modes of nutrition, and reproduction of animals

Animals are multicellular organism with eukaryotic cells that do not have cell walls surrounding their plasma membranes. Animals have several possible structural body forms. Animals can be relatively simple in structure such as sponges, which do not have a nervous system. Other animals are more complex with cells organized into tissues, and tissues organized into organs, and organs even further organized into systems. Invertebrates such as arthropods, nematodes, and annelids have complex body systems. Vertebrates including fish, amphibians, reptiles, birds, and mammals are the most complex with detailed systems such as those with gills, air sacs, or lungs designed to exchange respiratory gases. All animals are heterotrophs and obtain their nutrition by consuming autotrophs or other heterotrophs. Most animals are motile, but some animals move their environment to bring food to them. All animals reproduce sexually at some point in their life cycle. Typically, this involves the union of a sperm and egg to produce a zygote.

Organizational hierarchy of multicellular organisms

Multicellular organisms are made up of cells, which are grouped together in tissues. Tissues are grouped together in organs. Organs are grouped together into organ systems. Organs systems are grouped together into a single organism. Cells are defined as the basic structural units of an organism. Cells are the smallest living units. Tissues are groups of cells that work together to perform a specific function. Organs are groups of tissues that work together to perform a specific function. Organ systems are groups of organs that work together to perform a specific function. An organism is an individual that contains several body systems.

Biotic and abiotic factors in an ecosystem

Every ecosystem consists of multiple abiotic and biotic factors. Abiotic factors are the nonbiological physical and chemical factors that affect the ecosystem. Abiotic factors include soil type, atmospheric conditions, sunlight, water, chemical elements such as acidity in the soil, wind, and natural disturbances such as forest fires. In aquatic ecosystems, abiotic factors include salinity, turbidity, water depth, current, temperature, and light. Biotic factors are all of the living organisms in the ecosystem. Biotic factors include plants, algae, fungi, bacteria, archaea, animals, and protozoa.

Significance of habitat and niche to a population

The habitat of an organism is the type of place where an organism usually lives. A habitat is a piece of an environmental area. A habitat may be a geographic area or even the body of another organism. The habitat describes an organism's natural living environment. A habitat includes biotic and abiotic factors such as temperature, light, food resources, and predators. Whereas a habitat describes an organism's "home," a niche can be thought of as an organism's "occupation." A niche describes an organism's functional role in the community. A niche can be quite complex because it should include the impacts that the organism has on the biotic and abiotic surroundings. Niches can be broad or narrow. The niche describes the way an organism uses its habitat.

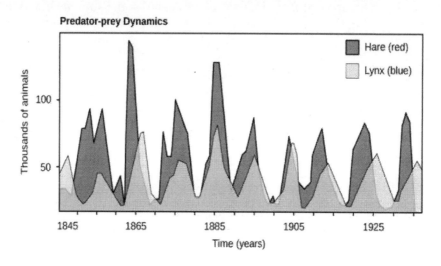

Influence of competition and predation on population size

Feeding relationships between organisms can affect population size. Competition and predation both tend to limit population size. Competition occurs when two individuals need the same resource. Predation occurs when one individual is the resource for another individual. Competition occurs when individuals share a resource in the habitat. This competition can be intraspecific, which is between members of the same species, or interspecific, which is between members of different species. Intraspecific competition reduces resources as that species' own population increases. This limits population growth. Interspecific competition reduces resources as a different species uses those same resources. Predation occurs when one species is a food resource for another species. Predator and prey populations can cycle over a range of years. If prey resources increase, predator numbers increase. An example of the predator-prey population cycle is the Canadian lynx and snowshoe hare.

<u>Predation</u>
Predation is a special nutritional relationship in which one organism is the predator, and the other organism is the prey. The predator benefits from the relationship, but the prey is harmed. The predator hunts and kills the prey for food. The predator is specially adapted to hunt its prey, and the prey is specially adapted to escape its predator. While predators harm (kill) their individual prey, predation usually helps the prey species. Predation keeps the population of the prey species under control and prevents them from overshooting the carrying capacity, which often leads to starvation. Also, predation usually helps to remove weak or slow members of the prey species leaving the healthier, stronger, and better adapted individuals to reproduce. Examples of predator-prey relationships include lions and zebras, snakes and rats, and hawks and rabbits.

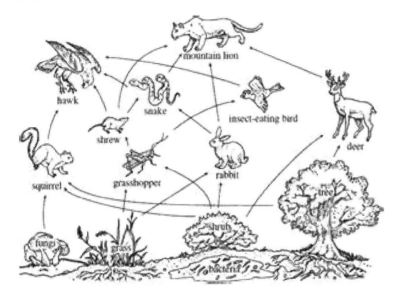

Energy flow in the environment using a food web

Energy flow through an ecosystem can be illustrated by a food web. Energy moves through the food web in the direction of the arrows. In the food web below, producers such as grass, trees, and shrubs use energy from the sun to produce food through photosynthesis. Herbivores or primary consumers such as squirrels, grasshoppers, and rabbits obtain energy by eating the producers. Secondary consumers, which are carnivores such as snakes and shrews, obtain energy by eating the primary consumers. Tertiary consumers, which are carnivores such as hawks and mountain lions, obtain energy by eating the secondary consumers. Note that the hawk and the mountain lion can also be considered quaternary consumers in this food web if a different food chain within the web is followed.

Natural disturbances that affect an ecosystem

A natural disturbance is an event caused by nature, not human activity. Natural disturbances can be brought on by weather such as fires from lightning, droughts, storms, wind, and freezing. Other natural disturbances include earthquakes, volcanic eruptions, and diseases. Natural disturbances can disrupt or disturb the ecosystem in many ways such as altering resources or removing individuals from the community. Natural disturbances can cover small regions, or they can affect an entire ecosystem. The effect may be long lasting and take several years to recover, or the effect may be minor and take only a few months to recover.

Affect of human population on ecological systems and biodiversity

Human population has been increasing at a near-exponential rate for the past 50 years. As the human population increases, the demand for resources such as food, water, land, and energy also increases. As the human population increases, species decrease largely due to habitat destruction, introduced species, and overhunting. The increased greenhouse gases and resulting climate changes have also significantly affected many ecosystems as temperatures rise and habitats are slowly changed or even destroyed. Increasing human population means increasing pollution, which harms habitats. Many animals have become extinct due to the effects of an exponentially increasing human population. High rates of extinction greatly reduce biodiversity.

Affect of introduced species on ecological systems and biodiversity

Introduced species are species that are moved into new geographic regions by humans. The introduction can be intentional such as the introduction of livestock including cattle, pigs, and goats to the United States or unintentional such as the introduction of Dutch elm disease, which has damaged and killed thousands of American elms. Introduced species are also called invasive or nonnative species. Introduced species typically cause a decrease in biodiversity. Introduced species can disrupt their new communities by using limited resources and preying on other members of the community. Introduced species are often free from predators and can reproduce exponentially. Introduced species are contributors or even responsible for numerous extinctions. For example, zebra mussels, which are native to the Black Sea and the Caspian Sea, were accidentally introduced to the Great Lakes. The zebra mussels greatly reduced the amount of plankton available for the native mussel species, many of which are now endangered.

Structure and Function of Earth Systems

Plate tectonics

Plate tectonics is a geological theory that was developed to explain the process of continental drift. The theoretical separation of the Earth's lithosphere and asthenosphere is based upon the mechanical properties of the materials in the two respective layers and is distinct from the chemical separation of Earth's crust, mantle, and core. According to the theory of plate tectonics, the Earth's lithosphere is divided into ten major plates: African, Antarctic, Australian, Eurasian, North American, South American, Pacific, Cocos, Nazca, and Indian; it floats atop the asthenosphere. The plates of the lithosphere abut one another at plate boundaries (divergent, convergent, or transform fault), where the formation of topological features of Earth's surface begins.

Volcanic eruption

Volcanic eruptions are classified by their degree of explosivity. *Explosive eruptions* expel gases, ash, and rocks (such as pumice) to incredible heights; these products affect areas miles away. An explosive eruption can affect atmospheric pressure and increase the electricity of the surrounding air. *Eruptions of intermediate explosivity* often occur in stratovolcanoes. They are similar to explosive eruptions but their effects are smaller in scale. *Quiet eruptions*, consistent with shield volcanoes, exhibit virtually no explosivity. Lava flows from the volcano instead of shooting out of it vertically. This type of eruption is often powered by the release of steam rather than the release of magmatic gases. *Fissure eruptions* are those during which lava flows from a series of small fissures, or fractures, in the Earth's crust instead of from a single volcanic vent. This type of eruption is usually accompanied by flood lava.

Interplate vs. intraplate earthquakes

An *interplate earthquake* occurs at a boundary between two tectonic plates. The slippage of rocks on either side of the boundary results in deformation of the surrounding land and the release of seismic waves. Interplate earthquakes are more common than intraplate earthquakes. Although plate tectonics envisions the Earth's surface as a series of plates moving past one another, we must remember that those plates are fractured aspects of the ancient crust. *Intraplate earthquakes* occur along highly stressed fault lines on the interior of tectonic plates. Because the faults that cause these earthquakes are often below the surface, they are difficult to predict or study.

Seismic waves

Seismic waves are mechanical disturbances that transfer energy. These waves are created by earthquakes or explosions. Body waves travel within the Earth's interior on curved pathways due to the various densities of the Earth's composite materials. The category of body waves is further subdivided into primary (P) waves and secondary (S) waves. P waves can travel through any material (although they move fastest in a solid), alternately compressing and dilating such materials in the direction of wave movement. They are similar to sound waves and move more quickly than S waves. S waves (or transverse waves) can only travel through solids. They displace the ground perpendicularly to the direction of wave movement to one side and then to the other. Surface waves, similar to water waves, travel above the Earth's surface and cause more damage than body waves due to their low frequencies. Rayleigh waves perpetuate ground roll during earthquakes: The Earth's surface ripples like the surface of water. Love waves move marginally more quickly than Rayleigh waves and cause horizontal shearing of the Earth's crust.

Runoff, watershed, groundwater and infiltration

Runoff is precipitation that does not experience evaporation, transpiration by plants, or infiltration (the process in which water transitions from surface water to groundwater). It is an important part of the hydrologic cycle. Runoff, or surface water, moves from the location where it falls as precipitation across the surface of the Earth to an ocean. Rivers and streams are the mechanisms of transportation for surface water. Moving runoff often picks up soil and other materials as it travels. A **watershed** is the area in which runoff moves toward a body of water; such a region is usually bounded by hills and/or mountains. **Groundwater** is precipitation that seeps through the upper layers of the Earth's surface. This process of **infiltration** is also referred to as groundwater recharge. Water moves underground back to the oceans from where it came at the beginning of the hydrologic cycle. When the water reaches its destination, it is deposited through groundwater discharge.

Processes by which surface water moves to the oceans

Precipitation that does not evaporate or seep into the Earth's surface may fall into a watershed, or it may be transported to one by gravity (if, for example, it falls on a hillside). Water that enters a watershed will eventually enter the area's associated body of water. This surface water may move directly to an ocean, or it may move into a transportation medium such as a river or stream (a smaller river); it may also move into a lake, where it will be temporarily stored. A river is a body of water with a detectable current (fluid motion). The velocity of moving water in a river depends largely on the gradient (downward slope); it is also influenced by the shape of the channel through which it moves, the texture of the inside surfaces of the channel, and the amount of sediment in the water.

Length, velocity, period and frequency

Wave *length* is defined as the horizontal distance between two equivalent wave phases (that is, the distance separating two sequential crests or troughs). The *velocity* of a wave is the distance it moves during a specified period of time. The *period* of a wave is the length of time required for two equivalent wave phases to pass a certain point. The number of periods that occur in a specified length of time is referred to as the *frequency* of the wave. These measurements vary greatly among waves. One of the largest such occurrences measured a wave length of 792 meters, a velocity of 126 kilometers per hour, and a period of 22.5 seconds.

Oceanic tides

Oceanic tides are the daily oscillations in sea level along coastlines. The number of times sea level changes and the differences in sea level vary with location, but all parts of the ocean experience this phenomenon. Tides occur due to the gravitational force and centripetal acceleration. Both the Sun and the Moon exert gravitational pulls on the Earth; however, the attraction of the Moon is more effective in tide formation, due to the fact that it is closer to our planet (because gravitational attraction varies with distance, among other things). As the Earth rotates, different areas of the oceans are closest to the Moon. Since water is not firmly affixed to the surface, it is disturbed by the Moon's gravitational pull, which creates an exceptionally long wave. Centripetal acceleration is the force that keeps the Earth and Moon in orbit around the Sun; this force is experienced equally at all points on the Earth's surface. The combined influence of these two forces produces the rhythmic pattern of oceanic tides.

Weather

Weather is the result of transfers of kinetic (heat) energy due to differences in temperature between objects as well as transfers of moisture in Earth's atmosphere. Most of the activity that produces the weather we experience on Earth takes place in the troposphere, the lowest level of the atmosphere (0-15 kilometers above Earth's surface). Atmospheric pressure, temperature, humidity, elevation, wind speed, and cloud cover are all factors in the formation of weather. A weather system is an organized atmospheric state, associated with a particular weather pattern such as cyclones or tornadoes. Meteorology, the study of weather, entails the observation of natural phenomena such as rain, fog, snow, and wind. The processes that occur at different stages in the hydrologic cycle form the basis of meteorological events.

Precipitation

Precipitation is water that falls back to Earth's surface from the atmosphere. This water may be in the form of rain, which is water in the liquid form. Raindrops are formed in clouds due to the process of condensation. When the drops become too heavy to remain in the cloud (due to a decrease in their kinetic energy), gravity causes them to fall down toward Earth's surface. Extremely small raindrops are called drizzle. If the temperature of a layer of air through which rain passes on its way down is below the freezing point, the rain may take the form of sleet (partially frozen water). Precipitation may also fall in the form of snow, or water molecules sublimated into ice crystals. When clumps of snowflakes melt and refreeze, hail is formed. Hail may also be formed when liquid water accumulates on the surface of a snowflake and subsequently freezes.

Types of clouds

The four main types of clouds are **cirrus**, **cumulous**, **nimbus**, and **stratus**.

A cirrus cloud forms high in a stable atmosphere, generally at altitudes of 6,000 meters or higher. Temperatures at these altitudes (in the troposphere) decrease with increased altitude; therefore, the precipitation in a cirrus cloud adopts the form of ice crystals. These usually thin traces of clouds may indicate an approaching weather depression.

A **cumulous cloud** is a stereotypical white, fluffy ball. Cumulous clouds are indicators of a stable atmosphere, and also of the vertical extent of convection in the atmosphere—condensation and cloud formation begin at the flat base of a cumulous cloud. The more humid the air, the lower a cumulous cloud will form.

A **nimbus cloud** is, generally speaking, a rain cloud. Nimbus clouds are usually low, dark, and formless, sometimes spanning the entire visible sky.

A **stratus cloud** is basically a cloud of fog which forms at a distance above the Earth's surface. This type of cloud forms when weak convective currents bring moisture just high enough to initiate condensation (if the temperature is below the dew point).

Biological, chemical, and physical properties that contribute to Earth's life-sustaining system

Life on earth is dependent on:
- All three states of water – gas (water vapor), liquid, and solid (ice)
- A variety of forms of carbon, the basis of life (carbon-based units)
- In the atmosphere, carbon dioxide in the forms of methane and black carbon soot produce the greenhouse effect that provides a habitable atmosphere.
- The earth's atmosphere and electromagnetic field, which shield the surface from harmful radiation and allow useful radiation to go through
- The earth's relationship to the sun and the moon, which creates the four seasons and the cycles of plant and animal life
- The combination of water, carbon, and nutrients, which provides sustenance for life and regulates the climate system in a habitable temperature range with non-toxic air.

Components of earth system science

The complex and interconnected dynamics of the continents, atmosphere, oceans, ice, and life forms are the subject of earth system science. These interconnected dynamics require an interdisciplinary approach that includes chemistry, physics, biology, mathematics, and applied sciences in order to study the Earth as an integrated system and determine (while considering human impact and interaction) the past, present, and future states of the earth. Scientific inquiry in this field includes exploration of:
- Extreme weather events as they pertain to a changing climate
- Earthquakes and volcanic eruptions as they pertain to tectonic shifts
- Losses in biodiversity in relation to the changes in the earth's ecosystems
- Causes and effects in the environment
- The sun's solar variability in relation to the earth's climate
- The atmosphere's increasing concentrations of carbon dioxide and aerosols
- Trends in the earth's systems in terms of changes and their consequences

Traditional earth science disciplines

Modern science is approaching the study of the earth in an integrated fashion that sees the earth as an interconnected system that is impacted by humankind and, therefore, must include social dimensions. Traditionally, though, the following were the earth science disciplines:

- Geology – This is the study of the origin and structure of the earth and of the changes it has undergone and is in the process of undergoing. Geologists work from the crust inward.
- Meteorology – This is the study of the atmosphere, including atmospheric pressure, temperature, clouds, winds, precipitation, etc. It is also concerned with describing and explaining weather.
- Oceanography – This is the study of the oceans, which includes studying their extent and depth, the physics and chemistry of ocean waters, and the exploitation of their resources.
- Ecology – This is the study of living organisms in relation to their environment and to other living things. It is the study of the interrelations between the different components of the ecosystem.

Hydrosphere and the hydrologic cycle

The hydrosphere is anything on earth that is related to water, whether it is in the air, on land, or in a plant or animal system. A water molecule consists of only two atoms of hydrogen and one of oxygen, yet it is what makes life possible. Unlike the other planets, earth is able to sustain life because its temperature allows water to be in its liquid state most of the time. Water vapor and ice are of no use to living organisms.

The hydrologic cycle is the journey water takes as it assumes different forms. Liquid surface water evaporates to form the gaseous state of a cloud, and then becomes liquid again in the form of rain. This process takes about 10 days if water becomes a cloud. Water at the bottom of the ocean or in a glacier is not likely to change form, even over periods of thousands of years.

Erosion

Erosion is the process that breaks down matter, whether it is a rock that is broken into pebbles or mountains that are rained on until they become hills. Erosion always happens in a downhill direction. The erosion of land by weather or breaking waves is called denudation. Mass wasting is the movement of masses of dirt and rock from one place to another. This can occur in two ways: mechanical (such as breaking a rock with a hammer) or chemical (such as pouring acid on a rock to dissolve it). If the material changes color, it indicates that a break down was chemical in nature. Whatever is broken down must go somewhere, so erosion eventually builds something up. For example, an eroded mountain ends up in a river that carries the sediment towards the ocean, where it builds up and creates a wetland or delta at the mouth of the river.

Layers of the earth

The earth has several distinct layers, each with its own properties:

- Crust – This is the outermost layer of the earth that is comprised of the continents and the ocean basins. It has a variable thickness (35-70 km in the continents and 5-10 km in the ocean basins) and is composed mostly of alumino-silicates.

- Mantle – This is about 2900 km thick, and is made up mostly of ferro-magnesium silicates. It is divided into an upper and lower mantle. Most of the internal heat of the earth is located in the mantle. Large convective cells circulate heat, and may cause plate tectonic movement.
- Core – This is separated into the liquid outer core and the solid inner core. The outer core is 2300 km thick (composed mostly of nickel-iron alloy), and the inner core (almost entirely iron) is 12 km thick. The earth's magnetic field is thought to be controlled by the liquid outer core.

Paleontology

Paleontology is the study of prehistoric plant and animal life through the analysis of fossil remains. These fossils reveal the ecologies of the past and the path of evolution for both extinct and living organisms. A historical science, paleontology seeks information about the identity, origin, environment, and evolution of past organisms and what they can reveal about the past of the earth as a whole. Paleontology explains causes as opposed to conducting experiments to observe effects. It is related to the fields of biology, geology, and archaeology, and is divided into several sub-disciplines concerned with the types of fossils studied, the process of fossilization, and the ecology and climate of the past. Paleontologists also help identify the composition of the earth's rock layers by the fossils that are found, thus identifying potential sites for oil, mineral, and water extraction.

Cycles in Earth Systems

Rock cycle

The **rock cycle** is the process whereby the materials that make up the Earth transition through the three types of rock: igneous, sedimentary, and metamorphic. Rocks, like all matter, cannot be created or destroyed; rather, they undergo a series of changes and adopt different forms through the functions of the rock cycle. Plate tectonics and the water cycle are the driving forces behind the rock cycle; they force rocks and minerals out of equilibrium and force them to adjust to different external conditions. Viewed in a generalized, cyclical fashion, the rock cycle operates as follows: rocks beneath Earth's surface melt into magma. This magma either erupts through volcanoes or remains inside the Earth. Regardless, the magma cools, forming igneous rocks. On the surface, these rocks experience weathering and erosion, which break them down and distribute the fragments across the surface. These fragments form layers and eventually become sedimentary rocks. Sedimentary rocks are then either transformed to metamorphic rocks (which will become magma inside the Earth) or melted down into magma.

Formation of igneous rocks

Igneous rocks can be formed from sedimentary rocks, metamorphic rocks, or other igneous rocks. Rocks that are pushed under the Earth's surface (usually due to plate subduction) are exposed to high mantle temperatures, which cause the rocks to melt into magma. The magma then rises to the surface through volcanic processes. The lower atmospheric temperature causes the magma to cool, forming grainy, extrusive igneous rocks. The creation of extrusive, or volcanic, rocks is quite rapid. The cooling process can occur so rapidly that crystals do not form; in this case, the result is a glass, such as obsidian. It is also possible for magma to cool down inside the Earth's interior; this type of igneous rock is called intrusive. Intrusive, or plutonic, rocks cool more slowly, resulting in a coarse-grained texture.

<u>Formation of sedimentary rocks</u>
Sedimentary rocks are formed when rocks at the Earth's surface experience weathering and erosion, which break them down and distribute the fragments across the surface. Fragmented material (small pieces of rock, organic debris, and the chemical products of mineral sublimation) is deposited and accumulates in layers, with top layers burying the materials beneath. The pressure exerted by the topmost layers causes the lower layers to compact, creating solid sedimentary rock in a process called lithification.

<u>Formation of metamorphic rocks</u>
Metamorphic rocks are igneous or sedimentary rocks that have "morphed" into another kind of rock. In metamorphism, high temperatures and levels of pressure change preexisting rocks physically and/or chemically, which produces different species of rocks. In the rock cycle, this process generally occurs in materials that have been thrust back into the Earth's mantle by plate subduction. Regional metamorphism refers to a large band of metamorphic activity; this often occurs near areas of high orogenic (mountain-building) activity. Contact metamorphism refers to metamorphism that occurs when "country rock" (that is, rock native to an area) comes into contact with high-heat igneous intrusions (magma).

Role of water in the cycling of Earth materials

Water plays an important role in the rock cycle through its roles in erosion and weathering: it wears down rocks; it contributes to the dissolution of rocks and minerals as acidic soil water; and it carries ions and rock fragments (sediments) to basins where they will be compressed into sedimentary rock. Water also plays a role in the metamorphic processes that occur underwater in newly-formed igneous rock at mid-ocean ridges. The presence of water (and other volatiles) is a vital component in the melting of rocky crust into magma above subduction zones.

Water cycle

The water cycle, also referred to as the hydrologic cycle, is a biogeochemical cycle that describes the continuous movement of the Earth's water. Water in the form of precipitation such as rain or snow moves from the atmosphere to the ground. The water is collected in oceans, lakes, rivers, and other bodies of water. Heat from the sun causes water to evaporate from oceans, lakes, rivers, and other bodies of water. As plants transpire, this water also undergoes evaporation. This water vapor collects in the sky and forms clouds. As the water vapor in the clouds cools, the water vapor condenses or sublimes depending on the conditions. Then, water moves back to the ground in the form of precipitation.

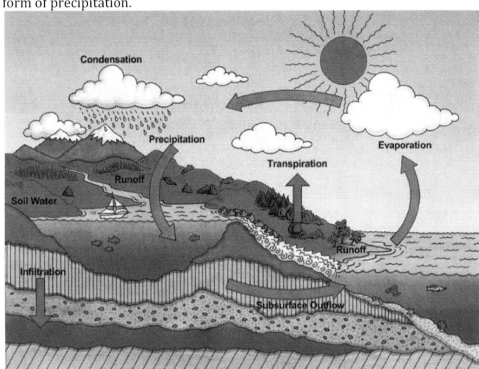

Carbon cycle

The carbon cycle is a biogeochemical cycle that describes the continuous movement of the Earth's carbon. Carbon is in the atmosphere, the soil, living organisms, fossil fuels, oceans, and freshwater systems. These areas are referred to as carbon reservoirs. Carbon flows between these reservoirs in an exchange called the carbon cycle. In the atmosphere, carbon is in the form of carbon dioxide. Carbon moves from the atmosphere to plants through the process of photosynthesis. Carbon moves from plants to animals through food chains. Carbon moves from living organisms to the soil when these organisms die. Carbon moves from living organisms to the atmosphere through cellular respiration. Carbon moves from fossil fuels to the atmosphere when fossil fuels are burned. Carbon moves from the atmosphere to the oceans and freshwater systems through absorption.

The carbon cycle

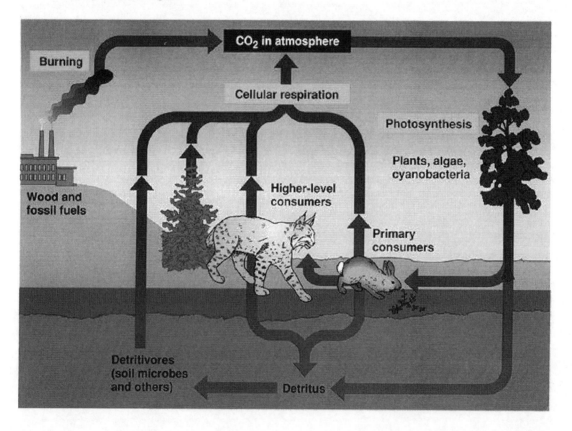

Nitrogen cycle

The nitrogen cycle is a biogeochemical cycle that describes the continuous movement of the Earth's nitrogen. Approximately 78% of the Earth's atmosphere consists of nitrogen in its elemental form N_2. Nitrogen is essential to the formation of proteins, but most organisms cannot use nitrogen in this form and require the nitrogen to be converted into some form of nitrates. Lightning can cause nitrates to form in the atmosphere, which can be carried to the soil by rain to be used by plants. Legumes have nitrogen-fixing bacteria in their roots, which can convert the N_2 to ammonia (NH_3). Nitrifying bacteria in the soil can also convert ammonia into nitrates. Plants absorb nitrates from the soil, and animals can consume the plants and other animals for protein. Denitrifying bacteria can convert unused nitrates back to nitrogen to be returned to the atmosphere.

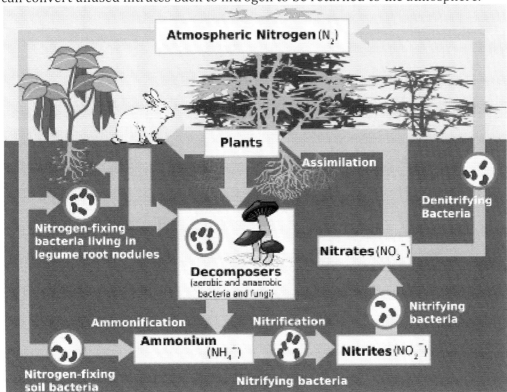

Energy in Weather and Climate

Hurricanes

Hurricanes form when several conditions are met: Oceanic water must be at least 26 degrees Celsius, the general circulation pattern of wind must be disrupted (this disruption usually takes the form of an atmospheric wave in the easterly trade winds), and the Coriolis force must be in effect. During hurricane season (June to November), easterly waves appear in the trade winds every few days. When such a wave occurs over a body of particularly warm, deep water, it is strengthened by the evaporation of warm air from below. Surrounding winds converge at the low-pressure zone created by the wave; air brought by these winds rises because it has nowhere else to go. The large body of warm, moist air rises high into the atmosphere and consequently condenses into huge clouds. As more and more humid air is drawn upward, this air begins to rotate around the area of low pressure. The storm continues to gain strength and may move toward land.

Measuring weather

Weather can be measured by a variety of methods. The simplest include measurement of rainfall, sunshine, pressure, humidity, temperature, and cloudiness with basic instruments such as thermometers, barometers, and rain gauges. However, the use of radar (which involves analysis of microwaves reflecting off of raindrops) and satellite imagery grants meteorologists a look at the big picture of weather across, for example, an entire continent. This helps them understand and make predictions about current and developing weather systems. Infrared (heat-sensing) imaging allows meteorologists to measure the temperature of clouds above ground. Using weather reports gathered from different weather stations spread over an area, meteorologists create synoptic charts. The locations and weather reports of several stations are plotted on a chart; analysis of the pressures reported from each location, as well as rainfall, cloud cover, and so on, can reveal basic weather patterns.

Creation of the seasons

The combined effects of Earth's revolution around the Sun and the tilt of the planet's rotational axis create the seasons. Earth's axis is not perfectly perpendicular to its orbital plane; rather, it is tilted about 23.5 degrees. Thus, at different times of the year, certain areas of the surface receive different amounts of sunlight. For example, during the period of time in Earth's orbit when the Northern Hemisphere is tipped toward the Sun, it is exposed to higher amounts of nearly direct sunlight than at any other time of year (days are longer, and the direction of Sun's rays striking the surface is nearly perpendicular). This period of time is summer in the Northern Hemisphere and winter in the Southern Hemisphere; on the opposite side of the orbit, the seasons are reversed in each hemisphere.

Types of climates

Scientists have determined the following different types of climates:
- Polar (ice caps)
- Polar (tundra)
- Subtropical (dry summer)
- Subtropical (dry winter)
- Subtropical (humid)
- Subtropical (marine west coast)
- Subtropical (Mediterranean)
- Subtropical (wet)
- Tropical (monsoon)
- Tropical (savannah/grasslands)
- Tropical (wet)

Several factors make up and affect climates. These include:
- Temperature
- Atmospheric pressure
- The number of clouds and the amount of dust or smog
- Humidity
- Winds

The moistest and warmest of all the climates is that of the tropical rainforest. It has daily convection thunderstorms caused by the surface daytime heat and the high humidity, which combine to form thunderclouds.

Revolution of the Earth and the tilt of the Earth on its axis

Major concepts in earth science include:
- The Earth revolves around the sun.
- The Earth is tilted on its axis.
- Earth's revolution around the sun and the tilt of the Earth on its axis cause the change of seasons.
- Summer occurs when a particular area is closer to the sun.
- Winter occurs when a particular area is farther from the sun.
- Summer and winter occur during opposite times of the year in the Northern and Southern hemispheres.
- Because the Earth is tilted on its axis, days are longer in the summer and shorter in the winter. Each year includes a longest day, a shortest day, and two days in which night and day are of equal length (equinoxes).

Solar System and the Universe

Earth's revolution around the Sun

Like all celestial objects in our solar system, planet Earth revolves around the Sun. This process takes approximately 365 1/4 days, the period of time that constitutes a calendar year. The path of the orbit of Earth around the Sun is not circular but elliptical. Therefore, the distances between the Earth and the Sun at points on either extreme of this counterclockwise orbit are not equal. In other words, the distance between the two objects varies over the course of a year. At perihelion, the minimum heliocentric distance, Earth is 147 million kilometers from the Sun. At aphelion, the maximum heliocentric distance, Earth is 152 million kilometers from the Sun. This movement of the Earth is responsible for the apparent annual motions of the Sun (in a path referred to as the ecliptic) and other celestial objects visible from Earth's surface.

Earth's Moon

Earth's Moon is historically one of the most studied celestial bodies. Its mass is approximately 1.2% of the Earth's mass, and its radius is just over one-fourth of the size of the Earth's radius. Measurements of the Moon's density suggest that its characteristics are similar to those of the rocks that make up Earth's crust. The landscape of the Moon consists mostly of mountains and craters formed by collisions of this surface with meteors and other interplanetary materials. The Moon's crust (estimated to be 50 to 100 kilometers in thickness) is made up of a layer of regolith (lunar soil) supported by a layer of loose rocks and gravel. Beneath the crust is a mantle made up of a solid lithosphere and a semiliquid asthenosphere. The Moon's core (the innermost 500 kilometers of the body) is not as dense as that of the Earth. The Moon is made up mostly of refractory elements with high melting and boiling points with low levels of heavy elements such as iron.

Earth-Moon system

While the Moon is commonly referred to as a satellite of the Earth, this is not entirely accurate. The ratio of the masses of the two bodies is much larger than that of any other planet-satellite system. Also, the Moon does not truly revolve around the Earth. Rather, the two bodies revolve around a common center of mass beneath the surface of the Earth (approximately 4,800 kilometers from Earth's core). The orbital planes of the Moon and the Earth are nearly aligned; therefore, the Moon moves close to the ecliptic, as seen from Earth. Due to the Moon's synchronous rotation (its rotation period and orbital period are equal), the same side of the Moon is always facing Earth. This occurs because of the mutual gravitational pull between the two bodies.

Terrestrial planets

The term *terrestrial planets* refers to the four planets closest to the Sun (Mercury, Venus, Earth, and Mars). They are classified together because they share many similarities that distinguish them from the giant planets. The terrestrial planets have high densities and atmospheres that constitute a small percentage of their total masses. These atmospheres consist mostly of heavy elements, such as carbon dioxide, nitrogen, and water, and are maintained by the gravitational field of the planets (which could not prevent hydrogen from escaping). These planets exhibit magnetic fields of varying intensity. An important characteristic that distinguishes the terrestrial planets from the giant planets is the evidence of various levels of internally generated activity, which caused these planets to evolve from their original states. These processes are thought to have been caused by constant meteoritic impacts during the first few hundred million years of the planets' existence. Radioactive decay of certain isotopes increased the internal temperatures of these planets, leading to volcanic activity on all of the terrestrial planets except Venus.

Giant planets

The large diameters of Jupiter, Saturn, Uranus, and Neptune gave rise to the name of the category into which they fall. The hypothetical icy cores of these planets cause them to exhibit primary atmospheres, because the large levels of mass they accreted prevented even the lightest elements from escaping their gravitational pulls. The atmospheres of the giant planets thus consist mostly of hydrogen and helium. The giant planets do not have solid surfaces like those of the terrestrial planets. Jupiter probably consists of a core (made of ice and rock) surrounded by a layer of metallic hydrogen, which is covered by a convective atmosphere of hydrogen and helium. Saturn is believed to have the same type of core and hydrogen mantle, enriched by the helium missing from the atmosphere, surrounded by a differentiation zone and a hydrogenic atmosphere. Uranus and Neptune probably have the same type of core, surrounded by ionic materials, bounded by methane-rich molecular envelopes. Uranus is the only giant planet that exhibits no evidence of internal activity.

Sun

The *Sun* is the vital force of life on Earth; it is also the central component of our solar system. It is basically a sphere of extremely hot gases (close to 15 million degrees at the core) held together by gravity. Some of these gaseous molecules are ionized due to the high temperatures. The balance between its gravitational force and the pressure produced by the hot gases is called hydrostatic equilibrium. The source of the solar energy that keeps the Sun alive and plays a key role in the perpetuation of life on Earth is located in the Sun's core, where nucleosynthesis produces heat energy and photons. The Sun's atmosphere consists of the photosphere, the surface visible from

Earth, the chronosphere, a layer outside of and hotter than the photosphere, the transition zone (the region where temperatures rise between the chronosphere and the corona), and the corona, which is best viewed at X-ray wavelengths. A solar flare is an explosive emission of ionized particles from the Sun's surface.

Binary star

Binary star systems, of which about fifty percent of the stars in the sky are members, consist of two stars that orbit each other. The orbits of and distances between members of a binary system vary. A visual binary is a pair of stars that can be visually observed. Positional measurements of a visual binary reveal the orbital paths of the two stars. Astronomers can identify astrometric binaries through long-term observation of a visible star—if the star appears to wobble, it may be inferred that it is orbiting a companion star that is not visible. An eclipsing binary can be identified through observation of the brightness of a star. Variations in the visual brightness of a star can occur when one star in a binary system passes in front of the other. Sometimes, variations in the spectral lines of a star occur because it is in a binary system. This type of binary is a spectroscopic binary.

Milky Way

The *Milky Way*, which houses the Earth's solar system, is a spiral galaxy. It consists of a central bulging disk, the center of which is referred to as a nucleus. Most of a galaxy's visible light comes from stars in this region. The disk is surrounded by a halo of stars and star clusters that spread above, next to, and beneath the nucleus. Globular clusters (dense, spherical clusters of ancient stars) are often found in the halo. Spiral arms of high-luminosity stars (from which this type of galaxy gets its name) fan out from the nucleus as well, with stars that are less bright in between. Interstellar dust populates the entire galaxy between celestial bodies. The entire galaxy rotates about the center. While Earth, the Sun, and its solar system are located on the disk, we are far from the center of the Milky Way. The galaxy's mass, determined through the application of Kepler's third law to the Sun's orbit, is about 1,011 solar masses.

History of the Earth System

Geological eras

Geologists divide the history of the earth into units of time called eons, which are divided into eras, then into periods, then into epochs and finally into ages. Dates are approximate of course, and there may be variations of a few million years. (Million years ago is abbreviated as Ma.) Some of the most commonly known periods are:
- Hadean Period – About 4.5 to 3.8 billion years ago
- Archaean Period – 3.8 to 2.5 billion years ago
- Proterozoic Period – 2.5 billion to 542 Ma
- Cambrian Period – 542 to 488 Ma
- Ordovician Period – 488 to 443 Ma
- Silurian Period – 443 to 416 Ma
- Devonian Period – 416 to 359 Ma
- Carboniferous Period – 359 to 290 Ma
- Permian Period – 290 to 248 Ma
- Triassic Period – 251 to 200 Ma

- Jurassic Period – 200 to 150 Ma
- Cretaceous Period – 150 to 65 Ma
- Paleogene Period – 65 to 28 Ma
- Neogene Period – 28 to 2 Ma
- Quaternary Period – about 2 Ma to the present

Development of life on earth

The evolution of life on earth is believed to have occurred as follows:
- Igneous rocks formed. (Hadean)
- The continents formed. (Archaean Eon)
- One-celled creatures such as hydras, jellyfish, and sponges appeared about 600 Ma.
- Flatworms, roundworms, and segmented worms appeared about 550 Ma.
- Moss, arthropods, octopus, and eels appeared. (Cambrian Period)
- Mushrooms, fungi, and other primitive plants appeared; sea animals began to use calcium to build bones and shells. (Ordovician Period)
- Fish with jaws appeared. (Silurian Period)
- Fish developed lungs and legs (frogs) and went on land; ferns appeared. (Devonian period)
- Reptiles developed the ability to lay eggs on land and pine trees appeared. (Carboniferous Period)
- Dinosaurs dominated the land during the Triassic and Jurassic Periods.
- Flying insects, birds, and the first flowering plants appeared; dinosaurs died out. (Cretaceous Period)
- Mammals evolved and dominated; grasses became widespread. (50 Ma)
- Hominids appeared more than 2 Ma.

Determining the order of geologic events

The Law of Superposition logically assumes that the bottom layer of a series of sedimentary layers is the oldest, unless it has been overturned or older rock has been pushed over it.

In addition, since igneous intrusions can cut through or flow above other rocks, these other rocks are older. For example, molten rock (lava) flows out over already present, older rocks.

Another guideline for the rock record is that rock layers are older than the folds and faults in them because the rocks must exist before they can be folded or faulted.

If a rock contains atomic nuclei, reference tables of the half lives of commonly used radio isotopes can be used to match the decay rate of known substances to the nuclei in a rock, and thereby determine its age.

Ages of rocks can also be determined from contact metamorphism, the re-crystallization of pre-existing rocks due to changes in physical and chemical conditions, such as heat, pressure, and chemically active fluids that might be present in lava or polluted waters.

Matching rocks and geologic events in one place with those of another

Geologists physically follow rock layers from one location to another by a process called "walking the outcrop." Geologists walk along the outcropping to see where it goes and what the differences and similarities of the neighboring locations they cross are.

Similar rock types or patterns of rock layers that are similar in terms of thickness, color, composition, and fossil remains tell geologists that two locations have a similar geologic history.

Fossils are found all over the earth, but are from a relatively small time period in earth's history. Therefore, fossil evidence helps date a rock layer, regardless of where it occurs.

Volcanic ash is a good time indicator since ash is deposited quickly over a widespread area. Matching the date of an eruption to the ash allows for a precise identification of time. Similarly, the meteor impact at the intersection of the Cretaceous and Tertiary Periods left a time marker. Wherever the meteor's iridium content is found, geologists are able to date rock layers.

Sequencing the earth's geologic history from the fossil and rock record

Reference tables are used to match specimens and time periods. For example, the fossil record has been divided into time units of the earth's history. Rocks can therefore be dated by the fossils found with them. There are also reference tables for dating plate motions and mountain building events in geologic history.

Since humans have been around for a relatively short period of time, fossilized human remains help to affix a date to a location.

Some areas have missing geologic layers because of erosion or other factors, but reference tables specific to a region will list what is complete or missing.

The theory of uniformitarianism assumes that geologic processes have been the same throughout history. Therefore, the way erosion or volcanic eruptions happen today is the same as the way these events happened millions of years ago because there is no reason for them to have changed. Therefore, knowledge about current events can be applied to the past to make judgments about events in the rock record.

Fossil and rock records and the earth's history

Fossils can show how animal and plant life have changed or remained the same over time. For example, fossils have provided evidence of the existence of dinosaurs even though they no longer roam the earth, and have also been used to prove that certain insects have been around forever. Fossils have been used to identify four basic eras: Proterozoic, the age of primitive life; Paleozoic, the age of fishes; Mesozoic, the age of dinosaurs; and Cenozoic, the age of mammals.

Most ancient forms of life have disappeared, and there are reference tables that list when this occurred. Fossil records also show the evolution of certain life forms, such as the horse from the eohippus. However, the majority of changes do not involve evolution from simple to complex forms, but rather an increase in the variety of forms.

Science Pedagogy

Scientific inquiry

Scientific inquiry is the impetus and catalyst for all scientific research and experimentation. It grows from questions about the observed world and gives us a template with which to apply the scientific method. Steps in scientific inquiry include the following principles:

1. Determination and scope of the questions to be investigated are the first step. These may range from simple to extremely complex questions to be explored by scientists.
2. The design, strategy, and method of the inquiry are then carefully considered, and a model for the inquiry is constructed.
3. The formulation of theories and models based on the careful observation of objective, unbiased data then follows. This formulation is derived from the scope of the scientific inquiry and the questions to be investigated.
4. Analysis of possible alternative conclusions drawn from the models and results of experimentation follows.
5. Postulating a theory or constructing a scientific statement based on conclusions is the next logical step.
6. Defending the scientific statement against alternative hypotheses is a critical function of scientific inquiry.
7. Defense of the theory or conclusion against critical analysis is the final step in the process.

Definition of science

Science is a method of acquiring and obtaining knowledge. It is the process of gaining reliable information about the real world, including the explanation of phenomena. It is the development of a body of knowledge about observable phenomena, using the best capabilities humans have at their disposal. The process of organizing and classifying knowledge, through objective observation and evaluation, is a major goal of science.

Science can be considered reliable, but it is not infallible. The limits of human knowledge are constantly growing, often making yesterday's science obsolete and simplistic. Science is thus never fixed; it is always subject to change as new information is gained and synthesized with existing knowledge.

Ultimately, science is the sum total of knowledge in any period of time, based on the current abilities of man to understand the world of phenomena, verifiable by observable data.

Limitations of science

There are clear limits on what science can explain. The demand for objectivity both strengthens knowledge we gain from scientific experiments and limits what we can explore. Beyond the realm of scientific inquiry are such questions as "Why does anything exist?" or "What is the meaning of life?" These are subjective questions that do not lend themselves easily to scientific inquiry. These questions, and others like them, come from within, and their conclusions, not validated by science, shape the very fabric of a society. They attempt to give meaning to what may be viewed as chaos. Periodically, science will impact these subjective conclusions with new evidence. For example, the theory of evolution is regarded as blasphemy by many religious fundamentalists. These conflicts may cause great upheavals in society, leaving many to wonder how science and religious belief can be reconciled. Ultimately, observation of the external world must stand as the true test of science.

Improvement of the human condition by science

Although basic science may have no stated goal or target, it provides many benefits to society:
1. Basic science contributes greatly to human understanding and culture, enriching society in many ways.
2. Basic science has been responsible for major breakthroughs that have great social and economic impact.
3. Basic science provides derivative solutions that can be used in applied science. For example, basic science was critical to the development of the space program, from which countless valuable applications have been derived.
4. Basic science contributes to education and research across the broad spectrum of society.

Overarching concepts of science

There are several concepts that transcend the branches of science and can be found as integral parts of physics, chemistry, biology, and other areas of study. One of these concepts is the system. A system is an arbitrarily sized group of entities that are taken to be a single unit. Systems may consist of physical bodies or of abstract concepts that intertwine. Systems will often be modeled by either mathematical expressions or physical-scale models, depending on the type of system and the purpose of the scale. In scale models, it is important to keep in mind that scale can have a huge effect on the behavior of a system. This can be seen in models of the solar system. The gravitational effects in a room-sized solar system model will be entirely negligible due to its reduced size. Other phenomena will only be observed on the atomic level. If the state of a system is constant, it is at equilibrium. Equilibrium may be either static or dynamic. A pair of side-by-side pools are in static equilibrium if there is no water being transferred between them. They are in dynamic equilibrium if equal amounts of water are being transferred between the pools in each direction. In the design of physical components, something that may be encountered is the interrelationship between form and function. If one of these two goals takes priority, that one will dictate the other. If the external appearance of a building is considered to be of higher importance than its utility, the functionality of the building may be limited.

Personal health portion of science class

Among the personal and social perspectives of science are the issues of personal and public health care. In this area, students learn such things as:
- The importance of regular exercise to the maintenance and improvement of health
- The need for risk assessment and educated decisions to prevent injuries and illnesses because of the potential for accidents and the existence of hazards
- The risk of illness and the social and psychological factors associated with the use of tobacco products
- The dangers of abusing alcohol and other drug substances, including addiction and damage to body functions
- The energy and nutrition values of various foods, their role in growth and development, and the requirements of the body according to variable factors
- The complexities of human sexuality and the dangers of sexually transmitted diseases
- The relationship between environmental and human health, and the need to monitor soil, water, and air standards

Personal and social perspectives of science

Risk analysis considers the type of hazard and estimates the number of people who might be exposed and the number likely to suffer consequences. The results are used to determine options for reducing or eliminating risks. For example, the Center for Disease Control must analyze the risk of a certain new virus strain causing a pandemic, how many people and what age groups need to be vaccinated first, and what precautions can be taken to guard against the spread of the disease.

Risk and benefit analysis involves having students consider the dangers of natural (major storms), chemical (pollution), biological (pollen and bacteria), social (occupational safety and transportation), and personal (smoking, dieting, and drugs) hazards. Students then use a systematic approach to think critically about these hazards, apply probability estimates to the risks, and compare them to estimated and perceived personal and social benefits.

Scientific Instruction

Scientific method of inquiry

The scientific method of inquiry is a general method by which ideas are tested and either confirmed or refuted by experimentation. The first step in the scientific method is formulating the problem that is to be addressed. It is essential to clearly define the limits of what is to be observed, since that allows for a more focused analysis. Once the problem has been defined, it is necessary to form a hypothesis. This educated guess should be a possible solution to the problem that was formulated in the first step. The next step is to test that hypothesis by experimentation. This often requires the scientist to design a complete experiment. The key to making the best possible use of an experiment is observation. Observations may be quantitative, that is, when a numeric measurement is taken, or they may be qualitative, that is, when something is evaluated based on feeling or preference. This measurement data will then be examined to find trends or patterns that are present. From these trends, the scientist will then draw conclusions or make generalizations about the results, intended to predict future results. If these conclusions support the original hypothesis, the experiment is complete and the scientist will publish his conclusions to allow others to test them by repeating the experiment. If they do not support the hypothesis, the results should then be used to develop a new hypothesis, which can then be verified by a new or redesigned experiment.

Skills necessary to the scientific process

Perhaps the most important skill in science is that of observation. A scientist must be able to take accurate data from his experimental setup or from nature without allowing bias to alter the results. Another important skill is hypothesizing. A scientist must be able to combine his knowledge of theory and of other experimental results to logically determine what should occur in his own tests. The data-analysis process requires the twin skills of ordering and categorizing. Gathered data must be arranged in such a way that it is readable and readily shows the key results. A skill that may be integrated with the previous two is comparing. A scientist should be able to compare his own results with other published results. He must also be able to infer, or draw logical conclusions, from his results. He must be able to apply his knowledge of theory and results to create logical experimental designs and determine cases of special behavior. Lastly, a scientist must be able to communicate his results and his conclusions. The greatest scientific progress is made when scientists are able to review and test one another's work and offer advice or suggestions.

Students as Learners and Science Instruction

Slide presentations can work well for presenting information to the classroom, but certain guidelines, if followed, can help these presentations be more effective.

- Be sure the presentation is structured so that students will be able to follow it easily.
- Be sure students will be able to see the presentation and read it easily even from the back of the classroom.
- Be sure all necessary equipment works and is appropriate to the size of the classroom.
- Always focus on the main message of the presentation.
- Be sure the presentation is consistent in presentation. Fonts, backgrounds, colors and transitions should be the same throughout the presentation.
- Keep individual slides simple and not overly busy so the information is more easily absorbed.

Scientific Assessment

A variety of software can be used to help students demonstrate their understanding of scientific concepts. Programs that present straightforward testing experiences are the most obvious application. In addition, students can make use of graphics programs to draw pictures, diagrams, or graphs that demonstrate their understanding of specific concepts such as the structure and components of a plant cell. Programs presenting problems for the student to solve can stimulate higher level thinking and demonstrate the student's knowledge. Simulations can give students the opportunity to experience situations that would be difficult to present in a classroom setting due to time, cost, or other issues. The teacher can use any of these applications as a tool for assessment.

Practice Test

English Language Arts and Reading

1. *Sea* and *see*, *fair* and *fare*, are called:
   a. Homophones
   b. Antonyms
   c. Homographs
   d. Twin words

2. Another name for a persuasive essay is:
   a. Dynamic essay
   b. Convincing essay
   c. Argumentative essay
   d. Position paper

3. A teacher is working with a group of third graders at the same reading level. Her goal is to improve reading fluency. She asks each child in turn to read a page from a book about mammal young. She asks the children to read with expression. She also reminds them they don't need to stop between each word; they should read as quickly as they comfortably can. She cautions them, however, not to read so quickly that they leave out or misread a word. The teacher knows the components of reading fluency are:
   a. Speed, drama, and comprehension
   b. Cohesion, rate, and prosody
   c. Understanding, rate, and prosody
   d. Rate, accuracy, and prosody

4. "Language load" refers to:
   a. The basic vocabulary words a first grader has committed to memory
   b. The number of unrecognizable words an English Language Learner encounters when reading a passage or listening to a teacher
   c. The damage that carrying a pile of heavy books could cause to a child's physique
   d. The number of different languages a person has mastered.

5. A syllable must contain:
   a. A vowel
   b. A consonant
   c. Both a vowel and a consonant
   d. A meaning

6. Of the three tiers of words, the most important words for direct instruction are:
   a. Tier-one words
   b. Common words
   c. Tier-two words
   d. Words with Latin roots

7. At the beginning of each month, Mr. Yi has Jade read a page or two from a book she hasn't seen before. He notes the total number of words in the section, and also notes the number of times she leaves out or misreads a word. If Jade reads the passage with less than 3% error, Mr. Yi is satisfied that Jade is:
    a. Reading with full comprehension
    b. Probably bored and should try a more difficult book
    c. Reading at her Independent reading level
    d. Comfortable with the syntactical meaning

8. The purpose of corrective feedback is:
    a. To provide students with methods for explaining to the teacher or classmates what a passage was about
    b. To correct an error in reading a student has made, specifically clarifying where and how the error was made so that the student can avoid similar errors in the future
    c. To provide a mental framework that will help the student correctly organize new information
    d. To remind students that error is essential in order to truly understand and that it is not something to be ashamed of

9. Which of the following best explains the importance prior knowledge brings to the act of reading?
    a. Prior knowledge is information the student gets through researching a topic prior to reading the text. A student who is well-prepared through such research is better able to decode a text and retain its meaning.
    b. Prior knowledge is knowledge the student brings from previous life or learning experiences to the act of reading. It is not possible for a student to fully comprehend new knowledge without first integrating it with prior knowledge.
    c. Prior knowledge is predictive. It motivates the student to look for contextual clues in the reading and predict what is likely to happen next.
    d. Prior knowledge is not important to any degree to the act of reading, because every text is self-contained and therefore seamless. Prior knowledge is irrelevant in this application.

10. Sight words are:
    a. Common words with irregular spelling
    b. Words that can easily be found on educational websites
    c. Any word that can be seen, including text words, words on signs, brochures, banners, and so forth
    d. There is no such thing; because oral language is learned before written language, all words are ultimately based on sound. The correct term is sound words and includes all words necessary to decode a particular text

11. *Phone, they, church.* The underlined letters in these words are examples of:
    a. Consonant blend
    b. Consonant shift
    c. Continental shift
    d. Consonant digraph

12. Phonemic awareness is a type of:
    a. Phonological awareness. Phonemic awareness is the ability to recognize sounds within words
    b. Phonics. It is a teaching technique whereby readers learn the relationship between letters and sounds
    c. Alphabetization. Unless a reader knows the alphabet, phonemic awareness is useless
    d. Syntactical awareness. Understanding the underlying structure of a sentence is key to understanding meaning

13. A fourth-grade teacher is preparing her students for a reading test in which a number of words have been replaced with blanks. The test will be multiple-choice; there are three possible answers given for each blank. The teacher instructs the children to read all the possible answers and cross out any answer that obviously doesn't fit. Next, the students should "plug in" the remaining choices and eliminate any that are grammatically incorrect or illogical. Finally, the student should consider contextual clues in order to select the best answer. This in an example of:
    a. Strategy instruction
    b. Diagnostic instruction
    c. Skills instruction
    d. Multiple-choice instruction

14. The term "common words" means:
    a. One-syllable words with fewer than three letters. Some examples are it, an, a, I, go, to, and in. They are the first words an emergent writer learns
    b. One-syllable words with fewer than five letters. Some examples include sing, goes, sit, rock, walk, and took
    c. Words that are ordinary or unexceptional; because they tend to flatten a piece of writing, they should be avoided
    d. Familiar, frequently used words that do not need to be taught beyond primary grades

15. *Train, brain, spring.* The underlined letters are examples of:
    a. Consonant digraph
    b. Consonant blend
    c. Consonant shift
    d. Continental shift

16. The most effective strategy for decoding sight words is:
    a. Segmenting sight words into syllables. Beginning readers are understandably nervous when encountering a long word that isn't familiar. Blocking off all but a single syllable at a time renders a word manageable and allows the reader a sense of control over the act of reading
    b. Word families. By grouping the sight word with similar words, patterns emerge
    c. A phonemic approach. When students understand the connection between individual words and their sounds, they will be able to sound out any sight word they encounter
    d. None; sight words cannot be decoded. Readers must learn to recognize these words as wholes on sight

17. Which of the following choices will be most important when designing a reading activity or lesson for students?
    a. Selecting a text
    b. Determining the number of students participating
    c. Analyzing the point in the school year at which the lesson is given
    d. Determining a purpose for instruction

18. Phonological awareness activities are:
  a. Oral
  b. Visual
  c. Both A and B
  d. Semantically based

19. A student is able to apply strategies to comprehend the meanings of unfamiliar words; can supply definitions for words with several meanings such as *crucial, criticism,* and *witness*; and is able to reflect on her background knowledge in order to decipher a word's meaning. These features of effective reading belong to which category?
  a. Word recognition
  b. Vocabulary
  c. Content
  d. Comprehension

20. When should students learn how to decode?
  a. Decoding is the most basic and essential strategy to becoming a successful reader. It should be introduced to kindergartners during the first two weeks of school
  b. Decoding is not a teachable skill. It is an unconscious act and is natural to all learners
  c. Decoding should be taught only after children have mastered every letter–sound relationship as well as every consonant digraph and consonant blend. They should also be able to recognize and say the 40 phonemes common to English words and be able to recognize at least a dozen of the most common sight words
  d. Decoding depends on an understanding of letter–sound relationships. As soon as a child understands enough letters and their correspondent sounds to read a few words, decoding should be introduced

21. *Since, whether,* and *accordingly* are examples of which type of signal words?
  a. Common, or basic, signal words
  b. Compare/contrast words
  c. Cause–effect words
  d. Temporal sequencing words

22. A class is reading *The Heart Is a Lonely Hunter*. The teacher asks students to write a short paper explaining the story's resolution. She is asking them to locate and discuss the story's:
  a. Outcome
  b. Highest or most dramatic moment
  c. Plot
  d. Lowest point

23. A student encounters a multisyllabic word. She's not sure if she's seen it before. What should she do first? What should she do next?
  a. Locate familiar word parts, then locate the consonants
  b. Locate the consonants, then locate the vowels
  c. Locate the vowels, then locate familiar word parts
  d. Look it up in the dictionary, then write down the meaning

The following passage pertains to the following questions 24 - 25:

The kindergarten teacher is concerned about three of her students. While they are enthusiastic about writing, they do not always recognize letters, confusing b, d, and p, or e and o. They do, however, know which sounds go with certain letters when they are orally drilled. When they write, they appear to be attempting letter–sound associations.

"Now I'm writing *M*," the teacher heard one boy say as he scripted a large *N* in the upper right corner of his paper. He studied it for a moment and added, "Nope, it needs another leg." The student then wrote an *I* beside the *N*. "There," he said. "Now you are an *M*. I can write the word, 'man,' because now I have *M*." The child then moved to the lower left corner of the paper. "M-A-N," he said to himself, slowly pronouncing each sound. "I already have that *M*. Here is where the rest of the word goes." He turned the paper sideways and wrote *N*.

The second child sang to herself as she gripped the crayon and scribbled lines here and there on her paper. Some of the lines resembled letters, but few actually were. Others were scribbles. As she "wrote," she seemed to be making up a story and seemed to believe she was writing the story down.

The third child didn't vocalize at all while he worked. He gripped the paper and carefully wrote the same letter over and over and over. Sometimes the letter was large, sometimes tiny. He turned the paper in every direction so that sometimes the letter was sideways or upside down. Sometimes he flipped it backward. "What are you writing?" the teacher asked him. "My name," the child told her. The teacher then realized the letter was, indeed, the first letter of his name. She gently told him he had done a fine job of writing the first letter of his name. Did he want her to help him write the rest of it? "Nope," he cheerfully told her, "it's all here." He pointed at one of the letters and "read" his full name. He pointed at another letter and again seemed to believe it represented all the sounds of his name.

24. The teacher might best encourage the three students in the above example by:
    a. Suggesting they write an entire book rather than just a single page. This will build confidence, teach them sequencing, and encourage the young writers to delve deeper into their ideas.
    b. Ask the students to read their stories to her. Suggest they visit other children in the class and read to each of them.
    c. Contact the local newspaper and invite a reporter to visit her class and write a story about her emergent writers. In this way, they are sure to see themselves as "real writers" and will more fully apply themselves to the task.
    d. Invite all the parents to visit the class the following week. This will give all classmates, regardless of where they are on the learning spectrum, time to memorize their stories. The children will be very excited and will begin to see themselves as "real writers."

25. At what point should the kindergarten teacher in the above example offer the three children picture books and ask them to read to her?

    a. When the three children are all able to script initial sounds, end sounds, and interior sounds they are ready to decode words. She should make her request at this point

    b. As each child reaches the stage in which he or she can script initial sounds, end sounds, and interior sounds, the teacher should ask only that child to read to her

    c. As each child reaches the stage in which he habitually writes from the top to the bottom of the page, moving left to right, the time has come. Books are intended to be read in this way, and until a child has had the experience of writing in the same manner, he won't be able to make sense of the words

    d. The teacher should encourage all students to "read" picture books from the first day of school. Talking about the pictures from page to page gives young readers the idea that books are arranged sequentially. Pictures also offer narrative coherence and contextual clues. Emergent readers who are encouraged to enjoy books will more readily embrace the act of reading. Holding a book and turning pages gives young readers a familiarity with them

26. A teacher is teaching students analogizing. She is teaching them to:

    a. Identify and use metaphors

    b. Identify and use similes

    c. Identify and use groups of letters that occur in a word family

    d. Identify and use figures of speech

27. A fifth grader has prepared a report on reptiles, which is something he knows a great deal about. He rereads his report and decides to make a number of changes. He moves a sentence from the top to the last paragraph. He crosses out several words and replaces them with more specific words. He circles key information and draws an arrow to show another place the information could logically be placed. He is engaged in:

    a. Editing

    b. Revising

    c. First editing, then revising

    d. Reviewing

28. *Bi, re,* and *un* are:

    a. Suffixes, appearing at the beginning of base words to change their meaning

    b. Suffixes, appearing at the end of base words to enhance their meaning

    c. Prefixes, appearing at the beginning of base words to emphasize their meaning

    d. Prefixes, appearing at the beginning of base words to change their meanings

29. Examples of CVC words include:

    a. Add, pad, mad

    b. Cat, tack, act

    c. Elephant, piano, examine

    d. Dog, sit, leg

30. Collaborative Strategic Reading (CSR) is a teaching technique that depends on two teaching practices. These practices are:

    a. Cooperative learning and reading comprehension

    b. Cooperative reading and metacognition

    c. Reading comprehension and metacognition

    d. Cooperative learning and metacognition

31. Context clues are useful in:
    a. Predicting future action
    b. Understanding the meaning of words that are not familiar
    c. Understanding character motivation
    d. Reflecting on a text's theme

32. Syllable types include:
    a. Closed, open, silent e, vowel team, vowel-r, and consonant-le
    b. Closed, open, silent, double-vowel, r, and le
    c. Closed, midway, open, emphasized, prefixed, and suffixed
    d. Stressed, unstressed, and silent

33. An eighth-grade student is able to decode most words fluently and has a borderline/acceptable vocabulary, but his reading comprehension is quite low. He can be helped with instructional focus on:
    a. Strategies to increase comprehension and to build vocabulary
    b. Strategies to increase comprehension and to be able to identify correct syntactical usage
    c. Strategies to improve his understanding of both content and context
    d. Strategies to build vocabulary and to improve his understanding of both content and context

34. Reading comprehension and vocabulary can best be assessed:
    a. With brief interviews and tests every two months to determine how much learning has taken place. Students learn in spurts, and in-depth assessments of comprehension and vocabulary are a waste of time
    b. Through a combination of standardized testing, informal teacher observations, attention to grades, objective-linked assessments, and systematized charting of data over time
    c. By giving students weekly self-assessment rubrics to keep them constantly aware of and invested in their own progress
    d. By having students retell a story or summarize the content of an informational piece of writing. The degree to which the material was comprehended, and the richness or paucity of vocabulary used in such work, provides efficient and thorough assessment

35. An ORF is:
    a. An Oral Reading Fluency assessment
    b. An Occasional Reading Function assessment
    c. An Oscar Reynolds Feinstein assessment
    d. An Overt Reading Failure assessment

36. Round-robin reading refers to the practice of allowing children to take turns reading portions of a text aloud to the rest of the group during class. Which of the following statements is least true about this practice?
    a. Students have the chance to practice reading aloud with this strategy
    b. This practice is ineffective in its use of time, leaving students who are not reading aloud to become bored or daydream
    c. Round-robin reading lacks the creativity or engaging qualities that will interest students in building literacy skills
    d. This practice helps students feel comfortable with reading aloud due to continuous practice and encouragement from the teacher and peers

37. Word-recognition ability is:
    a. Equally important to all readers
    b. Used only by fluent readers
    c. Another term for "word attack"
    d. Especially important to English Language Learners and students with reading disabilities

38. Research indicates that developing oral language proficiency in emergent readers is important because:
    a. Proficiency with oral language enhances students' phonemic awareness and increases vocabulary
    b. The more verbally expressive emergent readers are, the more confident they become. Such students will embrace both Academic and Independent reading levels
    c. It encourages curiosity about others. With strong oral language skills, students begin to question the world around them. The more they ask, the richer their background knowledge
    d. It demonstrates to students that their ideas are important and worth sharing

A teacher has given the first paragraph of an essay to her students to analyze and discuss. Read the paragraph and answer the following questions 39-42:

> Americans have struggled with cigarettes far too long. Until now, it has been a personal choice to smoke (or not), but the time for change is rapidly approaching. Local legislation has already begun for schools, restaurants, arenas, and other public places to be smoke-free. Years ago cigarette smoking was presented by the media as being fashionable, even sexy. In magazines, movies, and later in television, celebrities would indulge themselves with a smoke and even be paid to endorse a brand. As recently as 1975, it was common for talk show hosts like Tom Snyder and Johnny Carson to keep a cigarette burning. Cigarette smoking in America has persisted in spite of frightening concerns like lung cancer and emphysema. Over the years, the tobacco industry has sought to diffuse strong evidence that smoking is harmful. However, the myth of "safe cigarettes," questions about nicotine addiction, and denials about the dangers of secondhand smoke have proven to be propaganda and lies.

39. This is a(n) _____ essay:
    a. Compare/contrast
    b. Persuasive
    c. Narrative
    d. Analytic

40. The thesis statement is:
    a. However, the myth of "safe cigarettes," questions about nicotine addiction, and denials about the dangers of secondhand smoke have proven to be propaganda and lies
    b. Americans have struggled with cigarettes far too long
    c. Until now, it has been a personal choice to smoke (or not), but the time for change is rapidly approaching
    d. In magazines, movies, and later in television, celebrities would indulge themselves with a smoke and even be paid to endorse a brand

41. The next three paragraphs in the essay will most likely address:
    a. Smoking as a personal choice, changes in local legislation, and how fashionable smoking once was
    b. How fashionable smoking once was, talk show hosts smoking on air, the myth of "safe cigarettes"
    c. Propaganda and lies, the myth of "safe cigarettes," and how long Americans have struggled with cigarettes
    d. The myth of "safe cigarettes," questions about nicotine addiction, and the dangers of secondhand smoke

42. *Caret, carrot, to, two and too* share something in common. They:
    a. Are nouns
    b. Are monosyllabic
    c. Are homophones
    d. Represent things in nature

Questions 43 – 45 pertain to the following paragraph:
    A class will visit an assisted living facility to interview residents about their lives. Each group of three has selected a theme such as love, work, or personal accomplishment and written several questions around that theme. Next each group practices interviewing one another. The teacher then asks all the students to discuss the questions that caused them to respond most thoughtfully, as well as those they were less inspired by. The students decided the questions that were easiest to respond to asked for very specific information; for example, one inspiring question was, "Please tell me about something you learned to do as a child that affected the direction of your life." Those that were uninspiring were too broad, for example, "Please tell me about your happiest memory."

43. After they interview the residents, each group of three students will work together to write a piece about the resident. This kind of approach is called:
    a. Collaborative learning
    b. Companion learning
    c. Bonded learning
    d. Group learning

44. The genre the teacher expects is:
    a. Memoir
    b. Historical fiction
    c. Biography
    d. Autobiography

45. The teacher wants the students to apply what they've learned across content areas. Which of the following strategies would be most effective?
    a. Students will interview a family member, asking the same questions
    b. Students will write a personal piece in which they address the same questions
    c. Students will do online research about the cultural, economic, or political events that were occurring during the specific time about which they've written
    d. Students pretend to be the interviewee and rewrite the piece from a first person point of view

The following passage pertains to questions 46 – 48:

A seventh-grade teacher asks the reading teacher to suggest a lesson students will find simultaneously challenging and fun. The reading teacher suggests the class read fairy tales from both Hans Christian Anderson and the Brothers Grimm and have a rapid-paced, energetic discussion about the many similarities and differences between the two while the teacher lists them on the board.

46. The individual strategies the students will employ are:
    a. Collaborative learning and genre
    b. Brainstorming and a compare/contrast strategy
    c. Collaborative learning and brainstorming
    d. Analyzing and genre

47. The lesson is asking the students to consider two different:
    a. Learning styles
    b. Genres
    c. Writing styles
    d. Reading styles

48. The primary benefit of this exercise is that it promotes students':
    a. Vocabulary
    b. Comprehension
    c. Fluency
    d. Word identification

49. The phrase "Pretty as a picture" is *best* described as a:
    a. Metaphor
    b. Cliché
    c. Simile
    d. Figure of speech

50. A fourth-grade teacher had her students write haiku in order to promote the students'
    _____.
    a. Reading comprehension
    b. Vocabulary
    c. Word identification skills
    d. Confidence

51. Examples of onomatopoeia are:
    a. Sink, drink, mink, link
    b. Their, there, they're
    c. Drip, chirp, splash, giggle
    d. *Think, in, thin, ink*

52. "Code knowledge" facilitates reading fluency because:
    a. It brings the entirety of the student's previous experience to bear on decoding a text
    b. It offers a framework for organizing new information by assigning code words to sets of ideas
    c. There is no such thing as "code knowledge." The correct term is "core knowledge"
    d. It offers a systematic approach to untangling the wide variety of vowel sounds when an unfamiliar word is encountered

53. The purpose of "targeted instruction" is to:
   a. Deliver instructions that are precise, clear, and direct so that students understand exactly what is expected
   b. Accurately rank a group of learners from low achievers to high achievers so that the teacher knows from the beginning of the school year which students have less ability and will therefore need support
   c. Teach students how to take information from a text and reorganize it into bulleted lists
   d. Assess and target areas needing improvement as well as areas of greatest strength for each student to ensure that all members of a class are receiving instruction tailored to their specific needs

54. Silent reading fluency can best be assessed by:
   a. Having the student retell or summarize the material to determine how much was understood
   b. Giving a written test that covers plot, theme, character development, sequence of events, rising action, climax, falling action, and outcome. A student must test at a 95% accuracy rate to be considered fluent at silent reading
   c. Giving a three-minute Test of Silent Contextual Reading Fluency four times a year. The student is presented with text in which spaces between words and all punctuation have been removed. The student must divide one word from another with slash marks, as in the following example: The/little/sailboat/bobbed/so/far/in/the/distance/it/looked/like/a/toy. The more words a student accurately separates, the higher her silent reading fluency score
   d. Silent reading fluency cannot be assessed. It is a private act between the reader and the text and does not invite critique

55. A high school teacher has given her students an assignment to write a non-rhyming poem of three lines. The first and last lines each contain five syllables, and the middle line contains seven syllables. The students are writing a:
   a. Limerick
   b. Metaphor
   c. Villanelle
   d. Haiku

56. Which of the following statements regarding the acquisition of language is false?
   a. Young children often have the ability to comprehend written language just as early as they can comprehend or reproduce oral language when given appropriate instruction.
   b. Oral language typically develops before a child understands the relationship between spoken and written word.
   c. Most young children are first exposed to written language when an adult reads aloud.
   d. A child's ability to speak, read, and write depends on a variety of physiological factors, as well as environmental factors.

57. Jamie's teacher presents her kindergarten class with a unit about Mexico that includes information about the customs, geography, language, and cuisine of the country. While the teacher is showing pictures of a traditional Mexican festival, Jamie raises his hand to share some of the object-names he remembers from his family's annual trip to Mexico. This scenario is an example of:
   a. Paradigm emergence
   b. Prior knowledge activation
   c. Chunking
   d. Immersion theory

58. Which of the following statements is most true?

a. Introducing oral and written texts from a variety of cultures can enhance students' understanding and appreciation of language.

b. Children typically learn language best when exposed primarily to texts exemplary of their own background or culture, thereby increasing their ability to identify personally with what they are learning.

c. Studying other languages will impair a student's ability to develop his or her own first language.

d. Students should be exposed to one type of text at a time to diminish genre confusion.

59. Which adult would be most effective in helping a student who frequently mispronounces sounds both in reading and in conversation?

a. A whole language specialist

b. A speech pathologist

c. A paraprofessional

d. A psychologist

60. Which of the following is least important in its effect on a child's language development?

a. Physical development of ears, mouth, and nose

b. The IQ and educational level of the child's parents

c. Interaction and conversation with fluent speakers

d. Developmental or psychological delay

61. Reading can be best described as:

a. A skill that is learned through sequential lessons and concepts, presented carefully in order of importance.

b. An understanding of the written word.

c. A complex task that involves multiple physical and cognitive processes.

d. The primary form of transmitting knowledge within a culture.

62. Which choice describes a common function of reading or writing?

a. Communication of ideas

b. Enjoyment

c. Language acquisition

d. All of the above

63. Learning to construct a reading response would be most beneficial in enhancing which language skill?

a. Oral presentation

b. Comprehension

c. Fluency

d. Learning a second language

64. Which text(s) are likely to foster the greatest enthusiasm for reading and literature among students?
    a. Free choice of reading texts, provided that students complete class assignments, projects, and discussions.
    b. An all-in-one textbook that includes all reading material for the year, study guides, and sample test questions.
    c. A variety of texts, including books, magazines, newspapers, stories from oral traditions, poetry, music, and films.
    d. A small selection of current best-selling books for children, some of which the children may already have read and liked.

65. Which exercise would be best for building fluency in young students?
    a. Allowing students to draw pictures that illustrate the texts they read if they are unable to write their responses.
    b. Using daily games and lessons to reinforce phoneme-identification skills.
    c. Placing the students into groups to read aloud to one another.
    d. Reading to the students every day from a variety of texts.

66. Piper is chosen to read to the class on Friday from a book of her choosing. The book she chooses is challenging for her to read. Her teacher observes that Piper is reading the book with approximately 80% accuracy in decoding. Piper is reading a text at what level?
    a. Independent
    b. Frustration
    c. Advanced
    d. Instructional

67. Which of the following is the best use of technology in a language arts classroom?
    a. Providing laptops to students to achieve more effective note-taking, access to word processing programs, and access to the internet.
    b. Encouraging the use of PowerPoint or similar programs to support lectures and oral presentations, as well as to organize pertinent class concepts.
    c. Incorporating a computer-based "language lab" in which students can listen to texts and engage in interactive word-study and comprehension activities.
    d. Whenever possible, watching film interpretations based on texts studied in class.

68. A reading teacher is assessing an eighth grader to determine her reading level. Timed at a minute, the student reads with 93% accuracy. She misreads an average of seven words out of 100. What is her reading level?
    a. She is reading at a Frustration level
    b. She is reading at an Excellence level
    c. She is reading at an Instructional level
    d. She is reading at an Independent level

69. Which choice describes an appropriate alternative to Round-robin reading?

    a. All students read together, simultaneously speaking the text aloud.

    b. Students break into pairs assigned by the teacher to take turns reading the text while the teacher circulates among the pairs to guide and assess the students.

    c. The teacher reads aloud to the students before engaging in a class discussion about what they have learned.

    d. Students work on independent assignments while the teacher listens to students read individually.

70. Which choice describes the most complete method of displaying student achievement or progress in language arts?

    a. A written report or story that demonstrates a student's knowledge of grammar, spelling, comprehension, and writing skills.

    b. Either a norm- or criterion-referenced test that breaks language skills into small sub-sets and provides achievement levels for each skill.

    c. A portfolio containing a log of stories or books the student has read, rates of reading fluency, writing samples, creative projects, and spelling, grammar, and comprehension tests/quizzes.

    d. A year-end project in which the student presents what he or she has learned from a student-chosen book; the student must read an excerpt of the story and display a visual aid highlighting important information from the story or literary techniques used by the author.

71. Which student is most likely to need referral to a reading specialist for assessment, special instruction, or intervention?

    a. Annabel: a 2nd-grade student who tends to skip over words or phrases when she reads, affecting her comprehension of the text.

    b. Cliff: a kindergarten student who is already reading simple chapter books with his parents at home or in class.

    c. Noelle: a 1st-grader who avoids any activity in which she must read, both aloud and silently, preferring to ask an adult to read the text for her first.

    d. Barrett: a 3rd-grader who often confuses the sounds of certain letters, such as /b/ and /d/ or /v/ and /u/.

72. Which assessment will determine a student's ability to identify initial, medial, blended, final, segmented, and manipulated 'units'?

    a. Phonological awareness assessment

    b. High-frequency word assessment

    c. Reading fluency assessment

    d. Comprehension quick-check

73. Activating prior knowledge, shared reading, and using graphic organizers are all examples of what type of instructional concept?

    a. Modeling

    b. Scaffolding

    c. Assessing

    d. Inspiring

74. Which text should a teacher choose in order to practice the skills of previewing and reviewing information?

    a. A poem

    b. A chapter from the students' science class textbook

    c. A library book of each student's own choosing

    d. A short story from language arts class

Mathematics

1. Determine the number of diagonals of a dodecagon.
   a. 12
   b. 24
   c. 54
   d. 108

2. A circular bracelet contains 5 charms, A, B, C, D, and E, attached at specific points around the bracelet, with the clasp located between charms A and B. The bracelet is unclasped and stretched out into a straight line. On the resulting linear bracelet, charm C is between charms A and B, charm D is between charms A and C, and charm E is between charms C and D. Which of these statements is (are) necessarily true?
   I.   The distance between charms B and E is greater than the distance between charms A and D.
   II.   Charm E is between charms B and D.
   III.   The distance between charms D and E is less than the distance of bracelet between charms A and C.
   a. I, II, and III
   b. II and III
   c. II only
   d. None of these is necessarily true.

3. In a town of 35,638 people, about a quarter of the population is under the age of 35. Of those, just over a third attend local K-12 schools. If the number of students in each grade is about the same, how many fourth graders likely reside in the town?
   a. Fewer than 100
   b. Between 200 and 300
   c. Between 300 and 400
   d. More than 400

4. Identical rugs are offered for sale at two local shops and one online retailer, designated Stores A, B, and C, respectively. The rug's regular sales price is $296 at Store A, $220 at Store B, and $198.00 at Store C. Stores A and B collect 8% in sales tax on any after-discount price, while Store C collects no tax but charges a $35 shipping fee. A buyer has a 30% off coupon for Store A and a $10 off coupon for Store B. Which of these lists the stores in order of lowest to highest final sales price after all discounts, taxes, and fees are applied?
   a. Store A, Store B, Store C
   b. Store B, Store C, Store A
   c. Store C, Store A, Store C
   d. Store C, Store B, Store A

5. Two companies offer monthly cell phone plans, both of which include free text messaging. Company A charges a $25 monthly fee plus five cents per minute of phone conversation, while Company B charges a $50 monthly fee and offers unlimited calling. Both companies charge the same amount when the total duration of monthly calls is
   a. 500 hours.
   b. 8 hours and 33 minutes.
   c. 8 hours and 20 minutes.
   d. 5 hours.

6. A dress is marked down by 20% and placed on a clearance rack, on which is posted a sign reading, "Take an extra 25% off already reduced merchandise." What fraction of the original price is the final sales price of the dress?

a. $\frac{9}{20}$

b. $\frac{11}{20}$

c. $\frac{2}{5}$

d. $\frac{3}{5}$

7. The ratio of employee wages and benefits to all other operational costs of a business is 2:3. If a business's operating expenses are $130,000 per month, how much money does the company spend on employee wages and benefits?

a. $43,333.33

b. $86,666.67

c. $52,000.00

d. $78,000.00

8. Zeke drove from his house to a furniture store in Atlanta and then back home along the same route. It took Zeke three hours to drive to the store. By driving an average of 20 mph faster on his return trip, Zeke was able to save an hour of diving time. What was Zeke's average driving speed on his round trip?

a. 24 mph

b. 48 mph

c. 50 mph

d. 60 mph

9. The graph below shows Aaron's distance from home at times throughout his morning run. Which of the following statements is (are) true?

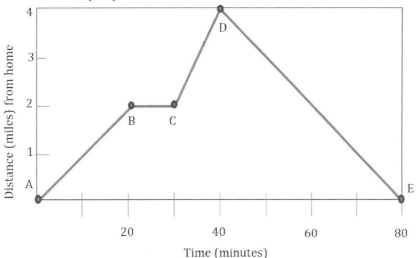

I.   Aaron's average running speed was 6 mph.
II.   Aaron's running speed from point A to point B was the same as his running speed from point D to E.
III. Aaron ran a total distance of four miles.
   a. I only
   b. II only
   c. I and II
   d. I, II, and III

10. If a, b, and c are even integers and $3a^2 + 9b^3 = c$, which of these is the largest number which must be factor of c?
   a. 2
   b. 3
   c. 6
   d. 12

11. Find $[g \circ f\,]x$ when $f(x) = 2x + 4$ and $g(x) = x^2 - 3x + 2$.
   a. $4x^2 + 10x + 6$
   b. $2x^2 - 6x + 8$
   c. $4x^2 + 13x + 18$
   d. $2x^2 - 3x + 6$

12. Given the partial table of values for $f(x)$ and $g(x)$, find $f(g(-4))$. (Assume that $f(x)$ and $g(x)$ are the simplest polynomials that fit the data.)

x	f(x)	g(x)
-2	8	1
-1	2	3
0	0	5
1	2	7
2	8	9

   a. 69
   b. 31

c. 18

d. –3

13. If $f(x)$ and $g(x)$ are inverse functions, which of these is the value of x when $f(g(x)) = 4$?

   a. –4

   b. $\frac{1}{4}$

   c. 2

   d. 4

14. A school is selling tickets to its production of *Annie Get Your Gun*. Student tickets cost $3 each, and non-student tickets are $5 each. In order to offset the costs of the production, the school must earn at least $300 in ticket sales. Which graph shows the number of tickets the school must sell to offset production costs?

a.

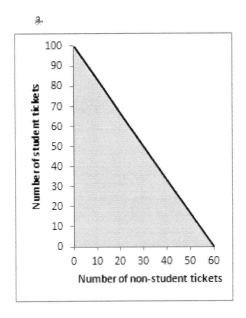

c.

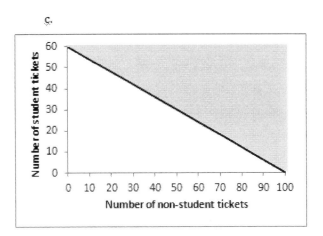

b.

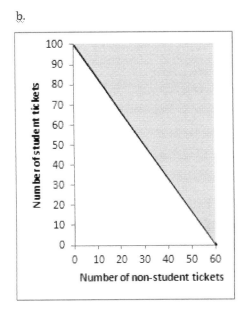

d.

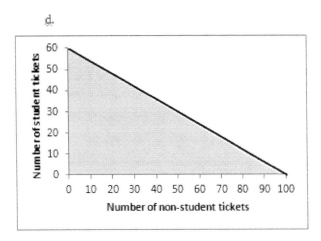

15. Which of these is the equation graphed below?
    a. $y = -2x^2 - 4x + 1$
    b. $y = -x^2 - 2x + 5$
    c. $y = -x^2 - 2x + 2$
    d. $y = -\frac{1}{2}x^2 - x + \frac{5}{2}$

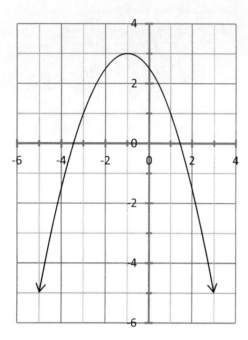

16. Solve the system of equations.

$$3x + 4y = 2$$
$$2x + 6y = -2$$

    a. $\left(0, \frac{1}{2}\right)$
    b. $\left(\frac{2}{5}, \frac{1}{5}\right)$
    c. $(2, -1)$
    d. $\left(-1, \frac{5}{4}\right)$

17. Which system of linear inequalities has no solution?
    a. $x - y < 3$
       $x - y \geq -3$

    b. $y \leq 6 - 2x$
       $\frac{1}{3}y + \frac{2}{3}x \geq 2$

    c. $6x + 2y \leq 12$
       $3x \geq 8 - y$

    d. $x + 4y \leq -8$
       $y + 4x > -8$

18. Solve $3x^3y^2 - 45x^2y = 15x^3y - 9x^2y^2$ for x and y.
    a. $x = \{0, -3\}$, $y = \{0, 5\}$
    b. $x = \{0\}$, $y = \{0\}$
    c. $x = \{0, -3\}$, $y = \{0\}$
    d. $x = \{0\}$, $y = \{0, 5\}$

19. If 1" on a map represents 60 ft, how many yards apart are two points if the distance between the points on the map is 10"?
    a. 1800
    b. 600
    c. 200
    d. 2

20. A developer decides to build a fence around a neighborhood park, which is positioned on a rectangular lot. Rather than fencing along the lot line, he fences x feet from each of the lot's boundaries. By fencing a rectangular space 141 yd^2 smaller than the lot, the developer saves $432 in fencing materials, which cost $12 per linear foot. How much does he spend?
    a. $160
    b. $456
    c. $3,168
    d. The answer cannot be determined from the given information.

21. Which of these is **NOT** a net of a cube?
    a.   b.   c.   d.

   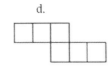

22. If the midpoint of a line segment graphed on the xy-coordinate plane is $(3, -1)$ and the slope of the line segment is -2, which of these is a possible endpoint of the line segment?
    a. $(-1, 1)$
    b. $(0, -5)$
    c. $(7, 1)$
    d. $(5, -5)$

23. The graph of $f(x)$ is a parabola with a focus of (a, b) and a directrix of $y = -b$, and $g(x)$ represents a transformation of $f(x)$. If the vertex of the graph of $g(x)$ is $(a, 0)$, which of these is a possible equation for $g(x)$ for nonzero integers a and b?
    a. $g(x) = f(x) + b$
    b. $g(x) = -f(x)$
    c. $g(x) = f(x + a)$
    d. $g(x) = f(x - a) + b$

24. A manufacturer wishes to produce a cylindrical can which can hold up to 0.5 L of liquid. To the nearest tenth, what is the radius of the can which requires the least amount of material to make?
    a. 2.8 cm
    b. 4.3 cm
    c. 5.0 cm
    d. 9.2 cm

25. Which of these would best illustrate change over time?
   a. Pie chart
   b. Line graph
   c. Box-and-whisker plot
   d. Venn diagram

Use the following data to answer questions 127-129:

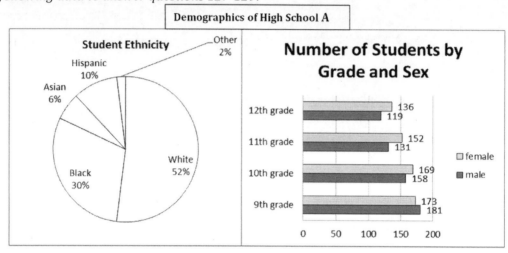

26. Which of these is the greatest quantity?
   a. The average number of male students in the 11ᵗʰ and 12ᵗʰ grades
   b. The number of Hispanic students at the school
   c. The difference in the number of male and female students at the school
   d. The difference in the number of 9ᵗʰ and 12ᵗʰ grade students at the school

27. Compare the two quantities.

Quantity A	Quantity B
The percentage of white students at the school, rounded to the nearest whole number	The percentage of female students at the school, rounded to the nearest whole number

   a. Quantity A is greater.
   b. Quantity B is greater.
   c. The two quantities are the same.
   d. The relationship cannot be determined from the given information.

28. An eleventh grader is chosen at random to represent the school at a conference. What is the approximate probability that the student is male?
   a. 0.03
   b. 0.11
   c. 0.22
   d. 0.46

29. A small company is divided into three departments as shown. Two individuals are chosen at random to attend a conference. What is the approximate probability that two women from the same department will be chosen?

	Department 1	Department 2	Department 3
Women	12	28	16
Men	18	14	15

a. 8.6%
b. 10.7%
c. 11.2%
d. 13.8%

30. A random sample of students at an elementary school were asked these three questions:

Do you like carrots?
Do you like broccoli?
Do you like cauliflower?

The results of the survey are shown below. If these data are representative of the population of students at the school, which of these is most probable?

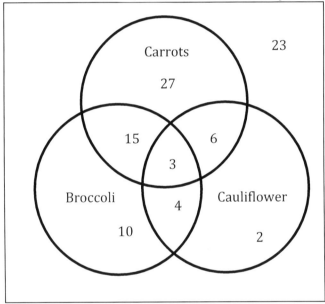

   a. A student chosen at random likes broccoli.
   b. If a student chosen at random likes carrots, he also likes at least one other vegetable.
   c. If a student chosen at random likes cauliflower and broccoli, he also likes carrots.
   d. A student chosen at random does not like carrots, broccoli, or cauliflower.

31. The intelligence quotients (IQs) of a randomly selected group of 300 people are normally distributed with a mean IQ of 100 and a standard deviation of 15. In a normal distribution, approximately 68% of values are within one standard deviation of the mean. About how many individuals from the selected group have IQs of at least 85?
   a. 96
   b. 200
   c. 216
   d. 252

32. Kim's current monthly rent is $800. She is moving to another apartment complex, where the monthly rent will be $1,100. What is the percent increase in her monthly rent amount?

a. 25.5%
b. 27%
c. 35%
d. 37.5%

33. Marlon pays $45 for a jacket that has been marked down 25%. What was the original cost of the jacket?
   a. $80
   b. $75
   c. $65
   d. $60

34. Which of the following statements is true?
   a. A number is divisible by 6 if the number is divisible by both 2 and 3.
   b. A number is divisible by 4 if the sum of all digits is divisible by 8.
   c. A number is divisible by 3 if the last digit is divisible by 3.
   d. A number is divisible by 7 if the sum of the last two digits is divisible by 7.

35. Which of the following is an irrational number?
   a. $4.\overline{2}$
   b. $\sqrt{2}$
   c. $\dfrac{4}{5}$
   d. $\dfrac{21}{5}$

36. Robert buys a car for $24,210. The price of the car has been marked down by 10%. What was the original price of the car?
   a. $25,900
   b. $26,300
   c. $26,900
   d. $27,300

37. Carlos spends $\dfrac{1}{8}$ of his monthly salary on utility bills. If his utility bills total $320, what is his monthly salary?
   a. $2,440
   b. $2,520
   c. $2,560
   d. $2,600

38. Jason decides to donate 1% of his annual salary to a local charity. If his annual salary is $45,000, how much will he donate?
   a. $4.50
   b. $45
   c. $450
   d. $4,500

39. Kendra uses the pie chart below to represent the allocation of her annual income. Her annual income is $40,000.

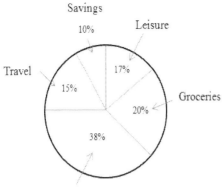

Which of the following statements is true?

    a. The amount of money she spends on travel and savings is more than $11,000.

    b. The amount of money she spends on rent and utilities is approximately $15,000.

    c. The amount of money she spends on groceries and savings is more than $13,000.

    d. The amount of money she spends on leisure is less than $5,000.

40. Which of the following correctly represents the expanded form of 0.867?

    a. $8 \cdot \dfrac{1}{10^0} + 6 \cdot \dfrac{1}{10^1} + 7 \cdot \dfrac{1}{10^2}$

    b. $8 \cdot \dfrac{1}{10^2} + 6 \cdot \dfrac{1}{10^3} + 7 \cdot \dfrac{1}{10^4}$

    c. $8 \cdot \dfrac{1}{10^3} + 6 \cdot \dfrac{1}{10^2} + 7 \cdot \dfrac{1}{10^1}$

    d. $8 \cdot \dfrac{1}{10^1} + 6 \cdot \dfrac{1}{10^2} + 7 \cdot \dfrac{1}{10^3}$

41. A dress is marked down 45%. The cost, after taxes, is $39.95. If the tax rate is 8.75%, what was the original price of the dress?

    a. $45.74

    b. $58.61

    c. $66.79

    d. $72.31

42. Amy saves $450 every 3 months. How much does she save after 3 years?

    a. $4,800

    b. $5,200

    c. $5,400

    d. $5,800

Social Studies

1. Emily West, a multiracial woman, who was captured by Santa Anna prior to the battle of San Jacinto and thought to have contributed to the Texans victory, is associated with which of the following symbols of Texas:
   a. The Lone Star
   b. The Yellow Rose
   c. The Blue Lacy
   d. The Bluebonnet

2. Which of the following is *not* true regarding the Virginia Companies?
   a. One of these companies, the Virginia Company of Plymouth, made its base in North America.
   b. One of these companies, the Virginia Company of London, made its base in Massachusetts.
   c. One company had a charter to colonize America between the Hudson and Cape Fear rivers.
   d. One company had a charter to colonize America from the Potomac River to north Maine.

3. Which of the following statements is *not* true regarding the colony of Jamestown?
   a. The colony of Jamestown was established by the Virginia Company of London in 1607.
   b. The colony of Jamestown became the first permanent English colony in North America.
   c. The majority of settlers in early Jamestown died of starvation, disease, or Indian attacks.
   d. John Smith's governance helped Jamestown more than John Rolfe's tobacco discovery.

4. Which of the following conquistadores unwittingly gave smallpox to the Indians and destroyed the Aztec empire in Mexico?
   a. Balboa
   b. Ponce de Leon
   c. Cortes
   d. De Vaca

5. Which of these factors was *not* a direct contributor to the beginning of the American Revolution?
   a. The attitudes of American colonists toward Great Britain following the French and Indian War
   b. The attitudes of leaders in Great Britain toward the American colonies and imperialism
   c. James Otis's court argument against Great Britain's Writs of Assistance as breaking natural law
   d. Lord Grenville's Proclamation of 1763, Sugar Act, Currency Act, and especially Stamp Act

6. Which of the following statements is *not* true regarding the Tea Act of 1773?
   a. The British East India Company was suffering financially because Americans were buying tea smuggled from Holland.
   b. Parliament granted concessions to the British East India Company to ship tea straight to America, bypassing England.
   c. Colonists found that even with added taxes, tea directly shipped by the British East India Company cost less, and they bought it.
   d. American colonists refused to buy less expensive tea from the British East India Company on the principle of taxation.

7. Which of the following were dispatch riders notifying Americans of British troop movements reported by American surveillance in 1775?
    a. Paul Revere
    b. William Dawes
    c. John Parker
    d. (a) and (b)

8. Which of the following is not a distinction achieved by a Texas-born woman during the 20th century:
    a. Oveta Culp Hobby was appointed the first secretary of the U.S. Department of Health, Education, and Welfare by Dwight Eisenhower.
    b. Barbara Jordan was the first African American woman elected to the U.S. House of Representatives.
    c. Frances Perkins was selected as the first female cabinet member (Secretary of Labor) by Franklin Roosevelt.
    d. Kay Bailey Hutchinson was elected as the first female U.S. Senator from Texas.

9. Which of the following is *not* a true statement regarding the Louisiana Purchase?
    a. Jefferson sent a delegation to Paris to endeavor to purchase only the city of New Orleans from Napoleon.
    b. Napoleon, anticipating U.S. intrusions into Louisiana, offered to sell the U.S. the entire Louisiana territory.
    c. The American delegation accepted Napoleon's offer, though they were only authorized to buy New Orleans.
    d. The Louisiana Purchase, once it was completed, increased the territory of the U.S. by 50% overnight.

10. Which of the following is *not* correct about the growth of America in the first half of the 19th century?
    a. By 1840, two thirds of all Americans resided west of the Allegheny Mountains.
    b. The population of America doubled every 25 years during this time period.
    c. The trend of westward expansion increased as more people migrated west.
    d. Immigration to America from other countries was not substantial prior to 1820.

11. Which of the following did *not* occur during the War of 1812?
    a. Early in the war, the U.S. executed a three-pronged invasion of Canada and succeeded on two of three fronts.
    b. Early in the war, Americans won naval battles against the British, but were soon beaten back by the British.
    c. Admiral Oliver Hazard Perry's fleet defeated the British navy on Lake Erie in September, 1813.
    d. William Henry Harrison invaded Canada and defeated the British and the Indians in the Battle of the Thames.

12. Which of the following is *not* correct concerning the growth of American labor unions?
    a. The new factory system separated workers from owners, which tended to depersonalize workplaces.
    b. The goal of attaining an 8-hour work day stimulated growth in labor organizing in the early 1800s.
    c. The first organized workers' strike was in Paterson, New Jersey in 1828, and was by child laborers.
    d. Recurring downturns in the economy tended to limit workers' demands for rights until the 1850s.

13. Which of the following is *not* true regarding public schools in the early 19th century?
    a. Virtually no public schools existed in America prior to around 1815.
    b. Schools were mainly financed by private corporate or religious groups.
    c. Thomas Jefferson's plan of a free school in Virginia was realized.
    d. American schools were elitist, catering to the rich and to males in academics.

14. Which of the following laws was instrumental in spurring westward migration to the Great Plains between 1860 and 1880?
    a. The Homestead Act
    b. The Timber Culture Act
    c. The Desert Land Act
    d. All of these laws were instrumental in spurring westward migration to the Great Plains during that period.

15. Which of the following groups associated with the advancement of minorities was ***not*** founded by a Texan during the 20th century?
    a. National Association for the Advancement of Colored People (NAACP)
    b. League of United Latin American Citizens (LULAC)
    c. Congress of Racial Equality (CORE)
    d. American GI Forum (AGIF)

16. Of the following international diplomatic conferences, which one made US-Soviet differences apparent?
    a. The Potsdam conference
    b. The conference at Yalta
    c. Dumbarton Oaks conference
    d. The Tehran conference

17. Which statement about relations between the Middle East and the US and Europe in the 1950s is incorrect?
    a. President Nasser of Egypt refused to align with the US in the Cold War.
    b. President Eisenhower removed US funding from the Aswan Dam in 1956.
    c. President Nasser nationalized the Suez Canal, which was owned by England.
    d. In 1956, Egypt attacked Israel, and England and France joined in the war.

18. Which of the following statements regarding events in the Middle East that took place during the Reagan administration is *not* correct?
    a. Israel invaded Lebanon to get rid of the Palestine Liberation Organization's camps there.
    b. When a terrorist bombing killed 240 US Marines, Reagan escalated military action.
    c. Lebanon was already in the midst of a civil war when Israeli troops invaded the country.
    d. President Reagan deployed US Marines to Lebanon in 1982 on a peacekeeping mission.

19. Of the following, which person or group was *not* instrumental in advancement of civil rights and desegregation during the 1940s and 1950s?
    a. The President
    b. The Supreme Court
    c. The Congress
    d. The NAACP

20. Of the programs enacted by President Lyndon B. Johnson's administration, which was most closely related to John F. Kennedy's legacy?
    a. The Economic Opportunity Act
    b. The Civil Rights Act
    c. The Great Society program
    d. All of these were equally related to JFK's legacy.

21. Which statement regarding US international trade policy in the 1990s is incorrect?
    a. In 1994, the General Agreement on Tariffs and Trade (GATT) was approved by Congress.
    b. The GATT included 57 countries who agreed they would remove or reduce many of their tariffs.
    c. The GATT created the World Trade Organization (WTO) to settle international trade differences.
    d. The NAFTA (North American Free Trade Agreement), ratified in 1994, had originally been set up by George H.W. Bush's administration.

22. Which of the following statements is not true regarding the social impact of the American Civil War on Texas?
    a. The contributions of women were more significant as many stepped up to fill in for men who were away at war.
    b. The number of slaves in the state increased as slave owners from other Confederate states fled to Texas
    c. The Union blockaded the port of Houston during the early part of the war, negatively impacting the trade of cotton
    d. Social tensions arose between groups in favor of and opposed to secession, particularly among German immigrants, a number of whom were massacred near the Nueces River in 1862.

23. During which of these periods were pyramids *not* built in Egypt?
    a. The Old Kingdom
    b. The Middle Kingdom
    c. The New Kingdom
    d. The Third Dynasty

24. The Indus Valley or Harappan civilization existed in what is now:
    a. Iran
    b. India
    c. Pakistan
    d. All of these

25. The Yellow River Valley began to emerge as a cultural center during the:
    a. Shang Dynasty
    b. Neolithic Era
    c. Xia Dynasty
    d. Paleolithic Era

26. Which statement is *not* true regarding ancient Greek democracy?
    a. Democracy began to develop approximately 500 B.C.E.
    b. One of the first, best-known democracies was in Athens
    c. It was a direct democracy, not using any representatives
    d. It was a democracy completely open to all of the public

27. Which of the following is *not* true about the Crusades?
    a. Their purpose was for European rulers to retake the Middle East from Muslims
    b. The Crusades succeeded at European kings' goal of reclaiming the "holy land"
    c. The Crusades accelerated the already incipient decline of the Byzantine Empire
    d. Egypt saw a return as a major Middle Eastern power as a result of the Crusades

28. Which of the following events did *not* contribute to the growth of the Italian Renaissance?
    a. The Black Death killed 1/3 of the population of Europe
    b. The lower classes benefited from the need for laborers
    c. The middle classes developed from a need for services
    d. All these events contributed to the Italian Renaissance

29. Which of the following is not true regarding the Texas State Government?
    a. Texas has a plural executive branch—nine executives including Governor, Lt. Governor, Attorney General, and Comptroller—who are elected independently and answerable directly to the electorate.
    b. Texas has a bicameral legislature including 150 House members and 31 senators.
    c. Texas' judiciary includes courts at the municipal, county, and district levels as well as a court of last resort, the Texas Supreme Court that consists of nine popularly elected judges
    d. Texas is a limited home rule state that allows cities of more than 5000 to adopt a home charter and a more generally a Dillon rule state in which the state government is preeminent over local governments

30. Of the following statements, which is true about the March on Versailles during the French Revolution?
    a. The March on Versailles was an action undertaken by equal numbers of both men and women
    b. The March on Versailles was an action undertaken primarily by women
    c. The March on Versailles happened prior to the storming of the Bastille
    d. The March on Versailles was not effective in accomplishing its purpose

31. Which of the following statements is accurate regarding the end of the First World War?
    a. The Treaty of Versailles brought peace among all countries involved in the war
    b. The Treaty of Versailles contained a clause for establishing the United Nations
    c. President Woodrow Wilson had proposed forming a coalition of world nations
    d. President Wilson succeeded in getting the USA to ratify the League of Nations

32. Which of the following empire(s) no longer existed following the armistice ending World War I?
    a. The Austro-Hungarian Empire
    b. The Ottoman Empire
    c. The German Empire
    d. All of these empires

33. During the decolonization of the Cold War years, which of the following events occurred chronologically latest?
    a. The Eastern Bloc and Satellite states became independent from the Soviet Union
    b. Canada became totally independent from British Parliament via the Canada Act
    c. The Bahamas, in the Caribbean, became independent from the United Kingdom
    d. The Algerian War ended, and Algeria became independent from France

34. Why was U.S. industrialization confined to the Northeast until after the Civil War?
    a. Because the Civil War delayed the development of water-powered manufacturing
    b. Because the Northeast had faster-running rivers than the rivers found in the South
    c. Because Slater's first cotton mill with horse-drawn production lost so much money
    d. Because the technical innovations for milling textiles had not as yet been invented

35. Which of the following statements is *not* an accurate statement about the Puritans in England?
    a. The Puritans unconditionally gave all their support to the English Reformation
    b. The Puritans saw the Church of England as too much like the Catholic Church
    c. The Puritans became a chief political power because of the English Civil War
    d. The Puritans' clergy mainly departed from the Church of England after 1662

36. What was Texas postal worker's Heman Sweatt's role in the national fight for civil rights during the second half of the 20th century?
    a. Sweatt successfully sued to have the poll tax eliminated in Texas
    b. Sweatt successfully sued for admission to the University of Texas' Law School.
    c. Sweatt unsuccessfully sued claiming that the white primary violated constitutional guarantees
    d. Sweatt unsuccessfully sued to overturn the segregation of Mexican American students via Jim Crow practices.

37. Which of the following statements is *not* true about the Gilded Age in America?
    a. The Gilded Age was the era of the "robber barons" in the business world
    b. The Gilded Age got its name from the excesses of the wealthy upper class
    c. The Gilded Age had philanthropy Carnegie called the "Gospel of Wealth"
    d. The Gilded Age is a term whose origins have not been identified clearly

38. Which of the following is *not* true about Democracy and the formation of the United States?
   a. The founding fathers stated in the Constitution that the USA would be a democracy
   b. The Declaration of Independence did not dictate democracy but stated its principles
   c. The United States Constitution stipulated that government be elected by the people
   d. The United States Constitution had terms to protect some, but not all, of the people

39. Which of the following statements does *not* describe the average European diet before the expansion of trade routes?
   a. Europeans ate for survival, not enjoyment.
   b. They had an abundance of preservatives such as salt that could make food last longer.
   c. Grain-based foods such as porridge and bread were staple meals.
   d. Spices were unavailable.

40. Which of the following statements is *not* true of daily life for the average European in the 1500s?
   a. Life was not significantly different from the medieval era.
   b. The majority of people worked in agriculture.
   c. Life expectancy was short.
   d. Most people were literate, due to well-financed public education programs.

41. Which of these is true concerning the French Revolution, America, and Europe?
   a. When France's revolution spread and they went to war with other European countries, George Washington allied with the French.
   b. During the time period around 1792, American merchants were trading with countries on both sides of the war.
   c. American traders conducted business with various countries, profiting the most from the British West Indies.
   d. The Spanish navy retaliated against America for trading with the French by capturing American trading ships.

42. Though the incorporation into the United State was favored by the majority of the Texas population when it became independent of Mexico in 1836, Texas was not annexed until the end of 1845. Which of the following was **not** a reason for the delay?
   a. Both major political parties feared that adding another slave state to the union would upset the volatile balance between pro-slavery and anti-slavery American factions.
   b. American politicians were afraid of triggering a war which Mexico, which did not want to recognize the independence of its former territory.
   c. The British government was suspected of trying to intervene in Texas affairs and arrange the emancipation of its slaves.
   d. The southern and western borders of Texas were not well defined. There was uncertainty as to what exact land area the United States was annexing.

Science

1. A student is working on a science project and is going through each step of the scientific method. After the student conducts his or her first experiment and records the results of the experimental test, what is the next step?
    a. Communicate the results
    b. Draw a conclusion
    c. Repeat the experiment
    d. Create a hypothesis

2. Once a hypothesis has been verified and accepted, it becomes a _____.
    a. fact
    b. law
    c. conclusion
    d. theory

3. Which of the following processes uses electrical charges to separate substances?
    a. Spectrophotometry
    b. Chromatography
    c. Centrifugation
    d. Electrophoresis

4. When using a light microscope, how is the total magnification determined?
    a. By multiplying the ocular lens power times the objective being used.
    b. By looking at the objective you are using only.
    c. By looking at the ocular lens power only.
    d. By multiplying the objective you are using times two.

5. After a science laboratory exercise, some solutions remain unused and are left over. What should be done with these solutions?
    a. Dispose of the solutions according to local disposal procedures.
    b. Empty the solutions into the sink and rinse with warm water and soap.
    c. Ensure the solutions are secured in closed containers and throw away.
    d. Store the solutions in a secured, dry place for later use.

6. The volume of water in a bucket is 2.5 liters. When an object with an irregular shape and a mass of 40 grams is fully submerged in the water, the total volume becomes 4.5 liters. What is the density of the object?
    a. 0.1 g/L
    b. 2 g/L
    c. 20 g/L
    d. 80 g/L

7. Which of the following represents a chemical change?
    a. Sublimation of water
    b. A spoiling apple
    c. Dissolution of salt in water
    d. Pulverized rock

8. The amount of potential energy an object has depends on all of the following except its
    a. mass.
    b. height above ground.
    c. gravitational attraction.
    d. temperature.

9. Elements on the periodic table are arranged into groups and periods and ordered according to
    a. atomic number.
    b. number of protons.
    c. reactivity.
    d. All of the above

10. The specific heat capacity of ice is half as much as that of liquid water. What is the result of this?
    a. It takes half the amount of energy to increase the temperature of a 1 kg sample of ice by 1°C than a 1 kg sample of water.
    b. It takes twice the amount of energy to increase the temperature of a 1 kg sample of ice by 1°C than a 1 kg sample of water.
    c. It takes a quarter the amount of energy to increase the temperature of a 1 kg sample of ice by 1°C than a 1 kg sample of water.
    d. It takes the same amount of energy to increase the temperature of a 1 kg sample of ice and a 1 kg sample of water by 1°C.

11. What happens to the temperature of a substance as it is changing phase from a liquid to a solid?
    a. Its temperature increases due to the absorption of latent heat.
    b. Its temperature decreases due to the heat of vaporization.
    c. Its temperature decreases due to the latent heat of fusion.
    d. Its temperature remains the same due to the latent heat of fusion.

12. A long nail is heated at one end. After a few seconds, the other end of the nail becomes equally hot. What type of heat transfer does this represent?
    a. Radiation
    b. Conduction
    c. Convection
    d. Entropy

13. Which of the following statements about heat transfer is not true?
    a. As the energy of a system changes, its thermal energy must change or work must be done.
    b. Heat transfer from a warmer object to a cooler object can occur spontaneously.
    c. Heat transfer can never occur from a cooler object to a warmer object.
    d. If two objects reach the same temperature, energy is no longer available for work.

14. The measure of energy within a system is called _____.
    a. temperature
    b. heat
    c. entropy
    d. thermodynamics

15. Which of the following is true of an isotope?
    a. It has a different number of protons than its element.
    b. It has a different number of electrons than its element.
    c. It has a different charge as compared to its element.
    d. It has a different number of neutrons than its element.

16. If an atom's outer shell is filled, what must be true?
    a. It reacts with other atoms through chemical reactions.
    b. It exchanges electrons to form bonds with other atoms.
    c. It has 32 electrons in its outer shell.
    d. It is a stable atom.

17. Which type of nuclear process features atomic nuclei splitting apart to form smaller nuclei?
    a. Fission
    b. Fusion
    c. Decay
    d. Ionization

18. Electrons with greater amounts of energy are found _____ the nucleus than electrons with less energy.
    a. closer to
    b. farther from
    c. more often inside
    d. more randomly around

19. The process whereby a radioactive element releases energy slowly over a long period of time to lower its energy and become more stable is best described as _____.
    a. combustion
    b. fission
    c. fusion
    d. decay

20. Which of the following is a type of simple machine?
    a. A bicycle
    b. A pair of scissors
    c. A screw
    d. A shovel

21. In which of the following scenarios is work not applied to the object?
    a. Mario moves a book from the floor to the top shelf.
    b. A book drops off the shelf and falls to the floor.
    c. Mario pushes a box of books across the room.
    d. Mario balances a book on his head.

22. A ball is resting on the front end of a boat. The boat is moving straight forward toward a dock. According to Newton's first law of motion, when the front of the boat hits the dock, how will the ball's motion change with respect to the boat?
   a. The ball will remain at rest.
   b. The ball will move backward.
   c. The ball will move forward.
   d. The ball will move sideways.

23. What two things are required for circular motion to occur?
   a. Acceleration and centripetal force
   b. Acceleration and gravitational force
   c. Constant speed and centripetal force
   d. Constant speed and gravitational force

24. According to Bernoulli's Principle, where will a gas flowing through a pipe exert the least amount of pressure?
   a. Where the pipe is widest
   b. Where the pipe is narrowest
   c. Where its velocity is lowest
   d. Where its kinetic energy is lowest

25. If a glass rod is rubbed with a cloth made of polyester, what will the resulting charge be on each material?
   a. The charge on the glass rod is positive and the charge on the cloth is negative.
   b. The charge on the glass rod is negative and the charge on the cloth is positive.
   c. The charge on the glass rod is neutral and the charge on the cloth is positive.
   d. The charge on the glass rod and the cloth both become neutral.

26. According to Ohm's Law, how are voltage and current related in an electrical circuit?
   a. Voltage and current are inversely proportional to one another.
   b. Voltage and current are directly proportional to one another.
   c. Voltage acts to oppose the current along an electrical circuit.
   d. Voltage acts to decrease the current along an electrical circuit.

27. A material becomes magnetic when the individual electrons of an atom _____, allowing their magnetic fields to add together.
   a. spin in pairs in opposite directions
   b. spin in pairs in the same direction
   c. spin unpaired
   d. stop spinning

28. In a parallel circuit, there are three paths: A, B and C. Path A has a resistance of 10 ohms, path B a resistance of 5 ohms and part C a resistance of 2 ohms. How do the voltage and current change for each path?
   a. Voltage and current are kept the same in each path.
   b. Voltage is greatest in path A and current is greatest in path C.
   c. Voltage is lowest in path C and current is greatest in path C.
   d. Voltage is the same for each path and current is greatest in path C.

29. Which of the following would cause a high angle of reflection of a light wave?
    a. A high angle of incidence of the wave
    b. A low angle of incidence of the wave
    c. A wave that travels through a medium of higher density
    d. A wave with a very short wavelength

30. What term is used to describe two waves that are out of phase as they come together to produce a new wave?
    a. Incomplete interference
    b. Distorted interference
    c. Constructive interference
    d. Destructive interference

31. What would happen to light waves if they hit a convex lens?
    a. They will be refracted and converge.
    b. They will be refracted and diverge.
    c. They will be reflected and converge.
    d. They will be reflected and diverge.

32. Salts are made from a combination of what two types of elements?
    a. A metal and a nonmetal
    b. A nonmetal and an alkaline earth metal
    c. A cation from a base and an anion from an acid
    d. A metal and a halogen

33. What group of the periodic table makes up the alkaline earth metals?
    a. Group 1
    b. Group 2
    c. Group 13
    d. Group 17

34. Which of the following elements is not a noble gas?
    a. Neon
    b. Argon
    c. Astatine
    d. Krypton

35. If an atom has a neutral charge, what must be true of the atom?
    a. The nucleus contains only neutrons and no protons.
    b. The atomic mass is equal to the number of neutrons.
    c. The atomic number is equal to the number of neutrons.
    d. The atomic number is equal to the number of electrons.

36. Most organic molecules have all of the following properties except
    a. high solubility in water.
    b. a tendency to melt.
    c. covalently bonded.
    d. high flammability.

37. What type of compound is formed by the combination of two or more non-metallic elements with one another?
    a. Organic
    b. Ionic
    c. Covalent
    d. Chemical

38. Which of the following does not describe a carboxyl group correctly?
    a. A carbon atom attached to an oxygen atom by a double bond and to a hydroxyl group by a single bond.
    b. A carbonyl group bonded to a hydroxyl group.
    c. A set of four atoms bonded together and abbreviated as CO2H.
    d. A carbon atom attached to a hydrogen atom by a double bond and to an oxygen atom by a double bond.

39. A gas is held in a closed container and held at constant temperature. What is the effect of increasing the volume of the container by 3 times?
    a. The pressure is tripled.
    b. The pressure increases by one third.
    c. The pressure decreases by one third.
    d. The pressure remains constant.

40. Which statement best describes the molecular arrangement of a liquid crystal?
    a. The molecular arrangement is random in some directions and regular in others.
    b. The molecular arrangement is a regularly, repeating pattern in all directions.
    c. The molecular arrangement is random in all directions.
    d. The molecular arrangement is reduced to one layer with a random pattern.

41. Which of the following is never true of a chemical reaction?
    a. Matter is neither gained nor lost.
    b. Heat is absorbed or released.
    c. The rate of the reaction increases with temperature.
    d. There are a different number of atoms for the products and the reactants.

42. Which of the following would increase the reaction rate of a chemical reaction?
    a. Low kinetic energy
    b. Low temperature
    c. High concentration
    d. High activation energy

Answers and Explanations

English Language Arts and Reading

1. A: Homophones. Homophones are a type of homonym that sound alike, but are spelled differently and have different meanings. Other examples are *two, to,* and *too; their, they're,* and *there.*

2. C: Argumentative essay. The goal of a persuasive essay is to convince the reader that the author's position or opinion on a controversial topic is correct. That opinion or position is called the argument. A persuasive essay argues a series of points, supported by facts and evidence.

3. D: Rate, accuracy, and prosody. Fluent readers are able to read smoothly and comfortably at a steady pace (rate). The more quickly a child reads, the greater the chance of leaving out a word or substituting one word for another (for example, *sink* instead of *shrink*). Fluent readers are able to maintain accuracy without sacrificing rate. Fluent readers also stress important words in a text, group words into rhythmic phrases, and read with intonation (prosody).

4. B: The number of unrecognizable words an English Language Learner encounters when reading a passage or listening to a teacher. Language load is one of the barriers English Language Learners face. To lighten this load, a teacher can rephrase, eliminate unnecessary words, divide complex sentences into smaller units, and teach essential vocabulary before the student begins the lesson.

5. A: A vowel. A syllable is a minimal sound unit arranged around a vowel. For example, *academic* has four syllables: *a/ca/dem/ic.* It is possible for a syllable to be a single vowel, as in the above example. It is not possible for a syllable to be a single consonant.

6. C: Tier-two words. Tier-two words are words that are used with high frequency across a variety of disciplines or words with multiple meanings. They are characteristic of mature language users. Knowing these words is crucial to attaining an acceptable level of reading comprehension and communication skills.

7. C: Reading at her Independent reading level. When reading independently, students are at the correct level if they read with at least 97% accuracy.

8. B: To correct an error in reading a student has made, specifically clarifying where and how the error was made so that the student can avoid similar errors in the future. A reading teacher offers corrective feedback to a student in order to explain why a particular error in reading is, in fact, an error. Corrective feedback is specific; it locates where and how the student went astray so that similar errors can be avoided in future reading.

9. B: Prior knowledge is knowledge the student brings from previous life or learning experiences to the act of reading. It is not possible for a student to fully comprehend new knowledge without first integrating it with prior knowledge. Prior knowledge, which rises from experience and previous learning, provides a framework by which new knowledge gained from the act of reading can be integrated. Every act of reading enriches a student's well of prior knowledge and increases that student's future ability to comprehend more fully any new knowledge acquired through reading.

10. A: Common words with irregular spelling. Sight words occur in many types of writing; they are high-frequency words. Sight words are also words with irregular spelling. Some examples of sight words include *talk, some,* and *the.* Fluent readers need to recognize these words visually.

11. D: Consonant digraph. A consonant digraph is group of consonants in which all letters represent a single sound.

12. A: Phonological awareness. Phonemic awareness is the ability to recognize sounds within words. Segmenting words and blending sounds are components of phonemic awareness. Phonological awareness includes an understanding of multiple components of spoken language. Ability to hear individual words within a vocalized stream and ability to identify spoken syllables are types of phonological awareness.

13. A: Strategy instruction. Strategic instruction involves teaching a methodic approach to solving a reading problem. It consists of strategies done in steps which aid the reader in eliminating incorrect responses.

14. D: Familiar, frequently used words that do not need to be taught beyond primary grades. Common or basic words are the first tier of three-tier words. These words are widely used across the spoken and written spectrum. Some examples are *walk, go, wish, the, look, happy,* and *always.* This essential vocabulary is taught early in a reader's instruction, and beyond that it need not be taught.

15. B: Consonant blend. Consonant blend refers to a group of consonants in which each letter represents a separate sound.

16. D: None; sight words cannot be decoded. Readers must learn to recognize these words as wholes on sight. Sight words have irregular spelling. Segmenting them into syllables or using a phonemic approach are ineffective strategies to aid a reader in recognizing a sight word, because these approaches depend on rules a sight word doesn't follow. Word families group words that share common patterns of consonants and vowels. The spelling of those words is therefore regular, because they follow a predictable pattern. Sight words are irregular and do not follow a predictable pattern and must be instantaneously recognized for writing fluency. No decoding is useful.

17. D: It is impossible to include every text desired into the language curriculum—there are simply too many good books, stories, poems, speeches, and media available. Teachers must first think about what skills their students need to acquire, as well as what skills they have already mastered. In designing activities for class, a good teacher will start first with the purpose for instruction (or perceiving oral or visual text such as video or music). For example, purposes of reading can include: reading for information; reading for enjoyment; understanding a message; identifying main or supporting ideas; or developing an appreciation for artistic expression/perception. Once the purpose or intended learning outcome has been identified, the teacher will have a much better idea of which texts, strategies, and activities will support that purpose.

18. A: Oral. Phonological awareness refers to an understanding of the sounds a word makes. While phonological awareness leads to fluent reading skills, activities designed to develop an awareness of word sounds are, by definition, oral.

19. B: Vocabulary. Strategizing in order to understand the meaning of a word, knowing multiple meanings of a single word, and applying background knowledge to glean a word's meaning are all

ways in which an effective reader enhances vocabulary. Other skills include an awareness of word parts and word origins, the ability to apply word meanings in a variety of content areas, and a delight in learning the meanings of unfamiliar words.

20. D: Decoding depends on an understanding of letter–sound relationships. As soon as a child understands enough letters and their correspondent sounds to read a few words, decoding should be introduced. The act of decoding involves first recognizing the sounds individual letters and letter groups in a word make and then blending the sounds to read the word. It's important to introduce the strategy as soon as a child knows enough letters and their corresponding sounds to read simple words.

21. C: Cause–effect words. Signal words give the reader hints about the purpose of a particular passage. Some signal words are concerned with comparing/contrasting, some with cause and effect, some with temporal sequencing, some with physical location, and some with a problem and its solution. The words *since, whether,* and *accordingly* are words used when describing an outcome. Outcomes have causes.

22. A: Outcome. Story action can be analyzed in terms of rising action, story climax, falling action, and resolution. Rising action consists of those events that occur before and lead up to the story's most dramatic moment, or climax. The climax occurs toward the end of the book, but rarely, if ever, right at the end. Following the climax, the consequences of that dramatic moment are termed falling action. The story reaches resolution with the outcome of the falling action.

23. C: Locate the vowels, then locate familiar word parts. Syllables are organized around vowels. In order to determine the syllables, this student should begin by locating the vowels. It's possible to have a syllable that is a single vowel (*a/gain*). It isn't possible to have a syllable that is a single consonant. Once the word has been broken into its component syllables the reader is able to study the syllables to find ones that are familiar and might give her a clue as to the word's meaning, such as certain prefixes or suffixes.

24. B: Ask the students to read their stories to her. Suggest they visit other children in the class and read to each of them. The teacher should encourage these students by "reading" what they have written, even if what she reads is incorrect. She might misread KJM as *Kathy jumped rope with Mandy*. Most children will not be upset by this, but will correct the teacher's misreading by reading what the letters really mean.

25. D: The teacher should encourage all students to "read" picture books from the first day of school. Talking about the pictures from page to page gives young readers the idea that books are arranged sequentially. Pictures also offer narrative coherence and contextual clues. Emergent readers who are encouraged to enjoy books will more readily embrace the act of reading. Holding a book and turning pages gives young readers a familiarity with them.

26. C: Identify and use groups of letters that occur in a word family. Analogizing is based on recognizing the pattern of letters in words that share sound similarities. If the pattern is found at the end of a family of words, it is called a *rhyme*. Some examples of rhyme are *rent, sent, bent,* and *dent*. If the pattern is found at the beginning of the family of words, it is frequently a consonant *blend* such as *street, stripe,* or *strong,* in which all the letters are pronounced, or the pattern is a consonant digraph, in which the letters are taken together to represent a single sound such as in *phone, phonics,* or *phantom*.

27. B: Revising. Revision (literally, re+vision) is the act of "seeing again." When revising, writers examine what they have written in order to improve the meaning of the work. Fine-tuning word choices, moving information to another location, and adding or deleting words are all acts of revision.

28. D: Prefixes, appearing at the beginning of base words to change their meanings. Suffixes appear at the end of words. Prefixes are attached to the beginning of words to change their meanings. *Un+happy, bi+monthly,* and *re+examine* are prefixes that, by definition, change the meanings of the words to which they are attached.

29. D: Dog, sit, leg. CVC words are composed of a consonant, a vowel, and a consonant. To learn to read them, students must be familiar with the letters used and their sounds. A teacher can present a word like *sit* to students who also know the consonants *b/f/h/p* and ask them to create a word family of other CVC words. The students will be able to read *bit, fit, hit,* and *pit* because they are similar to the word *sit* they have just learned.

30. A: Cooperative learning and reading comprehension. Cooperative learning occurs when a group of students at various levels of reading ability have goals in common. Reading comprehension is achieved through reading both orally and silently, developing vocabulary, a reader's ability to predict what will occur in a piece of writing, a reader's ability to summarize the main points in a piece of writing, and a reader's ability to reflect on the text's meaning and connect that meaning to another text or personal experience.

31. B: Understanding the meaning of words that are not familiar. Context clues offer insight into the probable meaning of unfamiliar words.

32. A: Closed, open, silent *e*, vowel team, vowel-*r*, and consonant-*le*. A closed syllable ends with a consonant, such as *cat*. Open syllables end with a vowel, such as *he*. Vowel team syllables contain two vowels working together, such as *main*. Vowel-*r* syllables such as *er* and *or* frequently occur as suffixes. Consonant-*le* syllables also typically occur as suffixes, such as *battle* or *terrible*.

33. A: Strategies to increase comprehension and to build vocabulary. The student should receive instruction focused on just those areas in which he is exhibiting difficulty. Improved vocabulary will give him greater skill at comprehending the meaning of a particular text. Strategies focused on enhancing comprehension together with a stronger vocabulary will provide the greatest help.

34. B: Through a combination of standardized testing, informal teacher observations, attention to grades, objective-linked assessments, and systematized charting of data over time. Reading comprehension and vocabulary cannot be sufficiently assessed with occasional, brief studies. Continuous observation, high-stakes and standardized testing, attention to grades, and closely tracking the outcomes of objective-linked assessments are interrelated tools that, when systematically organized, offer a thorough understanding of students' strengths and weaknesses.

35. A: An Oral Reading Fluency assessment. ORF stands for oral reading fluency. This assessment measures the words correct per minute (WCPM) by subtracting the number of errors made from the total number of words orally read in a one- to two-minute period of time. It is used to find a student's Instructional reading level, to identify readers who are having difficulties, and to track developing fluency and word recognition over time.

36. D: Round-robin reading is a common practice in language arts classes and has been for many years. In this process, students take turns reading aloud for their peers. Other students are asked to follow along silently in their texts while a peer is reading. This strategy does provide a way for students to read texts in class and include as many students as possible, which is often the intended outcome. However, this process often creates a boring atmosphere, since only one student at a time is actively engaged. While that student is reading, other students may become distracted by their own thoughts, other school work, or off-task interaction with each another; all of these issues subvert the intended outcome of the process. There is rarely enough time for each student to practice reading aloud to build students' reading fluency or comprehension in significant ways.

37. D: Especially important to English Language Learners and students with reading disabilities. Word recognition is required for reading fluency and is important to all readers, but it is especially so to English Language Learners and students with reading disabilities. It can be effectively taught through precisely calibrated word study instruction designed to provide readers with reading and writing strategies for successful word analysis.

38. A: Proficiency with oral language enhances students' phonemic awareness and increases vocabulary. Understanding that words are scripted with specific letters representing specific sounds is essential to decoding a text. Students cannot effectively learn to read without the ability to decode. An enhanced vocabulary supports the act of reading; the larger an emergent reader's vocabulary, the more quickly he will learn to read. He will be able to decode more words, which he can organize into word families, which he can use to decode unfamiliar words.

39. B: Persuasive. A persuasive essay takes a strong position about a controversial topic and offers factual evidence to support this position. The goal of a persuasive paper is to convince the audience that the claim is true based on the evidence provided.

40. A: However, the myth of "safe cigarettes," questions about nicotine addiction, and denials about the dangers of secondhand smoke have proven to be propaganda and lies. A thesis statement offers a hypothesis or opinion that the remainder of the paper then sets out to prove. Oftentimes, the thesis statement also offers a clear road map of the paper, foreshadowing the focuses of the paragraphs that follow and the order in which they will appear.

41. D: The myth of "safe cigarettes," questions about nicotine addiction, and the dangers of secondhand smoke. These three foci are presented in the thesis statement in this order and will be fleshed out in the following three paragraphs as the body of the essay.

42. C: Are homophones. Homophones are words that are pronounced the same, but differ in meaning. For example, a bride wears a 2 caret ring, but a horse eats a carrot.

43. A: Collaborative learning. A group of students working together on a project are applying numerous learning strategies at once. Collaborative learning is a hands-on approach that actively involves students in the learning process. Students involved in collaborative learning typically retain the lesson better.

44. C: Biography. A biography relates information about part of the life of an individual. An autobiography is a biography about the writer's own life. A memoir is also autobiographical, but focuses on a theme. Historical fiction uses a setting or event based in historical fact as the background for characters and/or action that is invented.

45. C: Students will do online research about the cultural, economic, or political events that were occurring during the specific time about which they've written. By researching the historic setting that cradled the events their interviewee discussed, students are simultaneously broadening their understanding of the context and working in a different content area.

46. B: Brainstorming and a compare/contrast strategy. Brainstorming is a prewriting activity in which an individual or group responds to a specific question by considering any and all responses that arise without editing, prioritizing, or selecting. Once the brainstorming session is complete, students look at the results and eliminate any responses that are not useful, then group and prioritize the remaining responses. In this example, the students are having a collaborative learning experience in that they are brainstorming together; however, collaborative learning is not a strategy per se, but is the outcome of a strategy. The students are also employing a compare/contrast strategy in that they are looking both at how the two writing styles share common elements and how they are distinct.

47. C: Writing styles. Both Anderson and the Grimms wrote in the same genre, that of fairy tales. Genre refers to types of writing. Mystery, romance, adventure, historical fiction, and fairy tales are some examples of genres. A genre can include many different authors and writing styles. These students are being asked to compare two distinct writing styles within a single genre in order to locate similarities and differences.

48. B: Comprehension. This exercise requires students to examine the authors' use of setting, plot, pacing, word choice, syntactical structures, narration, mood, metaphors, point of view, voice, and character development to find ways in which they are similar as well as different. In so doing, the students are discovering that language shapes meaning in ways both subtle and profound.

49. B: Cliché. While "Pretty as a picture" is a simile (comparison of two unlike things using *like* or *as*), its overuse has turned it into a cliché. A cliché is a trite platitude.

50. B: Vocabulary. The tightly controlled syllabic requirements will cause students to search for words outside their normal vocabularies that will fit the rigid framework and still express the writer's intended meanings. Often, students will rediscover a word whose meaning they know, but they don't often use.

51. C: *Drip, chirp, splash, giggle.* Onomatopoeia refers to words that sound like what they represent.

52. D: It offers a systematic approach to untangling the wide variety of vowel sounds when an unfamiliar word is encountered. Code knowledge, also called orthographic tendencies, is a helpful approach to decoding a word when multiple pronunciation possibilities exist. Example in the words *toe, go, though,* and *low*, the long O sound is written in a variety of ways. A code knowledge approach teaches a reader to first try a short vowel sound. If that doesn't help, the reader should consider the different ways the vowel or vowel groups can be pronounced, based on what he knows about other words.

53. D: Assess and target areas needing improvement as well as areas of greatest strength for each student to ensure that all members of a class are receiving instruction tailored to their specific needs.

54. C: Giving a three-minute Test of Silent Contextual Reading Fluency four times a year. The student is presented with text in which spaces between words and all punctuation have been

removed. The student must divide one word from another with slash marks, as in the following example: *The/little/sailboat/bobbed/so/far/in/the/distance/it/looked/like/a/toy*. The more words a student accurately separates, then the higher her silent reading fluency score. Silent reading fluency can be monitored over time by giving the Test of Silent Contextual Reading Fluency (TSCRF) four times a year. A similar assessment tool is the Test of Silent Word Reading Fluency (TOSWRF), in which words of increasing complexity are given as a single, undifferentiated, and unpunctuated strand. As with the TSCRF, three minutes are given for the student to separate each word from the next. *Itwillcannotschoolbecomeagendaconsistentphilosophysuperfluous* is an example of such a strand.

55. D: Haiku. Based on a Japanese form of poetry, haiku have become popular with students and teachers alike. Reading and writing haiku helps younger students become aware of syllables and helps older students learn about subtleties of vocabulary.

56. A: Most adults can understand the relationship between oral and written language: components of oral language have representational symbols that can be written and decoded. However, most normally-developing children acquire spoken language first and begin to develop reading and writing skills as they approach school-age. Many children are first exposed to the concept of written language when an adult introduces books or other written texts. However, a child's ability to read and write develops over time and is dependent on the development of physiological processes such as hearing, sight, and fine motor skills for writing. Written language development also typically requires direct instruction. Most children must be taught to read and write and rarely learn these skills simply by observing others.

57. B: Jamie's teacher is teaching the class about many aspects of Mexican culture. It can be assumed that Jamie has prior knowledge of this topic, which comes in part from his family's past travels. While Jamie is engaged in the lesson, the verbal instruction and photographs "activate" or inspire recall of his prior knowledge of Spanish vocabulary. Jamie would not likely have been able to access this information without the visual and verbal cues, although it was still stored in his long-term memory.

58. A: Students are completely capable of understanding and appreciating oral traditions and written texts from other world cultures, as well as those originating from cultures in the students' own community. In fact, introducing a variety of material can increase some students' appreciation of language and literature, as it enables them to learn about the world around them. Language skills emerge at a point in most children's development during which students are fascinated with learning new concepts. Introducing a variety of texts also benefits students in a classroom who belong to other cultures; these students are able to learn concepts from texts that represent their family, culture, or country of origin.

59. B: There are many different adults who can assist children in acquiring various types of language. If a child inconsistently mispronounces certain sounds in reading, he or she may simply need a reminder or instruction from a teacher. Often, children will not acquire knowledge of certain letters or sounds until a certain age. However, the child in this scenario mispronounces words consistently both in reading and in conversation. This combination suggests that the child is not physically able to make certain speech sounds. A speech-language pathologist can assist in determining whether or not the child's mispronunciations indicate the need for therapy. This type of therapist can also work directly with the child to help him or her learn how to make certain sounds.

60. B: Children develop language skills, both oral and written, based on a variety of physical, psychological, emotional and environmental factors. In order to speak, a child must have a developed physiology of the mouth, ears, nose, and other relevant physical features. Children will also learn to speak and read when they interact and receive instruction from fluent adults or older children. There are also times when a developmental or psychological delay can impair language acquisition. However, the IQ and education level of a child's parents is not necessarily relevant to the child's ability to acquire language (although parental intelligence or education may affect the type of exposure a child will encounter outside of school).

61. C: Reading is a process that involves several physical and neurological processes. In order to read, an individual must employ the use of his or her body to access and physically see the written words. The brain must then use schemata to decode or recognize the words and determine their meaning. Often, a reader uses prior knowledge and deductive reasoning to understand the meaning of non-literal text. The skills necessary to read evolve simultaneously and cannot necessarily be taught in exactly the same way for each person. A reader engages in both understanding *and* creating meaning from a text.

62. D: Reading can achieve a variety of purposes. Initially, students learn to read as a form of language acquisition. This process also enables them to learn about various concepts through written texts, both inside and outside of school. Individuals will write and read to share thoughts, stories, and ideas with others. As language develops, many individuals will view reading as a common form of entertainment or enjoyment, regardless of the text's perceived instructional value or content. Each answer choice describes a widely-accepted purpose of the reading process.

63. B: Reading responses can take various forms. The most common form of reading response is likely to be targeted student writing. Students may use journals, worksheets, or other formats to construct written responses to something they have read. The purpose of this type of assignment can range from fostering an appreciation of written text to helping a student prepare for an activity in class. Students may also engage in creating an oral reading response in the form of a presentation or debate. Ultimately, reading response increases a student's capacity to understand what he or she has read and to analyze personal responses to the text.

64. C: Students can easily become bored or disinterested in reading if they are not exposed to a variety of reading texts. Also, reading can be overwhelming or frustrating for students who are still learning to read fluently or to comprehend what they read. By incorporating media, oral stories, and various types of print, students of all ability levels can build both fluency and comprehension skills. This approach also enables the teacher and students to discuss the relationship between all aspects of literacy, including speaking, listening, thinking, viewing, and reading.

65. B: Reading fluency combines accuracy, speed, and inflection while reading aloud. As children are learning to read, they work on all of these skills simultaneously with writing, thinking, viewing, listening, and comprehension. By using daily games or specific lessons, a teacher can directly affect students' ability to read the individual sounds in words (phonemes). As students identify more sounds correctly, they will read more accurately. Practicing reading aloud can increase fluency, but only if the child's reading partner is able to correct and encourage him or her to read more accurately. By reading aloud to the students, a teacher models correct speed and inflection, but this will affect the students' skills less directly than lessons and games in phonetics.

66. B: There are three generally-accepted reading levels: independent, instructional, and frustration. Independent-level texts are those that a student can decode with 95% or better

accuracy and more than 75% comprehension. Instructional-level texts are read at a range between 93-95% accuracy and better than 60% comprehension. Piper's book falls below these percentages, placing it at frustration level. Often students will choose books that are too easy for them to read because they enjoy being successful; other times, sometimes students will choose texts that are at frustration level because they want to read the book. However, when reading aloud, it may be best to guide the student to choose an independent-level or instructional-level text.

67. C: There is currently a wide variety of technology resources available that can support class instruction. However, teachers must choose carefully in order to ensure that the technology is useful and relevant to his or her intended learning outcomes for the class. The language lab described allows students to experience text through listening *and* reading, thereby utilizing different processes in the brain. The interactive modules also support decoding and comprehension skills that go along with the texts. This use of technology reinforces important skills in a way that will be unique and interesting for the students.

68. C: She is reading at an Instructional level. In one minute, a student who misreads one or less than one word per twenty words, or with 95%–100% accuracy, is at an Independent reading level. A student who misreads one or less than one word per ten words, or with 90%–95% accuracy, is at an Instructional level. A student misreading more than one word out of ten, or with less than 90% accuracy, is at a Frustration level.

69. B: The intention of Round-robin reading is to provide practice reading aloud with appropriate fluency. This practice is also used to cover a large quantity of text with the entire class during the class period. By pairing the students, each child will get more practice reading aloud. He or she will also be more likely to stay engaged when working with only one partner, as there will be less time and fewer opportunities to become distracted. The teacher can then circulate amongst the groups to encourage focus and concentration, as well as provide guidance on fluency and comprehension of the text. As long as the students are paired carefully, this strategy is most likely preferable to the Round-robin method.

70. C: Literacy skills are various and include a number of different sub-skills: reading fluency, comprehension, application of knowledge, listening, speaking, grammar, spelling, writing, and more. It is important for teachers to track student development for lesson design and to communicate with the student, future teachers, and parents. Therefore, it is best to keep samples of a variety of assessments, including descriptions of reading fluency, writing samples, projects, and formal assessments of grammar, spelling, and other skills. All of these skills develop simultaneously, but at different rates. Therefore, it is impossible to judge a student's literacy based only on one measure of assessment.

71. D: Teachers will observe a variety of developmental arcs when teaching reading, since all students learn differently. It is very important to understand which instances are normal in the course of learning and which signal a learning difficulty. Barrett is still exhibiting confusion over certain letter-sounds, typically when the letters look similar. At his age, this difficulty could suggest that Barrett has an issue with reading that could be addressed by a reading specialist. The other three choices describe normal behaviors that are commonly exhibited by children when they are learning to read. Choice C, Noelle, may describe an instance in which a student is having a learning problem. However, the teacher will need more information about Noelle's reading skills besides her reluctance to read before making a determination about how to proceed.

72. A: The words in this question prompt are most often used to refer to *sounds* made while reading. Initial/onset, medial, and final sounds are decoded in the beginning, middle, and end of words. When a teacher needs to assess an emergent or struggling reader's ability to differentiate between sounds in words, he or she may use a phonological awareness assessment. This tool will provide the teacher with information about the student's current ability to decode or encode words.

73. B: Scaffolding refers to any kind of special instruction designed to help students learn a new or challenging concept. There are countless forms of scaffolding techniques. The three techniques mentioned in the question prompt are all used to facilitate student understanding of a given text or a concept taught within the text. Scaffolding should not be confused with modeling strategies, which refer to the process of demonstrating how something should be done before a student tries it on his or her own.

74. B: Previewing and reviewing are skills that assist in learning detailed or large amounts of information. Using these concepts, students learn skills such as skimming and outlining to get an idea of what the text is about before actually reading it. After reading, the students learn to review the information they learned and compare it to their initial previews. This method is particularly helpful when individuals are reading in order to learn new information, as they would be when reading their science texts.

Mathematics

1. C: Because drawing a dodecagon and counting its diagonals is an arduous task, it is useful to employ a different problem-solving strategy. One such strategy is to draw polygons with fewer sides and look for a pattern in the number of the polygons' diagonals.

	3	0
	4	2
	5	5
	6	9
Heptagon	7	14
Octagon	8	20

A quadrilateral has two more diagonals than a triangle, a pentagon has three more diagonals than a quadrilateral, and a hexagon has four more diagonals than a pentagon. Continue this pattern to find that a dodecagon has 54 diagonals.

2. B: The problem does not give any information about the size of the bracelet or the spacing between any of the charms. Nevertheless, creating a simple illustration which shows the order of

the charms will help when approaching this problem. For example, the circle below represents the bracelet, and the dotted line between A and B represents the clasp. On the right, the line shows the stretched out bracelet and possible positions of charms C, D, and E based on the parameters.

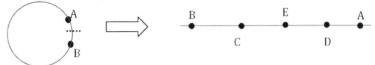

From the drawing above, it appears that statement I is true, but it is not necessarily so. The alternative drawing below also shows the charms ordered correctly, but the distance between B and E is now less than that between D and A.

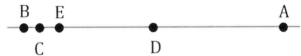

Statement II must be true: charm E must lie between B and D. Statement III must also be true: the distance between charms E and D must be less than that between C and A, which includes charms E and D in the space between them.

3. B: The population is approximately 36,000, so one quarter of the population consists of about 9,000 individuals under age 35. A third of 9,000 is 3,000, the approximate number of students in grades K-12. Since there are thirteen grades, there are about 230 students in each grade. So, the number of fourth graders is between 200 and 300.

4. A: The final sales price of the rug is $1.08(0.7 \cdot \$296) = \$223.78$ at Store A, $1.08(\$220 - \$10) = \$226.80$ at Store B, and $\$198 + \$35 = \$233$ at Store C.

5. C: The expression representing the monthly charge for Company A is $\$25 + \$0.05m$, where m is the time in minutes spent talking on the phone. Set this expression equal to the monthly charge for Company B, which is $50. Solve for m to find the number of minutes for which the two companies charge the same amount:

$$\$25 + \$0.05m = \$50$$
$$\$0.05m = \$25$$
$$m = 500$$

Notice that the answer choices are given in hours, not in minutes. Since there are 60 minutes in an hour, $m = \frac{500}{60}$ hours = $8\frac{1}{3}$ hours. One-third of an hour is twenty minutes, so m = 8 hours, 20 minutes.

6. D: When the dress is marked down by 20%, the cost of the dress is 80% of its original price; thus, the reduced price of the dress can be written as $\frac{80}{100}x$, or $\frac{4}{5}x$, where x is the original price. When discounted an extra 25%, the dress costs 75% of the reduced price, or $\frac{75}{100}\left(\frac{4}{5}x\right)$, or $\frac{3}{4}\left(\frac{4}{5}x\right)$, which simplifies to $\frac{3}{5}x$. So the final price of the dress is three-fifths of the original price.

7. C: Since the ratio of wages and benefits to other costs is 2:3, the amount of money spent on wages and benefits is $\frac{2}{5}$ of the business's total expenditure. $\frac{2}{5} \cdot \$130,000 = \$52,000$.

8. B: Since rate in mph $= \frac{\text{distance in miles}}{\text{time in hours}}$, Zeke's driving speed on the way to Atlanta and home from Atlanta in mph can be expressed as d/3 and d/2, respectively, when d=distance between Zeke's house and his destination . Since Zeke drove 20 mph faster on his way home, $\frac{d}{2} - \frac{d}{3} = 20$.

$$6\left(\frac{d}{2} - \frac{d}{3} = 20\right)$$
$$3d - 2d = 120$$
$$d = 120$$

Since the distance between Zeke's house and the store in Atlanta is 120 miles, Zeke drove a total distance of 240 miles in five hours. Therefore, his average speed was $\frac{240 \text{ miles}}{5 \text{ hours}} = 48$ mph.

9. C: Aaron ran four miles from home and then back again, so he ran a total of eight miles. Therefore, statement III is false. Statements I and II, however, are both true. Since Aaron ran eight miles in eighty minutes, he ran an average of one mile every ten minutes, or six miles per hour; he ran two miles from point A to B in 20 minutes and four miles from D to E in 40 minutes, so his running speed between both sets of points was the same.

10. D: Since a and b are even integers, each can be expressed as the product of 2 and an integer. So, if we write $a = 2x$ and $b = 2y$, $3(2x)^2 + 9(2y)^3 = c$.
$$3(4x^2) + 9(8y^3) = c$$
$$12x^2 + 72y^3 = c$$
$$12(x^2 + 6y^3) = c$$
Since c is the product of 12 and some other integer, 12 must be a factor of c. Incidentally, the numbers 2, 3, and 6 must also be factors of c since each is also a factor of 12.

11. A: $[g \circ f]x = g(f(x)) = g(2x + 4) = (2x + 4)^2 - 3(2x + 4) + 2 = 4x^2 + 16x + 16 - 6x - 12 + 2 = 4x^2 + 10x + 6$.

12. C: One way to approach the problem is to use the table of values to first write equations for $f(x)$ and $g(x)$: $f(x) = 2x^2$ and $g(x) = 2x + 5$. Then, use those equations to find $f(g(-4))$.
$$g(-4) = 2(-4) + 5 = -3$$
$$f(-3) = 2(-3)^2 = 18$$
So, $f(g(-4)) = 18$.

13. D: By definition, when $f(x)$ and $g(x)$ are inverse functions, $f(g(x)) = g(f(x)) = x$. So, $f(g(4)) = 4$.

14. B: $5n + 3s \geq 300$ when $n =$ number of non-student tickets which must be sold and $s =$ number of student tickets which must be sold. The intercepts of this linear inequality are $n = 60$ and $s = 100$. The solid line through the two intercepts represents the minimum number of each type of ticket which must be sold in order to offset production costs. All points above the line represent sales which result in a profit for the school.

15. D: The vertex form of a quadratic equation is $y = a(x - h)^2 + k$, where $x = h$ is the parabola's axis of symmetry and (h, k) is the parabola's vertex. The vertex of the graph is (-1,3), so the equation can be written as $y = a(x + 1)^2 + 3$. The parabola passes through point (1,1), so $1 = a(1 + 1)^2 + 3$.

Solve for a:

$$1 = a(1 + 1)^2 + 3$$
$$1 = a(2)^2 + 3$$
$$1 = 4a + 3$$
$$-2 = 4a$$
$$-\frac{1}{2} = a$$

So, the vertex form of the parabola is $y = -\frac{1}{2}(x + 1)^2 + 3$. Write the equation in the form $y = ax^2 + bx + c$.

$$y = -\frac{1}{2}(x + 1)^2 + 3$$
$$y = -\frac{1}{2}(x^2 + 2x + 1) + 3$$
$$y = -\frac{1}{2}x^2 - x - \frac{1}{2} + 3$$
$$y = -\frac{1}{2}x^2 - x + \frac{5}{2}$$

16. C: A system of linear equations can be solved by using matrices or by using the graphing, substitution, or elimination (also called linear combination) method. The elimination method is shown here:

$$3x + 4y = 2$$
$$2x + 6y = -2$$

In order to eliminate x by linear combination, multiply the top equation by 2 and the bottom equation by –3 so that the coefficients of the x-terms will be additive inverses.

$$2(3x + 4y = 2)$$
$$-3(2x + 6y = -2)$$

Then, add the two equations and solve for y.

$$6x + 8y = 4$$
$$\underline{-6x - 18y = 6}$$
$$-10y = 10$$
$$y = -1$$

Substitute -1 for y in either of the given equations and solve for x.

$$3x + 4(-1) = 2$$
$$3x - 4 = 2$$
$$3x = 6$$
$$x = 2$$

The solution to the system of equations is $(2, -1)$.

17. C: The graph below shows that the lines are parallel and that the shaded regions do not overlap. There is no solution to the set of inequalities given in Choice C.

$6x + 2y \leq 12$
$2y \leq -6x + 12$
$y \leq -3x + 6$

$3x \geq 8 - y$
$y \geq -3x + 8$

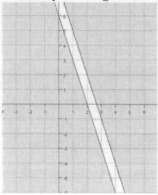

As in Choice C, the two lines given in Choice A are parallel; however, the shading overlaps between the lines, so that region represents the solution to the system of inequalities.

The shaded regions for the two lines in Choice B do not overlap except at the boundary, but since the boundary is same, the solution to the system of inequalities is the line $y = -2x + 6$.

Choice D contains a set of inequalities which have intersecting shaded regions; the intersection represents the solution to the system of inequalities.

18. A: First, set the equation equal to zero.
$$3x^3y^2 - 45x^2y = 15x^3y - 9x^2y^2$$
$$3x^3y^2 - 15x^3y + 9x^2y^2 - 45x^2y = 0$$

Then, factor the equation.
$$3x^2y(xy - 5x + 3y - 15) = 0$$
$$3x^2y[x(y - 5) + 3(y - 5)] = 0$$
$$3x^2y[(y - 5)(x + 3)] = 0$$

Use the zero product property to find the solutions.
$$\begin{array}{ccc} 3x^2y = 0 & y - 5 = 0 & x + 3 = 0 \\ x = 0 & y = 5 & x = -3 \\ y = 0 & & \end{array}$$
So, the solutions are $x = \{0, -3\}$ and $y = \{0,5\}$.

19. C: If 1" represents 60 feet, 10" represents 600 ft, which is the same as 200 yards.

20. C: If l and w represent the length and width of the enclosed area, its perimeter is equal to $2l + 2w$; since the fence is positioned x feet from the lot's edges on each side, the perimeter of the lot is $2(l + 2x) + 2(w + 2x)$. Since the amount of money saved by fencing the smaller are is $432, and since the fencing material costs $12 per linear foot, 36 fewer feet of material are used to fence around the playground than would have been used to fence around the lot. This can be expressed as the equation $2(l + 2x) + 2(w + 2x) – (2l + 2w) = 36$.

$$2(l + 2x) + 2(w + 2x) - (2l + 2w) = 36$$
$$2l + 4x + 2w + 4x - 2l - 2w = 36$$
$$8x = 36$$
$$x = 4.5 \text{ ft}$$

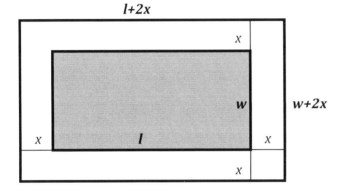

The difference in the area of the lot and the enclosed space is 141 yd^2, which is the same as 1269 ft^2. So, $(l + 2x)(w + 2x) - lw = 1269$. Substituting 4.5 for x,

$$(l + 9)(w + 9) - lw = 1269$$
$$lw + 9l + 9w + 81 - lw = 1269$$
$$9l + 9w = 1188$$
$$9(l + w) = 1188$$
$$l + w = 132 \text{ ft}$$

Therefore, the perimeter of the enclosed space, $2(l + w)$, is $2(132) = 264$ ft. The cost of 264 ft of fencing is $264 \cdot \$12 = \$3,168$.

21. B: A cube has six square faces. The arrangement of these faces in a two-dimensional figure is a net of a cube if the figure can be folded to form a cube. Figures A, C, and D represent three of the eleven possible nets of a cube. If choice B is folded, however, the bottom square in the second column will overlap the fourth square in the top row, so the figure does not represent a net of a cube.

22. D: The point $(5, -5)$ lies on the line which has a slope of -2 and which passes through $(3, -1)$. If $(5, -5)$ is one of the endpoints of the line, the other would be $(1,3)$.

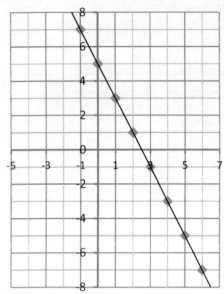

23. B: The graph of $f(x)$ is a parabola with a focus of (a, b) and a directrix of $y = -b$. The axis of symmetry of a parabola passes through the focus and vertex and is perpendicular to the directrix. Since the directrix is a horizontal line, the axis of symmetry is $x = a$; therefore, the x-coordinate of the parabola's vertex must be a. The distance between a point on the parabola and the directrix is equal to the distance between that point and the focus, so the y-coordinate of the vertex must be $y = \frac{-b+b}{2} = 0$. So, the vertex of the parabola given by $f(x)$ is $(a, 0)$.

If $g(x)$ were a translation of $f(x)$, as is the case for choices A, C, and D, the vertices of $f(x)$ and $g(x)$ would differ. Since the vertex of the graph of $g(x)$ is $(a, 0)$, none of those choices represent the correct response. However, if $g(x) = -f(x)$, the vertices of the graphs of both functions would be the same; therefore, this represents a possible relation between the two functions.

24. B: The manufacturer wishes to minimize the surface area A of the can while keeping its volume V fixed at 0.5 L = 500 mL = 500 cm^3. The formula for the surface area of a cylinder is $A = 2\pi rh + 2\pi r^2$, and the formula for volume is $V = \pi r^2 h$. To combine the two formulas into one, solve the volume formula for r or h and substitute the resulting expression into the surface area formula for r or h. The volume of the cylinder is 500 cm^3, so $500 = \pi r^2 h \rightarrow h = \frac{500}{\pi r^2}$. Therefore, $A = 2\pi rh + 2\pi r^2 \rightarrow 2\pi r\left(\frac{500}{\pi r^2}\right) + 2\pi r^2 = \frac{1000}{r} + 2\pi r^2$. Find the critical point(s) by setting the first derivative equal to zero and solving for r. Note that r represents the radius of the can and must therefore be a positive number.

$$A = 1000r^{-1} + 2\pi r^2$$
$$A' = -1000r^{-2} + 4\pi r$$
$$0 = -\frac{1000}{r^2} + 4\pi r$$
$$\frac{1000}{r^2} = 4\pi r$$
$$1000 = 4\pi r^3$$
$$\sqrt[3]{\frac{1000}{4\pi}} = r$$

So, when r≈4.3 cm, the minimum surface area is obtained. When the radius of the can is 4.30 cm, its height is $h \approx \frac{500}{\pi(4.30)^2}$≈8.6 cm, and the surface area is approximately $\frac{1000}{4.3} + 2\pi(4.3)^2 \approx 348.73$ cm^2. Confirm that the surface area is greater when the radius is slightly smaller or larger than 4.3 cm. For instance, when r=4 cm, the surface area is approximately 350.5 cm², and when r=4.5 cm, the surface area is approximately 349.5 cm².

25. B: A line graph is often used to show change over time. A Venn diagram shows the relationships among sets. A box and whisker plot shows displays how numeric data are distributed throughout the range. A pie chart shows the relationship of parts to a whole.

26. A: The average number of male students in the 11th and 12th grades is 125 (calculated as $\frac{131+119}{2}$). The number of Hispanic students at the school is 10% of 1219, which is 122 students (rounded up from 121.9). The difference in the number of male and female students at the school is $630 - 589 = 41$, and the difference in the number of 9th and 12th grade students at the school is 354 – 255 = 99.

27. C: 52% of the student population is white. There are 630 female students at the school out of 1219 students, so the percentage of female students is $\frac{630}{1219} \cdot 100\% \approx 52\%$. The percentages rounded to the nearest whole number are the same.

28. D: 131 of 283 eleventh graders are male. Given that an 11th grader is chosen to attend the conference, the probability that a male is chosen is $\frac{\text{number of males}}{\text{number of 11th graders}} = \frac{131}{283} \approx 0.46$. Note that this is **NOT** the same question as one which asks for the probability of selecting at random from the school a male student who is in eleventh grade, which has a probability of $\frac{131}{1219} \approx 0.11$.

29. B:

	Department 1	Department 2	Department 3	Total
Women	12	28	16	56
Men	18	14	15	47
Total	30	42	31	103

There are three ways in which two women from the same department can be selected: two women can be selected from the first department, or two women can be selected from the second department, or two women can be selected from the third department. The probability that two women are selected from Department 1 is $\frac{12}{103} \cdot \frac{11}{102} = \frac{132}{10506}$, the probability that two women are selected from Department 2 is $\frac{28}{103} \cdot \frac{27}{102} = \frac{756}{10506}$, and the probability that two women are selected from Department 3 is $\frac{16}{103} \cdot \frac{15}{102} = \frac{240}{10506}$. Since any of these is a discrete possible outcome, the probability that two women will be selected from the same department is the sum of these outcomes: $\frac{132}{10506} + \frac{756}{10506} + \frac{240}{10506} \approx 0.107$, or 10.7%.

30. B: The number of students who like broccoli is equal to the number of students who like all three vegetables plus the number of students who like broccoli and carrots but not cauliflower plus the number of students who like broccoli and cauliflower but not carrots plus the number of students who like broccoli but no other vegetable: $3 + 15 + 4 + 10 = 32$. These students plus the numbers of students who like just cauliflower, just carrots, cauliflower and carrots, or none of the vegetables represents the entire set of students sampled: $32 + 2 + 27 + 6 + 23 = 90$. So, the probability that a randomly chosen student likes broccoli is $\frac{32}{90} \approx 0.356$.
The number of students who like carrots and at least one other vegetable is $15 + 6 + 3 = 24$. The number of students who like carrots is $24 + 27 = 51$. So, the probability that a student who likes carrots will also like at least one other vegetable is $\frac{24}{51} \approx 0.471$.
The number of students who like cauliflower and broccoli is $4 + 3 = 7$. The number of students who like all three vegetables is 3. So, the probability that a student who likes cauliflower and broccoli will also like carrots is $\frac{3}{7} \approx 0.429$.
The number of students who do not like carrots, broccoli, or cauliflower is 23. The total number of students surveyed is 90. So, the probability that a student does not like any of the three vegetables is $23/90 \approx 0.256$.

31. D: A score of 85 is one standard deviation below the mean. Since approximately 68% of the data is within one standard deviation of the mean, about 32% (100%-68%) of the data is outside of one standard deviation within the mean. Normally distributed data is symmetric about the mean, which means that about 16% of the data lies below one standard deviation below the mean and about 16% of data lies above one standard deviation above the mean. Therefore, approximately 16% of individuals have IQs less than 85, while approximately 84% of the population has an IQ of at least 85. Since 84% of 300 is 252, about 252 people from the selected group have IQs of at least 85.

32. D: The percent increase is represented as $\frac{1100-800}{800}$, which equals 0.375 or 37.5%.

33. D: The original cost may be represented by the equation $45 = x - 0.25x$ or $45 = 0.75x$. Dividing both sides of the equation by 0.75 gives $x = 60$.

34. A: If a number is divisible by 2 and 3, it is also divisible by the lowest common multiple of these two factors. The lowest common multiple of 2 and 3 is their product, 6.

35. B: The decimal expansion of an irrational number does not terminate or repeat. The decimal expansion of $\sqrt{2}$ does not terminate or repeat.

36. C: The original price may be represented by the equation $24{,}210 = x - 0.10x$ or $24{,}210 = 0.9x$. Dividing both sides of the equation by 0.9 gives $x = 26{,}900$.

37. C: His monthly salary may be modeled as $\frac{1}{8}x = 320$. Multiplying both sides of the equation by 8 gives $x = 2{,}560$.

38. C: The amount he donates is equal to $0.01(45{,}000)$. Thus, he donates \$450.

39. B: The amount she spends on rent and utilities is equal to $0.38(40{,}000)$, or \$15,200, which is approximately \$15,000.

40. D: The 8 is in the tenths place, the 6 in the hundredths place, and the 7 in the thousandths place. Thus, 0.867 is equal to the sum of the product of 8 and $\frac{1}{10}$, the product of 6 and $\frac{1}{100}$, and the product of 7 and $\frac{1}{1000}$.

41. C. The original price may be modeled by the equation, $(x - 0.45x) + 0.0875(x - 0.45x) = 39.95$, which simplifies to $0.598125x = 39.95$. Dividing each side of the equation by the coefficient of x gives $x \approx 66.79$.

42. C: There are 36 months in 3 years. The following proportion may be written: $\frac{450}{3} = \frac{x}{36}$. The equation $3x = 16200$, may be solved for x. Dividing both sides of the equation by 3 gives $x = 5{,}400$.

Social Studies

1. B: The Bluebonnet is the state flower of Texas. The Blue Lacy is the state dog and the Lone Star is the state symbol. The song Yellow Rose of Texas dates back to at least the 1850's though it true origins are unknown. In approximately the 1950's Emily West, a folk hero from the Texas revolution, came to be associated with the song.

2. B: The Virginia Company of London was based in London, not Massachusetts. It had a charter to colonize American land between the Hudson and Cape Fear rivers (c). The other Virginia Company was the Virginia Company of Plymouth, which was based in the American colony of Plymouth, Massachusetts (a). It had a charter to colonize North America between the Potomac River and the northern boundary of Maine (d). Both Virginia Companies were joint-stock companies, which had often been used by England for trading with other countries.

3. D: It is not true that John Smith's governance helped Jamestown more than John Rolfe's discovery that a certain type of East Indian tobacco could be grown in Virginia. Smith's strong leadership from 1608-1609 gave great support to the struggling colony. However, when Smith's return to England left Jamestown without this support, the future of the colony was again in question. In 1612, however, when John Rolfe found that an East Indian tobacco strain popular in Europe could be

farmed in Virginia, the discovery gave Jamestown and Virginia a lucrative crop. Therefore, both Smith's time in office and Rolfe's discovery were beneficial to Jamestown. Jamestown was established by the Virginia Company of London in 1607 (a), and it became the first permanent settlement by the English in North America (b). It is also true that Jamestown survived in spite of the fact that most of its early settlers died from starvation, disease, and Indian attacks (c). It is also true that many of Jamestown's settlers came from the English upper class and were unwilling to farm the land, while others came hoping to find gold or other treasures, and persisted in their search for these instead of working to make the land sustainable.

4. C: Hernando Cortes conquered the Mexican Aztecs in 1519. He had several advantages over the Indians, including horses, armor for his soldiers, and guns. In addition, Cortes' troops unknowingly transmitted smallpox to the Aztecs, which devastated their population as they had no immunity to this foreign illness. Vasco Nunez de Balboa (a) was the first European explorer to view the Pacific Ocean when he crossed the Isthmus of Panama in 1513. Juan Ponce de Leon (b) also visited and claimed Florida in Spain's name in 1513. Cabeza de Vaca (d) was one of only four men out of 400 to return from an expedition led by Panfilio de Narvaez in 1528, and was responsible for spreading the story of the Seven Cities of Cibola (the "cities of gold"). Hernando de Soto led an expedition from 1539-1541 to the southeastern part of America.

5. A: The attitudes of American colonists after the 1763 Treaty of Paris ended the French and Indian War was not a direct contributor to the American Revolution. American colonists had a supportive attitude toward Great Britain then, and were proud of the part they played in winning the war. Their good will was not returned by British leaders (b), who looked down on American colonials and sought to increase their imperial power over them. Even in 1761, a sign of Americans' objections to having their liberty curtailed by the British was seen when Boston attorney James Otis argued in court against the Writs of Assistance (c), search warrants to enforce England's mercantilist trade restrictions, as violating the kinds of natural laws espoused during the Enlightenment. Lord George Grenville's aggressive program to defend the North American frontier in the wake of Chief Pontiac's attacks included stricter enforcement of the Navigation Acts, the Proclamation of 1763, the Sugar Act (or Revenue Act), the Currency Act, and most of all the Stamp Act (d). Colonists objected to these as taxation without representation. Other events followed in this taxation dispute, which further eroded Americans' relationship with British government, including the Townshend Acts, the Massachusetts Circular Letter, the Boston Massacre, the Tea Act, and the resulting Boston Tea Party. Finally, with Britain's passage of the Intolerable Acts and the Americans' First Continental Congress, which was followed by Britain's military aggression against American resistance, actual warfare began in 1775. While not all of the colonies wanted war or independence by then, things changed by 1776, and Jefferson's Declaration of Independence was formalized. James Otis, Samuel Adams, Patrick Henry, the Sons of Liberty, and the Stamp Act Congress also contributed to the beginning of the American Revolution.

6. C: Colonists did find that tea shipped directly by the British East India Company cost less than smuggled Dutch tea, even with tax. The colonists, however, did not buy it. They refused, despite its lower cost, on the principle that the British were taxing colonists without representation (d). It is true that the British East India Company lost money as a result of colonists buying tea smuggled from Holland (a). They sought to remedy this problem by getting concessions from Parliament to ship tea directly to the colonies instead of going through England (b) as the Navigation Acts normally required. Boston Governor Thomas Hutchinson, who sided with Britain, stopped tea ships from leaving the harbor, which after 20 days would cause the tea to be sold at auction. At that time, British taxes on the tea would be paid. On the 19th night after Hutchinson's action, American protestors held the Boston Tea Party, dressing as Indians and dumping all the tea into the harbor to

destroy it so it could not be taxed and sold. Many American colonists disagreed with the Boston Tea Party because it involved destroying private property. When Lord North and the British Parliament responded by passing the Coercive Acts and the Quebec Act, known collectively in America as the Intolerable Acts, Americans changed their minds, siding with the Bostonians against the British.

7. D: Paul Revere (a) and William Dawes (b) were both dispatch riders who set out on horseback from Massachusetts to spread news of British troop movements across the American countryside around the beginning of the War of Independence. John Parker (c) was the captain of the Minutemen militia, who were waiting for the British at Lexington, Massachusetts.

8. C: All the accomplishments described are accurate, however, Frances Perkins was from New York.

9. D: The Louisiana Purchase actually increased the U.S.'s territory by 100% overnight, not 50%. The Louisiana territory doubled the size of the nation. It is true that Jefferson initially sent a delegation to Paris to see if Napoleon would agree to sell only New Orleans to the United States (a). It is also true that Napoleon, who expected America to encroach on Louisiana, decided to avoid this by offering to sell the entire territory to the U.S. (b). It is likewise true that America only had authority to buy New Orleans. Nevertheless, the delegation accepted Napoleon's offer of all of Louisiana (c). Due to his belief in strict interpretation of the Constitution, Jefferson did require approval from Congress to make the purchase. When his advisors characterized the purchase as being within his purview based on the presidential power to make treaties, Congress agreed.

10. A: By 1840, more than one third of all Americans lived west of the Alleghenies, but not two thirds. It is correct that in the first half of the 19th century, the American population doubled every 25 years (b). It is also correct that westward expansion increased as more people moved west (c) during these years. It is correct that there was not a lot of immigration to the U.S. from other countries before 1820 (d). It is also true that foreign immigration to America increased quickly around that time, with most immigrants coming from the British Isles.

11. A: The U.S. did carry out a three-pronged invasion of Canada early in the war, but they did not succeed on two fronts. Instead, they lost on all three. Americans did win sea battles against the British early in the war, but were soon beaten back to their homeports and then blockaded by powerful British warships (b). Admiral Perry did defeat the British on Lake Erie on September 10, 1813 (c). Perry's victory allowed William Henry Harrison to invade Canada (d) in October of 1813, where he defeated British and Indians in the Battle of the Thames. *Old Ironsides* was one of the ships that won early naval battles during the war before Britain drove American ships to retreat.

12. B: Growth in labor organizing was stimulated by organizers wanting to achieve the goal of a shorter workday. However, what they were aiming for in the 1800s was a 10-hour day, not an 8-hour day, which was not realized until 1936. It is true that when the factory system supplanted the cottage industry, owners and workers became separate, and this depersonalized workplaces (a). Child laborers did conduct the first organized workers' strike in Paterson, N.J., in 1828 (c). Although the first strike did occur this early, there were not a lot of strikes or labor negotiations during this time period due to periodic downturns in the economy (d), which had the effect of keeping workers dependent and less likely to take action against management. The campaign to attain a 10-hour work day did stimulate a period of growth in labor organizing, but this growth period ended with the depression of 1837.

13. C: Thomas Jefferson did describe a plan for Virginia to have a free school, but it was not realized. Jefferson's plan was never implemented. It is true that there were really no public schools worth mentioning in America before around 1815 (a). Once there were schools, they were mainly paid for by private organizations – corporate ones in the Northeastern states and religious ones in the Southern and Mid-Atlantic states (b). America's early schools did cater to rich people, and specialized in providing academic instruction to males (d). The few schools for females in existence taught homemaking and fine arts rather than academic subjects. The New York Free School was a very unusual instance of an early American school that provided education for the poor. This school tried out the Lancastrian system, wherein older students tutor younger students, which not only employed a sound educational principle, but also helped the school to operate within its limited budget.

14. D: All the laws named were instrumental in spurring westward migration to the Great Plains. The Homestead Act (a), passed in 1862, gave settlers 160 acres of land at no monetary cost in exchange for a commitment to cultivating the land for five years. The Timber Culture Act (b), passed in 1873, gave the settlers 160 acres more of land in exchange for planting trees on one quarter of the acreage. The Desert Land Act (c), passed in 1877, allowed buyers who would irrigate the land to buy 640 acres for only 25 cents an acre. Thus,, all of these laws were instrumental to spurring westward migration to the Great Plains during that period, is correct.

15. A: The NAACP was founded in 1909 in New York City by W.E.B. DuBois and others. The first NAACP chapter in Texas was founded in 1912 in Houston and fought to eliminate voting obstacles (e.g., the white primary and poll tax) and desegregate both schools and larger society. In 1942, Texas native James L. Farmer was among the co-founders of the group that would become the Congress of Racial Equality. During the Civil Rights Movement, Farmer and CORE organized the 1961 Freedom Ride. The League of United Latin American Citizens was founded in Corpus Christi in 1929 by veterans of World War I to end ethnic discrimination against Latinos. The American GI Forum was founded in Corpus Christi in 1948 by Dr. Hector Perez Garcia to address the concerns of Mexican-American veterans of World War II who were segregated from other veterans groups.

16. A: The postwar conference that brought US-Soviet differences to light was (a) the Potsdam conference in July of 1945. The conference at Yalta (b), in February of 1945, resulted in the division of Germany into Allied-controlled zones. The Dumbarton Oaks conference (c) (1944) established a Security Council, on which with the US, England, Soviet Union, France, and China served as the five permanent members. Each of the permanent members had veto power, and a General Assembly, with limited power, was also established. The Tehran conference (d) included FDR's proposal for a new international organization to take the place of the League of Nations. This idea would later be realized in the form of the United Nations. Earlier in 1943, at the Casablanca Conference, President Roosevelt and Prime Minister Churchill agreed to a policy of unconditional surrender for all enemies of the Allied powers .

17. D: In 1956, Egypt did not attack Israel. On October 29, 1956, Israel attacked Egypt. England and France did join this war within two days. It is true that Egyptian President Gamal Abdul Nasser refused to take America's side in the Cold War (a). In reaction to his refusal, President Eisenhower's administration pulled its funding from the Aswan Dam project in Egypt (b). Nasser then nationalized the British-owned Suez Canal (c). Eisenhower further declared in 1957 that America would provide aid to any country in the Middle East facing Communist control. Pursuant to Eisenhower's declaration, the US invaded Lebanon in 1958 to resolve a conflict in government.

18. B: Reagan escalated military action in response to a terrorist bombing that killed 240 US Marines, is not true. Reagan sent the Marines to Lebanon in 1982 as part of a peacekeeping effort (d) after Israel invaded Lebanon on a mission to eradicate its PLO camps (a). At the time, Lebanon was already engaged in a civil war (c). When the terrorist attack killed 240 Marines, Reagan withdrew the rest of the troops rather than escalate the action. In 1988, an uprising of Palestinians known as the First Intifada started on the Jordan River's much-contested West Bank. In response to this uprising, Reagan initiated peace talks with the PLO's leader, Yasser Arafat. However, the goal of peace in the Middle East never materialized.

19. C: The person or group *not* instrumental in advancing civil rights and desegregation immediately after WWII was (c), Congress. As African American soldiers came home from the war, racial discord increased. President Harry Truman (a) appointed a Presidential Committee on Civil Rights in 1946. This committee published a report recommending that segregation and lynching be outlawed by the federal government. However, Congress ignored this report and took no action. Truman then used his presidential powers to enforce desegregation of the military and policies of "fair employment" in federal civil service jobs. The National Association for the Advancement of Colored People (NAACP) (d) brought lawsuits against racist and discriminatory practices, and in resolving these suits, the Supreme Court (b) further eroded segregation. For example, the Supreme Court ruled that primaries allowing only whites would be illegal, and it ended the segregation of interstate bus lines. The landmark civil rights laws were not passed by Congress until the 1960s

20. B: Of the programs enacted by Johnson, the one most closely related to JFK's legacy was (b), the Civil Rights Act, which Johnson pushed through Congress using allusions to Kennedy's and his goals. While Kennedy received congressional backing for a raise in minimum wage and public housing improvements, his efforts regarding civil rights were thwarted by conservative Republicans and Southern Democrats in Congress. However, as the Civil Rights movement progressed through the campaigns of the Freedom Riders, Kennedy developed a strong commitment to the cause. The Economic Opportunity Act gave almost $1 billion to wage Johnson's War on Poverty. The Great Society (c) was Johnson's name for his comprehensive reform program which included a variety of legislation.

21. B: The GATT countries did agree to abolish or decrease many of their tariffs, but this agreement did not include only 57 countries. Then number of signatories was much larger, totaling 117 countries. The GATT was approved by Congress in 1994 (a). In addition to having 117 countries agree to increase free trade, the GATT also set up the World Trade Organization (WTO) for the purpose of settling any differences among nations related to trade (c). Another instance of free trade policy established in the 1990s was the Senate's ratification of NAFTA. The negotiation of this agreement was originally made by the first Bush administration, with President Bush and the leaders of Canada and Mexico signing it in 1992 (d), but it still needed to be ratified. When he was elected President following the senior Bush's second term, Bill Clinton also supported NAFTA, and the Senate ratified it in 1994.

22. C: The Union blockaded the port of Galveston during the early part of the war, negatively impacting the trade of cotton. The port of Houston was not created until the 20th century.

23. C: The New Kingdom was the period during which no more pyramids were built in Egypt. The Pyramids were built between the years of 2630 and 1814 B.C.E., and the New Kingdom spanned from circa 1550-1070 B.C. As a result, the last pyramid was built approximately 264 years before the New Kingdom began. 2630 B.C.E. marked the beginning of the reign of the first Pharaoh, Djoser, who had the first pyramid built at Saqqara. 1814 B.C.E. marked the end of the reign of the last

Pharaoh, Amenemhat III, who had the last pyramid built at Hawara. In between these years, a succession of pharaohs built many pyramids. The Old Kingdom (a) encompasses both the Third (d) and Fourth Dynasties; therefore, all three of these choices encompass pyramid-building periods. Djoser's had his first pyramid built during the Third Dynasty (d). The Pharaohs Kufu, Khafre, and Menkaure, respectively, build the famous Pyramids of Giza during the Fourth Dynasty during their reigns at different times between circa 2575 and 2467 B.C.E., the period of the Fourth Dynasty. The Middle Kingdom (b) encompassed the 11th through 14th Dynasties, from circa. 2080 to 1640 B.C.E.—also within the time period (2630-1814 B.C.E.) when pyramids were built by the Pharaohs.

24. D: The ancient Indus Valley civilization, also known in its mature phase as the Harappan civilization, existed in what now encompasses all of the listed countries today. This culture flourished from circa 2600-1900 B.C.E., during the Bronze Age. This civilization included the most eastern portion of Balochistan in what is now Iran (a); the most western parts of what is now India (b); the majority of what is now Pakistan (c); and the southeastern part of Afghanistan.

25. B: Historians have determined that the Yellow River Valley in China began to develop into a cultural center during the Neolithic Era between c. 12,000-10,000 B.C.E. The Shang Dynasty (a) occurred between c. 1700-1046 B.C.E.—still part of the Ancient Era, but very long after the Neolithic era. The Xia Dynasty (c) ruled between circa 2100-1600 B.C.E., preceding the Shang Dynasty but still long after the Neolithic Era. The Paleolithic Era (d) came even before the Neolithic Era. Archaeological evidence exists of Homo erectus in China from more than a million years ago, during the Paleolithic Era, but the Yellow River Valley was not an emergent cultural center that long ago. The Zhou Dynasty ruled from circa 1066-221 B.C.E., later than the Neolithic Era, the Xia Dynasty, and overlapping with and then succeeding the Shang Dynasty.

26. D: Ancient Greek democracy was not completely open to all of the public. However, participating persons were not chosen or excluded based on their respective socioeconomic levels. The city-state of Athens had one of the first and most well-known democracies in ancient Greece (b). It began around 500 B.C.E. (a). The experiment of Athenian democracy was unique in that it was a direct democracy, meaning people voted directly for or against proposed legislation without any representation (c) such as the House of Representatives and the Senate, as we have in modern democracies.

27. B: It is not true that the Crusades succeeded at Christians' reclaiming the "holy land" (the Middle East) from Muslims. Despite their number (nine not counting the Northern Crusades) and longevity (1095-1291 not counting later similar campaigns), the Crusades never accomplished this purpose (a). While they did not take back the Middle East, the Crusades did succeed in exacerbating the decline of the Byzantine Empire (c), which lost more and more territory to the Ottoman Turks during this period. In addition, the Crusades resulted in Egypt's rise once again to become a major power (d) of the Middle East as it had been in the past. It is also true that during the Crusades, some Christians and Muslims became allies against common enemies. For example, during the Fifth Crusade, in Anatolia, Christian Crusaders with German, Dutch, Flemish, and Frisian soldiers allied themselves with the Sultanate of Rûm, a Seljuk Turk Sultanate that attacked the Ayyubids in Syria, in order to further their aim of attacking and capturing the port of Damietta in Egypt.

28. D: All these events contributed to the Italian Renaissance. After the Black Death killed a third of Europe's population (a), the survivors were mainly upper classes with more money to spend on art, architecture, and other luxuries. The plague deaths also resulted in a labor shortage, thereby creating more work opportunities for the surviving people in lower classes (b). As a result, these survivors' positions in society appreciated. Once plague deaths subsided and population growth in

Europe began to reassert itself, a greater demand existed for products and services. At the same time, the number of people available to provide these products and services was still smaller than in the past. Consequently, more merchants, artisans, and bankers emerged in order to provide the services and products people wanted, thereby creating a class of citizens between the lower class laborers and the upper class elite (c). After the two major Italian banks collapsed, wealthy investors who would normally have reinvested their disposable income did not do this, since the economy did not favor it. Instead, they invested their money in artistic and cultural products.

29. C: Texas has a bifurcated judiciary with two last resort courts— the Texas Supreme Court for civil cases and the Texas Court of Appeals for criminal cases— that both consist of nine popularly elected judges

30. B: The only true statement is the March on Versailles was made primarily by women. Therefore, an equal number of both men and women did not undertake the March on Versailles (a). The women took action because of the dire economic conditions from which they suffered, especially the high prices on bread and food shortages. The storming of the Bastille occurred on July 14, 1789; the March on Versailles occurred on October 5, 1789, almost three months later, not prior to it (c). (The date of July 14th is so famous as Bastille Day in France that generally it is familiar in other countries as well.) It is not true that the March on Versailles was not effective in accomplishing its purpose (d). In fact, the marchers did achieve their goal: They stormed the palace and killed several guards. La Fayette, in charge of the National Guard to control the mob, convinced the royals to move from Versailles to Paris and to stop blocking the National Assembly, and the royal family complied with these demands. The women did not march right to Versailles with no preliminaries. First, they assembled in markets around Paris and marched to the Hôtel de Ville. There they made their demands of the Paris city officials. When those officials did not give acceptable responses, the women then joined a march to the palace at Versailles. While the march to Versailles included men and weapons, some 7,000 women made up the majority of the marchers.

31. C: The only accurate statement about the end of WWI is that President Wilson had proposed that the nations of the world form a coalition to prevent future world wars. While he did not give the coalition a name, he clearly expressed his proposal that such a group form in the fourteenth of his Fourteen Points. The Treaty of Versailles (1919) did not bring peace among all countries involved in the war (a); Germany and the United States arrived at a separate peace in 1921. Furthermore, the Treaty of Versailles did not contain a clause for establishing the United Nations (b); it contained a clause for establishing the League of Nations. The League of Nations was created as dictated by the treaty, but when the Second World War proved that this group had failed to prevent future world wars, it was replaced by the United Nations after World War II. President Wilson did not succeed in getting the USA to ratify the League of Nations (d). Although he advocated vigorously for the League of Nations, the U.S. Senate never ratified the proposal. While the USA signed the League of Nations charter, the Senate never ratified it, and the USA never joined the League of Nations.

32. D: All of these empires no longer existed following the armistice ending WWI. The Austro-Hungarian Empire (a), the Ottoman Empire (b), and the German Empire (c) were all among the Central powers that lost the war. As empires capitulated, armistices and peace treaties were signed and the map of Europe was redrawn as territories formerly occupied by Central powers were partitioned. For example, the former Austro-Hungarian Empire was partitioned into Austria, Hungary, Czechoslovakia, Yugoslavia, Transylvania, and Romania. The Treaty of Lausanne (1923) gave Turkey both independence and recognition as successor to the former Ottoman Empire after Turkey refused the earlier Treaty of Sèvres (1920), and Mustafa Kemal Ataturk led the Turkish

Independence War. Greece, Bulgaria, and other former Ottoman possessions became independent. The Lausanne Treaty defined the boundaries of these countries as well as the boundaries of Iraq, Syria, Cyprus, Sudan, and Egypt. The Russian Empire was among the Allied powers. Russia not only sustained losses in WWI, but Russia also lost additional numbers in the Russian Revolution of 1917, which destroyed the Empire. Bolsheviks took power in Russia under Lenin and signed the Treaty of Brest-Litovsk with Germany in 1918, thereby formally ending Russia's part in WWI and ending the Eastern Front theatre of the war. The former Russian Empire territories of Latvia, Lithuania, Estonia, Finland, and Poland became independent. Therefore, by the end of the Second World War, these four multinational empires no longer existed.

33. A: The latest occurring decolonization event was the Eastern Bloc and Soviet Satellite states of Armenia, Azerbaijan, Estonia, Georgia, Kazakhstan, Kyrgyzstan, Latvia, Lithuania, Moldova, Russia, Tajikistan, Turkmenistan, Ukraine, and Uzbekistan all became independent from the Soviet Union in 1991. (Note: This was the last decolonization of the Cold War years, as the end of the Soviet Union marked the end of the Cold War.) Canada completed its independence from British Parliament via the Canada Act (b) in 1982. In the Caribbean, the Bahamas gained independence from the United Kingdom (c) in 1973. Algeria won its independence from France when the Algerian War of Independence, begun in 1954, ended in 1962 (d). In Africa, Libya gained independence from Italy and became an independent kingdom in 1951.

34. B: U.S. industrialization was confined to the Northeast until after the Civil War because the Northeast had faster-running rivers than the South. The earliest American factories used horse-drawn machines. When waterpower was developed and proved superior, the Northeast's faster rivers were more suited to water-powered mills than the South's slower rivers. The war did not delay the development of water power (a). Waterpower was developed before the Civil War in the late 1790s. Steam power, a more efficient alternative to water power, was developed after the Civil War and eventually replaced waterpower. With steam-powered engines, industry could spread to the South, since steam engines did not depend on rapidly running water like water-powered engines. While British emigré Samuel Slater's first cotton mill using horse-drawn production did lose a lot of money (c), this was not a reason for industrial delay. In fact, Slater's Beverly Cotton Manufactory in Massachusetts, the first American cotton mill, in spite of its financial problems, was successful in both its volume of cotton production and in developing the water-powered technology that ultimately would succeed the horse-drawn method. Slater's second cotton mill in Pawtucket, Rhode Island, was water-powered. Industrial delay was not because milling technology had not yet been invented (d). Slater learned of new textile manufacturing techniques as a youth in England, and he brought this knowledge to America in 1789. Resistance of Southern owners of plantations and slaves did not slow the spread of industrialism. Rather, as seen in (b) above, the South did not have the geographic capability to sustain waterpower. Once steam power was developed, the South joined in industrialization.

35. A: The inaccurate statement is the Puritans unconditionally supported the English Reformation. While they agreed with the Reformation in principle, they felt that it had not pursued those principles far enough and should make greater reforms. Similarly, they felt that the Church of England (or Anglican Church), though it had separated from the Catholic Church in the Protestant Reformation, still allowed many practices they found too much like Catholicism (b). The Puritans did become a chief political power in England because of the first English Civil War (c) between Royalists and Parliamentarians. The Royalists had a profound suspicion of the radical Puritans. Among the Parliament's elements of resistance, the strongest was that of the Puritans. They joined in the battle initially for ostensibly political reasons as others had, but soon they brought more attention to religious issues. Following the Restoration in 1660 and the Uniformity Act of 1662,

thereby restoring the Church of England to its pre-English Civil War status, the great majority of Puritan clergy defected from the Church of England (d). It is also accurate that the Puritans in England disagreed about separating from the Church of England. Some Puritans desired complete separation; they were known first as Separatists and after the Restoration as Dissenters. Others did not want complete separation but instead desired further reform in the Church of England. While they remained part of the Church of England, they were called Non-Separating Puritans, and after the Restoration, they were called Nonconformists.

36. B: Though he was otherwise qualified, Hermann Sweatt was originally denied admission to the University of Texas law school because of his race by the school's president Theophilus Painter. The case Sweatt vs. Painter was decided in his favor in 1950. The case was later part of the basis on which the Brown vs. Board case was decided. The 24th amendment barred the poll tax in federal elections. The poll tax for state elections was not eliminated until 1969. The white primary in Texas was overruled 1927. The American GI Forum and LULAC joined forces to fight the segregation of Mexican American students in public schools. In 1957 school segregation for these students was ended by the Supreme Court in its *Hernandez* decision.

37. D: It is not true that the Gilded Age is a term whose origins have not been identified clearly. In 1873, Mark Twain and Charles Dudley Warner co-authored a book entitled The Gilded Age: A Tale of Today. Twain and Warner first coined this term to describe the extravagance and excesses of America's wealthy upper class (b), who became richer than ever due to industrialization. Furthermore, the Gilded Age was the era of the "robber barons" (a) such as John D. Rockefeller, Cornelius Vanderbilt, J.P. Morgan, and others. Because they accumulated enormous wealth through extremely aggressive and occasionally unethical monetary manipulations, critics dubbed them "robber barons" because they seemed to be elite lords of robbery. While these business tycoons grasped huge fortunes, some of them—such as Andrew Carnegie and Andrew Mellon—were also philanthropists, using their wealth to support and further worthy causes such as literacy, education, health care, charities, and the arts. They donated millions of dollars to fund social improvements. Carnegie himself dubbed this large philanthropic movement the "Gospel of Wealth" (c). Another characteristic of the Gilded Age was the Beaux Arts architectural style, a neo-Renaissance style modeled after the great architectural designs of the European Renaissance. The Panic of 1893 ended the Gilded and began a severe four-year economic depression. The Progressive Era followed these events.

38. A: It is not true that the founding fathers specifically stated in the Constitution that the USA would be a democracy. The founding fathers wanted the new United States to be founded on principles of liberty and equality, but they did not specifically describe these principles with the term "Democracy." Thus, the Declaration of Independence, like the Constitution after it, did not stipulate a democracy, although both did state the principles of equality and freedom (b). The Constitution also provided for the election of the new government (c), and for protection of the rights of some, but not all, of the people (d). Notable exceptions at the time were black people and women. Only later were laws passed to protect their rights over the years. Because (b), (c), and (d) are all true, answer, these statements are all untrue, is incorrect.

39. B: is the answer. Preservatives such as salt were only introduced to the European diet after trade routes opened and these goods could be brought to Europe.

40. D: is the answer. Despite the growing amount of literacy in the 1500s, due principally to the invention of the printing press and the availability of texts, the majority of Europeans remained illiterate.

41. B: In 1792, when the French Revolution turned into European war, American traders conducted business with both sides. It is not true that Washington allied with the French (a) at this time. Washington issued a Proclamation of Neutrality in 1792 when the French went to war with European countries. While they did trade with both sides, American merchants profited the most from the French West Indies, not the British West Indies (c). The Spanish navy did not retaliate against America for trading with the French (d). Though Spain was an ally of Britain, it was the British who most often seized American ships and forced their crews to serve the British navy. Edmond-Charles Genêt, or Citizen Genêt, a French ambassador to the United States during the French Revolution, defied Washington's policy of neutrality by encouraging the American people to support the French. Washington was embarrassed by this violation. He did not agree with it.

42. C: The possibility of British interference aimed towards outlawing slavery in the territory, which the British has done throughout its empire three years before Texas gained its independence from Mexico, and the possibility that Texas emancipation might undermine American slavery was a key factor in the choice by President John Tyler to seek the annexation of Texas. Fears of both unrest over the issue of slavery and a possible Mexican conflict had to be addressed before annexation was brought before congress. At the time of annexation, the border issues remained unsettled. The southern Texas border was not set until the 1848 Treaty of Guadalupe-Hidalgo. The western border was not settled until the Compromise of 1850.

Science

1. C: Repeat the experiment. Repeating the experiment validates data. Each separate experiment is called a repetition. Results of experiments or tests should be able to be replicated. Similar data gathered from many experiments can also be used to quantify the validity of the hypothesis. Repeating the experiments allows for the observation of variation in the results. Variation in data can be caused by a variety of errors or may be disproving the hypothesis.

2. D: theory. Once a hypothesis has been verified and accepted, it becomes a theory. A theory is a generally accepted explanation that has been highly developed and tested. A theory can explain data and be expected to predict outcomes of tests. A fact is considered to be an objective and verifiable observation; whereas, a scientific theory is a greater body of accepted knowledge, principles, or relationships that might explain a fact. A law is an explanation of events by which the outcome is always the same. A conclusion is more of an opinion and could be based on observation, evidence, fact, laws, or even beliefs.

3. D: Electrophoresis. Electrophoresis, also known as gel electrophoresis, uses electrical charges to separate substances such as protein, DNA and RNA. Depending upon the electrical charge and size of the molecules, they will travel through a porous gel at different rates when a charge is applied. Spectrophotometry refers to the measurement of visible light, near-ultraviolet, and near-infrared wavelengths. Chromatography refers to a number of techniques that separate mixtures of chemicals based on the differences in the compound's affinity for a stationary phase, usually a porous solid, and a mobile phase, which can be either a liquid or a gas. Centrifugation separates mixtures by spinning to generate centripetal force, which causes heavier particles to separate from lighter particles.

4. A: By multiplying the ocular lens power times the objective being used. When using a light microscope, total magnification is determined by multiplying the ocular lens power times the

objective being used. The ocular lens refers to the eyepiece, which has one magnification strength, typically 10x. The objective lens also has a magnification strength, often 4x, 10x, 40x or 100x. Using a 10x eyepiece with the 4x objective lens will give a magnification strength of 40x. Using a 10x eyepiece with the 100x objective lens will give a magnification strength of 1,000x. The shorter lens is the lesser magnification; the longer lens is the greater magnification.

5. A: Dispose of the solutions according to local disposal procedures. Solutions and compounds used in labs may be hazardous according to state and local regulatory agencies and should be treated with such precaution. Emptying the solutions into the sink and rinsing with warm water and soap does not take into account the hazards associated with a specific solution in terms of vapors or interactions with water, soap, and waste piping systems. Ensuring the solutions are secured in closed containers and throwing them away may allow toxic chemicals into landfills and subsequently into fresh water systems. Storing the solutions in a secured, dry place for later use is incorrect as chemicals should not be re-used due to the possibility of contamination.

6. C: 20 g/L. One way to measure the density of an irregularly shaped object is to submerge it in water and measure the displacement. This is done by taking the mass (40 grams), then finding the volume by measuring how much water it displaces. Fill a graduated cylinder with water and record the amount. Put the object in the water and record the water level. Subtract the difference in water levels to get the amount of water displaced, which is also the volume of the object. In this case, 4.5 liters minus 2.5 liters equals 2 liters. Divide mass by volume (40 grams divided by 2 liters) to get 20 g/L (grams per liter).

7. B: A spoiling apple. A spoiling apple is an example of a chemical change. During a chemical change, one substance is changed into another. Oxidation, a chemical change, occurs when an apple spoils. Sublimation of water refers to the conversion between the solid and the gaseous phases of matter, with no intermediate liquid stage. This is a phase change, not a chemical reaction. Dissolution of salt in water refers to a physical change, since the salt and water can be separated again by evaporating the water, which is a physical change. Pulverized rock is an example of a physical change where the form has changed but not the substance itself.

8. D: temperature. The amount of potential energy an object has depends on mass, height above ground and gravitational attraction, but not temperature. The formula for potential energy is PE = mgh, or potential energy equals mass times gravity times height. Answers A, B, and C are all valid answers as they are all contained in the formula for potential energy. Potential energy is the amount of energy stored in a system particularly because of its position.

9. D: All of the above. Elements on the periodic table are arranged into periods, or rows, according to atomic number, which is the number of protons in the nucleus. The periodic table illustrates the recurrence of properties. Each column, or group, contains elements that share similar properties, such as reactivity.

10. A: It takes half the amount of energy to increase the temperature of a 1 kg sample of ice by 1°C than a 1 kg sample of water. Heat capacity refers to the amount of heat or thermal energy required to raise the temperature of a specific substance a given unit. A substance with a higher heat capacity requires more heat to raise its temperature than a substance with a lower heat capacity. The comparison here is that the specific heat capacity of ice is half as much as that of liquid water, so it takes half the amount of energy to increase the same amount of ice one temperature unit than it would if it were liquid water.

11. D: Its temperature remains the same due to the latent heat of fusion. The temperature of a substance during the time of any phase change remains the same. In this case, the phase change was from liquid to solid, or freezing. Latent heat of fusion, in this case, is energy that is released from the substance as it reforms its solid form. This energy will be released and the liquid will turn to solid before the temperature of the substance will decrease further. If the substance were changing from solid to liquid, the heat of fusion would be the amount of heat required to break apart the attractions between the molecules in the solid form to change to the liquid form. The latent heat of fusion is exactly the same quantity of energy for a substance for either melting or freezing. Depending on the process, this amount of heat would either be absorbed by the substance (melting) or released (freezing).

12. B: Conduction. A long nail or other type of metal, substance or matter that is heated at one end and then the other end becomes equally hot is an example of conduction. Conduction is energy transfer by neighboring molecules from an area of hotter temperature to cooler temperature. Radiation, or thermal radiation, refers to heat being transferred without the need for a medium by electromagnetic radiation. An example is sunlight heating the earth. Convection refers to heat being transferred by molecules moving from one location in the substance to another creating a heat current, usually in a gas or a liquid. Entropy relates to the second law of thermodynamics and refers to how much heat or energy is no longer available to do work in a system. It can also be stated as the amount of disorder in a system.

13. C: Heat transfer can never occur from a cooler object to a warmer object. While the second law of thermodynamics implies that heat never spontaneously transfers from a cooler object to a warmer object, it is possible for heat to be transferred to a warmer object, given the proper input of work to the system. This is the principle by which a refrigerator operates. Work is done to the system to transfer heat from the objects inside the refrigerator to the air surrounding the refrigerator. All other answer choices are true.

14. B: heat. The measure of energy within a system is called heat. Temperature is a measurement of the average kinetic energy of molecules in a substance. A higher temperature means greater kinetic energy or faster moving molecules. Entropy is the amount of energy that is no longer available for work, related to the second law of thermodynamics. Thermodynamics is the study of the conversion of energy into heat and work in a system.

15. D: It has a different number of neutrons than its element. An isotope is a variation of an element that has a different number of neutrons. The element and its various isotopes continue to have the same numbers of protons and electrons. For example, carbon has three naturally occurring isotopes, carbon-12, carbon-13 and carbon-14, which is radioactive. Isotopes of an element differ in mass number, which is the number of protons and neutrons added together, but have the same atomic number, or number of protons.

16. D: It is a stable atom. If an atom's outer shell is filled, it is a stable atom. The outer shell refers to one of many energy levels, or shells, that electrons occupy around a nucleus. An atom whose outer shell is not filled wants to become stable by filling the outer shell. It fills its outer shell by forming bonds. The atom can do this by gaining electrons or losing electrons in ionic compounds, or if the atom is a part of a molecule, by sharing electrons. If an atom has a full outer shell, such as the noble gases, it does not readily react with other atoms and does not exchange electrons to form bonds. These atoms are known as inert. Therefore, Answers A and B cannot be true. Answer C, It has 32 electrons in its outer shell, is not necessarily true because not all elements have the fourth shell that can hold 32 electrons. Some have fewer shells that hold fewer electrons.

17. A: Fission. Fission is a nuclear process where atomic nuclei split apart to form smaller nuclei. Nuclear fission can release large amounts of energy, emit gamma rays and form daughter products. It is used in nuclear power plants and bombs. Answer B, Fusion, refers to a nuclear process whereby atomic nuclei join to form a heavier nucleus, such as with stars. This can release or absorb energy depending upon the original elements. Answer C, Decay, refers to an atomic nucleus spontaneously losing energy and emitting ionizing particles and radiation. Answer D, Ionization, refers to a process by which atoms obtain a positive or negative charge because the number of electrons does not equal that of protons.

18. B: farther from. Electrons with greater amounts of energy are found farther from the nucleus than electrons with less energy. The principle quantum number describes the level or shell that an electron is in. The lower the number, the closer the electron is to the nucleus and the lower it is in energy.

19. D: decay. The process whereby a radioactive element releases energy slowly over a long period of time to lower its energy and become more stable is best described as decay. The nucleus undergoing decay, known as the parent nuclide, spontaneously releases energy most commonly through the emission of an alpha particle, a beta particle or a gamma ray. The changed nucleus, called the daughter nuclide, is now more stable than the parent nuclide, although the daughter nuclide may undergo another decay to an even more stable nucleus. A decay chain is a series of decays of a radioactive element into different more stable elements.

20. C: A screw. A screw is a type of simple machine. A screw is an inclined plane wrapped around a shaft. A wedge is also an inclined plane. A compound machine is a machine that employs two or more simple machines. Answer A, a bicycle, is a compound machine, consisting of a combination of the simple machines: wheels, levers, pulleys and wedges (used as stoppers). Answer B, a pair of scissors, is also a compound machine consisting of two wedges (the blades) that pivot on a lever. Answer D, a shovel, is a compound machine consisting of a lever (the handle) and a wedge (the head of the shovel).

21. D: Mario balances a book on his head. In this example, work is not applied to the book because the book is not moving. One definition of work is force acting on an object to cause displacement. In this case, the book was not displaced by the force applied to it. Mario's head applied a vertical force to the book to keep it in the same position.

22. C: The ball will move forward with respect to the boat. Newton's first law of motion states that an object in motion tends to stay in motion until a force acts to change it. The ball is initially at rest with respect to the boat, but the boat is moving forward. When the front of the boat hits the dock, the boat quickly decelerates, but the ball does not. It continues to move forward because the force acting to stop the boat does not significantly affect the ball. With the ball now moving forward faster than the boat, the ball's motion relative to the boat is forward motion.

23. A: Acceleration and centripetal force. Acceleration and centripetal force are required for circular motion to occur. Acceleration is defined as a change in direction of velocity. Centripetal force is force directed toward the center, or inward force. The force of gravity is not required for circular motion, nor is constant speed.

24. B: Where the pipe is narrowest. A fluid, either a gas or a liquid, will flow faster through a narrow section of a pipe than a wider section of pipe. Bernoulli's Principle says that the faster a

fluid flows, the less pressure the fluid exerts. Therefore, a fluid will exert a lower amount of pressure in the narrow section of pipe. A fluid moving through the pipe has the same flow throughout the wider and narrow portions. This means that the same volume and mass of fluid must go a specific distance in a certain amount of time. In a narrow portion of pipe, there is less area for the same volume and mass of fluid to flow, so the fluid must move faster to maintain the same flow as in the wider portion of pipe. A fluid moving faster through a narrow portion of pipe will exert less pressure and a fluid moving slower through a wide section of pipe will exert a greater pressure.

25. A: The charge on the glass rod is positive and the charge on the cloth is negative when the glass rod is rubbed with a cloth made of polyester. This is an example of static electricity — the collection of electrically charged particles on the surface of a material. A static charge can be quickly discharged, commonly called a "spark", or discharged more slowly by dissipating to the ground. A static charge occurs because different materials have a capacity for giving up electrons and becoming positive (+), or for attracting electrons and becoming negative (-). The triboelectric series is a list of materials and their propensities for either giving up electrons to become positive or to gain the electrons to become negative. Polyester has a tendency to gain electrons to become negative and glass has a tendency to lose electrons to become positive.

26. B: Voltage and current are directly proportional to one another. Ohm's Law states that voltage and current in an electrical circuit are directly proportional to one another. Ohm's Law can be expressed as V=IR, where V is voltage, I is current and R is resistance. Voltage is also known as electrical potential difference and is the force that moves electrons through a circuit. For a given amount of resistance, an increase in voltage will result in an increase in current. Resistance and current are inversely proportional to each other. For a given voltage, an increase in resistance will result in a decrease in current.

27. C: spin unpaired. In an atom with paired electrons, the opposite spins of each electron in the pair cancel out the magnetic field of each electron. A material becomes magnetic when the individual electrons of an atom spin unpaired thus allowing their magnetic fields to add together. The spin of an unpaired electron generates its own magnetic field. This can be used to make a magnet. When an external magnetic field is applied, these spins are lined up and the combined forces make a magnet.

28. D: Voltage is the same for each path and current is greatest in path C. In a parallel circuit, the voltage is the same for all three paths. Because the resistance is different on each path but the voltage is the same, Ohm's law dictates that the current will also be different for each path. Ohm's law says that current is inversely related to resistance. Therefore, the current will be greatest in path C as it has the least resistance, 2 ohms.

29. A: A high angle of incidence of the wave. A high angle of incidence will cause a high angle of reflection of a light wave. The angle of incidence is the angle of the incoming light and the angle of reflection is the angle of the light after being reflected. They are equal. A low angle of incidence of the wave would cause an equally low angle of reflection. A wave that travels through a medium of higher density would cause an angle of refraction, not reflection. Wavelength is not changed by reflection.

30. D: Destructive interference. Destructive interference describes two waves that are out of phase as they come together to produce a new wave. Out of phase refers to the crest of one and the trough of another arriving together. Interference, when used to discuss wave phenomenon, is the

interaction of two or more waves passing the same point, which could be either destructive or constructive. Incomplete interference and distorted interference are not real terms. Constructive interference refers to wave interference that results in higher peaks than the waves singularly because the waves arrive in phase with one another (the crests arrive together).

31. A: They will be refracted and converge. When light waves hit a convex lens they are refracted and converge. A convex lens curves or bulges with the middle being thicker and the edges thinner. A magnifying glass is an example. Light rays are refracted by different amounts as they pass through the lens. After light rays pass through, they converge at a point called the focus. An object viewed with a magnifying glass looks bigger because the lens bends the rays inwards. Answer B would indicate a concave lens as it would cause the light to be refracted and diverge. Light is not reflected in this case, so neither C nor D would be applicable.

32. C: A cation from a base and an anion from an acid. A salt is a general term for the neutral ionic product of a neutralization reaction between an acid and a base. Often, table salt, or sodium chloride, is mistakenly characterized as "salt", indicating that all salts are this compound. Although it is very common for a salt to be composed of a metal and a nonmetal, this is not always true, as in the case of the salt ammonium chloride. The ammonium ion (NH_4^+) is a polyatomic ion composed of non-metals. Likewise, many salts are composed of an alkali or alkaline earth metal and a halogen, but this is not always the case.

33. B: Group 2. Group 2 makes up the alkaline earth metals on the periodic chart of elements. There are 18 groups, or vertical columns, on the periodic table. In general, Group 2, alkaline earth metals, are characterized by silver colored, soft metals that melt at high temperatures. They also combine well with halogens to form salts and have two electrons in their valence level. Group 1 elements are called the alkali metals or lithium family. Group 13 is the boron family. Group 17 elements are known as the halogens or fluorine family.

34. C: Astatine. Astatine is not a noble gas (Group 18). Astatine is a halogen (Group 17). It is believed to be the rarest naturally occurring element. Its symbol is At and has an atomic number of 85. It is radioactive and has a short half life. Neon, Argon, and Krypton are all noble gases. These gases have low reactivity as their valence levels are filled with 8 electrons, except for helium, whose valence level is filled with 2 electrons.

35. D: The atomic number is equal to the number of electrons. An atom has a neutral charge if its atomic number is equal to its number of electrons. The atomic number (Z) of an element refers to the number of protons in the nucleus. If an atom has fewer or more electrons than its atomic number, then it will be positively or negatively charged, respectively. Cations are positively charged ions; anions are negatively charged ones. Answers A and B both describe a nucleus containing only neutrons with no protons. An element of this nature is referred to as neutronium, but is theoretical only.

36. A: high solubility in water. Most organic molecules have all of the following properties except high solubility in water. A tendency to melt, covalently bonded, and high flammability are all characteristics of organic molecules. Organic molecules are those that contain carbon molecules, with a few exceptions. Organic molecules tend to be less soluble in water than inorganic salts. They are good at forming unique structures and there are many organic compounds. Examples of organic compounds include hydrocarbons, carbohydrates, lipids and proteins.

37. C: Covalent. Covalent compounds are usually formed by the combination of two or more non-metallic elements with one another. In these compounds atoms share electrons. Ionic compounds are most often formed between a metal and a non-metal. Organic compounds are covalent compounds which contain carbon and hydrogen atoms. "Chemical compounds" is a general term that can mean any type of compound, either ionic or covalent.

38. D: A carbon atom attached to a hydrogen atom by a double bond and to an oxygen atom by a double bond. This is not a correct description of the carboxyl group. Hydrogen can never have more than one bond since it only has a 1s level and can only accommodate two electrons. The other answers are correct, as a carboxyl group does have a carbon atom attached to an oxygen atom by a double bond and to a hydroxyl (-OH) group by a single bond and is a set of four atoms bonded together and abbreviated as CO_2H.

39. C: The pressure decreases to one third. A gas in a closed container at constant temperature will decrease in pressure to one third when the volume of the container is tripled. The ideal gas law is $PV = nRT$ where P is pressure, V is volume, n is the moles of the gas, R is the gas constant and T is temperature. A variation to solve for pressure is:
$P = nRT/V$. Boyle's Law indicates that pressure and volume are inversely proportional. The pressure cannot be increased because that would imply that pressure and volume are directly proportional.

40. A: The molecular arrangement is random in some directions and regular in others. This best describes the molecular arrangement of a liquid crystal. A liquid crystal may seem like a contradiction as it seems to refer to two different states of matter. Liquid crystals have properties of both liquids and solids. The molecules of a liquid crystal are loosely bound allowing them to flow, like a liquid, yet they arrange themselves in a repeating pattern, like the molecules of a solid which are rigidly fixed in a pattern. Liquid crystals can also organize into layers, but with randomness in the layers.

41. D: There may be a different number of atoms for the products and the reactants. This is not true of a chemical reaction. Chemical equations must be balanced on each side of the reaction. Balancing means the total number of atoms stays the same, but their arrangement within specific reactants and products can change. The law of conservation of matter states that matter can never be created or destroyed. Heat may be absorbed or released in a reaction; these are classified as endothermic and exothermic reactions, respectively. The rate of the reaction increases with temperature for most reactions.

42. C: High concentration. A higher concentration could increase the reaction rate of a chemical reaction. The rate of reaction is affected by concentration, pressure and temperature. A higher concentration would allow for more potential collisions that set off the reaction. Low kinetic energy would lead to a lower rate of reaction, as does a lower temperature (usually). The term activation energy refers to the specific threshold that must be overcome for a reaction to occur. If the activation energy is lowered, for example, by a catalyst or enzyme, then the reaction can occur quicker. This rules out high activation energy.

Secret Key #1 - Time is Your Greatest Enemy

Pace Yourself

Wear a watch. At the beginning of the test, check the time (or start a chronometer on your watch to count the minutes), and check the time after every few questions to make sure you are "on schedule."

If you are forced to speed up, do it efficiently. Usually one or more answer choices can be eliminated without too much difficulty. Above all, don't panic. Don't speed up and just begin guessing at random choices. By pacing yourself, and continually monitoring your progress against your watch, you will always know exactly how far ahead or behind you are with your available time. If you find that you are one minute behind on the test, don't skip one question without spending any time on it, just to catch back up. Take 15 fewer seconds on the next four questions, and after four questions you'll have caught back up. Once you catch back up, you can continue working each problem at your normal pace.

Furthermore, don't dwell on the problems that you were rushed on. If a problem was taking up too much time and you made a hurried guess, it must be difficult. The difficult questions are the ones you are most likely to miss anyway, so it isn't a big loss. It is better to end with more time than you need than to run out of time.

Lastly, sometimes it is beneficial to slow down if you are constantly getting ahead of time. You are always more likely to catch a careless mistake by working more slowly than quickly, and among very high-scoring test takers (those who are likely to have lots of time left over), careless errors affect the score more than mastery of material.

Secret Key #2 - Guessing is not Guesswork

You probably know that guessing is a good idea. Unlike other standardized tests, there is no penalty for getting a wrong answer. Even if you have no idea about a question, you still have a 20-25% chance of getting it right.

Most test takers do not understand the impact that proper guessing can have on their score. Unless you score extremely high, guessing will significantly contribute to your final score.

Monkeys Take the Test

What most test takers don't realize is that to insure that 20-25% chance, you have to guess randomly. If you put 20 monkeys in a room to take this test, assuming they answered once per question and behaved themselves, on average they would get 20-25% of the questions correct. Put 20 test takers in the room, and the average will be much lower among guessed questions. Why?

1. The test writers intentionally write deceptive answer choices that "look" right. A test taker has no idea about a question, so he picks the "best looking" answer, which is often wrong. The monkey has no idea what looks good and what doesn't, so it will consistently be right about 20-25% of the time.
2. Test takers will eliminate answer choices from the guessing pool based on a hunch or intuition. Simple but correct answers often get excluded, leaving a 0% chance of being correct. The monkey has no clue, and often gets lucky with the best choice.

This is why the process of elimination endorsed by most test courses is flawed and detrimental to your performance. Test takers don't guess; they make an ignorant stab in the dark that is usually worse than random.

$5 Challenge

Let me introduce one of the most valuable ideas of this course—the $5 challenge:

You only mark your "best guess" if you are willing to bet $5 on it.
You only eliminate choices from guessing if you are willing to bet $5 on it.

Why $5? Five dollars is an amount of money that is small yet not insignificant, and can really add up fast (20 questions could cost you $100). Likewise, each answer choice on one question of the test will have a small impact on your overall score, but it can really add up to a lot of points in the end.

The process of elimination IS valuable. The following shows your chance of guessing it right:

If you eliminate wrong answer choices until only this many remain:	Chance of getting it correct:
1	100%
2	50%
3	33%

However, if you accidentally eliminate the right answer or go on a hunch for an incorrect answer, your chances drop dramatically—to 0%. By guessing among all the answer choices, you are GUARANTEED to have a shot at the right answer.

That's why the $5 test is so valuable. If you give up the advantage and safety of a pure guess, it had better be worth the risk.

What we still haven't covered is how to be sure that whatever guess you make is truly random. Here's the easiest way:

Always pick the first answer choice among those remaining.

Such a technique means that you have decided, **before you see a single test question**, exactly how you are going to guess, and since the order of choices tells you nothing about which one is correct, this guessing technique is perfectly random.

This section is not meant to scare you away from making educated guesses or eliminating choices; you just need to define when a choice is worth eliminating. The $5 test, along with a pre-defined random guessing strategy, is the best way to make sure you reap all of the benefits of guessing.

Secret Key #3 - Practice Smarter, Not Harder

Many test takers delay the test preparation process because they dread the awful amounts of practice time they think necessary to succeed on the test. We have refined an effective method that will take you only a fraction of the time.

There are a number of "obstacles" in the path to success. Among these are answering questions, finishing in time, and mastering test-taking strategies. All must be executed on the day of the test at peak performance, or your score will suffer. The test is a mental marathon that has a large impact on your future.

Just like a marathon runner, it is important to work your way up to the full challenge. So first you just worry about questions, and then time, and finally strategy:

Success Strategy

1. Find a good source for practice tests.
2. If you are willing to make a larger time investment, consider using more than one study guide. Often the different approaches of multiple authors will help you "get" difficult concepts.
3. Take a practice test with no time constraints, with all study helps, "open book." Take your time with questions and focus on applying strategies.
4. Take a practice test with time constraints, with all guides, "open book."
5. Take a final practice test without open material and with time limits.

If you have time to take more practice tests, just repeat step 5. By gradually exposing yourself to the full rigors of the test environment, you will condition your mind to the stress of test day and maximize your success.

Secret Key #4 - Prepare, Don't Procrastinate

Let me state an obvious fact: if you take the test three times, you will probably get three different scores. This is due to the way you feel on test day, the level of preparedness you have, and the version of the test you see. Despite the test writers' claims to the contrary, some versions of the test WILL be easier for you than others.

Since your future depends so much on your score, you should maximize your chances of success. In order to maximize the likelihood of success, you've got to prepare in advance. This means taking practice tests and spending time learning the information and test taking strategies you will need to succeed.

Never go take the actual test as a "practice" test, expecting that you can just take it again if you need to. Take all the practice tests you can on your own, but when you go to take the official test, be prepared, be focused, and do your best the first time!

Secret Key #5 - Test Yourself

Everyone knows that time is money. There is no need to spend too much of your time or too little of your time preparing for the test. You should only spend as much of your precious time preparing as is necessary for you to get the score you need.

Once you have taken a practice test under real conditions of time constraints, then you will know if you are ready for the test or not.

If you have scored extremely high the first time that you take the practice test, then there is not much point in spending countless hours studying. You are already there.

Benchmark your abilities by retaking practice tests and seeing how much you have improved. Once you consistently score high enough to guarantee success, then you are ready.

If you have scored well below where you need, then knuckle down and begin studying in earnest. Check your improvement regularly through the use of practice tests under real conditions. Above all, don't worry, panic, or give up. The key is perseverance!

Then, when you go to take the test, remain confident and remember how well you did on the practice tests. If you can score high enough on a practice test, then you can do the same on the real thing.

General Strategies

The most important thing you can do is to ignore your fears and jump into the test immediately. Do not be overwhelmed by any strange-sounding terms. You have to jump into the test like jumping into a pool—all at once is the easiest way.

Make Predictions

As you read and understand the question, try to guess what the answer will be. Remember that several of the answer choices are wrong, and once you begin reading them, your mind will immediately become cluttered with answer choices designed to throw you off. Your mind is typically the most focused immediately after you have read the question and digested its contents. If you can, try to predict what the correct answer will be. You may be surprised at what you can predict.

Quickly scan the choices and see if your prediction is in the listed answer choices. If it is, then you can be quite confident that you have the right answer. It still won't hurt to check the other answer choices, but most of the time, you've got it!

Answer the Question

It may seem obvious to only pick answer choices that answer the question, but the test writers can create some excellent answer choices that are wrong. Don't pick an answer just because it sounds right, or you believe it to be true. It MUST answer the question. Once you've made your selection, always go back and check it against the question and make sure that you didn't misread the question and that the answer choice does answer the question posed.

Benchmark

After you read the first answer choice, decide if you think it sounds correct or not. If it doesn't, move on to the next answer choice. If it does, mentally mark that answer choice. This doesn't mean that you've definitely selected it as your answer choice, it just means that it's the best you've seen thus far. Go ahead and read the next choice. If the next choice is worse than the one you've already selected, keep going to the next answer choice. If the next choice is better than the choice you've already selected, mentally mark the new answer choice as your best guess.

The first answer choice that you select becomes your standard. Every other answer choice must be benchmarked against that standard. That choice is correct until proven otherwise by another answer choice beating it out. Once you've decided that no other answer choice seems as good, do one final check to ensure that your answer choice answers the question posed.

Valid Information

Don't discount any of the information provided in the question. Every piece of information may be necessary to determine the correct answer. None of the information in the question is there to throw you off (while the answer choices will certainly have information to throw you off). If two seemingly unrelated topics are discussed, don't ignore either. You can be confident there is a relationship, or it wouldn't be included in the question, and you are probably going to have to determine what is that relationship to find the answer.

Avoid "Fact Traps"

Don't get distracted by a choice that is factually true. Your search is for the answer that answers the question. Stay focused and don't fall for an answer that is true but irrelevant. Always go back to the question and make sure you're choosing an answer that actually answers the question and is not just a true statement. An answer can be factually correct, but it MUST answer the question asked. Additionally, two answers can both be seemingly correct, so be sure to read all of the answer choices, and make sure that you get the one that BEST answers the question.

Milk the Question

Some of the questions may throw you completely off. They might deal with a subject you have not been exposed to, or one that you haven't reviewed in years. While your lack of knowledge about the subject will be a hindrance, the question itself can give you many clues that will help you find the correct answer. Read the question carefully and look for clues. Watch particularly for adjectives and nouns describing difficult terms or words that you don't recognize. Regardless of whether you completely understand a word or not, replacing it with a synonym, either provided or one you more familiar with, may help you to understand what the questions are asking. Rather than wracking your mind about specific detailed information concerning a difficult term or word, try to use mental substitutes that are easier to understand.

The Trap of Familiarity

Don't just choose a word because you recognize it. On difficult questions, you may not recognize a number of words in the answer choices. The test writers don't put "make-believe" words on the test, so don't think that just because you only recognize all the words in one answer choice that that answer choice must be correct. If you only recognize words in one answer choice, then focus on that one. Is it correct? Try your best to determine if it is correct. If it is, that's great. If not, eliminate it. Each word and answer choice you eliminate increases your chances of getting the question correct, even if you then have to guess among the unfamiliar choices.

Eliminate Answers

Eliminate choices as soon as you realize they are wrong. But be careful! Make sure you consider all of the possible answer choices. Just because one appears right, doesn't mean that the next one won't be even better! The test writers will usually put more than one good answer choice for every question, so read all of them. Don't worry if you are stuck between two that seem right. By getting down to just two remaining possible choices, your odds are now 50/50. Rather than wasting too much time, play the odds. You are guessing, but guessing wisely because you've been able to knock out some of the answer choices that you know are wrong. If you are eliminating choices and realize that the last answer choice you are left with is also obviously wrong, don't panic. Start over and consider each choice again. There may easily be something that you missed the first time and will realize on the second pass.

Tough Questions

If you are stumped on a problem or it appears too hard or too difficult, don't waste time. Move on! Remember though, if you can quickly check for obviously incorrect answer choices, your chances of guessing correctly are greatly improved. Before you completely give up, at least try to knock out a couple of possible answers. Eliminate what you can and then guess at the remaining answer choices before moving on.

Brainstorm

If you get stuck on a difficult question, spend a few seconds quickly brainstorming. Run through the complete list of possible answer choices. Look at each choice and ask yourself, "Could this answer the question satisfactorily?" Go through each answer choice and consider it independently of the others. By systematically going through all possibilities, you may find something that you would otherwise overlook. Remember though that when you get stuck, it's important to try to keep moving.

Read Carefully

Understand the problem. Read the question and answer choices carefully. Don't miss the question because you misread the terms. You have plenty of time to read each question thoroughly and make sure you understand what is being asked. Yet a happy medium must be attained, so don't waste too much time. You must read carefully, but efficiently.

Face Value

When in doubt, use common sense. Always accept the situation in the problem at face value. Don't read too much into it. These problems will not require you to make huge leaps of logic. The test writers aren't trying to throw you off with a cheap trick. If you have to go beyond creativity and make a leap of logic in order to have an answer choice answer the question, then you should look at the other answer choices. Don't overcomplicate the problem by creating theoretical relationships or explanations that will warp time or space. These are normal problems rooted in reality. It's just that the applicable relationship or explanation may not be readily apparent and you have to figure things out. Use your common sense to interpret anything that isn't clear.

Prefixes

If you're having trouble with a word in the question or answer choices, try dissecting it. Take advantage of every clue that the word might include. Prefixes and suffixes can be a huge help. Usually they allow you to determine a basic meaning. Pre- means before, post- means after, pro - is positive, de- is negative. From these prefixes and suffixes, you can get an idea of the general meaning of the word and try to put it into context. Beware though of any traps. Just because con- is the opposite of pro-, doesn't necessarily mean congress is the opposite of progress!

Hedge Phrases

Watch out for critical hedge phrases, led off with words such as "likely," "may," "can," "sometimes," "often," "almost," "mostly," "usually," "generally," "rarely," and "sometimes." Question writers insert these hedge phrases to cover every possibility. Often an answer choice will be wrong simply because it leaves no room for exception. Unless the situation calls for them, avoid answer choices that have definitive words like "exactly," and "always."

Switchback Words

Stay alert for "switchbacks." These are the words and phrases frequently used to alert you to shifts in thought. The most common switchback word is "but." Others include "although," "however," "nevertheless," "on the other hand," "even though," "while," "in spite of," "despite," and "regardless of."

New Information

Correct answer choices will rarely have completely new information included. Answer choices typically are straightforward reflections of the material asked about and will directly relate to the question. If a new piece of information is included in an answer choice that doesn't even seem to relate to the topic being asked about, then that answer choice is likely incorrect. All of the information needed to answer the question is usually provided for you in the question. You should not have to make guesses that are unsupported or choose answer choices that require unknown information that cannot be reasoned from what is given.

Time Management

On technical questions, don't get lost on the technical terms. Don't spend too much time on any one question. If you don't know what a term means, then odds are you aren't going to get much further since you don't have a dictionary. You should be able to immediately recognize whether or not you know a term. If you don't, work with the other clues that you have—the other answer choices and terms provided—but don't waste too much time trying to figure out a difficult term that you don't know.

Contextual Clues

Look for contextual clues. An answer can be right but not the correct answer. The contextual clues will help you find the answer that is most right and is correct. Understand the context in which a phrase or statement is made. This will help you make important distinctions.

Don't Panic

Panicking will not answer any questions for you; therefore, it isn't helpful. When you first see the question, if your mind goes blank, take a deep breath. Force yourself to mechanically go through the steps of solving the problem using the strategies you've learned.

Pace Yourself

Don't get clock fever. It's easy to be overwhelmed when you're looking at a page full of questions, your mind is full of random thoughts and feeling confused, and the clock is ticking down faster than you would like. Calm down and maintain the pace that you have set for yourself. As long as you are on track by monitoring your pace, you are guaranteed to have enough time for yourself. When you get to the last few minutes of the test, it may seem like you won't have enough time left, but if you only have as many questions as you should have left at that point, then you're right on track!

Answer Selection

The best way to pick an answer choice is to eliminate all of those that are wrong, until only one is left and confirm that is the correct answer. Sometimes though, an answer choice may immediately look right. Be careful! Take a second to make sure that the other choices are not equally obvious. Don't make a hasty mistake. There are only two times that you should stop before checking other answers. First is when you are positive that the answer choice you have selected is correct. Second is when time is almost out and you have to make a quick guess!

Check Your Work

Since you will probably not know every term listed and the answer to every question, it is important that you get credit for the ones that you do know. Don't miss any questions through careless mistakes. If at all possible, try to take a second to look back over your answer selection and make sure you've selected the correct answer choice and haven't made a costly careless mistake (such as marking an answer choice that you didn't mean to mark). The time it takes for this quick double check should more than pay for itself in caught mistakes.

Beware of Directly Quoted Answers

Sometimes an answer choice will repeat word for word a portion of the question or reference section. However, beware of such exact duplication. It may be a trap! More than likely, the correct choice will paraphrase or summarize a point, rather than being exactly the same wording.

Slang

Scientific sounding answers are better than slang ones. An answer choice that begins "To compare the outcomes…" is much more likely to be correct than one that begins "Because some people insisted…"

Extreme Statements

Avoid wild answers that throw out highly controversial ideas that are proclaimed as established fact. An answer choice that states the "process should used in certain situations, if…" is much more likely to be correct than one that states the "process should be discontinued completely." The first is a calm rational statement and doesn't even make a definitive, uncompromising stance, using a hedge word "if" to provide wiggle room, whereas the second choice is a radical idea and far more extreme.

Answer Choice Families

When you have two or more answer choices that are direct opposites or parallels, one of them is usually the correct answer. For instance, if one answer choice states "x increases" and another answer choice states "x decreases" or "y increases," then those two or three answer choices are very similar in construction and fall into the same family of answer choices. A family of answer choices consists of two or three answer choices, very similar in construction, but often with directly opposite meanings. Usually the correct answer choice will be in that family of answer choices. The "odd man out" or answer choice that doesn't seem to fit the parallel construction of the other answer choices is more likely to be incorrect.

Special Report: How to Overcome Test Anxiety

The very nature of tests caters to some level of anxiety, nervousness, or tension, just as we feel for any important event that occurs in our lives. A little bit of anxiety or nervousness can be a good thing. It helps us with motivation, and makes achievement just that much sweeter. However, too much anxiety can be a problem, especially if it hinders our ability to function and perform.

"Test anxiety," is the term that refers to the emotional reactions that some test-takers experience when faced with a test or exam. Having a fear of testing and exams is based upon a rational fear, since the test-taker's performance can shape the course of an academic career. Nevertheless, experiencing excessive fear of examinations will only interfere with the test-taker's ability to perform and chance to be successful.

There are a large variety of causes that can contribute to the development and sensation of test anxiety. These include, but are not limited to, lack of preparation and worrying about issues surrounding the test.

Lack of Preparation

Lack of preparation can be identified by the following behaviors or situations:

Not scheduling enough time to study, and therefore cramming the night before the test or exam
Managing time poorly, to create the sensation that there is not enough time to do everything
Failing to organize the text information in advance, so that the study material consists of the entire text and not simply the pertinent information
Poor overall studying habits

Worrying, on the other hand, can be related to both the test taker, or many other factors around him/her that will be affected by the results of the test. These include worrying about:

Previous performances on similar exams, or exams in general
How friends and other students are achieving
The negative consequences that will result from a poor grade or failure

There are three primary elements to test anxiety. Physical components, which involve the same typical bodily reactions as those to acute anxiety (to be discussed below). Emotional factors have to do with fear or panic. Mental or cognitive issues concerning attention spans and memory abilities.

Physical Signals

There are many different symptoms of test anxiety, and these are not limited to mental and emotional strain. Frequently there are a range of physical signals that will let a test taker know that he/she is suffering from test anxiety. These bodily changes can include the following:

Perspiring
Sweaty palms
Wet, trembling hands
Nausea
Dry mouth
A knot in the stomach
Headache
Faintness
Muscle tension
Aching shoulders, back and neck
Rapid heart beat
Feeling too hot/cold

To recognize the sensation of test anxiety, a test-taker should monitor him/herself for the following sensations:

The physical distress symptoms as listed above
Emotional sensitivity, expressing emotional feelings such as the need to cry or laugh too much, or a sensation of anger or helplessness
A decreased ability to think, causing the test-taker to blank out or have racing thoughts that are hard to organize or control.

Though most students will feel some level of anxiety when faced with a test or exam, the majority can cope with that anxiety and maintain it at a manageable level. However, those who cannot are faced with a very real and very serious condition, which can and should be controlled for the immeasurable benefit of this sufferer.

Naturally, these sensations lead to negative results for the testing experience. The most common effects of test anxiety have to do with nervousness and mental blocking.

Nervousness

Nervousness can appear in several different levels:

The test-taker's difficulty, or even inability to read and understand the questions on the test
The difficulty or inability to organize thoughts to a coherent form
The difficulty or inability to recall key words and concepts relating to the testing questions (especially essays)
The receipt of poor grades on a test, though the test material was well known by the test taker

Conversely, a person may also experience mental blocking, which involves:

Blanking out on test questions
Only remembering the correct answers to the questions when the test has already finished.

Fortunately for test anxiety sufferers, beating these feelings, to a large degree, has to do with proper preparation. When a test taker has a feeling of preparedness, then anxiety will be dramatically lessened.

The first step to resolving anxiety issues is to distinguish which of the two types of anxiety are being suffered. If the anxiety is a direct result of a lack of preparation, this should be considered a normal reaction, and the anxiety level (as opposed to the test results) shouldn't be anything to worry about. However, if, when adequately prepared, the test-taker still panics, blanks out, or seems to overreact, this is not a fully rational reaction. While this can be considered normal too, there are many ways to combat and overcome these effects.

Remember that anxiety cannot be entirely eliminated, however, there are ways to minimize it, to make the anxiety easier to manage. Preparation is one of the best ways to minimize test anxiety. Therefore the following techniques are wise in order to best fight off any anxiety that may want to build.

To begin with, try to avoid cramming before a test, whenever it is possible. By trying to memorize an entire term's worth of information in one day, you'll be shocking your system, and not giving yourself a very good chance to absorb the information. This is an easy path to anxiety, so for those who suffer from test anxiety, cramming should not even be considered an option.

Instead of cramming, work throughout the semester to combine all of the material which is presented throughout the semester, and work on it gradually as the course goes by, making sure to master the main concepts first, leaving minor details for a week or so before the test.

To study for the upcoming exam, be sure to pose questions that may be on the examination, to gauge the ability to answer them by integrating the ideas from your texts, notes and lectures, as well as any supplementary readings.

If it is truly impossible to cover all of the information that was covered in that particular term, concentrate on the most important portions, that can be covered very well. Learn these concepts as best as possible, so that when the test comes, a goal can be made to use these concepts as presentations of your knowledge.

In addition to study habits, changes in attitude are critical to beating a struggle with test anxiety. In fact, an improvement of the perspective over the entire test-taking experience can actually help a test taker to enjoy studying and therefore improve the overall experience. Be certain not to overemphasize the significance of the grade - know that the result of the test is neither a reflection of self worth, nor is it a measure of intelligence; one grade will not predict a person's future success.

To improve an overall testing outlook, the following steps should be tried:

Keeping in mind that the most reasonable expectation for taking a test is to expect to try to demonstrate as much of what you know as you possibly can.
Reminding ourselves that a test is only one test; this is not the only one, and there will be others.
The thought of thinking of oneself in an irrational, all-or-nothing term should be avoided at all costs.
A reward should be designated for after the test, so there's something to look forward to. Whether it be going to a movie, going out to eat, or simply visiting friends, schedule it in advance, and do it no matter what result is expected on the exam.

Test-takers should also keep in mind that the basics are some of the most important things, even beyond anti-anxiety techniques and studying. Never neglect the basic social, emotional and biological needs, in order to try to absorb information. In order to best achieve, these three factors must be held as just as important as the studying itself.

Study Steps

Remember the following important steps for studying:

Maintain healthy nutrition and exercise habits. Continue both your recreational activities and social pass times. These both contribute to your physical and emotional well being.
Be certain to get a good amount of sleep, especially the night before the test, because when you're overtired you are not able to perform to the best of your best ability.
Keep the studying pace to a moderate level by taking breaks when they are needed, and varying the work whenever possible, to keep the mind fresh instead of getting bored.
When enough studying has been done that all the material that can be learned has been learned, and the test taker is prepared for the test, stop studying and do something relaxing such as listening to music, watching a movie, or taking a warm bubble bath.

There are also many other techniques to minimize the uneasiness or apprehension that is experienced along with test anxiety before, during, or even after the examination. In fact, there are a great deal of things that can be done to stop anxiety from interfering with lifestyle and performance. Again, remember that anxiety will not be eliminated entirely, and it shouldn't be. Otherwise that "up" feeling for exams would not exist, and most of us depend on that sensation to perform better than usual. However, this anxiety has to be at a level that is manageable.

Of course, as we have just discussed, being prepared for the exam is half the battle right away. Attending all classes, finding out what knowledge will be expected on the exam, and knowing the exam schedules are easy steps to lowering anxiety. Keeping up with work will remove the need to cram, and efficient study habits will eliminate wasted time. Studying should be done in an ideal location for concentration, so that it is simple to become interested in the material and give it complete attention. A method such as SQ3R (Survey, Question, Read, Recite, Review) is a wonderful key to follow to make sure that the study habits are as effective as possible, especially in the case of learning from a textbook. Flashcards are great techniques for memorization. Learning to take good notes will mean that notes will be full of useful information, so that less sifting will need to be done to seek out what is pertinent for studying. Reviewing notes after class and then again on occasion will keep the information fresh in the mind. From notes that have been taken summary sheets and outlines can be made for simpler reviewing.

A study group can also be a very motivational and helpful place to study, as there will be a sharing of ideas, all of the minds can work together, to make sure that everyone understands, and the studying will be made more interesting because it will be a social occasion.

Basically, though, as long as the test-taker remains organized and self confident, with efficient study habits, less time will need to be spent studying, and higher grades will be achieved.

To become self confident, there are many useful steps. The first of these is "self talk." It has been shown through extensive research, that self-talk for students who suffer from test anxiety, should be well monitored, in order to make sure that it contributes to self confidence as opposed to sinking the student. Frequently the self talk of test-anxious students is negative or self-defeating, thinking that everyone else is smarter and faster, that they always mess up, and that if they don't do well, they'll fail the entire course. It is important to decreasing anxiety that awareness is made of self talk. Try writing any negative self thoughts and then disputing them with a positive statement instead. Begin self-encouragement as though it was a friend speaking. Repeat positive statements to help reprogram the mind to believing in successes instead of failures.

Helpful Techniques

Other extremely helpful techniques include:

Self-visualization of doing well and reaching goals
While aiming for an "A" level of understanding, don't try to "overprotect" by setting your expectations lower. This will only convince the mind to stop studying in order to meet the lower expectations.
Don't make comparisons with the results or habits of other students. These are individual factors, and different things work for different people, causing different results.
Strive to become an expert in learning what works well, and what can be done in order to improve. Consider collecting this data in a journal.
Create rewards for after studying instead of doing things before studying that will only turn into avoidance behaviors.
Make a practice of relaxing - by using methods such as progressive relaxation, self-hypnosis, guided imagery, etc - in order to make relaxation an automatic sensation.
Work on creating a state of relaxed concentration so that concentrating will take on the focus of the mind, so that none will be wasted on worrying.
Take good care of the physical self by eating well and getting enough sleep.
Plan in time for exercise and stick to this plan.

Beyond these techniques, there are other methods to be used before, during and after the test that will help the test-taker perform well in addition to overcoming anxiety.

Before the exam comes the academic preparation. This involves establishing a study schedule and beginning at least one week before the actual date of the test. By doing this, the anxiety of not having enough time to study for the test will be automatically eliminated. Moreover, this will make the studying a much more effective experience, ensuring that the learning will be an easier process. This relieves much undue pressure on the test-taker.

Summary sheets, note cards, and flash cards with the main concepts and examples of these main concepts should be prepared in advance of the actual studying time. A topic should never be eliminated from this process. By omitting a topic because it isn't expected to be on the test is only setting up the test-taker for anxiety should it actually appear on the exam. Utilize the course syllabus for laying out the topics that should be studied. Carefully go over the notes that were made in class, paying special attention to any of the issues that the professor took special care to emphasize while lecturing in class. In the textbooks, use the chapter review, or if possible, the chapter tests, to begin your review.

It may even be possible to ask the instructor what information will be covered on the exam, or what the format of the exam will be (for example, multiple choice, essay, free form, true-false). Additionally, see if it is possible to find out how many questions will be on the test. If a review sheet or sample test has been offered by the professor, make good use of it, above anything else, for the preparation for the test. Another great resource for getting to know the examination is reviewing tests from previous semesters. Use these tests to review, and aim to achieve a 100% score on each of the possible topics. With a few exceptions, the goal that you set for yourself is the highest one that you will reach.

Take all of the questions that were assigned as homework, and rework them to any other possible course material. The more problems reworked, the more skill and confidence will form as a result. When forming the solution to a problem, write out each of the steps. Don't simply do head work. By doing as many steps on paper as possible, much clarification and therefore confidence will be formed. Do this with as many homework problems as possible, before checking the answers. By checking the answer after each problem, a reinforcement will exist, that will not be on the exam. Study situations should be as exam-like as possible, to prime the test-taker's system for the experience. By waiting to check the answers at the end, a psychological advantage will be formed, to decrease the stress factor.

Another fantastic reason for not cramming is the avoidance of confusion in concepts, especially when it comes to mathematics. 8-10 hours of study will become one hundred percent more effective if it is spread out over a week or at least several days, instead of doing it all in one sitting. Recognize that the human brain requires time in order to assimilate new material, so frequent breaks and a span of study time over several days will be much more beneficial.

Additionally, don't study right up until the point of the exam. Studying should stop a minimum of one hour before the exam begins. This allows the brain to rest and put things in their proper order. This will also provide the time to become as relaxed as possible when going into the examination room. The test-taker will also have time to eat well and eat sensibly. Know that the brain needs food as much as the rest of the body. With enough food and enough sleep, as well as a relaxed attitude, the body and the mind are primed for success.

Avoid any anxious classmates who are talking about the exam. These students only spread anxiety, and are not worth sharing the anxious sentimentalities.

Before the test also involves creating a positive attitude, so mental preparation should also be a point of concentration. There are many keys to creating a positive attitude. Should fears become rushing in, make a visualization of taking the exam, doing well, and seeing an A written on the paper. Write out a list of affirmations that will bring a feeling of confidence, such as "I am doing well in my English class," "I studied well and know my material," "I enjoy this class." Even if the affirmations aren't believed at first, it sends a positive message to the subconscious which will result in an alteration of the overall belief system, which is the system that creates reality.

If a sensation of panic begins, work with the fear and imagine the very worst! Work through the entire scenario of not passing the test, failing the entire course, and dropping out of school, followed by not getting a job, and pushing a shopping cart through the dark alley where you'll live. This will place things into perspective! Then, practice deep breathing and create a visualization of the opposite situation - achieving an "A" on the exam, passing the entire course, receiving the degree at a graduation ceremony.

On the day of the test, there are many things to be done to ensure the best results, as well as the most calm outlook. The following stages are suggested in order to maximize test-taking potential:

Begin the examination day with a moderate breakfast, and avoid any coffee or beverages with caffeine if the test taker is prone to jitters. Even people who are used to managing caffeine can feel jittery or light-headed when it is taken on a test day.
Attempt to do something that is relaxing before the examination begins. As last minute cramming clouds the mastering of overall concepts, it is better to use this time to create a calming outlook.
Be certain to arrive at the test location well in advance, in order to provide time to select a location that is away from doors, windows and other distractions, as well as giving enough time to relax before the test begins.
Keep away from anxiety generating classmates who will upset the sensation of stability and relaxation that is being attempted before the exam.
Should the waiting period before the exam begins cause anxiety, create a self-distraction by reading a light magazine or something else that is relaxing and simple.

During the exam itself, read the entire exam from beginning to end, and find out how much time should be allotted to each individual problem. Once writing the exam, should more time be taken for a problem, it should be abandoned, in order to begin another problem. If there is time at the end, the unfinished problem can always be returned to and completed.

Read the instructions very carefully - twice - so that unpleasant surprises won't follow during or after the exam has ended.

When writing the exam, pretend that the situation is actually simply the completion of homework within a library, or at home. This will assist in forming a relaxed atmosphere, and will allow the brain extra focus for the complex thinking function.

Begin the exam with all of the questions with which the most confidence is felt. This will build the confidence level regarding the entire exam and will begin a quality momentum. This will also create encouragement for trying the problems where uncertainty resides.

Going with the "gut instinct" is always the way to go when solving a problem. Second guessing should be avoided at all costs. Have confidence in the ability to do well.

For essay questions, create an outline in advance that will keep the mind organized and make certain that all of the points are remembered. For multiple choice, read every answer, even if the correct one has been spotted - a better one may exist.

Continue at a pace that is reasonable and not rushed, in order to be able to work carefully. Provide enough time to go over the answers at the end, to check for small errors that can be corrected.

Should a feeling of panic begin, breathe deeply, and think of the feeling of the body releasing sand through its pores. Visualize a calm, peaceful place, and include all of the sights, sounds and sensations of this image. Continue the deep breathing, and take a few minutes to continue this with closed eyes. When all is well again, return to the test.

If a "blanking" occurs for a certain question, skip it and move on to the next question. There will be time to return to the other question later. Get everything done that can be done, first, to guarantee all the grades that can be compiled, and to build all of the confidence possible. Then return to the weaker questions to build the marks from there.

Remember, one's own reality can be created, so as long as the belief is there, success will follow. And remember: anxiety can happen later, right now, there's an exam to be written!

After the examination is complete, whether there is a feeling for a good grade or a bad grade, don't dwell on the exam, and be certain to follow through on the reward that was promised...and enjoy it! Don't dwell on any mistakes that have been made, as there is nothing that can be done at this point anyway.

Additionally, don't begin to study for the next test right away. Do something relaxing for a while, and let the mind relax and prepare itself to begin absorbing information again.

From the results of the exam - both the grade and the entire experience, be certain to learn from what has gone on. Perfect studying habits and work some more on confidence in order to make the next examination experience even better than the last one.

Learn to avoid places where openings occurred for laziness, procrastination and day dreaming.

Use the time between this exam and the next one to better learn to relax, even learning to relax on cue, so that any anxiety can be controlled during the next exam. Learn how to relax the body. Slouch in your chair if that helps. Tighten and then relax all of the different muscle groups, one group at a time, beginning with the feet and then working all the way up to the neck and face. This will ultimately relax the muscles more than they were to begin with. Learn how to breathe deeply and comfortably, and focus on this breathing going in and out as a relaxing thought. With every exhale, repeat the word "relax."

As common as test anxiety is, it is very possible to overcome it. Make yourself one of the test-takers who overcome this frustrating hindrance.

Additional Bonus Material

Due to our efforts to try to keep this book to a manageable length, we've created a link that will give you access to all of your additional bonus material.

Please visit http://www.mometrix.com/bonus948/texescore48 to access the information.

Made in the USA
San Bernardino, CA
28 January 2018